Intermediate
Tropical
Agriculture
Series

General Editor

W. J. A. Payne
Consultant in Tropical Livestock Production

Cattle and Buffalo Meat Production in the Tropics

Desmond Hill, CBE, DVM, MRCVS

formerly Professor of Veterinary Medicine, University of Ibadan, Nigeria

Longman
Scientific &
Technical

Longman Scientific and Technical
Longman Group UK Limited,
Longman House, Burnt Mill, Harlow,
Essex CM20 2JE, England
and Associated Companies throughout the world

First published 1988

British Library Cataloguing in Publication Data

Hill, Desmond
    Cattle and buffalo meat production in the tropics. –
    (Intermediate tropical agriculture series).
    1. Beef cattle – Tropics   2. Buffaloes – Tropics
    I. Title   II. Series
    636.2′13′0913   SF196.T7

ISBN 0-582-60895-3

Set in 9½/11 Times Roman.

Produced by Longman Singapore Publishers (Pte) Ltd
Printed in Singapore

Other titles in the Intermediate Tropical Agriculture Series

Already published:

H. T. B. Hall, *Diseases and Parasites of Livestock in the
Tropics*, Second Edition
Describes the causes, symptoms, treatment and control of the
main diseases of livestock in the Tropics.

J. C. Abbott and J. P. Makeham, *Agricultural Economics and
Marketing in the Tropics*
Describes the inter-relations of agriculture, farm management,
marketing and their economics, as they occur in the Tropics.

C. N. Williams, W. Y. Chew and J. H. Rajaratnam, *Tree and
Field Crops of the Wetter Regions of the Tropics*

Details are supplied of the botany, climatic and soil
requirements, cultivation and management, harvesting and,
where appropriate, processing of a large number of crops.

J. A. Eusebio, *Pig Production in the Tropics*
Covers all aspects of pig raising in tropical areas, including
nutrition, housing, breeding and marketing, with relevant
biological details.

M. E. Adams, *Agricultural Extension in Developing Countries*
Explains the background and practicalities of extension work in
the developing world.

H. F. Heady and E. B. Heady, *Range and Wildlife Management
in the Tropics*
Covers all aspects of rangeland from planting and maintenance
to cultural considerations.

D. Y. Coy, *Accounting and Finance for Managers in Tropical
Agriculture*
A useful guide to modern accounting practice for both students
of agriculture and farm managers.

C. Devendra and G. B. McLeroy, *Goat and Sheep Production
in the Tropics*
Provides comprehensive coverage of how to rear and maintain
healthy, productive goats and sheep in the Tropics. Includes
sections on breeds, nutrition, reproduction, health and breed
improvement.

D. S. Hill and J. M. Waller, *Pests and Diseases of Tropical
Crops. Volume 1: Principles and methods of control* A
A comprehensive coverage of chemical control including
methods of application together with information on biological
and integrated control methods.

E. Heath and S. Olusanya, *Anatomy and Physiology of Tropical
Livestock*
Based on body systems, this covers a wide range of agricultural
animals including less familiar livestock.

D. Gibbon and A. Pain, *Crops of the Drier Regions of the
Tropics*
Part 1 deals with basic ecological principles while Part 2 is a
survey of different crops. Problems and potential for future
development are considered in the final section.

Titles in preparation:

D. S. Hill and J. M. Waller, *Pests and Diseases of Tropical
Crops. Volume 2: Field Handbook*
R. L. Humphreys, *Tropical Pastures and Fodder Crops*, Second
Edition
A. Chamberlain, *Milk Production in the Tropics*

Contents

Acknowledgements and sources

The Publishers are grateful to the following for their permission to reproduce photographs:-

Country Life Newspaper, Australia for figs 3.17 and 3.21; East African Common Services for figs 3.14 and 8.4; Editor Dos Criadores Sao Paulo for fig 3.20; F.A.O. for fig 9.10; Farmers Weekly for fig 3.15, Fiji Public Relations Office Suva for fig 7.14; Indian Council of Agricultural Research for fig 3.3; Penrose Pictures for figs 7.17, 9.8, 9.13, 9.15 and 9.18; Tobin Armstrong for fig 3.18; Tropix Photo Library for fig 9.3; and Wellcome Foundation Ltd for fig 8.8a & b.

Figs 2.5, 3.5, 3.6, 3.7. 3.8, 3.9, 3.10, 3.11, 3.12, 3.13, 5.7, 7.2, 7.8, 7.13, 7.22, 8.3, 8.4, 8.5, 8.6, 8.7, 9.2, 9.14, 9.18 were supplied by Desmond Hill. Figs 2.1, 2.2, 2.6, 3.2, 3.3, 3.4, 3.14, 3.16, 3.18, 3.19, 3.22 by Dr. W. J. A. Payne and Figs 9.3, 9.4, 9.5, 9.6, 9.7, 9.9, 9.10, 9.11, 9.12 by I. Mann.

The author wishes to thank all his friends and colleagues whose work has contributed towards the book and also his wife Heather and daughter Jenny for their assistance with editing.

The sources of the figures are as follows:

Fig. 2.3: after Lee, D. H. K. (1955). *Manual of field studies on the heat tolerance of domestic animals*. FAO: Rome. Agric. Devel. Paper no. 38. p. 40. Fig. 2.4: McDowell, R. E. (1972). Responses of animals to warm environments. In *Improvement of livestock production in warm climates*. W. H. Freeman: San Francisco. Fig. 2.7: Turner, H. G. and Schleger, A. V. (1960). The significance of coat types in cattle. *Aust. J. of Agric. Res.*, 11. Fig. 3.1: Williamson, G. and Payne, W. J. A. (1978). *An introduction to animal husbandry in the tropics*. 3rd edn. Longman: London. p. 54. Fig. 4.1: after Sisson, S. S. and Grossman, J. D. (1938). *The anatomy of domestic animals*. 3rd edn. W. B. Saunders: London. Fig. 4.2: after Dyce, K. M and Wending, C. J. G. (1971). *Essentials of bovine anatomy*. Lea and Febiger: Philadelphia. Fig. 4.3: modified from Williamson, G. and Payne, W. J. A. (1978). *An introduction to animal husbandry in the tropics*. 3rd edn. Longman: London. p. 156. Fig. 4.4: Netke, S. P., Kalpatel, B. G. and Gambhur, R. K. (1970). Climate and animal production. In *The pastoral industries of Australia*, ed. G. Alexander and O. B. Williams. Sydney University Press. p. 348. Figs. 5.1 and 5.2: compiled from Mahadevan, P. (1970). Breeding methods. In *Cattle production in the tropics*, ed. W. J. A. Payne. Longman: London. Figs 5.3, 5.4, 5.5, 5.6: D. H. Hill (adapted). Fig. 6.1: Buttery, P. J. (1976). Protein synthesis in the rumen. In *Principles of cattle production*, ed. H. Swan and W. H. Broster. Butterworth: London. Fig. 7.1: ILCA (1980). *The first years*. Livestock Centre for Africa: Addis Ababa. Fig. 7.3: von Kaufmann, R. (1979). A generalised simulation approach to agriculture sector analysis with special reference to Nigeria. In *Livestock production in the subhumid zone of West Africa*. Systems Study No. 2. ILCA: Addis Ababa. Fig. 7.4: Cartographic Unit, Range Management Branch, Ministry of Livestock Development, Kenya. Fig. 7.5: ILCA (1982). *Annual Report*. p. 33. ILCA: Addis Ababa. Fig. 7.6: Hill, D. H. and Upton, M. (1964). Growth performance of ranch reared N'Dama and Keteku cattle and their crosses in the derived Guinea savannah zone. *Western Nigeria Trop. Agric.*, 41 (2). Fig. 7.7: Veiga, J. S. (1955). Improving Indian breeds in Brazil. In *Breeding beef cattle in unfavourable environments*. Univ. of Texas Press: Austin. Figs 7.9, 7.10, 7.11, 7.12, 7.15: A.P.R.U. Beef production and range management in Botswana. Animal Production and Research Unit, Ministry of Agriculture, Gaborone, Botswana Govt. Printer, Gaborone. Fig. 7.16: Tipping horn, D. H. Hill. Figs. 7.19, 7.20, 7.21: Brands, branding on gaskin, earnotching. D. H. Hill. 7.22: Miller, E. E. (1975). The raising and marketing of beef in Central America and Panama. *J. Trop. Geog.*, 41. Fig. 8.1: Acquisition of immunity. D. H. Hill. Fig. 8.2: Tsetse fly. Williamson, G. and Payne, W. J. A. (1978). *An introduction to animal husbandry in the tropics*. 3rd edn. Longman: London, p. 59. Fig 8.8: Engorged ticks. Hall, H. T. B. (1985) *Diseases and parasites of livestock in the tropics*. 2nd edition. ITAS, Longman. Fig. 8.9: (a) The essential features of a good cattle spray Fig. 8.11 (c) Hand pump spray A.P.R.U. (See 7.9–15). Fig. 9.1: Buchanan, K. M., Pugh, J. C., (1955) *Land and people in Nigeria*. Univ. of London Press. Fig. 9.2: Transporting cattle by boat. D. H. Hill. Fig. 9.3 to 9.12: Mann, I. (1960). *Meat handling in underdeveloped countries*. FAO Agric. Devel. Paper no. 70, pp. 13, 29–32, 37. Fig 9.14 Smoke house D. H. Hill. Figs. 9.16 and 9.17: Preston, T. R. and Willis, M. B. (1982). *Intensive beef production*. 2nd edn. Pergamon: Oxford, p. 40. Everitt, (1964), cited in Preston and Willis (1982).

The sources of the tables are as follows:

Tables 1.1 to 1.4: compiled from FAO (1982). *Production yearbook*, 36. Food and Agriculture Organisation: Rome. Tables 1.5 and 1.6: FAO (1982). *Production yearbook* and *Trade yearbook*, 35 and 36. Table 1.7: compiled from FAO (1982). *Trade yearbook*, 36. Table 2.1: Hutchinson, J. C. D. and Brown, G. D. (1969). Penetration of cattle by radiation. *J. of Applied Physiology*, 26. Table 3.1: Growth and reproduction of N'dama cattle p. 37 (data D. H. Hill) (unpublished). Table 3.2 Growth and reproduction of West African Shorthorn p. 29 (data D. H. Hill) (unpublished). Table 3.3: Growth and carcass data of Africander cattle p. 34. Compiled from Types and Breeds of African Cattle. Prepared by Joshi, N. R., McLaughlin, E. A., and Phillips R. W., (1957) Food and Agriculture Organisation of the United Nations p. 277–279. Table 3.4: FAO (1985). *Production yearbook*, 39. Table 3.5 Average measurements of swamp and river buffalo (cm) Compiled from data provided by McDowell, R. E., (1972) *Improvement of livestock Production in warm climates*. W. H. Freeman and Co., San Francisco p. 566 Table 4.2: compiled from Fahimuddin, M. (1975). *Domestic water buffalo*. Oxford and IBH Publ. Co.: New Delhi. Table 5.1: Animal Prod. Res. Unit, Botswana (1980). *Beef production and range management in Botswana*. Min. of Agric.: Gaborone. Also Robertson, A. (1950). A preliminary report on the herd of White Fulani cattle at Shika, Nigeria. Conference on Improvement of Livestock under Tropical Conditions, Edinburgh. Also Foster, W. H. (1960). The breeding of White Fulani cattle at Shika, Nigeria.

Samaru Res. Bull., **2**. Also Olaloku, E. A., Hill, D. H. and Oyenaga, V. A. (1971). Observations on the White Fulani (Bunaji) Zebu cattle of Northern Nigeria in a Southern Nigerian environment. Trop. Agric., **48**. Also Touchberry, R. W. (1967). A study of the N'dama cattle at the Maasai animal husbandry station in Sierra Leone. Univ. of Illinois Agric. Exper. Sta. Bull., **724**. Also Dettmers, A. and Hill, D. H. (1974). Animal breeding in Nigeria. Proceedings of the 1st World Congress on Genetics applied to Livestock Production. Madrid. Also ILCA (1978). Evaluation of the productivities of Maure and Peul cattle breeds at the Sahelian station, Nioni, Mali. Monograph no. 1. ILCA: Addis Ababa. Also Mahadevan, P. (1970). Breeding methods. In Cattle production in the tropics, ed. W. J. A. Payne. Longman: London. **Tables 5.2, 5.3 and 5.4**: Dalton, Clive (1980). An introduction to practical animal breeding. Granada: London. **Tables 5.5 and 5.6**: Hill, D. H. (1967). Cattle breeding in Brazil. Commonwealth Agricultural Bureau and Rev. Reprint no. 74. **Table 6.1**: Butterworth, M. H. (1963). Digestibility trials on forages in Trinidad and their use in the prediction of nutritive value. J. Agric. (Camb.), 60. Also Butterworth M. H. (1964). The digestible energy of some tropical forages. J. Agric. Sci. (Camb.), **64**. **Table 6.2**: derived from Butterworth, M. H. and Diaz, J. A. L. (1970). Use of equations to predict the nutritive value of tropical grasses. J. of Range Management, **23**. **Table 6.3**: NAS (1976). Nutrient requirements of beef cattle. 5th edn. Nat. Acad. of Sci.: Washington. **Table 6.4**: NAS (1971). Nutrient requirements of dairy cattle. 4th edn. Nat. Acad. of Sci.: Washington. **Table 6.5**: Kay, H. D. (1974). Milk and milk production. In The husbandry and health of the domestic buffalo, ed. W. Ross Cockrill. FAO: Rome. **Table 6.6**: NAS (1976). Nutrient requirements of beef cattle. 5th edn. Nat. Acad. of Sci.: Washington. **Table 6.7**: derived from Huss, D. L. (ed.) (1964). A glossary of terms used in range management. American Society of Range Management: Portland, Oregon. **Table 6.9**: NAS (1976). Nutrient requirements of beef cattle. 5th edn. Nat. Acad. of Sci.: Washington. **Table 6.10**: Ognjanovic, A. (1974). Meat and milk production. In The husbandry and health of the domestic buffalo, ed. W. Ross Cockrill. FAO: Rome. Also Charles, D. D. and Johnson, E. R. (1975). Liveweight gains and carcass composition of buffalo (Bubalus bubalis) steers on four feeding regimes. Aust. J. Agric. Res. **26**. Also Johnson, E. R. and Charles, D. D. (1975). Comparisons of liveweight gain and changes in carcass composition between buffalo (Bubalus bubalis) and Bos taurus steers. Aust. J. Agric. Res., **26**. Also Matsukawa, T., Tilakaratne, N. and Buvanandran, V. (1976). Growth and carcass characteristics of cattle and buffalo breeds reared on a dry zone pasture in Sri Lanka (Ceylon). Trop. Anim. Health Prod., **8**. Also Shute, (1966). DTA thesis (unpublished) ICTA, Trinidad. Also Houghton, T. R. (1960). The water buffalo in Trinidad. J. Agric. Soc. Trin. Tob., **60**. Also Bennet, S. P. (1964), cited by Rastogi, R. et al. (1978). Beef type water buffalo of Trinidad: Buffalypso. Wld. Rev. Anim. Prod., **14**. Also Wahid, A. (1973). Pakistani buffaloes. Wld. Anim. Rev., **7**. **Table 6.11**: Ledger, H. P. (1965). The body and carcass composition of East African ruminants. 1 The composition of 'improved Boran' Bos indicus steer carcasses. J. Agric. Sci. (Camb.), **65**. **Table 6.12**: derived from Johnson, E. R., and Charles, D. D. (1975). Comparisons of liveweight gain and changes in carcass composition between buffalo (Bubalus bubalis) and Bos taurus steers. Aust. J. Agric. Res., **26**.

Table 7.1: Payne, W. J. A. (1976). Systems of Beef Production in developing countries, pp. 118–131: Beef cattle production in developing countries ed. A. J. Smith, in Proceedings of the conference held in Edinburgh 1–6 Sept 1974. Centre for Tropical Veterinary Medicine, University of Edinburgh. **Table 7.2**: modified from Williamson, G. and Payne, W. J. A. (1978). An introduction to animal husbandry in the tropics. 3rd edn. Longman: London. **Table 7.3**: Herd structure; ranch 6,400 ha. A.P.R.U. Beef production and range management in Botswana Animal Production and Research Unit, Ministry of Agriculture, Botswana Government Printer, Gaberone. **Table 7.4**: Walter Fonseca (1977). O búfalo-Sinonimo de carne, leite, manteiga e trabalho. 3rd edition. Revista Atualizada Ampliada. Ministerio da Agricultura. DNPA-DAGE. Associacão Brasileira de Criadores de Bufalos. CENAGRI. **Table 7.5**: Afifi, Y. A., Shanin, M. A., Omara, S. F. and Youssef, T. (1974). Animal Production Research Institute, Agric. Res. Centre, Cairo. Agric. Res. Rev. (abstr.). **Table 7.6**: Stocking rate on Nigerian Pastures, Oyenuga, V. A. (1969) Meeting nutrient requirements of range cattle for optimum yield. "Animal Production in Africa." The Abidjan Conf. 1968 3 p. 32–50. **Table 7.7**: Vincente-Chandler, J., Caro-Costas, R., Pearson, R. W., Abruña, F., Figarella, J. and Silva, S. (1964). The intensive management of tropical forages in Puerto Rico. University of Puerto Rico. Agricultural experiment station. Bull, 187. Also Quinn, L. R. C., Motl, G. O. and Bisschoff, W. N. A. (1968). Brief presentation of 6 tropical grasses in central Brazil. Proceedings Ninth International Grassland Congress, Brazil, pp. 1017–1020. **Table 7.8**: Alarcon, **8**. Alarcon, E, and Lotero, J (1969) Establecimiento, fertilizacion y manejo de los principales gramineas y leguminoses forrajeras en dos pisas termicas de Columbia, ACIA, Curso Asist. Tec., Monizalos. Publ. ICA, Palmira, Columbia. **Table 7.9**: Stobbs, T. H. (1976). Beef production from sown and planted pastures in the tropics. In Beef cattle production in developing countries, ed. A. J. Smith. Centre for Trop. Vet. Medic.: Edinburgh. **Table 7.10**: Olayiwole, M. B., and Fulani, I. J. (1978). Economics of commercial beef production under feedlot systems of management. Nat. Anim. Prod. Res. Inst. Ahmadu Bello Univ. Zaria, Nigeria. **Table 7.11**: Data from Preston, T. R. (1974) (unpublished). Also Willis, M. B. and Preston, T. R. (1970). Performance testing for beef. Animal Production 11, 12, 45. Also Creek, M. et al. (1973). A case study in the transfer of technology. Proceedings of the 3rd World Conference on Animal Production. Melbourne, Aust. Preston, T. R. (1976) Prospects for the intensification of production in developing countries: Beef cattle production in developing countries, in Proceedings of the Conference held in Edinburgh 1–6 Sept 1974. Centre for Tropical Veterinary Medicine. Univ. of Edinburgh. **Table 8.1**: Selected information on some infectious diseases of cattle and buffaloes. D. H. Hill. Compiled from various sources. **Table 8.2**: Some health problems associated with intensive management systems. D. H. Hill. Compiled from various sources. **Tables 8.3 to 8.5**: compiled from ILCA (1979). Trypanotolerant livestock in West and Central Africa. ILCA: Addis Ababa. vol. 1, p. 303 and vol. 2, p. 147. Data for Table 8.6 from Service d'élevage, Mali. **Table 9.1**: compiled from Okorie, I. I., Hill, D. H. and McIlroy, R. J. (1965). The productivity and volume of tropical grass/legume pastures rotationally grazed by N'dama cattle at Ibadan, Nigeria. J. Agric. Sci., **64**. **Table 9.2**: compiled from Olayiwole, M. B.

and Fulani, I. J. (1978). Economics of commercial beef production under the feedlot system of management. Nat. Anim. Prod. Res. Inst., Ahmadu Bello Univ.: Zaria. **Table 9.3**: compiled from Charles, D. D. and Johnson, E. R. (1970). Composition of the water buffalo (*Bubalus bubalis*). *Austr. J. Agric. Res*, **23**, 905, (ABA-41, 1508).
Also Ragat, M. T., Darwish, M. Y. H. and Malek, A. G. A., (1966). Meat production from Egyptian buffalo. Development changes and dressing percentage of a group of buffalo males. *J. Anim. Prod., U.A.R. 6.9.*

Table 9.4: Kassir, S. M., McFetridge, D. G., and Hansen, N. G. (1969). Studies on the growth, feed costs and carcass composition of young male cattle and buffalo fed under comparable conditions. *Tech. Rep. Anim. Husb. Res. Train. Proj.* Baghdad. No. 21. Rome, F.A.O. pq (A.B.A. 38:2237).
Table 9.5: Charles, D. D. and Johnson, E. R. (1975). Comparisons of liveweight gain and changes in carcass composition between buffalo (Bubalus bubalis) and *Bos indicus* bulls. *Austr. J. Agric. Res. 26*, 407–413.

Glossary

abomasum The fourth compartment of the digestive tract of a ruminant; sometimes known as the true stomach.

abortion A miscarriage during prenatal development.

acaricide A fluid or powder consisting of one or more insecticides, diluted at a recommended rate for use in a dip tank or spray to kill ectoparasites.

acquired characteristic A change of the structure or function of an organism which has been brought about during the life of the individual.

aerobe A micro-organism which can live and grow in the presence of oxygen.

alopecia Baldness; deficiency of hair.

alternate husbandry An agricultural system in which crop production alternates with grass leys at 3–5 year intervals.

mean temperature The temperature of the surroundings averaged over 24 hours.

anaerobe A micro-organism that grows in the absence of oxygen.

anastomosis (vascular) The union of two normally distinct vascular systems.

anorexia Loss of appetite for food.

antiserum A serum that contains antibodies.

artificial insemination (AI) Semen is collected from selected bulls and impregnated into the cow (in cattle, buffalo, etc.).

ascaridiosis Infestation with worms of the genus *Ascaridia*.

ascites Accumulation of a clear straw-coloured fluid in the abdominal cavity, causing enlargement of the abdomen.

aseptic Free from infection, a state brought about by prevention of entry of micro-organisms or by their destruction if they are already present.

ataxia Failure of muscular coordination; irregularity of muscular action.

attenuated Reduced in virulence; said of a micro-organism, and usually brought about by passage through a succession of abnormal hosts, thus reducing the virulence for the original host.

auscultation The act of listening for sounds within the body, for determining abnormality, chiefly in the lungs.

autogenous vaccine A vaccine prepared from a micro-organism from the animal to be vaccinated, as distinct from a vaccine from a stock culture.

autosome Any chromosome other than the sex chromosomes.

avitaminosis Deficiency of vitamins in the diet; sometimes the missing vitamin is indicated also, e.g. avitaminosis A.

back cross A cross between a hybrid and either of its parental types.

bacteraemia The presence of bacteria in the blood.

bagasse Fibrous residue from processing of sugar cane.

balanced lethals Lethal factors located in chromosomes of opposite gametes and each lethal closely linked with the normal allelomorph of the other lethal; thus crossing-over is infrequent, and generally no obvious harm results from the lethals.

biometry The branch of science dealing with the statistical investigation of organic differences.

blaze A broad, white band of hair between the horn base and the nose.

blood serum The clear liquid which separates from the blood when it is allowed to clot.

body capacity A somewhat loose term based upon the overall depth of the animal's body.

breed A group of individuals having a common origin and possessing certain distinguishing characteristics not common to other members of the same species.

buccal mucosae The mucous membranes lining the cavity of the mouth.

calving interval The period between births of two successive calves from one cow.

carbohydrate Constituents of the food with the general formula $C_x(H_2O)_y$, such as sugars, starch and cellulose; they are a major source of energy for the animal.

carrying capacity The unit area that will carry one mature stock unit.

vii

catarrhal stomatitis Inflammation of the mucous membrane of the mouth, characterised by the presence of a free, fluid discharge.

chlorophyll A green colouring matter of plants by which with the association of sunlight and carbon dioxide, photosynthesis is accomplished.

cicatrisation A healing process which leaves a scar (i.e. a cicatrix).

cloven hoof Divided hoof as in cattle and buffalo.

cold dressed weight (CDW) The weight of a carcass after being dressed, i.e. rejecting the entrails, head, feet, etc., and allowing for shrinkage which occurs in the first 12–24 hours after it has been placed in a cold store.

compensatory growth Growth in an individual that takes place after a period of underfeeding and during which lost weight is regained.

conformation The visual shape or appearance of the live animal.

conjunctivitis Inflammation of the conjunctiva.

contagious A disease communicated from one animal to another by contact or discharges.

coronet The line where the pastern and hoof meet.

corral (kraal) Enclosure.

cow A bovine female which has had at least one calf.

crepitation A crackling sound which is heard e.g. in some lung diseases when the ear is placed close to the thorax; or when the fingers are pressed into the skin covering a gaseous lesion such as occurs in black-quarter.

cull To remove unwanted animals from a herd.

cyanosis A blueness of the skin or mucous membrane, due to insufficient oxygenation of the blood, often found in cardiac insufficiency or occlusion of main veins.

cyclic development Development in the life cycle stages of a parasite.

dam Mother; also an artificial lake made by constructing a wall across a river or stream.

deferred grazing The closing of an area to livestock for the latter half to three-quarters of the rainy period; the pasture being allowed to grow and seed; afterwards used as standing hay.

dehydration Removal of water from a body or tissue; or the condition which results from loss of water.

dentition Teeth; by an examination of the lower incisors an estimate can be made of the animal's age.

diluting factor A minor factor which by itself has no noticeable effect but which lessens the effect of another factor.

diploid The condition in which both members of each chromosome pair are present; the chromosome number which usually and normally occurs in the somatic cell of a species, twice the gametic or haploid number.

dominance (a) *in genes*
One that produces the same characteristic when present in the heterozygous as in the homozygous state (as in **dominant**).
(b) *in plants*
The major plant in a plant population. Dominance may be complete, partial, absent or greater than complete; in the latter case it is known as overdominance.

dominant The term applied to the member of an allelomorphic pair which manifests an effect wholly or partly to the exclusion of the effect of the other allelomorph.

dressing percentage The percentage of liveweight which is represented by the CDW.

dual purpose cattle Breeds of cattle with two productive purposes, e.g. milk and meat.

dun A dull greyish brown colour.

dyspnoea Difficult or laboured breathing.

ecchymosis An effusion of blood into the tissues causing irregular patches visible on the surface of an organ or tissue.

ectoparasites Insects which live on the skin of cattle.

encephalitis Inflammation of the brain.

endocardial The inner surface of the heart.

endoparasites Parasites which live inside the animal's body.

epidermis The outermost, non-vascular layer of the skin.

epistatic That condition in which one factor prevents a factor other than its allelomorph from exhibiting its normal effect on the development of the individual.

epizootic A disease of animals, spreading rapidly and widely distributed.

epizootiology The study of epidemic diseases.

eructation Belching up of wind from the stomach.

erythema A redness of the skin; a rash.

erythrocytes The red corpuscles of the blood.

exudate A substance issuing from a tissue either as a normal process or because of disease in the tissue.

eye muscle A cross section of the *longissimus dorsi* muscle cut at a specific point.

family A group of individuals within a breed, all of which have pedigrees which trace directly in the female line to a common ancestress called the foundress of the family; at times used in reference to the male line of descent, in which case it is used interchangeably with line breeding.

farmyard manure (FYM) Cattle faeces usually mixed with straw or similar material.

feral and semi-feral Previously domesticated animals gone wild or semi-wild.

fibrinous pericarditis An inflammation of the heart sac characterised by the excess accumulation of a straw-coloured or haemorrhagic fluid containing fibrin, a whitish insoluble protein derived from the blood.

fomite An article or substance, other than food, which can harbour and carry micro-organisms and transmit them from one animal to another, thus disseminating a disease.

foster mother A cow used to suckle one or more calves in addition to her own.

freemartin Females born as twins with bull calves.

gene One of the biological units which transmit hereditary characteristics; genes are self-reproducing, and are located at specific points on specific chromosomes of the nucleus of the cell.

gene complex The balanced state of several (perhaps many) genes which collectively affect a given character or group of characters.

gene interaction The action of different genes upon each other.

genera Plural of genus, the term used in classification for a group or category of plants or animals, subordinate to a tribe or family, and superior to a species.

genotype An individual's constitution as regards the factors composing its germ plasm; the hereditary factors which it may transmit to its offspring.

gestation Pregnancy.

grade An individual, one of whose parents is a purebred, usually the sire, and the other a scrub or grade.

haploid The usual chromosome number occurring in the gametes in which only one member of each chromosome pair is present; one-half the diploid number.

heart girth Virtually the chest measurement with the tape measure immediately behind the elbows.

heat The time when a female is receptive to the bull.

heat tolerance test A measure of adaptation to high temperatures as shown by the least rise in body temperature.

heifer A bovine female from birth to calving herself.

hermaphrodite An organism which contains both male and female sexual organs.

heterosis The increased stimulus for growth and vigour often exhibited by the crossbred individual; hybrid vigour.

heterozygous A condition in which the homologous chromosomes carry dissimilar genes.

hybrid An individual resulting from the mating of individuals belonging to different genotypes.

hydropericardium A condition in which the pericardial sac (the fibrous tissue sac in which the heart is contained) is filled with an excess of fluid.

hyperaesthesia Excessive sensitiveness of the skin, usually in the area of a diseased tissue.

ileo-caecal (valve) The valve formed by a projection of the mucous membrane at the junction of the ileum (last section of the small intestine) and the caecum (the large blind gut).

inbreeding The mating of related individuals.

in situ In the original situation.

karyotype Characteristics of a set of chromosomes (size, shape and number) of a typical somatic cell of a species.

keratitis Inflammation of the cornea.

kerato-conjunctivitis Inflammation of the cornea and conjunctiva.

killing-out percentage See cold dressed weight or dressing percentage.

lachrimal discharge A discharge of tears of fluid similar to tears from the eyes.

lachrimation Secretion and discharge of tears.

larva Pre-adult form which in some animals hatches from the egg.

larval or 'seed' ticks Immature stages in tick development.

larval stage The first stage after leaving the egg in the development of an insect.

latent Concealed; not clearly visible or defined; not manifest.

leggy Cattle or buffalo long in the legs.

lesion Any pathological or traumatic abnormality in a tissue.

lethal Destructive of life.

let-down The reflex release of the milk in response to various stimuli, e.g. calf presence or noises accompanying milking time.

leys Pastures of planted grasses and/or legumes.

limpid Clear (usually with reference to eyes).

line breeding A rather indefinite term used somewhat loosely, applied to a group of individuals which have descended from one individual; used more frequently and correctly with reference to male lines of descent; more recently it is used to designate an inbred and closely related family.

linkage A form of inheritance in which certain genes tend to remain together in the process of segregation and transmission from one generation to the next, owing to their being located on the same chromosome.

livestock unit (LSU) A subjective liveweight unit (usually 330–400 kg) used to represent the overall liveweights of livestock of mixed age, sex or species.

liveweight (LW) The weight of a live animal.

liveweight gain (LWG) The rate of liveweight gain expressed on a time basis.

locus (plural loci) A definite point or region in a chromosome at which a genetic factor is located.

macroscopic Visible to the unaided eye, without the microscope.

mature stock unit (MSU) Another method of expressing LSUs.

medulla Cavity or hollow inside a fibre.

metazoan The multicellular members of the animal kingdom, as opposed to the protozoa, or unicellular members.

mineral A substance, one of the elements of nature, which either in inorganic or organic combination with other elements is essential in the nutrition or physiological function of the body.

morbidity The condition of being diseased; the morbidity rate is the proportion of sick to healthy animals.

morphology The visible shape, form, or structure of individuals.

multiple factors Two or more factors all of which are needed to produce a maximum effect.

mutant An individual the genotypic constitution of which differs from that of its parents and ancestors because of a definite change in the germ plasm, not brought about by segregation or crossing-over.

mutation The process by which a mutant is produced.

myiasis The migration of larval forms of flies (maggots) under the skin.

myocarditis Inflammation of the muscular wall of the heart.

nares The openings into the nasal cavity.

naso-pharynx The part of the pharynx which lies above the level of the soft palate.

necropsy A postmortem examination.

necrosis Death of a cell or more often a group of cells which are in contact with, or form part of, a living tissue.

neonatal Newly born.

nymphs The intermediate stage in the life cycle of arthropods such as ticks, between the larval and adult stages, and usually having much the same morphological appearance as the adult.

obligate parasite A parasite which is obliged to live on or in its host, as distinct from a facultative parasite, which has the ability to live on or in the host or away from it.

oedema The presence of abnormally large quantities of fluid in the intercellular tissue of the body.

oestrus The recurrent restricted period of sexual receptivity in female animals, marked by intense sexual urge.

oocysts A part of the sporogony phase of protozoa which occurs after macrogametes have been fertilised by microgametes in the intermediate host; the subsequent multiplication of cells produces an oocyst, each cell then becoming a sporozoite which is subsequently injected into the final host.

opisthotonus A form of spasm in which the muscles of the back are violently contracted causing the head and tail to come nearer each other and the abdomen to be protruded forward.

orchitis Inflammation of the testes.

order (pertaining to classification) A category used in taxonomic classification which is subordinate to a Class and superior to a Family.

ordinance An authoritative direction or decree (e.g. by government).

oviparous Producing young from an egg, hatched outside the body of the mother, as distinct from ovoviviparous.

ox A castrated cattle male.

oxytocin A hormone secreted by the pituitary gland and released into the bloodstream which induces let-down of milk.

panzootic contagious disease One contracted over a very wide area by contact.

paraplegia Paralysis of the hind legs and posterior part of the body.

parenterally Referring to injections, given by subcutaneous, intravenous or intramuscular route, as distinct from administration by mouth.

paresis Paralysis which is partial only; slight paralysis.

parturient Referring to birth; connected with the act of parturition.

pathogen A disease-producing micro-organism.

pedigree A list of the individual's ancestors; usually only those of the five closest generations.

perinatal Around the time of birth.

peritoneal (fluid) Pertaining to the peritoneum, the smooth serous lining of the abdominal cavity, covering the inside of the wall of the abdomen and reflected over the abdominal viscera; the cavity contained by the peritoneum is filled with a clear straw-coloured fluid when normal.

petechiae Small pinpoints of haemorrhage usually numerous and giving the tissue a red spotted appearance; they indicate a pathological condition.

phenotype An individual's constitution in regard to the visible characters; contrast with genotype.

pheronome Chemical released by an animal that influences the behaviour and/or development of other individuals of the same species.

pica A tendency to eat abnormal articles as food, e.g. the consumption of wood, earth, faeces, stones, and in the case of herbivores, the eating of bones.

placenta The membrane, together with its accessories which covers the foetus in the uterus, that establishes communication including blood supply between mother and foetus; at birth the membrane is broken to release the offspring, and soon after, the umbilical cord which is integral with the placenta is detached from the umbilicus; later, the placenta is detached from the inner surface of the uterus of the mother and is shed.

polled Having no horns.

postmortem Subsequent to death; often used as a term to describe an examination after death, the word examination being inferred.

pregnancy diagnosis (PD) The determination

by manual examination via the rectum of the cow's internal genitalia whether or not she is in-calf.

prehension The act of seizing, usually the act of taking food with the mouth.

prepotency The ability possessed by certain individuals to impress their characteristics upon their offspring to a marked degree.

prepuce The fold of skin covering the anterior end of the penis.

proliferation The multiplication of similar forms, usually cells, or micro-organisms.

prophylactic Pertaining to prophylaxis, the prevention of disease.

prostaglandin Any one of a group of compounds, formed from C_{20} fatty acids containing a 5-member ring, that affect various hormonal reproductive activities.

protein Complex organic nitrogenous substance forming the principal constituent of living cells. Protein is made up of amino acids, sometimes linked to other molecules. There are many types of protein, and many different amino acids; protein is an essential constituent of food.

pruritus Intense itching.

puberty Sexual maturity.

purebred An animal which is registered or eligible to registration in the record books of its breed; it is the descendant, in all lines of its ancestry, of individuals of the same type as itself.

pure line A strain that has resulted from continued inbreeding, the individual members of which are closely related and highly purified.

quicklime Caustic or 'unslaked' lime.

raddling Painting the male's chest so that he leaves a mark on the female which indicates her acceptance in mating.

recessive The opposite of dominant.

rectum The last part of the large intestine before the anus; in large animals approximately the last 30 cm.

refractory A wound or disease that does not respond to treatment.

repeatability Statistical term used to describe the chances of a particular trait being repeated; usually measured to indicate herd or overall breed performance.

rib spread Good curvature of ribs, rather than flat-sided as in many Zebu cattle, but not the buffalo.

riverine Associated with a river and the area adjacent to it.

rotational grazing Moving cattle methodically from one paddock to another in a rotation of paddocks, resting each in turn.

salivation A discharge of saliva.

saprophyte A living organism that lives on dead or decaying matter.

scrub An animal of nondescript breeding and having no definite type; an inferior individual.

segregation The process by which genetic factors become separated and included in different gametes by the process of gametogenesis.

septicaemia Blood poisoning due to pathogenic bacteria and/or their toxins.

service Also joining, mating, mounting, covering. The mounting of a bull on a female resulting in the deposition of semen in the female's genital tract.

set-stocking The opposite of rotational grazing; keeping the same animals in one area.

sex chromosome A chromosome other than the autosomes and one which has been identified with one or the other of the sexes; one member of a pair of chromosomes which differ morphologically or physiologically from the autosomes and carry a factor or factors for sex.

sex-limited Applied to characters which are exhibited by one sex only.

sex ratio The proportion of males to females of a population.

shute Fenced alley where animals can be guided and restrained during handling for vaccination etc.; the crush is a more restricted portion of the shute.

sire Father.

species A category used in the taxonomic classification of living organisms which is subordinate to a genus; it is generally the final category and is composed of individuals having common characteristics which distinguish them from other categories, e.g. two of the species of the genus *Bos* are *Bos taurus* (temperate-type cattle) and *Bos indicus* (Zebu-type cattle).

springing (also freshening). The signs shown by a cow indicating the approach of calving.

standing hay Grass which has matured and dried out while standing.

staring coat A symptom noted in sick animals in which the hairs of the coat, instead of lying flat and being smooth and shiny, are standing up with the ends clear of each other and are dull and lustreless.

steaming-up Feeding a cow or heifer before calving to increase her subsequent lactation yield.

steer A castrated male being reared for meat; also referred to as a bullock.

sternum The breast bone.

stirrup pump A hand pump held at base by placing the foot through a metal ring or stirrup.

stomatitis Inflammation of the membrane lining the inside of the mouth.

strain A rather loose term applied to a group of individuals within a breed and differing in one or more characters from the other members of the breed, e.g. the Milking Shorthorns or Polled Herefords.

sub-clinical A condition in an animal which is diseased, but in which the symptoms are not sufficiently serious to be clinically manifest.

subcutaneous Under the skin.

surveillance To keep under close observation.

syndrome A set of symptoms that occur together; the total signs that collectively indicate an abnormal state; a complex of symptoms.

teaser bull A male bull or buffalo used to detect females on heat; operations may be done to cause deflection of the penis, or vasectomy, or by the simple use of an apron tied round the male's belly so that he may not successfully mate the female.

tenesmus Straining; especially ineffectual and painful straining at defaecation or urination.

terrain An area of land, including its geological formation, its vegetation and animal life.

tranquilliser A drug used to sedate or quieten an animal.

tribe (pertaining to classification) The category used in classification which is subordinate to a Class and superior to a Family.

udder quarter One of the four quarters into which the udder of cows is physically divided.

umbilicus The navel; the scar marking the point of attachment of the umbilical cord in the foetus.

uterus (also womb). The organ in the female in which the foetus develops during pregnancy.

vaccine A suspension of killed or attenuated micro-organisms, or of products derived from them, which on injection stimulate the production of antibodies against the disease which the micro-organisms cause.

vasectomy Surgical removal of part of the vas deferens so that semen on ejaculation does not enter the female at mating.

vector A carrier, especially the arthropod which carries an infective agent from one host to another.

vesicle Blister. A small circumscribed swelling of the epidermis containing a clear fluid.

viraemia The presence of viruses in the circulating blood.

viral Pertaining to viruses.

viscerotropic virus A virus which attacks primarily the viscera; having a predilection for the abdominal or thoracic viscera.

vitamin An organic substance occurring in small amounts in food and which is necessary for the proper functioning of the body.

viviparous Giving birth to live young, as distinct from oviparous, i.e. laying eggs.

wall-eyed Discolouration (usually bluish) of the iris in the eye.

withers The highest point at the shoulder in

humpless cattle, or just behind the hump in Zebu cattle.

yearling An animal of either sex somewhere between the ages of 12–20 months.

zero grazing A system of management where all feed is transported to the animal which is confined.

zoonosis A disease which is transmissible between animals and man.

1 Introduction

Developing countries contributed some 27.8 per cent of world beef and veal production in 1974–76, rising to 33.3 per cent in 1982. However, as will be seen from Table 1.1, the average cattle carcass weight in developing countries was much lower than that in developed countries and is not increasing as rapidly. Therefore, despite a large increase in the number slaughtered between 1974–76 and 1982 the contribution of developing countries to the world's beef supplies has not increased proportionally. In view of the immense cattle resources of developing countries, some 65.2 per cent of the world's total (Table 1.2), a priority development objective in the tropics, where the majority of developing countries are located, must be to increase productivity per head of cattle.

Out of a world population of 122 m head of buffalo in 1982 (Table 1.2), 11.9 per cent were in Africa, 87.2 per cent in Asia and 0.9 per cent in Europe and the USSR. There was a 15 per cent increase in the total number of buffalo between 1974–76 and 1982, Asia accounting for 12.8 per cent of this increase. Asia also accounted for 88.5 per cent of the world output of 1 352 mt of buffalo meat in 1982. However, improvements in carcass weight in the developing countries were negligible compared with improvements in developed countries, 0.7 per cent as against 5.8 per cent (Table 1.3). Thus, as with beef cattle, the objective should be to augment carcass weight through improved nutrition and management. That this can be accomplished has been demonstrated in the tropics.

Table 1.1 World output of beef and veal by region

Region	'000 head slaughtered		Carcass wt (kg)		Production '000 (mt)		Percentage change in production
	1974–76	1982	1974–76	1982	1974–76	1982	
World	228 984	233 861	193	195	4 428	45 656	3.1
Developing market economies							
Africa	13 415	15 777	124	126	1 667	1 989	19.3
Latin America	37 821	41 977	193	193	7 299	8 091	10.9
Near East	7 044	9 105	115	115	808	1 047	29.6
Far East	7 241	8 438	121	122	877	1 033	17.8
Other	73	81	163	165	12	13	8.3
Developed market economies							
North America	50 333	43 475	247	246	12 452	11 471	−7.9
Western Europe	38 116	35 186	215	234	8 185	8 219	0.4
Oceania	12 263	11 914	170	175	2 083	2 090	0.3
Other	3 721	3 978	231	257	861	1 021	18.6
Centre planned economies							
Asian CPE	11 037	14 110	149	149	1 644	2 105	28.0
Eastern Europe and USSR	47 921	49 820	175	172	8 392	8 578	2.2
Developed total	152 353	144 373	210	217	31 975	31 379	1.9
Developing total	76 631	89 488	144	145	12 308	14 277	16.0

Table 1.2 World meat production by region and contribution of domestic animal species

Livestock population ('000 head)

	World total	Developed market economies	Developing market economies	Percentage of world total (developing markets)
Beef cattle	1 226 433	427 190	799 243	65.2
Buffaloes	122 053	770	121 283	99.4
Sheep	1 167 690	542 923	624 767	53.9
Goats	472 784	25 681	447 103	94.6
Pigs	763 813	332 963	430 850	56.4
Horses	65 044	22 160	42 884	65.9
Camels	17 050	211	16 839	98.8
Poultry	6 578 484	3 110 166	34 688 318	52.7

Table 1.3 Total meat produced, number slaughtered and carcass weight of buffalo on the world market

	(1) '000 head slaughtered		(2) Carcass wt (kg)		Percentage change		Total meat ('000 mt)	
	1974–76	1982	1974–76	1982	(1)	(2)	(1)	(2)
Developed market economies	84	78	190	201	−7.2	5.8	15.9	15.6
Developing market economies	8 011	9 240	144	145	15.3	0.7	1 152	1 337 (16.1%)

For example, in Bangladesh, Brunei, Burma, Vietnam, Brazil and northern Australia, improved buffalo carcass weights compare favourably with those in the developed buffalo meat market economies of Greece, Bulgaria and Romania.

Australia and Brazil are currently the largest producers of buffalo meat on a commercial basis. In tropical northern Australia in 1982, 32 913 feral buffaloes were slaughtered for the export trade and a further 7 076 at local abattoirs. In addition 111 live buffaloes were exported. Of a total of 308 350 head of buffaloes in Latin America 300 000 (92.5 per cent) are located in Brazil. A total of 1 060 mt of dressed buffalo carcass was recorded recently from seven of the large meat packing companies in Brazil.

The contribution by the developing market economy countries to international trade refers more specifically to inter-regional exports, e.g. between Argentina and North America and Europe, and between Botswana and the EEC coun-

tries. There is also considerable exchange of livestock and livestock products across international borders in neighbouring tropical countries, of which much remains unrecorded in the official registers. The FAO has developed and is further developing what is termed a 'matrix' to account for this type of international trading and this is being incorporated in the FAO Production Yearbooks. In this context total beef and veal production listed in Table 1.1 includes the meat equivalent of exported animals. In other words, the totals presented are not all available for domestic consumption. Attempts to meet this demand are made through importations (Table 1.4) from neighbouring countries. Such importations are often extensive. Many countries in Africa, for example, especially those with nomadic pastoralist peoples, have large numbers of livestock within their national boundaries. Despite this, increased numbers of live cattle are imported annually to meet local demands for meat. In three major cattle producing countries in

West Africa, Niger, Nigeria and Senegal, with an estimated total of some 18 million head of cattle, over 40 000 head were imported in 1982 from neighbouring countries. This does not hold true in all cases. Mali, also in West Africa and with over 5 million head of cattle, was a net exporter of 250 000 head of cattle in 1982.

In many African countries widespread and prolonged drought has affected supplies of cattle from traditional pastoralist sources and this, coupled with rising prices due to inflation, has lowered consumer demand in the private sector. Substantial demands for meat, however, still continue in those countries supporting large standing armies and other security forces.

In the international export market for fresh bovine meat in 1982 developing Latin American countries accounted for about one-quarter of the total (Table 1.4) with Argentina being the largest exporter. Some 1 per cent of the total was exported from Africa, mainly from Botswana (30 000 mt),

Zimbabwe (2 432 mt in 1981), Madagascar (867 mt) and Kenya (220 mt).

In addition to fresh bovine meat, Argentina and Brazil between them exported in 1982 a further 197 831 mt of canned meat, much of this beef. In Africa, Kenya came first with canned meat exports of 2 230 mt and Ethiopia second with about half this quantity; there were small contributions also from Madagascar, Ivory Coast, Senegal, Tanzania and Tunisia. Fresh offal forms a considerable import and export trade between neighbouring countries, besides dried and salted meats, all of which add substantially to total meat supplies.

India dominated the meat market in Asia with a steadily rising output of fresh bovine meat (42 000 mt) for export in 1982. There were virtually no imports. Indonesia, the Korean Republic and Singapore, despite substantial exports in these commodities, were nonetheless, along with most other countries in Asia, net importers. Asian countries with centrally planned economies, however, showed a markedly favourable balance of exports over imports in fresh bovine meat. This favourable balance was due, however, to exports from China and Mongolia. The overall imports for the same commodities in the developing market economy countries in tropical areas of the region exceeded total exports by 37.3 per cent.

World market prices for imports and exports in 1982 of various kinds of meat are given in Table 1.5. Prices per kg of meat are calculated from the total quantities involved in metric tonnes, and their equivalent values in US dollars. The price of beef is markedly lower for the developing meat exporting countries in Africa and Latin America (Table 1.6). The high cost of sheep meat in Africa, on the other hand, at prices over one-third of those

Table 1.4 Import and export of fresh bovine meat on the world market (1982)

Region	Import (mt)	Export (mt)
Developed market economies	2 162 918	2 422 738
North America	681 054	139 901
Western Europe	1 307 951	1 506 710
Oceania	1 805	776 108
Other	172 108	19
Developing market economies	761 295	658 082
Africa	130 328	34 592
Latin America	99 605	861 999
Near East	389 875	15 600
Far East	124 433	45 391
Other	17 054	500
Centre planned economies	485 530	227 937
Asian CPE	19 777	30 000
Eastern Europe and USSR	465 753	197 937
Developed total	2 628 671	2 620 675
Developing total	781 072	688 082

Table 1.5 Cost of various meats on the world market in 1982 (US $ per kg)

Meat class	Developed market economies		Developing market economies	
	Import	Export	Import	Export
Bovine (fresh)	2.7	2.6	2.1	1.8
Sheep	2.3	1.7	2.0	2.2
Pig	2.3	1.9	1.9	2.1
Poultry	1.6	1.2	1.3	1.1

in Latin America and Australia, may be due, to a large extent, to high demands during Muslim festivals. At such times prices paid bear little relation to carcass values.

Table 1.6   Price of beef exported from major developing market economies in 1982 (US $ per kg)

	Export
Latin America	
Argentine	1.9
Brazil	2.0
Uruguay	1.4
Africa	
Botswana	2.2
Kenya	2.1
Zimbabwe	2.4

World demand for beef

Estimated world demand for all meats and beef for 1980 are provided in Table 1.7. Using these figures as a baseline, demands for 1982 have been calculated on the arbitrary basis of increases in world human population in the developed market economy countries since 1980 of 1.5 per cent, and of 4.2 per cent for the developing market economy countries.

Table 1.7 indicates a shortfall of some 3.1 per cent and 8.6 per cent for total meat production and beef, respectively, in the developed market economy countries. Among these, both Western Europe and Oceania were equal to or slightly in excess of projected demands in 1982. In the developing market economy countries the total shortfall for beef was 10.3 per cent but total meat production was in excess of estimated demands. Africa was close to meeting demands for beef in 1982, perhaps due to reduced purchasing power on the part of the average consumer. Beef production in Latin America equalled estimated demands during the same period, but in the Near and Far East it was well below estimated demand. Such a situation would be compensated for, to a considerable extent, by the availability of buffalo meat. Asian, East European and the USSR countries in the centrally planned economy areas were also below the estimated demand figures for beef but, as opposed to the general shortfall elsewhere, total meat production from other livestock sources was 11.2 per cent above estimated demand.

The potential of developing market economy countries in the tropics may be seen from the considerable expansion in production of both the beef and buffalo meat producing countries referred to above. Much of this output stems from production in the traditional sector and on this account international livestock aid programmes are giving increasing recognition of the importance of socio-economic and other factors relating to the more traditional methods of animal husbandry.

Many barriers to the export trade need to be overcome by those countries wishing to enter the world market, including tariffs, levies, trade licences, quarantine regulations and the problem of international monetary exchange rates. Disease control on an international basis is necessary for developing countries to compete on the livestock and livestock products export market. An essential factor in this respect is the establishment of major disease free zones which would facilitate meat trading between countries included in the zones. Some of these have already been or are in the

Table 1.7   World meat demand and production

	Estimated demand 1982[1] ('000 mt)		Production 1982 ('000 mt)		Shortfall ('000 mt)	
	All meats	Beef	All meats	Beef	All meats	Beef
Developed market economies	66 744	27 934	64 738	22 801	2 006	5 184
Developing market economies and centre planned economies	71 823	27 006	79 876	22 856	8 053(+)	4 150

[1] Calculated on the basis of FAO estimates for 1980 plus population growth of 1.5% for developed and 4.2% for other market economies.

process of being established in Kenya, Somalia, the Sudan, Turkey, Thailand and Colombia. Other countries, including Ethiopia, Tanzania, Indonesia and the Philippines, are considering their establishment.

Possibilities for increasing the production of beef

The two major sectors in which beef production in the tropics could most rapidly be improved are in perennial crop production systems and commercial ranching in the humid and sub-humid tropics. New methods and organisations are required for the proper exploitation of agro by-product feed resources by large bovines in the perennial crop areas. In a specific situation in Africa considerable interest has been revived in utilising the small but comparatively efficient trypano-tolerant cattle in tsetse fly inhabited areas in both extensive and more intensive management situations.

Improvement in meat productivity in the sedentary subsistence cultivation systems in which the largest number of cattle and buffalo are at present raised, will continue to be slow and difficult, involving certain changes in crop management that must be acceptable to the farmer. Not least among these will be changes in cereal crop cultivation and the judicious use of tropical legumes.

For nomadic and transhumant systems to survive and develop in tropical Africa innovations to existing systems need to be adequately tested in order to ensure that they fit into the pastoralist's traditional way of life. Cooperative ranching schemes for those pastoralists willing to accept some measure of government managerial control also offer opportunities for more efficient land use.

Both water and swamp buffaloes, in large areas of the tropics otherwise unsuited to domestic ruminants, continue to provide the main domestic source of meat. There is now, however, mounting evidence that buffalo calves under proper conditions of intensive feeding and management and slaughtered at the right age can compete with similarly managed beef cattle. Under extensive management regimes the feral buffalo of northern Australia and the semi-feral and ranch-reared buffalo of Brazil show the greatest potential for providing an export market in buffalo meat. There is particular need for further research on the buffalo as a world competitor on the international meat market. This could well be directed towards research in nutrition, breeding and selection and the identification of the most suitable meat producing types under a given environmental situation.

Some of the systems of cattle and buffalo meat production currently operating in the tropics and their potential for development under more extensive or intensive management are more fully discussed in subsequent chapters.

Further reading

Crolty, R. (1980) *Cattle, economics and development.* Commonwealth Agric. Bureau: Farnham Royal, UK.

Crump, D. K. (1973). Cattle and buffalo in Southeast Asia – their past and present role in the economy of the region – a philosophy for development. *New Zealand Agric. Sci.*, **9**, 138–143.

Hall, W. J. A. and **De Boer, A. J.** (1977). Increasing ruminant productivity in Asia. *Wld. Rev. Anim. Prod.*, **13** (3), 9–16.

Mahadevan, P. (1978). Water buffalo research – possible future trends. *Wld. Anim. Rev.*, **25**, 2–7.

Rao, M. K. and **Nagarcenkar, R.** (1977). Potentialities of the buffalo. *Wld. Rev. Anim. Prod.*, **13** (3), 53–61.

Spedding, C. R. W. and **Hoxey, A. M.** (1974). The potential for conventional meat animals. In *Meat: proceedings of the 21st Easter school in agricultural science, Univ. of Nottingham.* Butterworth: London.

2 The effects of climate on production

General considerations

Pastoral enterprises are carried out in a wide variety of climates throughout the world. Grazing animals therefore encounter climatic conditions that can markedly affect their levels of production. The study of the behaviour and performance of animals in different climates is referred to by numerous terms, the best known being climate physiology, environmental physiology, or bioclimatology. During the past few decades much attention has been given to the performance of livestock in hot environments. *Bos indicus* cattle, for example, have been observed to withstand both dry and humid tropical environments better than most *Bos taurus* breeds, and in addition Australian cattlemen in tropical Queensland have observed greater resistance to ectoparasites in *Bos indicus* breeds or crossbreds compared with *Bos taurus* breeds, under the same conditions of management.

Within tropical areas regional differences in productivity reflect climatic effects on vegetation and animals, as well as on differences in breed, or strain of animal. Such regional differences are often most marked in upland and lowland areas of the tropics. For example, the long-legged, rangy Rahaji or Red Bororo of the Sahel zone of West Africa, that is usually considered to be a poor beef animal, will under good management produce excellent beef on the pastures of the Cameroon montane border uplands and crosses admirably with the local humped Adamawa upland breeds (figs 2.1 and 2.2). Such variations in the productivity of local types, or their crosses, can be demonstrated in the comparatively narrow confines of a selected tropical zone – in this case West Africa. Climatic effects on growth of pasture are thus probably the most important of the influences of climate on the productivity of meat from cattle and buffalo. In parts of the tropics, variations in 'summer' and 'winter' rainfall have the most marked effect. In much of the tropics, however, the seasonal pattern of rainfall is more clearly identified, as the rainy and the dry season.

fig. 2.1 Red Bororo

fig. 2.2 Adamawa

It can be seen, therefore, that livestock production in the tropics is markedly influenced by environmental variables. The term variable in this instance refers to those variations in the climate which have either a direct, or an indirect effect upon animal growth and production. The livestock producer in the tropics is particularly concerned with these variables since extremes of heat and humidity can greatly affect such physiological functions as growth, reproduction, milk secretion and egg production.

Air temperatures of 13–18 °C are considered to be ideal for optimum growth and production in cattle and buffaloes, combined with an average relative humidity of 55–65 per cent, a wind velocity of 5–8 km/hr and a medium level of sunshine. Such ideal conditions seldom exist and certainly not in the major part of the tropics. This is the reason why many temperate breeds of beef or dairy cattle in the tropics can rarely – despite some acclimatisation and good feeding – express their optimum genetic capacity in terms of production. Much of the producer's time is spent in trying to improve environmental conditions and in breeding and selecting breeds most suited to local conditions that will give greater economic returns than local unimproved animals.

In cattle, which are in any event polyoestrous and thus have regular reproductive cycles, the period of light or day-length in the 24 hours (photoperiod) is of little importance compared with other factors such as nutrition. This is particularly so in the arid tropics, where the long dry season and consequent lack of feed have a marked influence on the productivity of indigenous cattle.

Biometeorological principles

The physical environment is generally thought of as the prevailing climatic conditions, but the latter are only a portion of the animal's environment. Climate can be defined as average weather conditions, whereas weather comprises the day-to-day changing meteorological conditions immediately surrounding the animal. Macroclimate refers to those further removed. The ambient temperature, sunshine, wind, light, precipitation and humidity are important elements of climate because they influence most of the other elements of the environment in one way or another. The conditions created by the climatic elements have both direct and indirect effects on the animal. Indirect effects influence the growth and quality of forage, the incidence of diseases and parasites, the efficiency of labour, and numerous other conditions.

Temperature is the chief climatic element which directly affects the physiological functions of an animal. Climates may have daily variation ranges from about 6 °C near the equator to 16–20 °C in desert regions. In West Africa, temperatures just before the rains in the southern coastal regions vary as little as 5–10 °C; whilst in the northern Sahel such variations may be as much as 30–35 °C, with bitterly cold nights at certain times of the year and scorching temperatures during the day.

A mean daily temperature in the range of 10 to 20 °C would not be likely to place cattle and buffalo under thermal stress; that is, there are no discernible changes in the animal's usual body processes within this range, which is generally referred to as the 'comfort zone'. Newborn animals, on the other hand, long acclimatised to the constant environment of the dam's uterus, are more sensitive to the thermal environment. The comfort zone in such cases may be restricted to ±1 or 2 °C. This is especially so, for example, in young pigs.

As the temperature conditions fall outside the comfort zone, other elements of the climate assume greater significance in the comfort of animals. The water-vapour content of the air or relative humidity becomes increasingly important as an interacting factor with any rise or fall in air temperature. Solar radiation and wind velocity also assume importance. For example, at low temperatures solar radiation raises the temperature of the animal's surroundings and so helps maintain thermal balance. At high temperatures, on the other hand, direct solar radiation will impose an excess heat load on the animal (fig. 2.3). Air velocity may have an opposite effect, since a good strong wind will increase the rate of movement of air away from the animal's body and hasten cooling by dissipating body heat into the atmosphere. It should be borne in mind however that when the ambient air temperature exceeds the temperature of the animal's skin surface the skin cannot lose heat to the atmosphere and this imposes a significant stress on the animal.

Grazing animals are exposed to all the elements including direct sunlight and rain. Rain helps the animal on a hot day (water sprays are used in many tropical dairies) but in cold weather rain can cause chills. In the tropics, sudden storms can cause quite

7

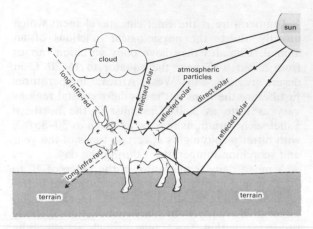

fig. 2.3 Channels of radiation exchange between an animal and its surroundings

marked changes in ambient temperatures which can increase stress and consequent susceptibility to infectious disease agents.

Altitude influences the prevailing air temperature pattern. Air temperature diminishes at the rate of about 0.65 °C per 100 m increase in elevation. However, as in parts of the Kenya uplands, local topography frequently upsets this relationship. Sheep, goats, and cattle managed at altitudes above 2 500 m or higher may exhibit altitude stress. In addition to low oxygen pressure, the dry atmosphere of high altitude is a further hazard for the newborn, affecting the body's water balance, temperature regulation, respiration, and vulnerability to diseases. Livestock tend nevertheless to become acclimatised to altitudes and can survive, for example, in Peru at altitudes above 4 000 m. However, very high altitudes do influence the growth-rate and nutritive value of plants and this is a further example of the indirect effect of climate on livestock. In spite of these disadvantages, reasonably productive livestock enterprises are carried on in the tropics or subtropics at altitudes of 2 000 to 3 000 m. Although certain diseases such as 'brisket disease', in which the heart and circulation are affected, do occur at high altitudes, ruminants in particular can become remarkably adapted to conditions of high altitude.

There are thus many environmental elements that have a major direct influence on an animal, with important interactions that influence their overall effect. The amount and quality of feed available is perhaps the single most important factor in livestock production. This determines not only the animal's growth rate and production, but it also contributes to resistance to other conditions, including many diseases.

Meat animals in the tropics have to maintain themselves in a state of thermal homeostasis or heat balance in order to sustain productive performance in terms of growth and/or reproduction. It is important to bear in mind that no matter what the genetic (hereditary) make-up of the meat animal, it cannot express its full potential unless the environment, that is, the climate, feed and management, and other factors, make this possible.

Mechanisms of heat production and heat loss

There are still differences of opinion as to the practical significance or value in the field of some of the experimental results obtained in the laboratory, but livestock husbandmen in the tropics are nevertheless aware of the importance of certain physiological and physical criteria in stock management and take note, from the practical standpoint, of many of these findings.

Adaptations to adverse conditions are mainly the result of adaptations or improvements in the physiological systems of the body that are common to all cattle and buffaloes and to most other warm-blooded animals. Adaptations in those systems concerned with heat regulation and body metabolism are of special importance. In tropical areas, regulating the heat system is mainly concerned with coping with excess heat production (heat load) and hence loss of heat. Heat production may be increased by several factors, for example the heat increment of feeding, the utilisation of body food reserves, the state of activity and even the posture of an animal.

Heat is produced by oxidations in the active protoplasm of the body. Muscle and gland are the most active tissues of the body and are therefore the principal areas of heat production. During strenuous work or exercise the greater portion of the heat is produced in skeletal muscle. Weight for weight, however, the liver is one of the most active and constant sources of heat.

The mechanism of heat production and heat loss covers a wide range of inter-related factors. The heat arising from the energy derived from the oxidation of food and body reserves, in addition to the ambient heat received by the animal from radiation, convection and conduction, is dissipated by radiation, convection, conduction, and evaporation. These in turn are influenced by the temperature of the surrounding environment, the air temperature, humidity and wind velocity. All of these methods of dissipating heat are themselves further influenced by the physical characteristics of the animal, such as the body surface area; the type, colour and texture of the body covering; skin and lung moisture vaporisation; water exchange (drinking and excretion); and the thermal conductivity of tissues peripheral to the blood flow.

An environmental temperature above or below certain levels raises the heat production of the body. There is an environmental temperature below which the rate of metabolism of an animal must be increased to prevent a fall of body temperature. This environmental temperature, known in the resting, fasting animal as the critical temperature, shows considerable inter- and intra-species variation. If the environmental temperature falls below the critical temperature, heat production by the animal must increase if the body temperature is to remain constant. If the environmental temperature is raised above the critical temperature, heat loss mechanisms must come into play so that the rate of metabolism and body temperature are not materially increased. However, if the environmental temperature is further raised, the warming of the active protoplasm by the rise of body temperature causes an increase in the metabolic rate.

In considering changes in body temperature, however, too much emphasis has perhaps been placed, in the past, on the constancy of the temperature of the body as a whole, and too little stress has been placed on its variability. The rectal temperature is a fair index of the internal temperature of the body, but there are gradients of temperature in the blood, tissues and rectum, the lowest temperatures being on the surface of the body. In addition normal variations in temperature may be due to sex, season, time of day, and may follow eating, drinking or exercise. In considering temperature changes in the body, therefore, these normal variations need to be taken into account before it is assumed that the animal may be responding adversely to increased ambient temperature and humidity. Rises in temperature may, of course, also be due to disease.

The nervous regulation of body temperature

Regulation against a rise of body temperature is under the control of the nervous system acting through the nerves of the vasomotor, sweat, and respiratory centres and the pilomotor nerves which control the erection of hairs or feathers. Regulation against a fall of body temperature can be achieved by vasoconstriction (constriction of peripheral blood vessels) in the skin, a decrease in the activity of the sweat glands and erection of hairs or feathers. When these responses are no longer effective, skeletal muscles are brought into play.

The centre for control of temperature regulation exists in that part of the brain known as the hypothalamus. This 'heat centre' is said to be activated according to the temperature of the blood bathing its cells. When the blood is cooled, the heat conserving area is stimulated and the body heat is conserved, or more heat is produced. The reverse takes place when the blood is warmed. The 'heat centre' is also activated by reflexes from the skin.

Regulation against cooling

Regulation against body cooling is brought about first by a reduction of cooling (physical regulation) and later by an increase of heat production (chemical regulation). In the first case, reduction of cooling or heat loss can be achieved by vasoconstriction, causing a diminished blood flow to the skin and thus reducing heat loss by radiation, conduction and convection. A well developed heat retaining mechanism betokens a low critical temperature. Man lowers his critical temperature by the use of clothing. Hair, fur, feathers, or subcutaneous fat act similarly in animals. Among the domestic animals cattle and sheep have been shown to have low critical temperatures and are thus able to withstand extremes of cold.

Heat production can be achieved by vigorous, voluntary bodily movements. Increased metabolism is also brought about by shivering, rapid reflex muscular contractions stimulated by the action of cold on receptors in the skin and by the action of blood of lowered temperatures reaching the heat regulating centres. An increased output of hormones from the thyroid gland and adrenal gland cortex may also play a part in the adjustment of the metabolic rate. It appears, however, that the emergency response to extreme cold is by shivering.

The body can also respond to an increased tendency to cool by an increased metabolism, a further form of regulation quite apart from those mentioned above. This form of regulation might likewise enter into account where surrounding temperatures are raised, by a reduced metabolism. It is, in fact, a regulation of heat production and not of loss of heat.

The means whereby an animal can vary its heat production are nonetheless very limited compared with its ability to conserve or eliminate heat. Most recent work on the larger farm animals has been concerned with the study of heat loss mechanisms.

Regulation against overheating

All body heat produced must be dissipated either by the non-evaporative channels (convection, radiation and conduction), or by the evaporative channel (moisture vaporisation from the skin and the lungs), or by both. Radiation is the transfer of energy across space without heating the space through which it passes. Conduction is the passage of heat energy from particle to particle of matter by increased molecular agitation. Convection is the transfer of heat energy by a circulation of heated material (gas, liquid) which is less dense than the cooler material. Convection facilitates heat exchange within the animal's body by means of the circulatory blood and on the skin surface by the rate of air flow.

Non-evaporative cooling Under ordinary conditions about 75 per cent of the heat lost from the body is dissipated via the non-evaporative channels. Heat loss by convection, i.e. the replacement of air next to the skin by cool air, is affected by the surface area of the animal and will thus vary with posture. It is also affected by the velocity of the air moving past the animal's surface, and by the temperature of the animal's surface and the ambient air.

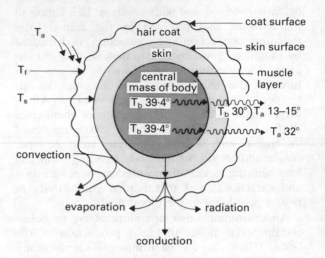

T_a = air temperature
T_b = temperature of central core
T_f = temperature of hair-coat surface
T_s = temperature of skin surface

fig. 2.4 The physical processes of heat dissipation from the animal's body and the influence of ambient air at 13–15 °C (rapid) and 32 °C (low) on the rate of exchange

Heat loss by conduction enables the animal to lose heat by physical contact with surrounding surfaces, and the magnitude of this loss will depend on the thermal conductivity of the contacting surfaces, their areas and temperatures. Heat is produced chiefly in the deeper body tissues and is diffused by conduction to the cooler parts and ultimately to the skin. The degree of conduction of heat through the tissues, however, is comparatively low and does not account for any appreciable degree of heat loss from the body except when the animal is in contact, for example, with cold cement floors, or in cold water wallows.

Heat loss by radiation from the animal's body is of considerable importance. Human skin, of whatever colour, radiates strongly in the long wavelengths and at a rate proportional to the fourth power of its absolute temperature. The body surface, therefore, exchanges heat with its surroundings, such as walls or rocks, at a rate proportional to the difference between the fourth powers of their temperatures. For example, if the temperature of wall or rock falls considerably, the radiation loss for a given skin temperature rapidly increases. Here again, however, the radiation loss will depend upon the posture of the animal (e.g. crowded or huddled together) and the emissivity of the skin, that is, how nearly the skin is a perfect absorber or emitter of heat. Furthermore, the nature and colouring of the animal's coat also affects considerably the degree of radiation. While the rate of heat loss by radiation is proportionate to the surface area of the animal, it is also necessary to take into account the fact that there is no heat loss by radiation between surfaces that touch each other, e.g. in the area of contact between the forelegs and chest. The physical processes of heat dissipation from the body and the influence of ambient air temperature are illustrated schematically in fig. 2.4.

Evaporative cooling Evaporation of water from the skin and respiratory surfaces accounts for much of the heat lost by an animal. The rate of such heat dissipated depends on the surface area of the animal; the vapour pressure of the surrounding air (humidity); the rate of air movement surrounding the animal; and the extent of respiratory activity. Evaporation of water from the skin is further modified by the temperature of the skin and degree of covering of the skin, e.g. wool or hair, and the amount of water available for evaporation.

Generally speaking, about 25 per cent of the heat produced in a resting animal at ordinary environmental temperatures is lost by water vaporisation from the skin and respiratory passages. This evaporative loss is proportional to the metabolic rate of the animal and is known as the insensible perspiration. Ordinarily, evaporation keeps pace with insensible perspiration so that no visible moisture collects on the skin.

At higher temperatures, however, the loss of heat through vaporisation of water from the skin is much more efficient in animals with well developed sweat glands. Some animals, though, have a comparatively inefficient sweating mechanism and vaporise a large amount of water from the lungs and from the tongue, as observed during panting. Panting occurs in other animals but it is most marked in the dog. Panting in cattle and buffalo is a sign of extreme heat distress. There are wide variations in the development of sweat glands in domestic animals. The goat, rabbit and chicken have none. The horse has the best developed sweat glands and like man sweats from the whole body surface. The dog has sweat glands distributed all over the body and both the dog and cat sweat from the footpads. It is doubtful, however, if sweating from the footpads is concerned in temperature regulation. Many studies now indicate that both sheep and cattle sweat and that sweat secretion is of some value in cooling their bodies. There is still some debate as to whether tropical breeds of cattle lose heat much more efficiently by sweating than do temperate breeds. In general, however, the sweating mechanism of the domestic animal is inferior to that of man.

Drinking helps to reduce the body temperature in view of the fact that the imbibed water becomes raised to body temperature. On the other hand, the vaporisation of a given unit of water from the skin is said to dissipate 15 times more heat from the animal than does drinking. Since the cow may drink 8 times more water than she vaporises, however, considerable benefit is obtained from drinking. A small amount of heat is lost from the body through the faeces and urine.

Practical implications

Coat hair characteristics, including overall coat thickness, colour, length, curliness, fibre thickness and internal hair fibre structure are all considered important in heat loss or for reduction of heat load by the non-evaporative channels of radiation, convection and conduction.

The coat hair as well as the skin are important in protecting the body from excess solar radiation. Solar radiation can impose a considerable heat load in the tropics. The coat protects the animal by reflecting heat away from the body and by insulating the body against part of the radiation. The absorptance (the proportion of incident radiation absorbed) varies with the colour of the coat.

Exposed to short wavelength (ultra-violet) radiation, cattle coats of any colour absorb almost all the incident solar radiant energy. The potentially damaging ultra-violet rays are, however, absorbed in a pigmented (coloured) skin and this renders them less harmful; it also protects the animal from photosensitisation.

On the other hand, light-coloured coats reflect away a considerable proportion of the solar energy contained in the visible and long, infra-red wavelengths. Since this energy generates considerable heat, the lighter coats such as white, brown and red, serve to protect the animal from this additional heat load. Many tropical breeds of cattle, e.g. the White Fulani (Bunaji) of West Africa (fig. 2.5) have the ideal combination of black skin, combined with a light-coloured coat. So also has the N'dama (fig. 2.6) which has reddish skin and a brown coat.

A larger surface area has also been claimed to be advantageous to the animal, so that the greater body area of Zebu cattle with their umbilical fold, hump and dewlap, assists heat loss. However, experimental evidence in the laboratory (regarding the contribution of the hump) and practical work in the field no longer entirely support this view.

For many years it was considered that cattle did not sweat, but it is now generally accepted that sweating provides a most important avenue of heat loss in cattle exposed to hot environments. Both *Bos indicus* and *Bos taurus* breeds have been shown to possess sweat glands. Humped Zebu cattle and humpless tropical breeds of cattle such as the N'dama, can sweat more effectively and at higher temperatures than temperate-type *Bos taurus* cattle. It has also been demonstrated that selection for sweating ability in *Bos taurus* can also be effective, as in the Australian Illawara Shorthorn breed, which has been selected over the years for both the cooler south, as well as for the tropical areas of the north of Australia.

Improved sweating ability in tropical breeds may be due to the increased number, volume and more sack-like shape of the sweat glands, and an improved supply of blood to the skin; the skin thickness and other factors may be involved. Sleek-coated animals are also reported to sweat more easily since their sweat glands are claimed to be associated with more actively growing hairs. Hair growth and coat shedding are also important characteristics associated with seasonal changes, so that the glossy summer coat, for example, is at the same time accompanied by increased sweat gland activity, in response to summer heat.

Coat type and ability to thrive are associated with efficient coat shedding. This is indicated by the number of new hairs produced at different periods of the year and appears to be closely related to the animal's gain in liveweight. Beef cattle with 'woolly' or curly coats do not thrive as well as those with

fig. 2.5 White Fulani

fig. 2.6 N'dama

Table 2.1 Proportion of total incident solar radiation absorbed by samples of cattle pelts

Sample	Absorptance (direct and diffuse radiation)
White 1	0.45
White 2	0.54
White 3	0.58
Brown 1	0.81
Brown 2	0.84
Black 1	0.91
Black 2	0.92

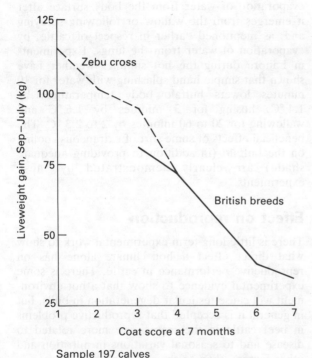

Sample 197 calves
Low scores indicate a sleek coat
High scores indicate a rough coat

fig. 2.7 Relation between subjective coat score and growth rate

sleek coats in a hot environment, especially in conditions of under-nutrition. The type of coat can reflect any one or more of several factors: seasonal changes in the coat, the nutritional status of the animal, debility due to disease, its genotype, and its individual ability to thrive. The 'coat score', in which the coat is examined and scored at a given time of the year, can be used to help predict the future potential of the animal and so is a useful additional criterion in breeding and selection programmes in a hot environment (Table 2.1 and fig. 2.7). Beef cattle producers have also demonstrated that clipping of the long coat can improve heat tolerance and consequently the growth performance of cattle on range.

There are reports of high heritability of coat colour in relation to production characteristics, although coat score accounted for only 16 per cent of variation in liveweight gain in a group of cattle 16 to 28 months of age. Opinions from other sources are that selection for a short coat will not necessarily improve performance, selection for liveweight gain and/or efficiency being far more effective in improving herd production. There is also some lack of agreement on the role of coat colour in heat tolerance; experiments in Central America indicating that black Holstein × Brahman crossbreds had a better production performance than whitish-grey Brahmans. Such differences in opinion arising from different trials may be expected, but the varying conditions under which experiments are conducted, such as breed differences, hybrid vigour, management and duration and season, particularly where there are cool nights or cooler spells allowing for a 'recovery period', may account for some of these. Generally speaking, however, the majority of tropical cattle breeds and types adapted to the semi-arid and sub-humid zones have lighter coloured, short and glossy coats which are shed and replaced throughout the year, as well as pigmented skins. It must be assumed that such characteristics are the most appropriate under prevailing conditions.

The view has also been expressed that too much emphasis has been placed in the past on the superiority of the heat loss mechanism in *Bos indicus* over *Bos taurus*. Experimental work in Central America has demonstrated that superior heat tolerance in a group of Red Sindhi × Holstein crossbreds over the Red Sindhi was due to their lower heat production both in absolute terms and per unit of body surface area. It was concluded that lower body temperatures and respiration rates in Zebu cattle are due more to overall lower heat production than to the possession of a superior heat exchange mechanism. Furthermore, although the Zebu had lower metabolic rates than the crossbred cattle, they required as much feed energy as the latter to maintain weight gains. Similar findings have been observed in experiments with Red Sindhi and Holstein × Red Sindhi crossbreds in Louisiana, USA. A high level of nutrition and low heat tolerance are to some extent incompatible. High productivity entails high feed intake with resultant high heat production arising from the 'heat increment' of feeding. The high fibre content of a feedstuff results in a higher heat increment and a good management practice in feedlot cattle in some hot climate areas is to reduce as far as possible the fibre content of the ration.

Young calves may be less able to withstand high temperatures during the first month of life due to a higher metabolic rate at this stage. Coat hair probably reaches maximum growth between 6 to 24 months of age, so that selection of calves, using various attributes for heat tolerance, can be useful at this age.

The thick, hard-to-the-touch skin of the buffalo is due to the greater percentage of total skin thickness accounted for by the horny layer (*stratum corneum*) than is the case with cattle. Pigment granules are also numerous. As in cattle, the hairs grow singly and each hair is associated with sweat and sebaceous glands. However, while the skins of temperate and tropical breeds of cattle are estimated to have some 800–1 000 and 1 500–1 700 hairs/cm², respectively, the skin of the buffalo may possess only 100–200 hairs/cm², or less than one-tenth the hair density of cattle. The density of hairs at birth is fixed, so that the density of both hairs and associated sweat and sebaceous glands diminishes as the animal grows and its surface area increases. About 80 per cent of hairs in the adult buffalo are short and fine, while the rest are long and coarse. The thick, hard skin of the buffalo may help protect it from insects and other pests, but there is little protection from the heat rays of the sun and so this species of domestic bovine needs periodic wallowing or ample shade for optimum growth and weight gains, as well as for milk production and work.

Studies in India on the density of sweat glands in the water buffalo have shown it to have not only a reduced number of glands per unit area of skin surface, but glands that are also considerably smaller in size when compared to those of Zebu cattle. From these and other observations, especially on the behaviour of the water buffalo, it is concluded that these animals have far less ability to dissipate heat from the body surface by sweating than do Zebu cattle.

Probably the major cooling mechanisms of the buffalo are due to the direct conduction of heat away from the animal's body during wallowing, by evaporation of water from the body surface after it emerges from the wallow or following spraying and, as mentioned earlier in respect of cattle, by evaporation of water from the lungs. Experiments in Lahore during the hot summer weather have shown that simple hand splashing with water for 10 minutes lowers buffalo body temperatures by 1.4 °C, hosing for 3 minutes by 1.6 °C and wallowing for 20 to 60 minutes by 2 to 2.3 °C. The beneficial effects of some sort of extraneous cooling on the buffalo (in addition to providing adequate shade) are clearly demonstrated by these experiments.

Effect on reproduction

There is little long-term experimental work to show what direct effect a hot climate alone has on reproductive performance in cattle. There is some experimental evidence to show that a hot environment will cause testicular degeneration in bulls, but in general it is accepted that reproductive problems in beef cattle in the tropics are more related to disease and to seasonal variations in nutrition and other factors, than to the direct effects of heat.

For example, under field conditions bulls poorly adapted to the environment may demonstrate periods of reduced libido for two reasons. In persistent tropical heat a bull may become less active and even separate himself from the cows. Furthermore, much of his time and energy on range is concerned with seeking feed. Hot climates may also affect calf growth and this may to some extent relate to depression of endocrine secretion and other physiological functions in the dam. Studies on cattle in the sub-tropical areas of Louisiana, USA have shown that the interaction of season, breed, age and lactation are important to the reproductive efficiency of beef herds.

There are somewhat conflicting reports regarding the effects of hot weather on the concentration and quality of buffalo semen, although there is adequate information to illustrate variation in reproductive parameters associated with seasonal changes. In the Philippines, for example, high sexual activity coincides with the rainy and cooler months and in India and Pakistan there is practically no incidence of oestrus in the buffalo during the hottest months of the year. Investigations at the Veterinary College, Mathure, India, indicate that failure of buffalo breeding during the summer months is basically an endocrine problem requiring further attention. Breeding and production programmes which are based on the seasonal variations in reproductive performance are discussed further in Chapter 5.

Effect on animal behaviour

In pre-agricultural times man studied the behaviour of wild animals in order to learn how to hunt them. As agricultural practices have developed through the ages livestockmen have continued to observe the behaviour of their animals from a practical standpoint, although the study of farm animal behaviour has become a more scientific study only during the past few decades.

Studies on behaviour include those of grazing, rumination, excretion, courtship and mating, birth and maternal care of the newborn, grooming, wallowing, resting, sleeping and so on. These may be regarded as the basic elements of behaviour and represent the ethogram of a species. A knowledge of the ethogram forms a foundation for a broader study as to how an animal can cope with new experiences, such as it may encounter on range, or in stall feeding and in other environments. An example of this is the way beef cattle may adapt or change their behaviour in order to survive under conditions that may include severe water shortage on range during drought, or during long transit by rail or trekking for hundreds of miles on foot: all factors which are relevant to beef cattle management in a tropical environment.

Daily behavioural cycle

This is largely dependent on climate, pasture, season and other factors. Grazing behaviour may be markedly influenced by watering routine or the availability of watering points. The degree of solar radiation and availability of shade may influence individuals or groups of animals and cause them to graze more intensively at cooler times, as in the evening or at night.

Grazing behaviour in cattle is generally common to a group or herd, which moves slowly across the ground, each animal tearing off the grass by prehending the food with the tongue, pinching the forage between the tongue and lower incisors (the dental pad occupies the position of the upper incisors) and so plucking off the grass.

A steer may travel 3 to 5 km daily to graze and sometimes considerably more. Obviously, an animal grazing on a quarter of a hectare of intensive pasture will not need to travel as far as an animal covering about 8 ha a day in the arid tropics, such as the Sahel in West Africa.

Cattle spend daily about 8 hours each in resting, sleeping and ruminating. Grazing periods number about 4 to 5 daily, but this varies with management and climate. Night grazing is common practice with temperate dairy breeds in the tropics. On range, however, beef cattle tend to rest up during the heat of the day, especially between 12.00 and 15.00 hours and graze mainly in the mornings, evenings, and to some extent at night. Zebu calves, running with their dams and with access to pasture from birth, begin to nibble leafy grass at about 10 to 14 days of age and may commence rumination from this age onwards. Tropical breeds – if given the opportunity – appear to develop this facility very early in life.

Cattle are well known for their 'selective grazing' behaviour and respond to various grazing stimuli. Shortage of good herbage makes them select other alternatives. Tropical breeds are, in fact, very efficient browsers on trees and shrubs and may depend on this forage during the dry season. It is often forgotten that browsing plays an important part in the feed intake of animals in the dry tropics and during the dry season in the wetter areas. Furthermore, it is possible that cattle enhance their mineral and trace element intake in this way.

Although cattle normally avoid poisonous plants, these may be eaten when there is extreme shortage of other feed; sometimes poisonous plants may be mixed accidentally with hay. Taste appears to be the main guide in selection, but the senses of smell and touch and other factors also play some part in the animal's choice of food.

Grazing intake depends upon whether the stock are feeding or ruminating. Grazing cattle chew very little during feeding and it is only during rumination that one observes 40 to 55 chewing movements before swallowing.

Rumination includes regurgitation, remastication, re-ensalivation and re-swallowing (redeglutition) of previously ingested feed. The ruminant is adapted to take in large qualities of fibrous feed and to deal with this at ease and at a suitable time. It is essential for the stockman to remember that cattle need time to rest (they may lie down or stand for this) in order to give optimum results and economic returns from the feed. The ratio of rumination to grazing time is called the R:G ratio or value. This will vary with quantity and quality of the feed, but as a general rule cattle will spend 8 hours feeding, 8 hours ruminating and 8 hours resting or sleeping. This pattern is not set. For example, temperate-type breeds managed in the tropics – if allowed – may spend more time grazing at night. But the overall period of hours assigned to each physiological process, feeding, ruminating and resting is, nonetheless, much the same in all climates. The important point to remember is that while a Zebu cow may graze contentedly at 15.00 hours on a hot, tropical, afternoon, temperate-type cows cannot so do and the stockman must therefore make available evening or night grazing to make up for this.

Special features of buffalo behaviour

The buffalo has, as one might expect with this humid tropical bovine species, a distinctive grazing behaviour not observed in cattle, unless one includes the great horned Kuri cattle of Lake Chad which also feed on aquatic plants. In their natural marshland environment buffalo will, after the sun has warmed them up, spend several hours during the day swimming and grazing on underwater plants. They swim with their heads parallel to the surface, nostrils, eyes, ears, horns and withers just above the water. They can stay under water to prehend their food for as long as a minute, after which they surface to chew and swallow it, before again submerging. They appear to graze in this way even when fodder is brought to them. In the Amazon basin of Brazil, where at times of the year much of the land is under water, except for isolated patches or *tesos*, and where buffalo are housed on raised platforms known as *marambas*, these animals still continue to swim and range freely during the day in search of aquatic plants.

During the rainy season in Oceania, when there is an abundance of green forage, swamp buffalo will graze for about 3 to 4 hours after sunrise, after which they will seek a wallowing area, or lie in the shade. In the afternoons they graze from about 14.30 hours until about 18.30 to 19.00 hours. During the drier months of the year herds tend to gather closer together in those areas where there is both feed and water. Grazing also includes a wide variety of plants on dry land.

Wallowing Buffalo wallow in order to lower their body temperature during the heat of the day and as a means of controlling their parasites. While wallowing they will rub their heads in the mud, sometimes tossing the mud up into the air with their horns and, after lowering themselves to the ground hindlegs first – as opposed to cattle which go down first on their forelegs – roll over onto one side, or sometimes almost onto their backs and stay in such a position for 10 minutes or so. They may continue to rest on their sides or in a standing position and at times ruminate. They will then move to a different wallowing area and repeat the process of rolling, resting and ruminating. It has been observed under range conditions that animals provided with a wallow will graze for one-half hour longer during the day than those without access to a wallow. More feed intake, of course, means additional daily weight gains.

Practical tests for heat tolerance

Meticulous experiments have been carried out in large animal climatological laboratories to obtain some basic data on the comparative response of temperate and tropical breeds of cattle under conditions of high ambient temperature and high humidity.

A simple field test was devised by Rhoad based upon the fact that the rectal temperature of cattle (38.3 °C), taken with an ordinary medical thermometer inserted 4 to 6 cm into the rectum, tends to increase with ambient temperatures above 10 °C. It is assumed in this test that if the ambient temperature is such that the cow or bull's rectal temperature increases markedly above the normal, this is an indication that the animal is unable to dissipate the excess heat load imposed upon it by the high environmental temperature. This test is known as the Iberia Heat Tolerance Test by which a 'heat tolerance coefficient' for cattle is calculated from the increase in rectal temperature above the accepted norm of 38.3 °C. The coefficient A is calculated as follows:

$$A = 100 - 10 (BT - 38.3)$$
[where BT is the body temperature of the animal in the sun in °C]

Many tropical breeds of cattle almost achieve coefficients of 100 whereas non-acclimatised temperate-type breeds may have coefficients of the order of 60 to 70. However, even between tropical herds the Iberia Heat Tolerance Test will indicate marked differences, the dwarf trypanotolerant cattle of West Africa demonstrating Iberia Heat Tolerance coefficients of below 70, compared to local Zebu breeds with coefficients of over 90. Results from Rhoad's work in the southern USA have shown a range of coefficients of 89 for Brahman and 59 for Angus cattle breeds. Heat tolerance appears to increase considerably in cattle up to about two years of age. High humidities only have a pronounced effect on the animal at temperatures within the zone of evaporative regulation. In other words, if the ambient temperature is above 32 °C and the relative humidity is such that this affects heat loss by evaporative channels, then cattle will be even more heat stressed since one of their major methods of heat loss will be blocked.

It should be stated that not all workers agree that marked rises above normal rectal temperatures in some individual animals are an indication of heat stress and low productivity. While this is true, culling on the basis of high rectal temperatures as an indicator of heat stress can be applied with some effect to those animals in the herd in which there is a strong correlation between high temperatures and lowered productivity in terms of reduced feeding activity and liveweight gain. Such individuals would be most likely to have markedly higher rectal temperatures than the average for the herd under the same conditions of climate stress.

There are other useful and comparatively straightforward field tests based upon both rectal temperature and respiration rate, rectal temperature following exercise and cooling, the coat score test already mentioned and an extremely useful technique described by Lee for coat hair sampling which assesses such characteristics as hair quality, hair count and stage of shedding.

Further reading

Amakiri, S. F. and **Hill, D. H.** (1975). Hair densities in Nigerian cattle breeds. *Int. J. Biometeor.*, **19**, 115.

Amakiri, S. F. and **Hill, D. H.** (1978). Seasonal and monthly cyclic changes in hair shedding in tropical cattle. *Bull. Anim. Health Prod. Afr.*, **26** (3), 264–267.

Bligh, J., Cloudsley-Thompson, J. L. and **Macdonald, A. G.** (eds.) (1976). *Environmental physiology of animals*. Blackwell Scientific: Oxford.

Bonsma, J. C. (1949). Breeding cattle for increased adaptability to tropical and subtropical environments. *J. Agric. Sci.*, **13**, 204.

Dowling, D. F. (1956). An experimental study of heat tolerance of cattle. *Aust. J. Agric. Res.*, **7**, 482.

Findlay, J. D. (1954). Environmental physiology of farm animals. In *Progress in the physiology of farm animals*, ed. **J. Hammond.** Butterworth: London. 252–298.

Lee, D. H. K. (1955). *Manual of field studies on the heat tolerance of domestic animals*. FAO Agric. Devel. Paper no. 38. FAO: Rome.

Lee, D. H. K. (1965). Climatic stress indices for domestic animals. *Int. J. Biometeor.*, **9**, 29.

McDowell, R. E. (1972). Responses of animals to warm environments. In *Improvement of livestock production in warm climates*, ed. **R. E. McDowell**. W. H. Freeman & Co.: San Francisco. 65–164.

Yousef, H. K. (1985). *Stress physiology in livestock*. Vol. 2: *Ungulates*. CRC Press Inc.: Boca Raton, Florida.

3 Cattle and buffalo breeds

The many breeds and types of cattle in the tropics include some indigenous breeds of *Bos taurus*, a large number of breeds of *Bos indicus*, and breeds in Southeast Asia that are derived wholly or partially from *Bos* (*Bibos*) spp.

Until the sixteenth century the distribution of cattle in the world was restricted to Asia, Europe and Africa, cattle being first introduced into the Americas at the end of the sixteenth century and into Australia and Oceania in more recent times. During the last two centuries exotic cattle have also been introduced into Asia and Africa, so that the present overall distribution of cattle breeds and types is now very complex.

Virtually all indigenous Asian and African cattle can be considered to be primarily beef and/or working-type cattle. Beef-type *Bos taurus* cattle have also been introduced into these continents from Europe. Until comparatively recent times the majority of cattle in the Americas, Australia and Oceania were also of the beef type.

All buffalo breeds and types in the world appear to have been derived from the wild Asian buffalo and breeds have not been as differentiated as have cattle breeds. Until comparatively recent times buffalo were restricted to Asia, Europe and North Africa, but they are also now being imported into the Americas, Africa south of the Sahara and elsewhere. There are no specific buffalo beef breeds but the majority of types are used for work and for beef production and there are some specific milking-type breeds.

World distribution of cattle

Cattle are now found in almost all parts of the world where there is vegetation to support them. They are, however, more or less excluded from certain verdant regions in Africa by the presence of the tsetse fly, unless they are genetically tolerant of trypanosomiasis or are protected by drugs (fig. 3.1).

Specialised beef cattle breeds have been developed in Western Europe and from there they have been taken to the range lands in the Americas, Australasia and some regions of Africa and Asia. Elsewhere in the world cattle were, and in most places still are, kept as dual, triple or general purpose animals. However, whether they are slaughtered at 3 months or 13 years of age almost all cattle can be eaten and usually are.

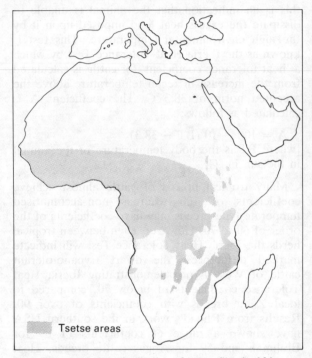

fig. 3.1 Approximate distribution of tsetse flies in Africa

The spread of different types of cattle

Longhorned cattle (*Bos primigenius*), the wild ox of Europe and Asia that is now extinct, were first domesticated, probably somewhere in the eastern Mediterranean or western Asia, some 10000 years ago. The appearance of the wild ox is probably best known from its representations in European cave paintings, and particularly in those from Lascaux, in France. It was a large animal with long lyre-shaped horns directed forwards and was usually dark in colour. Its early domesticated descendants were naturally similar and remains of this *primigenius* type have been found in Neolithic sites throughout Europe.

In western Asia domesticated longhorned cattle are known from ancient Mesopotamia and the Indus valley civilisation. Domestic cattle possibly came first to Egypt as early as the late fifth millenium BC. Tomb paintings from the Old Kingdom show humpless longhorns – the so-called Hamitic Longhorn. From Egypt they appear to have been taken westwards along the Maghreb and southwards up the Nile valley through Sudan and Ethiopia.

The archaeological record (*c*. 3000 BC) also reveals a type named *Bos brachyceros*, since its most striking feature is its short horns. It was smaller than the original *primigenius* type. It is possible that this type was selected primarily for milk production – its short horns and small size would have made it easier to handle. Certainly in representations from ancient Egypt and Sudan, where they co-existed with the Hamitic Longhorn, it is the new shorthorned cattle which are more often shown with conspicuous udders and depicted in milking scenes. These *brachyceros* cattle are found in archaeological remains throughout Europe along with the preceding *primigenius* cattle.

It is probable that man's ingenuity in genetically manipulating the morphology of his domestic animals combined with the effects of natural selection for an animal adapted to a hot, dry environment to produce humped cattle or Zebu. Archaeological information is available on the existence of the Zebu (*Bos indicus*) from both Baluchistan and ancient Mesopotamia (*c*. 3000 BC), so it is not known whether they were first developed in one of these regions or, possibly, somewhere in modern Iran. Migrating peoples spread Zebu cattle throughout the Indian sub-continent and they were selected in different regions for coat colour and horn shape and for draught or milk production, but not for beef production. From India they were taken to Southeast Asia where they interbred with *Bos* (*Bibos*) spp. and possibly into southwestern Asia.

There appear to have been two major migrations of peoples with their Zebu cattle into northeastern Africa. It is believed that Zebu cattle first came to ancient Egypt from the 'Land of Punt' (present day Somalia). There are diagrammatic representations of humped cattle in rock engravings from this period in Somalia. They probably interbred with local Hamitic Longhorn cattle to form the so-called Sanga cattle. Typically, Sanga cattle have long horns and small humps. From their cradle of origin in Ethiopia they were taken south by migrating peoples to form some of the various breeds of central and southern Africa.

Major immigrations of Zebu into Africa date from the time of the Arab invasions which commenced in AD 669. They gradually displaced the Sanga breeds from large areas of northeastern and eastern Africa, from Ethiopia to as far south as the Zambezi. In the whole of this area the dominant breed is now the East African Short-horned Zebu type.

From the Sudan, thoracic humped Zebu cattle were taken into West Africa along the broad belt between the desert to the north and the tsetse-fly area to the south. Crossbreeding with the indigenous humpless cattle produced various local populations of intermediates. The Fulani breeds of West Africa with their long horns, for example, appear to have derived from the Hamitic Longhorn.

Until recently cattle in these areas were not used for draught purposes, and beef was only a by-product. Therefore it is possible that the spread of the Zebu throughout much of East, Central and West Africa can be attributed to its adaptation to dry tropical conditions and to milk production in arid and semi-arid environments. However, the major advantage that the Zebu had over the Sanga was that it was more resistant to rinderpest. It was not until the great pandemic of rinderpest at the end of the nineteenth century that Zebu replaced Sanga cattle in many regions, a situation that has continued to the present time.

Cattle were first introduced into the Americas in the latter part of the sixteenth century. Originally all the introduced cattle were of *Bos taurus* type of European origin – Spanish, Portuguese, French, Dutch and British. Latterly other European breeds were introduced, as well as *Bos indicus* type cattle from Asia, Sanga type cattle from South Africa and *Bos taurus* type cattle from West Africa.

Today there are Criollo breeds in Central and South America, descendents of the original unimproved European type *Bos taurus* cattle that were imported throughout the Americas, beef and dairy breeds of improved *Bos taurus* European type cattle, *Bos indicus* breeds and a considerable variety of semi-stabilised and stabilised crossbred breeds.

Recently improved European type *Bos taurus* breeds have been imported into Asia and Africa. They are used as purebreds in the more temperate areas as in the montane tropics or for crossbreeding with indigenous cattle elsewhere.

In Australia, the first imports of cattle were of British breeds, and specifically the Beef Shorthorn. It did not flourish in the tropical areas of northern Queensland and so the Hereford was introduced. This was a satisfactory solution for a time, possibly due to hybrid vigour in the crosses, but there was soon degeneration of the breeding stock. Instead of trying to develop an adapted breed, new imports into Queensland were made from southern Australia and from the UK.

Finally, the solution of introducing an adapted breed was made, partly by chance and partly by design. Chance led to a few imported Zebu bulls producing progeny that were obviously superior to the existing British cattle and to the development of a new breed – the Droughtmaster – based on early Zebu × Shorthorn crossbreds. Deliberately designed breeding programmes also led to the import of America Brahman, Santa Gertrudis and Africander cattle. The Africander has already fathered another local breed – the Belmont Red. Now it is estimated that the majority of cattle in northern Queensland possess some Zebu blood. Furthermore, it is in Queensland that investigations have demonstrated most vividly the characteristics which make Zebu cattle and their crossbreds better adapted than the British beef breeds to tropical range conditions. The ability to withstand the burden of parasitic worms and ticks is one of the most important of these.

Classification of tropical cattle

Of two earlier proposals for the classification of the great numbers of breeds and types of cattle of India and Pakistan, one was based upon identification of the main groups according to area of origin and certain phenotypic characteristics such as coat colour and head and horn size, the other on the basis of utility (e.g. dairy, medium or heavy draught) in addition to certain phenotypic characteristics. Classification along these lines had most merit when related to local breeds. What was still needed, however, was some form of classification that would embrace all tropical cattle breeds and types or groups on an inter-continental basis.

The following classification is compiled from that of Payne who proposed that it be used as a tentative guide in this complex field. This, and the work of other researchers in the same field, have been listed in the 'Further reading' at the end of the chapter.

Breeds

These are classed into three categories according to continent of recent origin, that is:
1 within continents on a regional basis;
2 within regions on a type basis;
3 within type on a major 'characteristics' basis (position of hump, angle, shape and length of horns).

Types

There are five of these:
1 humpless (*Bos taurus*);
2 humped (*Bos indicus*);
3 humpless × humped crossbreds (in Africa the Sanga);
4 *Bos* (*Bibos*) domesticated species;
5 *Bos* (*Bibos*) × humpless and/or humped cattle.

Groups

These include types that have been subdivided into three groups:
1 generally accepted established indigenous breeds developed over time from crosses of major types;
2 intermediate types probably still in process of formation;
3 breeds of comparatively recent introduction based on planned breeding programmes.

The list below is drawn up directly from Payne's work; the five types are prefixed by the letters A to E, the related groups numerically under these and the breed names for all types follow in parenthesis.

Asia
Western Asia
A Humpless cattle (Oksh)
B Humped cattle (Aden, Iraqi)
C Humpless × humped cattle
(1) Stabilised indigenous (Damascus, Lebanese, Persian)

Indian subcontinent and Sri Lanka
B Humped cattle
(1) Shorthorned Zebu (Bachaur, Bhagnari, Gaolao, Hariana, Krishna Valley, Mewati, Nagori, Ongole, Rath)
(2) Lateral-horned Zebu (Gir, Dangi, Deoni, Nimari, Dhanni, Red Sindhi, Sahiwal)
(3) Lyre-horned Zebu (Kankrej, Malvi, Tharparkar, Hissar)
(4) Longhorned Zebu (Amrit Mahal, Hallikar, Kangayam, Khillari, Bargur, Alambadi)
(5) Small shorthorned or lyre-horned Zebu (Kumauni, Lohani, Ponwar, Shahabadi, Punganoor, Sinhala)
C Humpless × humped cattle
(1) Stabilised indigenous (Siri)
(3) Recent (Taylor)
D Bos (Bibos) spp. (Gaur)
E Bos (Bibos) spp. × humpless and/or humped cattle
(2) Intermediate (Gayal)

China and Southeast Asia
A Humpless cattle (Chinese Yellow, Batangas)
B Humped cattle (South Chinese Zebu, Taiwan Zebu)
C Humpless × humped cattle
(1) Stabilised indigenous (Burmese, Thai, Indo-Chinese, Sumatran, Batangas, Kedah var. Kelantan)
(2) Intermediate (Chinese Yellow)
D Bos (Bibos) spp. (Kouprey, Banteng, Bali)
E Bos (Bibos) spp. × humpless and/or humped cattle
(1) Stabilised indigenous (Madura)
(3) Recent (Grati)

Africa
North Africa
A Humpless cattle (Libyan, Brown Atlas)

C Humpless × humped cattle
(1) Stabilised indigenous (Egyptian)
(3) Recent (Meknes Black Pied)

West Africa
A Humpless cattle (Kuri, N'dama, Dwarf Shorthorn, N'dama × Dwarf Shorthorn crossbreds)
B Humped cattle
(1) Shorthorned Zebu (Maure, Azaouak, Shuwa, Sokoto)
(2) Medium-horned Zebu (Adamawa, Diali)
(3) Lyre-horned Zebu (Senegal Fulani, Sudanese Fulani, White Fulani)
(4) Long lyre-horned Zebu (Red Bororo)
C Humpless × humped cattle
(1) Stabilised indigenous (Bambara, Biu, Borgu, Keteku)
(2) Intermediate (Kuri × Zebu crossbreds, N'dama crossbreds, N'dama × Dwarf Shorthorn × Zebu crossbreds)

Northeast and East Africa
B Humped cattle (Sudanese, Ethiopian, Small Somali Zebu, Boran, Karamajong, Small East African Zebu)
C Humpless × humped cattle
(1) Stabilised indigenous (Nilotic, Danakil, Ankole)
(2) Intermediate (Arado, Nuba Mountain, Tuni, Nganda, Alur, Sukumu)
(3) Recent (Kasai)

Central Africa
B Humped cattle (Angoni)
C Humpless × humped cattle
(1) Stabilised indigenous (Sanga)
   (i) Longhorned Sanga (Barotse, Tuli, Angolan)
   (ii) Medium-horned Sanga (Tonga, Mashona)
(2) Intermediate (Matabele, Baila)
(3) Recent (Mateba, Kisantu)

Southern Africa
C Humpless × humped cattle
(1) Stabilised indigenous (Sanga)
   (i) Longhorned Sanga (Bechuana, Ovambo)
   (ii) Medium-horned Sanga (Nguni, Basuto)
   (iii) Lateral-horned Sanga (Africander)
(3) Recent (Drakensberger, Bonsmara)

Offshore islands
A Humpless cattle (Mauritius Creole)
B Humped cattle (Madagascar Zebu)
C Humpless × humped cattle
(1) Stabilised indigenous (Baria)
(3) Recent (Rana)

The Americas
North America
A Humpless cattle (Texas Longhorn)
B Humped cattle (Brahman)
C Humpless × humped cattle
(3) Recent (Santa Gertrudis, Beefmaster, Brangus, Charbray, other crossbred types)

Central America and the Caribbean
A Humpless cattle (Criollo, Nelthropp)
B Humped cattle (Jamaica Brahman)
C Recent (Jamaica Black, Jamaica Red Poll, Jamaica Hope)

South America
A Humpless cattle (Caracú, Criollo)
B Humped cattle (Indo-Brazilian or Indu-Brasil)
C Humpless × humped cattle
(3) Recent (Malabar, Canchim, Ocampo)

Oceania
Australia
C Humpless × humped cattle
(3) Recent (Droughtmaster, Australian Milking Zebu)

Details of some potential beef breeds and types

The above list includes all types of tropical cattle: *Bos taurus, Bos indicus* and *Bos (Bibos)* spp. Those breeds and/or types which are considered most suitable for beef production are now described in some detail, bearing in mind that almost all tropical breeds are dual or triple purpose animals.

Western Asian cattle
Oksh (synonyms: Bedouin, Chaissi, Kleiti) Related types of humpless cattle, including the Jaulan, Kundi and Anatolian, are widely dispersed in western Asia, both in the west and north where the climate is of the Mediterranean type and in the south and southeast, subtropical semi-arid type climate. They are believed to be descendants of the ancient Shorthorn humpless (*Bos brachyceros*) cattle.

Most types are relatively small, the Jaulan of the Golan Hills of Syria being the largest and the Kundi and other hill types smaller, liveweights ranging from 220–420 kg for males and 200–363 kg for females. Coat colours range from black, often with light or white markings, to black and white, roan or pied. The horns are short or absent and many are naturally polled. The Kundi type is the best meat producer.

Indian subcontinent cattle
There are some 25 breeds of Zebu cattle to be found in the Indian subcontinent and Sri Lanka. Many of these are dual or triple purpose animals and since they are for the most part not reared as beef animals in their place of origin, only those breeds, namely the Kankrej, Ongole, Gir, Krishna Valley, Hariana and Bhagnari, which have provided much of the genetic basis of the North American Brahman Zebu and the South American Indu-Brasil Zebu, will be described in any detail.

Bhagnari (synonyms Nari, Kachhi) It is found principally in the Kachhi division of the Kalat State of Baluchistan between latitudes 27° 53′ and 29° 35′ N and longitudes 67° 11′ and 67° 28′ E. The area is a plain surrounded by hills. It has been suggested that these animals are direct descendants of cattle that were introduced by the Vedic Aryans. The natural habitat is subtropical and semi-arid with a total rainfall of 203 to 254 mm per annum and is very hot in the summer.

This animal is long, compact, deep-bodied and sturdy with a short powerful neck. The colour of the coat is white or grey deepening to black in the males particularly over the neck, shoulders and hump. In the females the coat colour darkens during winter or in advanced stages of pregnancy. Grey bulls usually change to white when castrated. The skin is pigmented, of medium thickness and generally loose. The head is long, the forehead flat and wide and the ears are medium-sized and semipendulous. The horns are stumpy and set well apart curving outwards, forwards and inwards. They are thick at the base and taper towards blunt points. The hump is moderately developed in the male and firmly fleshed. The dewlap is small, of medium thickness but not pendulous. The sheath of the male is moderate in length and semipendulous. In the female the navel flap is medium in size and hangs freely.

This breed is primarily used for draught purposes, though it is a fair milker when properly managed and it might be suitable for beef production. It is a docile and willing worker.

These cattle are usually managed in small herds. They have been exported to the Punjab and used for upgrading purposes. They are also widely used for heavy field operations in the irrigated areas of the Sind.

Hariana The breed is found in the Hariana tract in East Punjab, India, situated between latitudes 28° 30′ and 30° N and longitudes 75° 45′ and 76° 30′ E. and in the states of Jind, Nabha, Patiala, Jaipur, Jodhpur, Loharu, Alwar, Bharatpur and the western districts of Uttar Pradesh. The habitat has an average altitude of 213 m. The climatic environment is subtropical and semi-arid, the annual rainfall being 457 mm.

This is a compact animal of graceful appearance. The coat colour is white or grey being darker over the quarters in the male. The skin is pigmented, fine, thin and tight. The face is long and narrow and there is a well-marked bony prominence at the centre of the poll. The ears are small and somewhat pendulous. The horns are fine and short, and thinner in the female than in the male. The hump is large and well developed in the male but of medium size in the female. The dewlap is moderately well developed but thin in the male and the sheath is short and tight. The navel flap is close to the body. The udder is relatively large and extends well forward. The teats are of medium size, the fore being longer than the hind.

This is a dual purpose milk–work breed and is one of the most important in northern India. The cows are quite good milkers and the bullocks make powerful work animals. They are widely used all over India.

The males are castrated for work purposes at 3 years of age. Syndactalysm (uncloven hoof) and flexed fetlock, both recessive characteristics, are common in the breed.

Krishna Valley This breed is found in the Krishna Valley tract of Hyderabad and in the south of Bombay State.

The habitat lies between latitudes 15° 8′ and 17° 8′ N and longitudes 74° to 78° E. The altitude of the area varies from 548 to 762 m. The climatic environment is tropical and moderately dry.

It demonstrates a variety of characteristics, as it is not a well-fixed type, but in general it is large with a massive frame. The body is short, the barrel large and well developed and the legs short and thick. The coat colour is usually grey to white, the males being darker on the quarters. The forehead has a distinct bulge surmounted by small, curved horns that vary in size and shape. The ears are small and pointed. The dewlap is well developed and pendulous, as is the sheath.

This is primarily a heavy draught breed used in the black cotton soil areas though it has some milking potential. It has soft feet and is not suitable for working on stony land.

In the area where it is reared the grazing is usually very limited and the animals are normally stall-fed. The calves suckle, male calves being allowed two teats and female calves one teat. At $2\frac{1}{2}$ years of age young males are broken in to work and at 3 to 4 years they are castrated and sold as bullocks. They have been exported to Brazil and to the USA.

Ongole (synonym Nellore) This breed (fig. 3.2) is found in the Kistna, Guntur and Nellore districts of Madras, between latitudes 15° and 16° 1′ N and longitudes 79° 4′ to 80° 2′ E. The habitat is more or less flat and the climate is tropical with a medium to low annual rainfall.

They are large, long-bodied animals with short necks and long limbs. The normal coat colour is white but the male has dark grey markings on the head, neck and hump and sometimes black points on the knees. Red, or red and white animals are occasionally seen. The skin is of medium thickness and often shows black mottled markings. The head is long and the ears are moderately long and slightly drooping. The horns are short and stumpy, growing outwards and backwards, and are thick at the base. The hump in the males is well developed and erect. The dewlap is large and fleshy and hangs

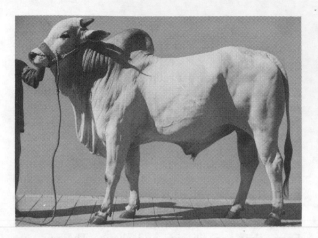

fig. 3.2 Ongole

fig. 3.3 Gir

in folds extending to the navel flap. The sheath is slightly pendulous.

These cattle are used for work and milk production. They are usually docile and the bullocks are very powerful and suitable for heavy field or transport work but not for light field work or for trotting purposes. The cows are fair milkers. They have been exported to Brazil, the USA, Sri Lanka, Fiji, Vietnam, Indonesia, Malaysia, the Philippines and the West Indies.

Gir (synonyms Deccan, Kathiawari, Surti, Sorthi) This breed (fig. 3.3) is found in the Gir hills and forest in the Kathiawar peninsula on the west coast of India; also in Baroda State, western Rajputana, the northern part of Bombay State and as far south as the western portion of Hyderabad State. The habitat is an undulating area rising to 610 m in altitude. The climatic environment is monsoon tropical.

These cattle are moderately large, heavy animals. The coat colour is characteristic and varies from yellowish red to black or white with dark red or chocolate brown patches distributed all over the body. The skin is loose, pliable and fine and the hair short and glossy. They possess a very prominent and broad forehead and the ears are long and pendulous. The horns are moderate in size. They curve away from the head in a downwards and backwards manner and then incline a little upwards and forwards, taking a spiral inward sweep and

finally end in a fine taper. The hump is large. The dewlap is only moderately developed while the sheath in the male is large and pendulous.

They are fairly good milkers and are used extensively for draught purposes though they are rather slow moving. They are very even tempered. Although they are not used in India for beef purposes, outside India they are reputed to be excellent beef animals. Large numbers have been exported to Brazil and they are one of the foundation breeds of the Indu-Brazilian and American Brahman. They are used all over India for upgrading purposes.

Kankrej (synonyms Bannai, Gujarati, Nagar, Talebda, Sanchore, Wagadia, Wagad, Vadhiyar, Wadhiar, Wadial) This breed is found in north Gujarat, Bombay Province, India, in an area situated between latitudes 21° to 24° N and longitudes 71° to 74° E. The habitat is varied and the climatic environment is tropical to subtropical and dry. Mean annual rainfall is 508 to 762 mm, the wet season being from July to October.

This is a large animal. The coat colour varies from silver to iron grey or steel black. The newborn calves are coloured a rusty red on the poll. The skin is pigmented and the hair is soft and short. The forehead is wide with prominent orbital arches. The ears are large and pendulous. The horns are large and lyre-shaped, and covered in skin to a much higher point than is normal in other breeds.

24

The hump is well developed. The dewlap is thin and pendulous, the males having pendulous sheaths.

This is a dual purpose milking–draught breed. They are powerful animals and are used for field work and for transport. It is believed that the breed has an excellent potential for beef production. They are usually grazed during the day and paddocked at night. Male calves are castrated at from 6 to 12 months of age and the steers are worked from 3 to 4 years onwards. They are very resistant to ticks but exhibit no tolerance of tuberculosis or brucellosis and they often suffer from a cancer of the horn.

Large numbers were exported to Brazil between 1870 and 1914, where they became one of the foundation breeds of the Indu-Brasil breed. This breed is also one of the foundation breeds of the American Brahman.

Southeast Asian cattle

All cattle breeds in Southeast Asia are used for draught purposes and finally as beef. One breed in particular, the Bali, is considered to produce excellent lean beef which is much in demand.

Bali (*Bos* (*Bibos*) *banteng*) This animal is considered to be a domesticated type of banteng. Cattle of this type (fig. 3.4) are found today in Bali, Lombok, Timor, Flores, south Sulawesi, East Java and Borneo, and in small numbers in Sabah and Sarawak. In Bali they comprise the majority of the cattle, except in some isolated western districts, where proximity to Java has encouraged cross-breeding with Zebu-type cattle. The habitat is varied and the climatic environment generally humid and tropical.

It is a medium-sized, deep-chested, fine-legged animal. The fore legs are more powerful than the hind, with the consequence that the hindquarters are poorly developed. The coat colour is usually red, though a golden colour and deep brown are known, white being very uncommon. The muzzle, feet and switch are black and the legs are white up to the knees and there is white under the thighs, and a distinct white oval patch on the hindquarters below the tail. The male is often darker than the female, the coat colour becoming dark brown to black at maturity. At birth the calves of both sexes

fig. 3..4 Bali

possess a golden to reddish-brown coat with typical light spots on the back of the legs, but this darkens, particularly in the male as the animals age. The reddish-brown coat colour returns if the male is castrated. The hair is short, fine and smooth. The skin is pigmented and fine. The head is broad, with a flat poll, and short; the ears are of medium size and are pointed. Those of the female are considerably smaller. The male possesses a crest and the dewlap is well developed in both sexes. The udder is poorly developed and covered with hair.

This breed is used for work purposes and is considered a good meat animal, possessing a high dressing percentage and exhibiting a low shrinkage during transit. It is considered by some to be superior to the Zebu as a work animal in a humid tropical climate and has the ability to thrive on feeds of very low nutritive value.

These cattle have been exported to Hawaii, the Philippines, Singapore and Malaysia for slaughter purposes and early in the last century to Australia. Small herds have been established in Malaysia and the Philippines and an experimental herd in Australia. It is an excellent browser as well as grazer.

African cattle

Perhaps no other continent can claim the variety of cattle breeds, *Bos taurus*, *Bos indicus* and their crossbreds, as can Africa.

25

It is not possible to classify many of these superbly adapted breeds or types solely as beef animals. More often than not they are dual purpose beasts, normally providing milk and some meat for the family or surplus animals for sale. Some are used to produce blood to support the family animal protein needs, as is the case of the Maasai and other non-Muslim or Christian peoples, who perform very efficient periodical bleeding from the jugular vein of their cattle for this purpose. The Zebu breeds may perform triple purpose functions, including meat and milk production and draught animal functions. Others, like the compact and medium-sized Azaouak Zebu and the Azaouak 'Adar' type of north-eastern Nigeria are also used as pack animals, providing safe and steady transport for women, smaller children and household equipment (fig. 3.5).

To classify many of these breeds or types of cattle solely as beef animals is therefore not tenable in the context of this book, although the majority of the breeds listed below contribute to a greater or lesser extent to the meat economy of the various countries, or neighbouring countries in which they are found. True beef types have been developed, however, such as the Boran of East Africa, the Africander of southern Africa and the Adamawa, Sokoto and Peul or Fulani breeds of West Africa. Some of the east-central African Zebus or small-humped Sanga types of Malawi and Zimbabwe may also be included as beef animals. The position of the European *Bos taurus* breeds as specialised beef animals will not be stressed but some reference must be made to the value of the infusion of exotic beef-type cattle blood, for example, the Hereford and Angus of southern Africa and the Red Devon of the eastern uplands of Nigeria and European breeds in the highlands of East Africa.

West African cattle

N'dama (synonyms Fouta Djallon (Guinea), Malinke, Madingo Boenca, Fouta Longhorn, Gambian Longhorn) It is believed that the N'dama (fig. 3.6) is a descendant of the ancient longhorn of the Nile Valley and that it may later have accompanied Berber migrants from southern Morocco. The Fouta Djallon plateau in Guinea is regarded as its centre of origin in West Africa. It is found today in Liberia, Guinea, the Gambia, southern Senegal, Ivory Coast, Sierra Leone, Benin, Burkina Faso (formerly Upper Volta), Nigeria, Mali and Guinea-Bissau. The northern and southern limits are, very approximately, at latitudes 14° N and 8° N in a belt of country more or less parallel to the equator and extending from the Atlantic coast in Senegal and Guinea to the Borgou district of Benin, and during recent decades eastwards to southern Nigeria.

fig. 3.5 Azaouak

fig. 3.6 N'dama

Large but isolated groups have also been developed commercially during the past 50 years in Zaire. The breed appears over the past century to have acclimatised itself to life on the edge or within the rain forests of West Africa.

In West Africa the N'dama has also interbred with the Zebu cattle of the sub-saharan savannas and the dwarf shorthorned cattle of the coastal areas, the Mere (Peul × N'dama cross) and the Bambara type of the Ivory Coast and Borgou of Benin being examples. The northern limits of the N'dama and its crosses approximate to the northern limits of the tsetse fly and to the natural southern limits of the Zebu.

It is a small, humpless animal with a straight topline and short, fine-boned limbs. The coat colour of the true N'dama of the Fouta Djallon plateau is usually yellow, fawn, light red or dun. A particularly hardy variety has dark to almost black colouring, especially of the head, neck and shoulders and a dark band of coat hair along the spine. The skin varies from almost black to red and the coat is short, soft and shiny. Coat colours that include areas of white indicate an admixture of other breeds. The head is short and broad with a straight profile, flat forehead and the orbital arches are not accentuated. The ears are small and horizontally placed. The horns are lyre-shaped, growing sideways, forwards and upwards from the poll. They may reach 45–50 cm in length in mature cattle. They are circular to oval in cross section at the base and with dark tips. Polled N'dama are quite common and are especially selected for in some commercial herds. The dewlap and umbilical fold are not prominent. The udder of the female is generally small and set high between the legs.

The N'dama is a poor milker, although lactations of over 680 kg have been recorded. For the most part, however, the cow produces just enough milk to raise her calf. If handled from birth they make good draught animals; under range management conditions they become extremely agile and wild with a temperament very different from the docile African or Asiatic Zebu. They are essentially beef animals, producing fairly good carcasses even under poor grazing conditions. On improved pastures the carcass is very good. They are fast becoming a much sought after beast for ranching in tsetse-infested areas due to their trypanotolerance which is enhanced by exposure to infection. This trypanotolerance appears to be inherited, although it can be broken down under stress. Present evidence indicates that they are also resistant to streptothricosis, a severe skin condition in West Africa, especially in extensively managed cattle.

Herds of N'dama established in West Africa, away from their native Guinea and the Sudan zone, have performed well and have been used extensively to improve local dwarf or semi-dwarf breeds. Importations to southern Nigeria from the Gambia and Guinea were first made between 1938 and 1947 and an improved beef-type N'dama, including a polled variety, was imported from Zaire as additional foundation stock for a cattle ranch in the derived Guinea savanna in 1955. Growth, reproduction and carcass data from livestock stations in Guinea, Ivory Coast, Sierra Leone and Nigeria are summarised in Table 3.1. N'dama cattle were exported from Senegal as early as 1825 and during the mid-nineteenth century to the islands of Martinique and Guadeloupe in the West Indies and later to the Virgin Islands where they were crossed with the British Red Poll to establish the Nelthropp breed. They have also been crossed with other

Table 3.1 Growth, reproduction and carcass data of N'dama cattle

Liveweight		
at birth (kg)	M	16
	F	14
at maturity (kg)	M	232–315
	F	210–300
Height at withers (cm)	M	94–119
	F	89–112
Milk production (kg)		
normal range		150–379
maximum		450
Age at first calving (months)		27–72
Length of lactation (days)		150–300
Calving interval (months)		14–42
Butter fat content %		6.5
Carcass dressing %		40–56

European breeds such as the Charolais and Aberdeen Angus.

In the Sudanese climatic zone of Nigeria and the Ivory Coast the herds are sedentary and are usually owned by Bambara villagers who employ Peul (Fulani) herdsmen to supervise their cattle. Besides natural pastures near the villages the herds graze on millet and maize stubble. In some areas, as in northern Benin and Borgou, there are short periods of several days' duration when herds move in search of green pastures. In northern Sierra Leone the cattle are managed under a more pastoral nomadic system; owners also feed supplementary leaves, roots, bark and other food residues during the dry season. In some areas they are used by farmers as work animals for tillage purposes.

West African Shorthorn (synonyms Dwarf Shorthorn, Nigerian Dwarf Shorthorn or 'Muturu', Somba (Benin), Bakosi and Race des Lagunes) The origin of this true dwarf type is obscure and has been discussed previously. Like the N'dama, it is considered to have been brought southwards by Berber tribesmen although some claim there is an infusion of 'blood' from European cattle imported to the West Coast by Portuguese navigators in the sixteenth and seventeenth centuries. Others claim they are descended from the isolated indigenous Somba cattle of the mountainous Attacora region of northern Benin. As with N'dama cattle, these dwarf types have considerable resistance to tsetse-borne trypanosomiasis. Their comparative segregation in the tsetse-inhabited coastal areas protected them from the devasting outbreaks among northern Zebu cattle of rinderpest or cattle plague which reached West Africa towards the end of the nineteenth century.

The true dwarf types are found in the southern coastal areas of the Ivory Coast, Togo, Benin and Nigeria. The 'Muturu' of Nigeria and the 'Race des Lagunes' are good examples (fig. 3.7). There are also West African Shorthorn types in the Gambia, Ghana and Liberia. The Ghana Shorthorn is a larger type, which is not a true dwarf shorthorn.

The land near the coast of much of the area inhabited by these cattle is low, sandy and often intercepted by lagoons and creeks. Isolated pockets of dwarf cattle are also found in non-forest or lagoon areas, for example among the villages of the Jos Plateau in Nigeria. The Ghana Shorthorn is also to be found in more open savannas such as the Accra Plains. For the most part, however, they are considered as a forest or lagoon type.

They are kept mainly for social and ritual purposes, allowed to roam freely around the villages during the day and confined at night in an open enclosure. In very wet lagoon areas they may spend some months housed on rafts during the rains. In the Baoulé and Somba areas of central Ivory Coast and northern Benin, respectively, sedentary cultivators may employ nomad or transhumant Peul herdsmen to look after the cattle. This also occurs in many areas of Nigeria, where the dwarf may be seen herded with semi-dwarf herds. There are no seasonal movements, however, grazing being entirely local.

The West African Shorthorn is a small, thick-set animal, with a comparatively large head, straight profile and concave forehead (frontal bone) accentuated by prominent orbital arches, the poll broad and straight and the horns short. Polled and loosely attached horn types also occur, the latter condition also being seen in West African Zebu breeds. The topline is generally straight and the back well muscled, the barrel round but often lacking in depth behind the shoulder, the hindquarters of medium length and depth, and the limbs short and fine-boned. The dewlap and umbilical fold are tight. The skin of the true dwarf breeds is usually unpigmented throughout although some variations

fig. 3.7 'Muturu'

will occur. The coat colour varies, often solid black, black and white or various shades of brown, and brown and white. Grey and dun coats are less common.

They are poor milkers compared with the Zebu, although they are sometimes milked on mission stations in the hinterland, or in 'bush' dairies. They are, however, well proportioned beasts and produce a good carcass of up to 55 per cent dressed weight and of excellent flavoured meat. Their chief value lies in their trypanotolerance and in a balanced state of premunition. Without undue stress, they provide security, and a capital asset to the farmer. They respond, in terms of growth rate and breeding performance, to improved management (Table 3.2) although their dwarf character remains constant.

Table 3.2 Growth, reproduction and carcass data of West African Shorthorn

Liveweight		
at birth (kg)	M	13
	F	12
at maturity (kg)	M	150–200
	F	145–185
Height at withers (cm)	M	90–117
	F	79–110
Milk production		
normal range (kg)		120–360
Age at first calving (months)		30–48
Length of lactation (days)		120–1
Calving interval (months)		12–24
Carcass dressing %		15–52

Kuri (synonyms Chad, Buduma) The Kuri (fig. 3.8), Lake Chad or Buduma humpless cattle are maintained by two closely related tribal groups, the Kuri and Buduma peoples who are believed to be descended from the Kanembou tribe which migrated to the Kanem district of the extreme northeast of Nigeria and southern Chad and Niger from Libya and the Sudan in historical times. Their unique characteristics are that they are truly lake dwellers, often grazing in water almost to the withers and with the herd-boy sitting on the back of the lead bull. Physically they are distinguished by their great size and height, over 500 kg liveweight and 135 cm at the withers for a mature bull, with gigantic bulbous horns. They bear little resemblance to any other cattle of Africa.

fig. 3.8 Kuri

Kuri cattle are found approximately between latitudes 13° and 16° N and longitudes 13° and 17° E, that is on the islands and shores of Lake Chad extending into Borno State of Nigeria, Chad territory and the N'Guigni Province of Niger. The type also extends into the area west and south of Lake Chad and to the borders of the Sahelian zone to its northwest. In the southern fringing areas the Kuri have been crossed with Zebu cattle to produce an intermediate type known as the Jotkor.

The area inhabited by the Kuri has a Sudanese type climate, with a severe dry season and rainy season of barely five months. Temperature varies from considerable cold at nights to extreme heat (49 °C) at noon during the hottest part of the year.

Kuri cattle are usually managed in herds of 30–35 cows and a bull, grazing mainly on lakeside grasses, or swimming or walking in the deeper waters. The breed is a good milker (one of the best in Nigeria) but it does not do well outside its somewhat unique environment. It is a good beef animal and is shipped annually by road or rail to the meat markets of southern Nigeria and across borders to neighbouring countries in considerable numbers.

It is a tall, heavily boned, humpless animal with enormous bulbous horns. The horns are of two types, the short type being only 20–30 cm long and over 50 cm in circumference or, more typically, 70–130 cm long and 35–55 cm in circumference at the base. They are comparatively light and porous or cellular in structure. The topline is straight and the withers are thick but without a hump. The common colour is white, but grey shading over shoulders and extremities occurs. Other coat colours, such as red and white, suggest admixture of Zebu blood.

Sokoto Gudali Like the majority of West African humped Zebu cattle, this breed (fig. 3.9) most closely resembles the heavy-humped, flop-eared grey-white breeds of India. Its ancestors, brought with the Arab invasions of East Africa, probably reached the West African littoral in early history via the southern Sahara route. In Nigeria it is the breed type of the semi-arid Sokoto State, lying approximately between latitudes 10° and 14° N.

It is a medium sized, deep-bodied Zebu, the coat colour in the female generally white or cream and light grey or cream with dark shading over the poll, neck, shoulders and tail in the male. Some males are coloured dun with blue-grey shading. The coat hair is short and the skin medium thick, loose and pigmented. The ears are markedly pendulous. The male has short, upturned horns projecting laterally and the female smaller but usually slightly longer horns. The hump is well developed in both sexes and in a near cervico-thoracic position. The dewlap and umbilical fold is also well developed in both sexes.

Although a good milker and a good draught breed the Sokoto Gudali is one of West Africa's best beef-type cattle.

· *Fulani (synonym Peul)* The pastoral tribe from which these cattle derive their name is referred to in English as Fulani and in French as Peul. The geographical area occupied by the Fulani extends from west of the River Senegal to east of Lake Chad and includes parts of Senegal, Mauritania, Mali, Niger, Nigeria and Cameroon.

There are four main groups of Fulani cattle: the Nigerian Fulani, the Senegal Fulani, the Sudanese Fulani and the White Fulani. Only the White Fulani will be described in any detail.

The Sudanese Fulani – a long lyre-horned type (fig. 3.10) – probably originates from cattle brought in by Semites when they invaded West Africa in the seventh century. The White Fulani, maintained in their pure form by nomadic Fulani in Nigeria, a pastoral people of Hamitic origin, is most likely, like other Zebu cattle, of Asiatic origin. Some claim, however, that it has affinities with more ancient breeds such as the Hamitic Longhorn and the lyre-shaped horns certainly support this conjecture.

White Fulani (synonyms Yakanaji (Fulani),

fig. 3.9 Sokoto Gudali

fig. 3.10 Sudanese Fulani

fig. 3.11 White Fulani

fig. 3.12 M'Bororo

Bunaji (Hausa), White Bororo (Bororo-nomad Fulani), Akou (Cameroon)) This is perhaps the most cosmopolitan in distribution of the West African lyre-horned group of Zebu cattle and this is probably due to its somewhat better tolerance to trypanosomiasis than other West African Zebu. It has been taken further southwards and has been crossed with the southern dwarf cattle over the past decades to form the intermediate semi-dwarf types of the derived guinea savanna such as the Borgou and Keteku.

Like the Sokoto Gudali it is a triple purpose animal of powerful frame and docile temperament, well fitted to cultivating and general pack or haulage purposes. Although it has been improved for milk production it is a good beef animal and despite the sloping Zebu sacrum has a well balanced hindquarter (fig. 3.11). It stands up well to dry-season ranging and responds well to more intensive grazing.

In its natural habitat over 95 per cent of these cattle are in the hands of nomadic or transhumant Fulani, for whom they represent a source of prestige as basic wealth and investment and, together with their products, provide the means of exchange for the purchase of daily needs. Milk and butter, sold by the women, provide daily revenue, while surplus males or barren females are sold as slaughter stock. Regrettably, pregnant females are sold when prices are temptingly high, or where

drought conditions necessitate reduction in herd numbers.

M'Bororo (synonyms Rahaji, Rahaza, Brahaza, Red Longhorn) This breed is believed to have originated from a possible westward migration in early history of the Sanga cattle of Upper Egypt. In francophone West Africa they are called Borori or M'Bororodji, after the subsidiary Fulani tribe of that name. This breed has also spread to the Cameroons, accompanying the eastward movement during the nineteenth century of the Bororodji Fulani, their cattle also forming an excellent dual purpose animal when crossed with the stockier upland Adamawa type.

The M'Bororo (fig. 3.12) is a tall (130–145 cm), rangy, long-legged animal, with horns up to 128 cm in length and a well developed cervico-thoracic hump and loose, pendulous sheath and dewlap. Its generally rangy, long-legged conformation adapts it to the extreme hardships of the southern Sahel, although it responds admirably to improved nutrition. The M'Bororo constitutes, with the White Fulani and Peul herds, a major source of meat supply for the southern, densely populated areas of West Africa.

Adamawa (synonyms Adamawa, Ngaundere, Banyo, Yola and Zebu Peul of Adamawa) Humped Zebu cattle found in the Cameroon uplands of West Africa. The breed is believed to be derived from M'Bororo cattle while the Yola variety has an admixture of West African Shorthorn and White Fulani blood.

Adamawa are medium-horned, low-set, stocky Zebu cattle characteristic of other breeds or types found in upland or mountain areas. The true Ngaundere Adamawa measures about 110–125 cm at the withers, with a heart girth of up to 150–160 cm and a liveweight of 350–560 kg. The Ngaundere hump is characteristically very heavy and flaccid, falling over one side of the withers. The Banyo Adamawa (see fig. 2.2 on page 6) is smaller, with a more erect hump. The Yola is the smallest type, with short horns.

Adamawa heifers, under traditional management, calve down between 3 and 4 years of age; first service for bulls at about 3 years. While being fair milkers, the Adamawa is best considered in local markets as a meat animal, with liveweight records of 400–520 kg at 4–5 years of age and 51–52 dressing percentage. They are also good draught animals.

Northeast and East African cattle

Sudanese cattle The Sudanese cattle breeds are considered for the most part to have reached North Africa from Asia in small numbers before the Arab invasion and subsequently in greater numbers. The various breeds may be considered mainly as milk or dual purpose animals.

Many resemble the Indian-type Zebu. The Kenana and White Nile are representative of the cattle of the nomadic tribes of northern Sudan semi-arid desert scrubland. They are good dual purpose breeds and have been improved by selection at livestock stations. The Butana are managed in a semi-arid zone lying between the Blue Nile and the Atbara rivers. The Baggara are a mixed type occupying the savanna regions between the Nile and the western frontiers of the Sudan.

Size and coat colour vary among the different types. The White Nile may be white, red, black, fawn and admixtures of these colours. The Butana coat colour is usually red; the Baggara white with red or black markings. Kenana cattle are commonly grey and their calves, although born with a red-brown coat, change to the adult grey between 3 and 6 months of age. The head is long and coffin shaped and the ears semi-pendulous. Horns are short and, as in West Africa, polled and loose-boned or scur

types occur. The Baggara has the smallest hump, often cervico-thoracic in position in the males.

The majority of the Sudanese breeds are kept by nomadic or semi-nomadic people. Many of the breeds are good milkers. Surplus males are sold for local slaughter.

Boran Boran cattle are indigenous to the semi-nomadic Borana tribe of southern Ethiopia and the adjoining parts of Somalia and northern Kenya. There are three related types today, the Somali Boran (Avai), Tanaland Boran or Galla and the Kenya Boran, the Kenya type having been selected for decades for its beef qualities and crossed with European breeds such as the Hereford. It is bred in the semi-arid montane uplands of Kenya.

Compared with the somewhat leggy, straight-ribbed Tanaland, the Ethiopian Boran is a fairly large, long-legged animal with good body conformation. The improved Boran of the Kenya upland ranches (fig. 3.13) is typically white with black spots, but other colours such as fawn, red, and black occur. Both the Kenya and Somali Boran usually have a pigmented skin, which is loose and pliable. The head is medium to long, the ears small and carried horizontally and the horns short and thick. The hump is large, especially in the male, thoracic in position and sometimes folded on one side. The improved ranch Boran has a straight topline and well developed hindquarters.

fig. 3.13 Boran

The improved Boran is today one of the outstanding beef breeds of Africa and produces a carcass suitable for the export market. Unlike the small East African Zebus they are highly susceptible to tick-borne diseases, especially to East Coast Fever (ECF). While having excellent beef qualities, therefore, they need skilled management and can only be kept in relatively tick-free areas.

Small East African Zebu (synonym East African Shorthorned Zebu) There are numerous types such as the Mongalla or Southern Sudan Nile Zebu, the Lugware, the Bukedi or Eastern Province or Uganda Zebu, the Nandi, Kikuyu, and the Maasai, Tanzania and Zanzibar Zebu. Their distribution and the climatic environment of their habitat are variable. They are generally most numerous in the wetter and more humid areas of East Africa, although their habitat ranges from sea-level to 2 740 m. They are considered fairly recent arrivals, probably replacing Sanga cattle. The ancestors of the present Lugware breed, for example, are believed to have moved southwards from the Nile valley with the Lugware tribes, to settle in the wooded plateau of Aru.

Most are small, stocky animals, of variable coat colours, medium sized head and short horns. The hump is well developed. They are dual and triple purpose animals; some, like the Nandi are good milkers. They produce a good, compact beef carcass.

Central African cattle These include the Angoni of Zambia, Malawi and Mozambique in an area south and west of Lake Nyasa. These types represent the southernmost extension of the East African Shorthorned Zebu. They occupy a variable but generally tropical and dry habitat. They are used for milk, meat, draught and ceremonial purposes.

Mashona (synonyms Shona, Nogmbe, Mombe, Makalanga) These cattle are considered to have accompanied tribes migrating from the north, southwards and across the Zambezi river into Zimbabwe. The type, named after the eastern Mashona tribe, has since spread more widely.

Conformation is compact, the animal is fine-boned and small in stature. Common colours are black, red-brown with yellow muzzle, brownish black with lighter black stripes along the spine, dun, and mixed colours of red and white, black and white and brindle; whole yellow and cream coats also occur. The head is short, and 'dished' (concave), horns medium and ears small and pointed. The hump is cervico-thoracic and medium in size, being larger in the male.

This is a good beef and draught animal, being very hardy and docile. During this century Mashona have been extensively crossed with temperate-type beef breeds and with the Africander of southern Africa for ranching purposes. Stabilised humpless × Mashona types have been established (fig. 3.14).

fig. 3.14 Mashona

South African cattle

Africander The present day Africander, one of the best beef–draught cattle of Africa, is generally believed to be derived from cattle owned by Hottentot tribes during the seventeenth and eighteenth centuries. Some authorities claim the Hottentot cattle were pure *Bos indicus*, in no way related to the Bantu cattle of southern Africa. They consider also that their forebears, the lateral-horned Zebu with cervico-thoracic humps, were brought into northern Africa in pre-history by Semitic tribes from Asia (fig. 3.15), from where they migrated southwards eventually to become established as Hottentot cattle. A less accepted theory is that the Africander originated from the Alentejo breed from Portugal as well as from Dutch cattle shipped to Africa with the early European settlers.

fig. 3.15 Africander

fig. 3.16 Modern Africander

Dutch settlers in the Cape acquired their first Africanders in 1652. Despite the ravages of rinderpest during the pandemic of 1896 to 1899, some dedicated farmers, especially in what was then the Orange River Colony, kept a few herds pure and intact and in 1912 the 'Africander Breeders Society' was founded. The habitat has been described as Mediterranean in Cape Province, to modified subtropical and tropical to the north. The breed has played one of its greatest commercial roles in the savanna country of the Transvaal and Botswana together with a strip of 'low veld' bordering the river Limpopo.

The modern Africander (fig. 3.16), improved by selection over several decades, has been modified from the powerful free-striding trek ox to a beef-type animal, strongly built, long-bodied and with good 'spring' of rib, fair depth of chest and strong well placed legs, well muscled above the hock. Table 3.3 shows average measurements and liveweights of Africanders at two research stations. For a mature African Zebu these are high liveweights, indicating how the animal will respond to improved management and nutrition. The head is long and coffin shaped characteristic of the Zebu, the horns oval in cross-section, long with a characteristic twist and downward and backward sweep where they leave the head. Horns of the female are longer than the male; the hump is cervico-thoracic and prominent in the male. The dewlap is large with folds and the umbilical fold is well developed.

This is the main breed found in the cattle ranches of southern Africa and while it is still used to some extent as a trek ox its chief value is as a commercial beef animal. It is well adapted to subtropical or tropical climates provided those are neither too arid nor too humid. These cattle have been exported in large numbers to other countries in Africa, to the USA, the Philippines and Australia. Crossbred European × Africander cattle show marked hybrid vigour in the first generation but higher grades of the European bulls do not adapt as much as the lower grades to rigours of the environment under ranch management. They cross well with the Shorthorn, Aberdeen Angus and other improved beef breeds. Crosses with the Boran in Kenya, however, are reported to do no better than purebred Borans.

Table 3.3 Growth and carcass data of Africander cattle

Liveweight		
at birth (kg)	M	30
	F	28
at maturity (kg)	M	454–947
	F	363–544
Height at withers (cm)	M	130–142
	F	123–137
Carcass dressing %		59–64

North American cattle

Texas Longhorn   Brief mention only will be made of this breed which, one hundred or so years ago, was the traditional beef breed of the American 'West'. It originated from the Spanish Longhorn breeds imported to the Americas from the Iberian Peninsula with Spanish settlers along with humpless cattle of Portuguese origin, described later. The Spanish Longhorn is a rangy, large boned, slab (flat) sided animal with long legs which was able to survive and multiply under the rigorous conditions of climate varying from temperate, to subtropical and semi-arid. Some herds of pure-type longhorns have been conserved and at the present time the breed is being used once again, now mainly for crossbreeding purposes on ranches in the warmer regions of North America.

Brahman (synonym American Brahman)   The breed (fig. 3.17) was developed in the Gulf area of the southwestern USA between 1854 and 1926. It is a Zebu derived mainly from strains of the Kankrej, Ongole, Gir, Krishna Valley, Hariana and Bhagnari breeds although the exact origin of the breed may never be known. The foundation animals were either imported directly into the USA or indirectly through Brazil and Mexico.

The climatic environment of the Gulf coast where the Brahman breed was originally developed can be described as humid and subtropical, but cattle of this breed are now bred in many regions of the tropical and subtropical world.

As might be expected, the breed exhibits some variability in physical characteristics. It is a large animal with a long body of moderate depth, with long to medium-length legs and a straight back. The colour of the coat is normally a very light grey, but it may be red or black. The mature male is usually darker in colour than the female, with darker areas on the neck, shoulders, lower thighs and flanks. Calves often possess a red coat at birth that quickly turns grey. The skin is loose, soft and pliable, of medium thickness and is usually pigmented. The head is normally long. The ears are pendulous. The horns are widely spaced, thick, medium in length; those of the female being thinner than those of the male. The hump is large in the male, smaller in the female. The dewlap is large, but the sheath and navel flaps are not very

fig. 3.17 American Brahman

pendulous. The udder in the female is of moderate size, as are the teats.

The Brahman is essentially a beef animal that grows well on poor, dry grazings and also responds to feedlot management. In the USA, Latin America and Australia it has been widely used for crossbreeding purposes, to produce Zebu × temperate-type beef animals that are well acclimatised to tropical or subtropical environments and exhibit hybrid vigour.

It has been less successful in West Africa where crosses, although of good conformation and growth rate, are more susceptible than local breeds to the skin disease streptothricosis under extensive management. When the Brahman is continuously handled, it is a docile animal, but if it is 'gathered' or brought in from range it can occasionally be very wild. It appears to have a long productive life, is not unduly troubled by ticks (a reason for its popularity in northern Australia), biting flies and mosquitoes, exhibits considerable tolerance to pink-eye and cancer-eye and is gregarious and a close herder, not responding well to hand mating. The American Brahman Breeders Association was organised in 1924 and Brahmans have been exported all over the world, in particular to countries in the Caribbean, Central and South America, and to Australia, the Pacific islands and the Philippines.

Santa Gertrudis   The Santa Gertrudis (fig. 3.18) is a crossbred, $\frac{3}{8}$ Zebu × $\frac{5}{8}$ Shorthorn developed on

fig. 3.18 Santa Gertrudis

the King Ranch in Texas. The breeding work undertaken in the evolution of the Santa Gertrudis is perhaps one of the best examples of constructive animal breeding in this century and the creation of this breed compares with the work of Robert Bakewell who established the Shorthorn breed in Britain in the eighteenth century. The King Ranch was originally stocked with Texas Longhorns and these were upgraded using Shorthorn and Hereford bulls. In 1910 the first crossbred Zebu were purchased by the ranch and between this date and 1940, by means of a well-planned breeding policy, the Santa Gertrudis breed was developed.

The original habitat is subtropical and semi-arid, but the breed has now been exported to many different regions of the tropical and subtropical world.

It is a large symmetrical, deep-bodied, strong-boned animal. The coat colour should be solid cherry-red, the hair short and straight and the skin thin, loose and pigmented red. The head is broad and the animal has a slightly convex forehead. The ears are medium to large and drooping. The horns are usually of the Shorthorn type, but polled animals exist. The hump is of medium size in the male but absent in the female. The dewlap is well developed. The sheath and navel flap are of medium size. The udder of the female is of medium size with well-placed teats.

This is a beef breed that is said to have cold-, as well as heat-tolerance characteristics, and to be resistant to ticks. Exports of cattle of this type have made a considerable impact on beef industries in countries in the Caribbean, Central and South America and in Australia. As with the American Brahman, it is also susceptible to streptothricosis in tropical West Africa, as are its crossbreds. Some doubts have been expressed as to the fertility of the breed.

Other crossbred 'breeds' A considerable number of Zebu × European-type beef breed crossbreds have been developed in North America for use in subtropical and tropical environments. Apart from the Santa Gertrudis breed, few of the 'crossbred breeds' are truly stabilised and the only other breed listed is the *Brangus*. This is a crossbred $\frac{3}{8}$ Brahman × $\frac{5}{8}$ Angus type, the earliest crosses of Brahman with Angus dating back to 1912. Early experimental crossbreeding was carried out at the USDA Experimental Station at Jeanerette in subtropical Louisiana, and also in Oklahoma, Texas and elsewhere. The breed was originally developed for use in the Gulf area where summers are hot and humid but the Brangus is now bred in many tropical and subtropical countries. This is a breed of hardy cattle that do well on range and fatten well in the feedlot.

Central American and Caribbean cattle

Jamaica Red Poll (synonyms Good Hope Red, Jamaica Red) The breed has been developed by the upgrading of indigenous Criollo and Zebu crossbreds using Red Poll bulls. A Jamaica Red Poll Cattle Breeders Society was founded in 1952 and the herdbook was closed in 1960. The habitat is varied and the climatic environment is tropical and generally humid.

It is a large animal with a good depth of body and medium-sized legs. The coat colour is dark to medium red; the hair sleek and dense; the skin fine; and the true to type animal should be polled.

The breed had been developed to produce beef at an early age off pasture and it is particularly well adapted to improved grass/legume pastures in a humid tropical environment. Cattle of this breed have been exported to Latin American countries and the breed appears to be flourishing, particularly in Venezuela.

Criollo (synonyms Creole (Guyana and West Indies), Puerto Rican Barrosa (Honduras and

Guatemala), Chino (Honduras)) These cattle have somewhat the same origin and history as the Criollo cattle of South America; that is, their ancestors were imported in past centuries from the Iberian Peninsula and the Cape Verde Islands. Once considered to be dual or triple purpose type cattle, they are disappearing in the Caribbean and Central America as they are being progressively upgraded to European temperate-type and Zebu (mainly Brahman) breeds.

Nelthropp (synonyms Senepol, Red Pied) This breed is of some interest because it originates from crossbreeding between the West African Senegal N'dama, described earlier, and the British Red Poll. N'dama were first imported into Martinique and Guadaloupe in 1825, to St Croix in 1860, to the British and American Virgin Islands between 1870 and 1914 and into Antigua in 1945.

Jamaica Brahman This is essentially the same type of animal as the American Brahman, being a breed that has been evolved from a mixture of Mysore, Ongole, Hissar and Kankrej cattle. Imports to Jamaica from India date back to 1850. American Brahman bulls have also been imported since 1948 to contribute to the formation of the breed. The Jamaica Brahman Breeders Society was formed in 1949.

Originally meant for work in the sugar plantations the breed is now bred specifically for beef production. It has been exported to Caribbean and South American countries.

South American cattle

Criollo cattle The Criollo type of cattle, found throughout the Caribbean and Central America, are mainly bred in South America by smallholders or small beef producers in humid, tropical and swampy areas, or in the coffee-growing montane uplands. They may be dual or triple purpose animals, although the milking Criollo of the Cauca Valley in Colombia is one of the most promising milking breeds in Latin America, adapted to grazing lowland pastures under fairly primitive husbandry methods. Beef or dual purpose types include the Romo-Sinuano, described below, but most beef is produced by the Zebu breeds or Zebu × Criollo crossbreds.

Romo-Sinuano (synonyms Coastal Polled, Moruno-Sinuano, Polled Sinu) This is a Criollo breed found in north Columbia around the Sinu river and in the province of Bolivar. They are believed to have originated from crossbreeding between Red Poll and/or Aberdeen Angus and Horned Sinu at the end of the last century. The habitat is either swampy or slightly undulating. The climatic environment is humid and tropical, the rainfall usually exceeds 1 780 mm per annum.

The Romo-Sinuano is a beef-type animal (fig. 3.19). The coat colour is red. The skin colour is deeply pigmented. The hair is scanty and short and many older animals possess a topline and rump completely devoid of hair. The breed is polled but scurs occur.

It is a beef breed that possesses a tendency to lay down localized 'gobs' of fat, a characteristic of the meat that is now considered undesirable. The breed is very docile and animals are easily herded.

fig. 3.19 Romo Sinuano

Zebu and Zebu crossbred cattle Zebu breeds used in the tropical regions of South America may be the descendants of imports from India and elsewhere, or more recently American Brahman, or a Zebu breed developed in Brazil and known as the Indu-Brasil. There are a number of locally developed European beef breed × Zebu crossbred types, one being the Canchim, while most of the North American crossbred types such as the Santa Gertrudis, Brangus and the Charbray are also used.

fig. 3.20 Indu-Brasil

fig. 3.21 Droughtmaster

Indu-Brasil (synonyms Hindu-Brazil, Inubereba) This breed originated from indiscriminate crossbreeding between Indian breeds imported into Brazil; mainly Gir, Kankrej and Ongole. The habitat is varied and the climatic environment tropical.

It is somewhat similar to the American Brahman, demonstrating characteristics from the foundation breeds (fig. 3.20). It is a beef breed and some of the best herds are now found in the states of Minas Gerais and Bahia in Brazil.

Canchim This breed has been developed in Brazil since 1940 by crossbreeding Charolais and Zebu breeds at the Sao Carlos Experimental Station. It is approximately $\frac{5}{8}$ Charolais × $\frac{3}{8}$ Zebu. It has been bred essentially for beef production and is showing great promise.

Australian cattle

The majority of cattle in the subtropical and tropical regions of Australia are still of the European *Bos taurus* type, the American Brahman and the Santa Gertrudis having been imported into northern Queensland only during the past few decades. Crossbreeding between temperate-type cattle such as the Hereford and Shorthorn has recently been extensively practised and new Australian types of Brahman, Santa Gertrudis, Brangus and Braford breeds have been established not dissimilar to their North American counterparts. Among these, the Droughtmaster demands special attention. The aim with Australian

breeders has been to infuse some of the basic hardiness and disease resistance – including that of greater resistance to the ectoparasite tick – with the better beef qualities of the European-type beef breeds.

Droughtmaster These are crossbred cattle with three-eighths to five-eighths Zebu blood, mainly derived from red American Brahman cattle imported from Texas. There is also some infusion of Santa Gertrudis blood. The temperate-type cattle inheritance has been derived from the Devon, Shorthorn, Hereford and Red Poll breeds, together with some genes from the Shorthorn inheritance in the Santa Gertrudis. A Droughtmaster Stud Breeders Society was formed in 1962. The climatic environment of the region in which they are utilised varies from humid tropical of the coast to semi-arid tropical and subtropical in the interior of the continent.

These cattle (fig. 3.21) are large, long-bodied and well fleshed. The coat is short and sleek and the skin loose and pliable. The coat colour is light or dark red. There are both horned and polled individuals. The dewlap and sheath in the male and the navel flap in the female are moderately developed. The udder of the female is of moderate size, possessing evenly placed teats.

This is a beef breed producing excellent quality meat. Animals of this breed are resistant to tick infestation and appear to be more tolerant to babesiosis than the British breeds. Droughtmaster cattle have been exported to New Guinea, and the

Solomon Islands and more recently in small numbers to West Africa. The Droughtmaster is Australia's own tropical beef cattle breed and its performance either on unimproved or improved (e.g. Pangola grasslands) range lands has shown it to be a highly adaptable breed able to thrive under very variable conditions of management.

Domestication and distribution of buffalo

Buffalo, like cattle, belong to the even-toed (artyodactyl) hoofed (ungulate) animals of the sub-order Ruminantia, sub-family Bovinae and tribe Bovini. There are two major types of wild buffalo, *Bubalis arnee*, the mainland Asiatic buffalo, and *Syncerus caffer*, the African buffalo.

It is generally accepted that the domesticated water buffalo, *Bos bubalus bubalis* originated from *Bos arnee*, the wild Indian buffalo, whose habitat in the past was the northeastern region of India, bordering on Burma and China. It is to be found today mainly in Assam.

The present world population of buffalo is by no means static. Due to its importance in the economies of Asian countries – as a principal source of tractor power for paddy cultivation in Southeast Asia and also as a source of milk and butter fat in India and Pakistan, coupled with the rapid increase in human population and consequent demand for animal products in these areas – the buffalo population has expanded. This has occurred in all the countries of the Far East region in the years following the Second World War and especially so in Burma, Kampuchea and the Philippines where the buffalo populations have doubled. India and Thailand have recorded increases of 33 per cent and 28 per cent respectively – a spectacular increase in the case of India which is the world's largest buffalo breeding country, with 44 per cent of the total number of buffalo in the world. The buffalo is thus increasing both in numbers and in popularity. In Sri Lanka, for example, the once popular tractor used on smallholdings is being replaced by the buffalo due to maintenance, fuel and 'spares' costs in mechanical cultivation. Recent statistics (Table 3.4) indicate that total world buffalo population during the past 15 years has increased from 114 to 150 million head, of which 75 per cent are located in Asian countries, providing the main source of milk and animal traction, in addition to their valuable contribution to local meat supplies.

In Africa the buffalo has had its greatest success in Egypt and much of the research on its growth and productivity cited in this book stems from the results of work done in that country. Although climate and environment in many other parts of Africa are suitable for the breeding and use of the water buffalo, there have been few importations over the past decades and most of these have had little success, projects being abandoned through inadequate management skills, or losses from local diseases, or a combination of these. Importations were made to the island of Madagascar from India in 1957. Elsewhere on the continent there were sporadic importations to Tanzania in the 1920s, to Zaire in the 1930s, from Sri Lanka and Indonesia to Uganda in 1971, to Mozambique from Italy in 1969 and more recently to Nigeria, and from Pakistan some years later. The Zaire importations were the most successful and although useful data on reproduction, growth rate, milk yield, carcass quality and susceptibility to local diseases were provided from this work the use of the water buffalo in central Africa has not been followed up. Heavy losses have been experienced in the Nigerian imports resulting from a severe skin disease (dermatophilosis or streptothricosis) that also affects Zebu cattle in Africa.

Importations of the water buffalo to the Americas and the Caribbean have occurred over the past 100 years, but mainly during the last two or three decades. The earliest imports to Trinidad and Tobago were of the Jafarabadi breed between 1900 and 1905. Guyana imported swamp buffalo in 1903 and Venezuela made its first imports from Trinidad in 1922. Large numbers of buffalo have been imported into Brazil where they have thrived in the Amazon region. Peru imported Brazilian buffalo for use in the Peruvian Amazon region in 1965 and Colombia as recently as 1967 from Trinidad. Promising results are reported from these last two recent imports where the hot humid environment of the Peruvian Amazon region and the high rainfall Pacific coastal region of Colombia are ideally suited to the buffalo.

Table 3.4 World distribution of buffalo

Continent	Country	Number in '000 1961–65	1985	Percentage increase/decrease from 1961–65 to 1985	As percentage of world total in 1985
Africa		1 559	2 415	+55	1.9
Tropics		–	–	–	
Other	Egypt	1 559	2 415	+55	
Americas		72	728	+911	0.6
Tropics	Brazil	67	720	+975	
	Trinidad & Tobago	5	8	+60	
Other		–		–	
Asia		113 184	125 413	+11	97.0
Tropics	Bangladesh	505	1 800	+256	
	Brunei	14	12	–14	
	Burma	1 117	2 100	+88	
	India	25 936	64 500	+149	49.9
	Indonesia	2 961	2 424	–18	
	Kampuchea	596	685	+15	
	Laos	527	1 200	+128	
	Malaysia	359	260	–28	
	Philippines	3 357	4 325	+29	
	Sri Lanka	855	990	+16	
	Thailand	6 859	6 250	–9	
	Vietnam	2 295	2 800	+22	
Other	China	28 318	19 547	–31	
	Bhutan		29		
	Iran		230		
	Iraq		145		
	Nepal	39 480	4 500	–53	
	Pakistan		13 070		
	Syria		2		
	Turkey		544		
Europe and USSR		792	727	–8	0.5
	Europe	407	407	–	
Other	USSR	385	320	–17	
Oceania		1	–	–100	
Tropics	Guam	1	–	–100	
Other		–		–	
World		115 608	129 283	+12	
Tropics		45 459	88 074	+94	68.1
Other		70 149	41 209	–41	31.9

No account is taken in these statistics of small numbers of domestic and land buffalo present in many countries.

The buffalo has been found to revert easily to the feral or semi-feral, that is, the wild or semi-wild state. Herds of feral animals exist in parts of Indonesia, Borneo, Brazil and Australia. In many instances, e.g. in Brunei, such animals serve as capital reserve for local farmers and in Brazil, female calves of feral or semi-feral buffalo are captured and domesticated as milk producers for the household. Swamp buffalo, imported from Timor some 150 years ago, and left to run wild in the coastal plains of the Northern Territory of Australia now number over 200 000 head and provide foundation stock for a growing buffalo meat industry.

Buffalo breeds and types with potential for beef production

Since the majority of buffalo breeds are either dual or triple purpose animals, only those breeds which have had the widest impact on meat production will be described here. Types within breeds may be selected for either their milking or meat propensities and it must be accepted that many of such dual purpose animals are also triple purpose, as valuable traction or pack animals for the community. The river buffalo breeds that will be described include the Murrah, Jafarabadi, Nagpuri, Nili and Mehsana. Many other breeds or types are used for meat production, in particular the swamp buffalo types found throughout Southeast Asia. Some authorities, such as Cockrill, group all swamp buffalo types together as one breed, but there are many variants to be found in swamp buffalo. For example, the swamp buffalo of Thailand may weigh at maturity over 900 kg, while the Carabao of the Philippines or the Borneo buffalo may weigh less than 400 kg.

General characteristics
Buffalo may be described in general terms, to include both the swamp and river types, as big boned, rather massive animals when compared to both Zebu and *Bos taurus* cattle breeds, with bodies set low on strong legs with large hooves. There is no dewlap or hump. The milk-type river buffalo has the body conformation of the dairy cow while that of the swamp type resembles the draught

Zebu breeds. A distinct feature is the horns which are more massive than those in cattle, not smooth and conical, but broad, flat and almost rectangular near the base with prominent ridges across the long axis. Swamp, and several breeds of river and nondescript types of buffalo, have backward-swept horns, although tightly curled horns are seen in two river buffalo breeds. Generally speaking, horns may vary in shape from the coiled Murrah type to the long sickle shape found in the Surti breed resembling the horns of the ram. Excessively long horns measuring more than three-quarters of the body length also occur.

Hair growth and density are also markedly different from cattle. At birth and in early calfhood buffalo have a good coat of soft hair like that of cattle, but this becomes much sparser and coarser as the animal grows to maturity. Colours vary from black, dun, creamy yellow, to dark or light grey, or white. Stars, blazes, socks and a white tail switch are common in river buffalo. White animals are found among swamp buffalo.

The swamp buffalo of Southeast Asia
The area of distribution of the domestic buffalo extends northward to the Yangtze Valley in China and westward to Assam. This includes Southeast China, Burma, Assam, Laos, Kampuchea, Vietnam, Thailand, Malaysia, Indonesia and the Philippines. The swamp buffalo are much closer to the wild type in many of these areas, e.g. in Sri Lanka and Assam, often running with and interbreeding with the latter. Likewise, the imported Murrah and Surti or Surati breeds were referred to as river buffalo because of their preference for river water and pools. The swamp buffalo has not been classed with breeds as applies to the river type, but as varieties, often bearing the name of the district or country in which they were bred, for example, the Kwai Tui or Kwai Jaew of north and northeast Thailand. The Carabao breed of the Philippines is the Spanish representation of the Malay word for buffalo.

The skin of the swamp buffalo is grey in colour, becoming slate blue as the calf grows. Horns, hooves and hair are normally of the same colour, the coat usually being described as dark grey. An albinoid type is sometimes found in the Philippines, West Malaysia and Thailand, that has white or yellowish hair and pink skin, but pigmented eyes. They are not therefore true albinos but commonly called such. Common features are light grey or white stockings and two white or light grey chevrons, one just below the jaw and the other below the neck on the front of the brisket. The horns grow outwards laterally and horizontally, curving outwards horizontally as the animal grows but remaining approximately in the plane of the forehead. Very long horns, 2.5 m from tip to tip, occur in Indonesia.

The general conformation is as follows:
trunk – heavy bodied and stockily built, with short body and somewhat pot-bellied appearance;
head – forehead flat, orbits prominent, short face and wide muzzle; in the male the forehead is narrow with long thin horns resembling the arnee;
neck – long and withers prominent;
legs – short and thin;
dorsal ridge – formed by spines of the first two thoracic vertebrae;
shoulders – heavy and powerful;
hindquarters – poorly developed;
tail – short, down to the hocks;
udder – small, set back between the hind legs;
genitalia – penis adheres to abdomen, the last few cm free or attached by small fold to the umbilicus, the scrotum has no neck, is about 10 cm long and carried high.

The river buffalo, by general comparison with the swamp type, has a relatively longer body and face, smaller girth, longer and thicker legs, prominent hocks and sacrum and heavier head and horns with greater variations between male and female. The penis hangs clear of the abdomen, attached by a triangular fold of skin running back from the umbilicus (more like Zebu cattle). The scrotum has a distinct neck and is 20–25 cm in length. Some details of average body measurements of river and swamp buffalo are provided in Table 3.5.

Indian subcontinent river buffalo

Murrah The home of the Murrah is in Haryana State and the Union territory of Delhi in India. They are also bred in large numbers in the State of Punjab in India, the Punjab province of Pakistan, the northern part of Uttar Pradesh in India and Sind in Pakistan. The best specimens of the breed are found in the Rohtak, Hissar and Jind districts of Haryana and the riverine tracts of Sind (Pakistan).

The head of the Murrah (fig. 3.22) is relatively small in proportion to body size, shapely and fine in the female, heavier and coarser in the male. The face is clean cut, with prominent, limpid, bright eyes. Ears are small, well shaped and drooping. Horns are short, tightly curled, growing upwards and backwards. The neck is long and thin in females but thick and massive in males. The chest is well developed and wide across the brisket. Legs are straight, short and strong with large black hooves.

The body frame is compact, deep and capacious, and in females it is as wedge-shaped as that of dairy cattle. The navel flap is small. The udder is of good size and well shaped, possessing prominent milk veins. The teats are well spaced, of good size and

Table 3.5 Average measurements of swamp and river buffalo (cm)

		Swamp buffalo	River buffalo
Height at withers	M	129–33	138
	F	127–30	132
Heart girth	M	199–228	209
	F	187–94	202
Length (point of shoulder to pin bone)	M	149–80	158
	F	134–52	148

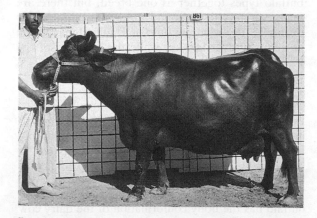

fig. 3.22 Murrah

fig. 3.23 Nili

fig. 3.24 Surti

long. The tail is long and thin reaching the fetlocks, often with white markings towards the end and usually ending with a white switch.

The skin is thin, soft and pliable with very little hair on the body in adult animals. The popular skin colour is jet black, but animals with fawn-grey body hair are not uncommon. White markings on the face or limbs are not liked.

Nili The home of Nili buffalo is partly in Pakistan and partly in India; the major part being in Pakistan. The animals are bred in the Montgomery, Multan and Lyallpur districts of Punjab province in Pakistan and the Ferozepur district of the State of Punjab in India. The best specimens of the breed are found in the valleys of the Ravi and Sutlej rivers. The name of the breed is supposedly derived from the deep blue colour (Nili) of the water of the Sutlej river.

The Nili buffalo (fig. 3.23) possesses a shapely, long head with a fine muzzle and wide nostrils. The head is rounded and convex at the top, depressed between the eyes and has a prominent nasal bone. The horns are small but broad, thick and tightly curled. Ears are medium sized and pointed at the apex. The neck is long, thin and fine in the female; thick and massive in the male.

The body frame is deep, of medium size and is set low on short, straight, strong, big-boned legs. The udder is well developed, shapely and well placed. The teats are of good size and are spaced well apart. The milk veins are prominent. The tail is long and fine, almost touching the ground, and invariably possesses a white switch.

The skin is smooth and soft and black colour is most common. Animals with brown colour are acceptable. The skin of the udder and brisket frequently shows pink patches. Animals with wall eyes (one or both) and with white markings on the forehead, face, muzzle and limbs are greatly valued.

Surti The home of the Surti is in the south-western part of Gujarat State in India. The best animals of the breed are found in the Kaira, Nadiad and Baroda districts.

The Surti (fig. 3.24) has a fairly broad, rather long head, with a convex shape at the top between the horns. The face and muzzle are clean cut and the nostrils are big. The eyes are bright, clear and prominent. Ears are medium sized and drooping and the skin on the inner side of the ear is pinkish in colour. Horns are flat, sickle-shaped and of good size with ridges across the long axis as in other buffalo. They grow in a downward and backward direction and then upwards at the tip, forming a hook. The neck is well shaped and long in the female; thick and heavy in the male. The chest is broad and the brisket is prominent.

The body is medium sized, well built and wedge-shaped, and set rather low on straight, strong legs with broad black hooves. No other breed of buffalo has as straight a back as the Surti. The tail is long, thin and flexible, usually with a white switch. The udder is well developed and finely shaped, and well placed between the hindlegs. The teats are medium

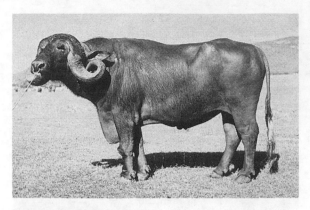

fig. 3.25 Jafarabadi

fig. 3.26 Nagpuri

in size and well spaced. The skin is rather thick but soft, smooth and pliable, having a sparse hair coat. The skin colour is black or brown and the colour of the hair varies from rusty brown to silvery grey. Good specimens have two white chevrons – one around the jaw extending from ear to ear and the other around the brisket.

Jafarabadi The home tract of the Jafarabadi buffalo lies in the Gir forest of Gujarat State in India.

It possesses (fig. 3.25) a rather heavy head with fairly large, thick, flat horns which tend to droop on each side of the neck and then turn up at the tips in a curl but not so tight as in the Murrah or Nili breeds. A noticeable feature of the breed is the very prominent bulging forehead of the animal. The neck is strong and well built.

The body is massive, relatively long and not very compact, and is set somewhat high on the legs, which are straight and strong. The udder is well developed and the teats are of good size and well placed. The usual colour is black.

Nagpuri (synonyms Barari, Ellichpuri, Gaulani, Gauli, Marathwada, Durna-Thali and Varadi) This is a breed (fig. 3.26) from central India. The colour is usually black, sometimes with white markings on the face, legs and switch. The horns are long, flat-curved and carried back nearly to the shoulder.

The Nagpuri is lighter in build than the breeds of northern India and Pakistan. The face is long and thin with a straight profile. The neck is

comparatively long and the limbs are long and light. The tail is short, hanging only a little below the hocks. Average bodyweights of Nagpuri range from 320 to 400 kg, while the average wither height is 142 cm in males and 132 cm in females.

The males are used for heavy draught but are slow. They are reputed to be more heat tolerant and to require less water externally as a cooling medium than other breeds.

Mehsana The Mehsana is used for milk production in Ahmadabad and Bombay but originates from around the town of Mehsana.

Horns vary from coiled horn approaching the Murrah type to the long sickle shape of the Surti; but typically they are intermediate, i.e. sickle-shaped but with more curve than the Surti and less than the Murrah. This gives them a ram's horn shape.

Compared with the Murrah, the Mehsana has a longer body, lighter limbs, and longer and heavier head. The forehead is wide with a slight depression in the middle sloping towards the root of the horns. The face is long and straight with a wide muzzle and wide open nostrils. Eyes are very prominent, black and bright, bulging from their sockets, with folds of skin on the upper lids. Ears are medium sized and pointed at the apex. The neck is long and well set on the shoulders.

The skin over the neck region has folds. In males, the neck is massive and dewlap is almost absent. The chest is deep with broad brisket. Shoulders are broad and blend well with the body. The legs are of medium to short length with clean bones and broad, black hoofs.

The barrel is long and deep, with well-sprung ribs. In males, the forequarters are massive and the hindquarters fairly wide. The back is comparatively straight and strong with the pelvic joint higher than the withers. The hindquarters are well developed, wide and deep.

The udder is well developed and well set and in good females carried well behind. Generally, the hindquarters are more developed than the forequarters – a good meat characteristic. The skin is thin, pliable and soft and usually black in colour, while hair is rough and scanty. The temperament is docile and so the animals are easy to handle. Mehsana animals differ little in size from those of the Surti breed.

Further reading

Epstein, H. (1972). *The origin of the domestic animals of Africa* (2 volumes). Africana Publ. Corp.: New York.

Fahimuddin, M. (1975). *Domestic water buffalo*. Oxford and IBH Publ. Co.: New Delhi.

Foster W. H. (1960). The breeding of White Fulani cattle at Shika, Nigeria. *Samaru Res. Bull.* (Nigeria), **2**.

ILCA (1978). *Evaluation of the productivities of Maure and Peul cattle breeds at the Sahelian station, Niono, Mali.* ILCA Monograph no. 1. International Livestock Centre for Africa: Addis Ababa.

Joshi, N. R. and Phillips, R. W. (1953). *Zebu cattle of India and Pakistan*. FAO Agric. Studies no. 19. FAO: Rome.

Mason, I. L. (1951). The classification of West African livestock. Commonwealth Bureau of Animal Breeding and Genetics Tech. Comm. no. 7. Commonwealth Agric. Bureau: Farnham Royal, UK.

Mason, I. L. (1973). The role of natural and artificial selection in the origin of breeds of farm animals. *Zeitschrift für Tierzuchtung und Zuchtungsbiologie*, **90**, 229–244.

Payne, W. J. A. (1970). *Cattle production in the tropics.* Vol. 1: *Breeds and Breeding*. Longman: London.

Plasse, D. (1975). The possibility of genetic improvement of beef cattle in developing countries with particular reference to Latin America. In *Beef cattle production in developing countries*, **ed. A. J. Smith.** Edinburgh Univ. Press: Edinburgh. 308–329.

Williamson, G. and Payne, W. J. A. (1978). *An introduction to animal husbandry in the tropics*. 3rd edn. Longman: London.

4 Reproduction and behaviour

Structure of the urogenital system

The urinary and reproductive organs of the male and female are known as the urogenital system. The reproductive organs of cattle and buffalo bulls consist of the testes or testicles contained in the scrotum, the epididymis and vas deferens, the penis contained in the prepuce and the accessory sex glands including the seminal vesicles, prostate and Cowper's glands, adjacent to the proximal part of the urethra and bladder of the urinary system (fig. 4.1). The cow and buffalo cow reproductive organs consist of the ovaries (which produce the ova or eggs) connected by the fallopian tube to the tip of the uterus. The uterus leads into the vagina via the cervix and the vagina leads to the exterior through the vulva which contains the small and sensitive homologue (counterpart) of the male penis known as the clitoris (fig. 4.2).

Fertilisation

Whereas the bull should show ready sexual vigour or libido when put into active service the cow will only accept the bull at mating or 'joining' when she is in oestrus, referred to by cattlemen as 'bulling' or 'on heat'. The signs of oestrus and the management of the cow during this period are discussed later. When the bull mounts the accepting cow he ejaculates over one million sperm (spermatozoa). During this mating process some of the sperm from the bull's epididymis are forced by strong muscular contractions along the vas deferens where, near the bladder area (fig. 4.1), they are diluted by secretions from the accessory glands. The function of the secretions of these glands is to make the sperm vigorous so that they may quickly ascend the female reproductive tract. The bull secretes about 5 ml of accessory gland secretions, the secretions and

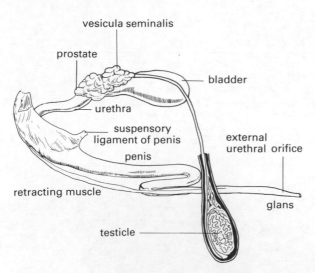

fig. 4.1 The genital organs of a bull

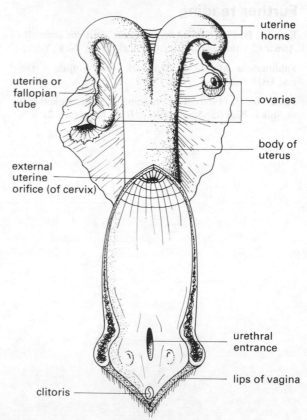

fig. 4.2 The reproductive organs of a cow

sperm together constituting the semen. The spermatozoa themselves are produced in the seminiferous tubules of the testicle and from there pass down to the duct of the lower part of the epididymis (fig. 4.1), where they mature, attain full motility and are stored. The spermatozoa remain fertile for about 40 days in the epididymis and if they are not used they disintegrate and are resorbed into the body. The interstitial cells between the seminiferous tubules secrete a substance into the blood (hormone) which causes development of male physical characteristics, also desire and ability to mate. Within the cow the semen is sprayed over the cervix of the uterus and upper end of the vagina. At the time of mating, or during artificial insemination, nerves are stimulated to act on the posterior pituitary gland which releases into the blood the hormone oxytocin to cause contractions of smooth muscle of the uterus and associated structures. These contractions hasten the passage of the spermatozoa up the horns of the uterus towards the entry point of the fallopian tubes (fig. 4.2) along which the ovum travels after release during ovulation from the ovary. The fusion of one sperm with the ovum constitutes fertilisation and the fertilised ovum is then known as the zygote. This process represents the only physical link between one generation and another, the zygote combining the genetic or hereditary make-up of the parent bull and cow. During oestrus the fallopian tubes, uterine horns and especially the cervix secrete a thin, watery mucus which forms a good medium in which the spermatozoa may travel.

The reproductive cycle

The reproductive cycle begins with fertilisation of the ovum and ends with parturition or birth of the calf. The period between these events is the gestation period and should not be confused with the oestrus or oestral cycle which is the period between heats or oestrus. The normal cow possesses two ovaries at the tip of the uterine horns, each ovary being adjacent to the funnel-like structure known as the fimbria (fig. 4.2) and into which the ovum is shed at ovulation, prior to being conveyed along the fallopian tube to the uterus. Normally, only one

ovulation occurs at a time from either one or the other ovary. The ovum, which is rather like a microscopic version of the yolk of a hen's egg, ripens into a follicle within the germinal epithelium or germinal layer of the ovary, the follicles containing an albuminous fluid. The follicles secrete a hormone known as oestrogen into the bloodstream which, besides promoting the development of physical and other female characteristics, brings about the symptoms of oestrus. After rupture of the follicle the ovum drops into the funnel-like structure of the fimbria and is washed into the fallopian tube by the albuminous fluid surrounding it. The cells of the empty wall of the ovarian follicle then proliferate rapidly and form the corpus luteum (CL) or yellow body which projects from the germinal surface of the ovary. The corpus luteum secretes the hormone progesterone which stimulates the lining of the uterus (endometrium) to receive and nourish the fertilised ovum, which has now become the developing embryo during its passage of 3 to 4 days down the fallopian tube. The embryo becomes attached to the uterine lining during the implantation stage. In the cow the corpus luteum remains present and active throughout pregnancy and its removal accidentally or deliberately will cause an abortion. The condition of the corpus luteum is of considerable importance in pregnancy diagnosis and examination for fertility and is carried out by manual palpation through the wall of the cow's rectum. The lining of the uterus produces what are known as prostaglandins and the foetal membranes placental gonadotrophins, both having an effect on ovarian activity.

The chemical substances circulating in the bloodstream – the hormones – play an important part in reproduction and the reproductive cycle, as indeed in growth and other metabolic functions. The glands that produce the hormones are known as endocrine or ductless glands in that they secrete directly through their cell walls into the bloodstream. Some endocrine glands have only one function, to secrete a specific hormone that acts on specific cells or organs, whereas the gonads or sexual reproductive organs, such as the testicles and ovaries, have a dual role in producing both sperm or ova, as well as certain hormones. The control centre of hormone production is situated in an area

47

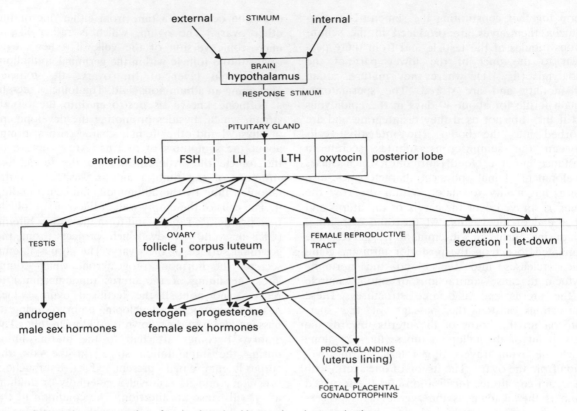

fig. 4.3 Schematic representation of endocrine gland interactions in reproduction

of the brain known as the hypothalamus, acting on the pituitary gland which in turn is involved in stimulating the gonads to produce sperm and ova. A schematic representation of the interactions of hormones with the reproductive tract is set out in fig. 4.3. The emphasis on hormones in this discussion is given to their role in reproduction. They can now be manufactured synthetically and hence more cheaply and are used a great deal in the treatment of reproductive disorders such as failure to come on heat and other malfunctions in reproduction and in the control of the breeding cycle.

Pregnancy (gestation)

Implantation of the fertilised ovum in the uterine lining takes place so that nutrition of the embryo

can commence at this critical stage. There are three major phases of pregnancy:

1 The 'blastocyst' stage – the ovum obtains its nutrients from secretions of the uterine glands (uterine 'milk').
2 The embryonic stage – the placenta (foetal membranes) are formed. The foetus is nourished via the placenta from the maternal tissues.
3 The foetal stage – foetal growth is rapid and occurs mainly by increase in cell size. The rate of growth of the foetus is very dependent on the nutrition of the mother and absorption of her nutrients through the placenta from her bloodstream.

The foetal membranes or placenta enveloping the foetus, described in more detail in relation to parturition, are not attached diffusely, as is the case in some animals, to the inner lining of the uterus, but to specially raised button-like structures called cotyledons that receive the caruncles or tufts of villi (minute finger-like structures) into their crypts. Nutrients are passed across the villi from the maternal circulation to the foetus and waste products of metabolism from the foetus are passed back to the dam, which she then disposes of through her own system. The maternal and foetal circulations are thus completely separate, communicating only across the linings of the two circulatory systems and intervening tissue layers.

In the early stages of pregnancy, therefore, much of the growth of the embryo consists of the placenta (allanto-chorion) and the amniotic and allantoic fluids surrounding it. In the second phase the foetus itself is making rapid growth and has priority over the dam's nutrition during mid-pregnancy. At this stage an inadequately fed cow may lose weight while the foetus gains. During the latter part of the pregnancy the nutritional level of the dam has an appreciable effect on the birthweight of the calf. The practical implications of this are considered in Chapter 7.

Reproductive behaviour of cattle

The oestrus cycle

The oestrus cycle in the cow refers to a rhythmic cycle of some 16 to 21 days culminating in ovulation. The duration of heat in European-type cattle in the temperate zone averages some 18 hours; it is considerably less for Zebu cattle as well as for European-type breeds in a tropical environment. Zebu cattle may have heat periods lasting only 4 to 8 hours and even less for cattle managed under stressful nomadic conditions. Such heat periods often occur at night. Heat periods in the buffalo average approximately 36 hours but are extremely variable (Table 4.1). Few studies have been carried out on tropical *Bos taurus* breeds or types. One such study on N'dama cattle under range management conditions in West Africa showed an average oestrus cycle of 19.4 days (range 10 to 30 days) and duration of oestrus of 3.4 ± 1.43 hours with ovulation occurring 20 ± 6.9 hours after the end of 'standing heat' that is, after the time when the cow will no longer stand for or accept the bull. Their heat period is thus considerably shorter than for European-type *Bos taurus* breeds and so also is the period from end of heat to ovulation. The interval between end of heat and ovulation in temperate cattle breeds in their own environment is reported to average 7.7 hours, which is a considerably shorter period than reported for the Brahman or the N'dama. The duration of the oestrus cycle varies little between the Zebu and tropical *Bos taurus* breeds, reports on duration of heat for the Zebu varying from as little as 1.4–4.8 to 6.7 hours. The general consensus of opinion seems to be that such variations are due to an effect of climate on the duration of heat rather than a breed characteristic, whether this applies to tropical or to temperate breeds managed in the tropics.

Signs of heat include restlessness, mounting of other cows or being mounted by them, slackening of the vulva and mucus discharge and the major feature of standing for the bull. The occurrence in temperate climates of oestrus in small ruminants such as sheep is influenced by changes in day length; in cattle this has no marked effect, the chief causes of absence, unnoticed or 'silent' heat being due to poor nutrition. Zebu cattle in the Sahel zone of Africa, for example, may conceive so as to produce only one calf every other year whereas better nourished cows in the more southerly grassland savanna zones may calve down every 14 to 18 months and even every 12 to 14 months under optimum management conditions.

Parturition

Parturition is the act of giving birth to the calf. It follows much the same pattern in the cow and buffalo cow and it is important that the livestockman should have a working knowledge of the sequence of events involved. Not all cows labour in the same way; the first-calving heifer on range or intensive management may be more excited or give more problems than the older cow. Likewise, the accepted normal sequence of events in dams of any age may not necessarily occur, for there may be premature or prolonged gestation periods (Table 4.1), or difficult parturition (dystocia) because of the malposition of the calf in the 'birth canal' during delivery. The following paragraphs describe the normal or average stages of parturition in a cow or buffalo.

Table 4.1 Some examples of reproductive behaviour in cattle and buffalo

Factor	Cattle	Buffalo
Age at puberty (mths)	Criollo 27–33 African Zebu 37	24–26
Age at first calving (mths)	Criollo 36–42 African Zebu 46 (31–52)* Indian Zebu 41–44	India 30–46 Pakistan 32–72 Egypt 40 (22–60) Brazil 36 Philip's 26
Gestation period (days)	283–291	315 (River 300–320 Swamp 325–330)
Calving interval (days)	Criollo 372–420 Indian Zebu 410–580 African Zebu 378–590	417.7 (Indian) 415.4 (Carabao) (403–730)
Period of oestrus (hrs)	N'dama 3.9 African Zebu 4.8–7.5 Brahman 6.7 (2–8)	24–36 (even 5 days: very variable)
Post-partum oestrus (days)	Criollo 40–80 African Zebu 40–100+	90 (35–170) Indian Murrah 185+ Philippine Murrah 49.6 Carabao 54
Oestrus cycle (days)	16–26 11 (2–22)	21 (very variable) 10 (5–24: very variable)
Ovulation post-oestrus (hrs)	N'dama 20+–6.9	
Service period (days)	Criollo 89–129 Indian Zebu 127–289 African Zebu 85–299	Indian Murrah 146.8 (42–202) Philippine Murrah 305 (29–522) Egyptian Murrah 177
Acceptance period (hrs)	11 before and 24 post-oestrus	
Longevity (yrs) (productivity post first calving)	Criollo 5 Indian Zebu 4–5+ African Zebu 5–10	Indian Murrah 146.8 (42–202) Philippine Murrah 305 (29–522) Egyptian Murrah 177
Heritability of factors		
Calving interval	0.1–0.3	–
Age first calving	0.08–0.25 (0.39 selected)	0.13
Reproductive efficiency (temperate-type dairy cattle)	0.0–0.1	–
Service period	0.07	–

* Figures in parenthesis indicate *range* of behaviour, figures outside parenthesis indicate the *average*

Early signs

1 The most certain indications of the approach of calving time occur in the visible appearance of the udder. Some weeks prior to parturition the udder begins to enlarge. Shortly before calving milk (colostrum) can be squeezed from the teats. The 'lips' of the vulva swell and become slack and normally there is a mucoid vulval discharge.

2 The immediate approach of labour can be recognised by changes in what is called the 'pelvic canal'.

The sacrosciatic ligaments become softened and relaxed, accompanied by a raising of the sacrum and tailhead. As the normally strong and tense ligaments from the tailhead to the pinbones (*tuber ischii*) soften and loosen, this signals the onset of parturition within a few hours.

3 The above changes are followed by the onset of labour, due to a complex of hormone influences arising in the pituitary gland (fig. 4.3), the ovaries, the suprarenal or adrenal glands, the placenta and possibly also the foetus and the uterus. The full cause of the 'time signal' for the onset of labour is as yet unclear.

Labour
For clarity the sequence of events during labour is divided into three stages. Events that occur between the first two phases may frequently overlap.

First stage: dilatation of the cervix The relaxed uterine cervix becomes dilated by the passage, in advance of the foetus, by that part of the foetal membranes known as the amniotic sack or 'water bag'. This is normally the first, balloon-like structure to appear between the vulval lips. There may be some straining and discomfort, especially in first-calving heifers. There is considerable variation in the intensity of symptoms, but signs of approaching parturition before the 'water bag' becomes apparent may last for 24 to 36 hours, or considerably less, even to the extent of the stockman being taken by surprise by a cow's easy, unexpected and rapid delivery.

Second stage: expulsion of the foetus This stage, often not clearly demarcated from the first, involves the expulsion of the foetus, preceded by the appearance of the 'water bag' at the vaginal orifice and the ejection through the vaginal lips of its fluid contents. It therefore serves to protect the foetus and lubricate the birth canal at the time of parturition. During this period intermittent straining by the cow also occurs and as the calf's head passes through the vulva the cow will usually go down and remain recumbent until the calf is born. There are occasions, however, when the emergent calf will literally take a 'nose-dive' to the ground behind the standing cow. This stage may take anything from

one-half to four hours or more. Longer periods may herald difficult parturition.

Third stage: expulsion of the foetal membranes This stage entails the expulsion of the foetal membranes and placenta, generally termed the 'afterbirth'. Visible, voluntary expulsion efforts have ceased but the involuntary uterine musculature contractions still continue to assist in expelling the placenta. This may normally occur in 2–24 hours, but retention after this period may indicate a 'retained' placenta and requires veterinary intervention.

After normal parturition, the beef cow needs little care and is, in fact, better left alone, especially cows on range. Management at weaning is important, however, and is discussed later in detail (Chapter 7).

Dystocia (difficult birth)
This implies some obstacle to parturition in which the calf cannot be delivered by the maternal effort of the cow alone and in consequence of which she requires external help. The situation is more common in dairy and more intensively managed beef herds, but far less so for cattle and buffalo under more extensive or traditional management systems. The normal position of the calf at parturition is that of the 'nose-dive' posture with both forefeet and nose appearing more or less together at the vulval lips. Sometimes, the calf may be too big to be expelled, as may occur with calves from large beef breed bulls crossed with smaller breeds, or with Zebu cows, the latter, in any event, having a smaller diameter of pelvic inlet/outlet than *Bos taurus* cows. Conversely, the head of a normal sized calf may be deflected to the left or right, so that only the shoulder is presented at the outlet. At other times, one of the calf's legs may be deflected, or it may be upside down, or in some other abnormal position in the birth canal. The experienced stockman can deal with minor problems such as the application of careful and steady traction to facilitate the delivery of a large calf, or one that has become dry around the head due to a prolonged delivery. Over and above this, veterinary assistance should be sought. There are occasions, however, especially under range management conditions,

when time-consuming assistance to the individual animal may not be considered desirable on economic grounds and under such circumstances cows giving problems at calving may be sold or slaughtered as commercially unproductive. This situation is different in smaller and more intensive holdings where individual animal rather than herd attention is more possible and of greater managerial consequence.

Reproductive behaviour of buffalo

There is considerable variation in reports on the reproductive behaviour of buffalo. Data on the more important traits are provided in Tables 4.1 and 4.2.

Table 4.2 Season of calving in water buffalo

Breed/type	Country	Month(s)	Season
Trinidad	Trinidad	July–Dec.	wet
Carabao	Philippines	July–Jan.	wet
Egyptian	Egypt	March–May	spring (wet)
Indian Murrah	India		
	(north)	June–Dec.	wet
Pakistan	Pakistan	Aug.–Oct.	wet

Age at puberty

Even under conditions of good nutrition the male buffalo attains sexual maturity rather later than *Bos taurus* or *Bos indicus* bulls. In Egypt, buffalo males are put to first service at an average age of 3.7 years, while in Pakistan service is a little earlier, between 3 and 3.5 years. Reduced potency has been reported at 6 to 7 years of age, males becoming senile, with generalised muscular weakness and impotency by 15 years. Other reports, however, indicate that under good conditions of feeding and management the buffalo male can remain in useful service up to 10 to 15 years of age and allowing one male to serve on an average 50 females in a year.

As with cattle there is no marked rutting (i.e. bulling) season. On the other hand, since the optimum buffalo breeding season is during the cooler months of the year, greater stress is put on the males at such times. In Egypt, for example, it has been observed that if males are put to the females as many as three times in a week and kept in continuous use over a breeding season of four months, lower conception rates and poorer semen quality are the result. As with cattle breeding, therefore, optimum conception rates depend to a considerable extent on management and nutrition.

Reproductive characteristics of the female buffalo are summarised in Table 4.1 and it will be seen that there are considerable variations in the data presented, depending to a large extent on standards of management and nutrition. Although first oestrus may occur as early as 15 to 18 months in the Egyptian buffalo, mating at this age is reported to result in possible abortions and, for the dairy farmer especially, subsequent loss in milk production. Reports on age at puberty vary from 15 to 18 months in Egypt, to 26 to 29 months in the Philippines and 36 months in Kampuchea.

Oestrus and oestrous cycle

The oestrous cycle in most buffalo breeds, as in cattle, is 21 days, although a range of 8 to 24 days has been reported in Egyptian, and 28 to 30 days in the West Malaysian buffalo. There are greater variations in the seasonal incidence of oestrus in buffalo females than in cattle in Pakistan, as well as differences in oestrus behaviour in these two bovine species. Behavioural differences are also reported during oestrus between certain buffalo breeds, for example, between the water buffalo of Egypt and India and the Carabao of the Philippines. Signs of oestrus and mating behaviour of the Egyptian and most swamp buffalo occur during the night and cease with the onset of daylight, whereas, in breeds of Indian water buffalo, these activities usually commence in the morning. The duration of oestrus is generally 1.5 days, varying from a few hours to as long as 4 to 5 days. Special exceptions are reported in the Malaysian water buffalo in which oestrus may last up to two weeks if fertilisation after mating did not take place. Ovulation time in different buffalo breeds occurs approximately 5 to 24 hours after the cessation of heat. Silent heat and anovular heat (oestrus without ovulation) post-partum is observed in Indian buffalo, and in Egyptian buffalo 30 per cent of heat periods after calving are silent.

Symptoms or signs of oestrus are more pronounced in the Carabao of the Philippines than in Indian buffalo and more marked than in female cattle. There are, however, reports to the effect that the thick, clear, viscid vulval mucus discharge in female cattle is absent in the Carabao although it is considered that this may be due to the frequent urination of the Carabao during the heat period. Oestrus during pregnancy, as with cattle, sometimes occurs.

Gestation period

Accepting the cow to carry her calf on an average for 278 to 290 days, it is generally agreed that the gestation period of the buffalo is longer and more variable. The majority of buffalo breeds have gestation periods of 300 to 320 days and above; the Egyptian buffalo ranges from about 316 to 319 days. For the swamp buffalo the range is 325 to 330 days so that for all practical purposes this represents about 10 to 10.5 calendar months, as compared to 9 months in the cow. Male calves are generally carried longer than female calves, although the opposite is occasionally reported. In some cases older females 6 to 8 years of age have longer gestation periods than younger females. There is also a significant correlation between length of gestation and calf weight at birth; gestations ending in winter (cool weather) calving are longest and those ending at the end of the hottest months are shortest.

Age at first calving

Studies on farm data for age at first calving in Egypt show a range of 22 to 60 months, with over 40 per cent of the females calving down at 38 to 42 months of age. The average in Pakistan in another study was 47 months, in Indian buffalo on breeding farms 40.4 months and in Brazil 36 months of age. These figures have been compiled from observations, not only on females of different breeds and from several countries, but also under varying systems of management, including small peasant holdings, government breeding stations, on range, or under selected farming systems. In a small group of buffalo imported to the Congo (Zaire) in the early 1950s first calving was reported on a livestock breeding station at 2.5 years of age.

Calving intervals vary from 334 to 650 days (Table 4.1). An average of a comparatively long calving interval of 15 months is considered mainly a function of management, due to a considerable extent to failure in detecting heat, especially during the 'summer' months in the tropics. Calving rate in summer (March–May) in Madras, India is down to 9.36 per cent and in the northeast monsoon (September–November) up to 43.17 per cent (fig. 4.4). Studies over a ten year period in Pakistan, indicated a strong correlation between decreasing day length and rainfall and conception rate. Studies on the effects of season on breeding of Murrah buffalo and their crosses with the indigenous swamp buffalo were made on herds at two government farms in Sri Lanka. The season of

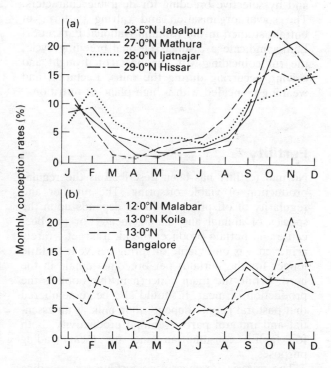

fig. 4.4 Monthly conception rates in Murrah river buffalo at several locations in India

53

birth of the dam had a significant effect on the age at first calving, and in addition there was a marked influence of season on the calving interval. Animals born during the period August–December calved earlier than those born during January–July, this being considered due also to the indirect result of changes in the plane of nutrition in the young calf. The length of the 'refractory' period, i.e. the service period or interval from parturition to the next fertile service, was also considered to be affected by seasonal changes in nutrition. A useful hypothesis in management was formulated in these studies, that the minimum refractory period following parturition was about 5 to 6 months, and that where conditions are favourable at the end of this period, animals return early to heat, thus shortening the calving interval. On this hypothesis, productivity could be increased by improved management through the conservation of fodder to ensure a uniform plane of nutrition throughout the year, through close scrutiny of the service period and by selective breeding for desirable characters. The social organisation and calving patterns of buffalo studied in the Ruhuna National Park in Sri Lanka indicate a distinct seasonal breeding cycle, the rut coinciding with the onset of drought and calving occurring during the rains. Lactation and weaning coincided with a high plane of nutrition.

Fertility

Normal fertility has been described as the regular production of viable offspring. The number and regularity of offspring produced depends upon the species of animal and management. For the beef cattle and buffalo producer the ideal target – rarely achieved – is one viable offspring per year (a little longer for the buffalo) per breeding female in the herd. While the main concern in this book is the production of meat, it should also be remembered that pastoral people depend upon milk as an essential and integral part of animal productivity, both for family consumption and for local trading purposes.

The criteria for measuring fertility (or breeding efficiency) include:

age at sexual maturity (puberty);
degree of sexual desire (libido);
the non-return rate (NR);
the pregnancy (conception) rate (CR);
the calving rate (CR);
calving interval (CI);
longevity (reproductive life) (L);
calving ability (normal or difficult) (CA).

To the above may be added various indices based on calving intervals, the number of days between calving and the first (post-partum) oestrus and age at first calving. Many producers consider the average number of offspring per breeding female in the herd weaned and marketed as the surest guide to productivity. Others attach great score to the average productive life (longevity), that is, the number of offspring produced in a lifetime.

The above may appear as a somewhat formidable list of criteria for measuring breeding efficiency but in practical terms for the cow and calf producer the most important indicator of productivity is the calving rate or calf crop. This may be expressed as the percentage of live calves (the inclusion of dead or stillborn calves distorts the index) per 100 breeding females. At the same time this gives a measure of the culling that may be necessary in the breeding herd.

The service period relates to the number of days from calving to the next successful service and conception. During this intervening period the female is technically referred to as being 'open'. The length of the service period is markedly influenced by management and nutrition and, in the buffalo, by season. The more adverse the environmental conditions, the longer the service period. Successful service and conception is measured by what is referred to as the 'non-return' rate, the success or failure from natural service or artificial insemination depending upon whether or not, for cattle, the cow will need to be re-bred or inseminated within a period of 60 to 90 days from last calving. Service periods beyond this range indicate progressive lowering in herd breeding efficiency.

Females with perennial difficulties at parturition (calving ability) should not be retained in the breeding herd. Their retention may be more acceptable in the more specialised dairy herds, if they are good milk producers, but for beef and buffalo meat production, especially under more extensive management conditions, early culling and disposal is essential.

Factors affecting fertility

The incidence of lethal and sub-lethal genes affecting reproduction is quite rare in tropical breeds; twinning does occur and, as with temperate breeds, is accompanied in the female by sterility due to incomplete development of the reproductive organs of the heifer calf born with the male twin ('freemartin'). In general Zebu bulls are more placid, if continuously handled, than temperate-type *Bos taurus* bulls. Short and subdued signs of oestrus are common in the Zebu. Behaviour during oestrus in the cow and buffalo cow were discussed earlier. Adaptability to the environment, disease resistance and resistance to many external parasites are cardinal virtues of tropical cattle breeds and the buffalo. Reproduction takes place under environmental conditions that the majority of temperate-type breeds cannot tolerate.

Breeding efficiency can be represented in terms of percentage calving performance, 100 per cent being optimum for one calf per annum, or for a period considered optimum for a given environment and type of animal, i.e. beef cattle or buffalo. Two ways of calculating breeding efficiency have been suggested:

$$\text{(i)} \quad \frac{365 \times (n - 1) \times 100}{D}$$

where D is the number of days from the dam's last calving and n is her total number of calvings;

(ii) A modification of (i)

$$\frac{[n(365) + 1\,040]\,100}{Ac + C_i}$$

where n is the total number of calving intervals, Ac the age at first calving and C_i the sum of calving intervals in days. The figure 1 040 is taken as the optimum age (in this example using the buffalo) at first calving in days.

Examples:

$$\text{(i)} \quad \frac{365 \times (4 - 1) \times 100}{1\,800} = \frac{1\,095}{1\,800} \times 100 = 60.8\%$$

$$\text{(ii)} \quad \frac{[3(365) + 1\,040]\,100}{912 + 1\,800} = \frac{[2\,135]100}{2\,712} = 78.7\%$$

In (ii) above the breeding efficiency was appreciably raised because this particular buffalo had a first calving age of 912 days as against the average for the herd of 1 040 days. In both cases the calving interval was 450 days over four calvings (1 800 days).

Variations in herd breeding efficiency

These may be ascribed to what are termed exogenous or environmental factors, such as breeding techniques, climate and nutrition, referred to earlier, and to endogenous or constitutional factors in the individual animal. In the case of exogenous factors much depends upon breeding techniques with bulls, particularly as regards their current health and reproductive records and, if available, any previous service records. The use of immature breeding males should be avoided as marked libido is needed. For the more sophisticated set-up, especially for the artificial insemination (AI) centre, semen quality may be assessed in the laboratory. Excessive use, particularly of young bulls, should be avoided although this is taken care of to a considerable extent under tropical pastoral conditions in that oestrus will be depressed during long, dry, hot periods.

Immature females should not be used for breeding and this involves careful herd management and segregation of age groups. At the same time, breeding of old but valuable females should be phased to achieve optimum lifetime productivity.

In any controlled breeding programme detection of heat is essential, the most obvious time for mating being at 'standing' heat, when the female is ready to accept the male. The livestockman may best recognise these signs by the behaviour of the females among themselves, or by the attentions paid by 'teaser' or entire bulls. Under natural conditions the male will mount the female at intervals sufficient to ensure conception, but for successful AI procedures, proper identification of the heat period and a knowledge of the time lapse between cessation of heat and ovulation are essential to the maintenance of herd fertility.

Strategies to improve fertility

The conditions relating to lowered fertility and comments on their treatment and/or prevention will be outlined briefly; detailed discussion on these is available in the recommended reading at the end of the chapter.

The breeding male Whether retained in the herd for natural breeding or for artificial insemination purposes the bull or male buffalo should be selected for pronounced libido, showing willingness to serve the standing female, or into the artificial vagina. In those cases where infertility is suspected to be due to some infectious agent, sample swabs may be collected from the crypt of the sheath (prepucial cavity) for laboratory check and subsequent treatment of the male based upon the laboratory findings.

The breeding female Defective functioning of the ovaries may be ascribed to:

1 the 'anaphrodisia complex', that is, failure to observe heat (behavioural heat) due to:
  (a) pregnancy (normal situation);
  (b) freemartinism (congenital defects);
  (c) 'silent' and missed heats (reduced expression or brief period of activity); and
2 true anoestrus with inactive ovaries due to:
  (d) congenital ovarian defects;
  (e) developed (normal) ovarian inactivity (anoestrus).

Absence of heat (anoestrus) during pregnancy is a normal condition but occurs rarely in either female cattle or buffalo. It can be verified by rectal palpation of the uterus by a competent technician. Freemartin mature females and calves have an enlarged clitoris and usually a 'blind' vagina beyond the urethral opening which can be identified manually, or by the use of a probe. Silent and missed heats are common in cattle and the buffalo and while silent heats can be accepted as normal in the early post-partum period, malnutrition, severe climatic stress, pain, exhaustion, excitement and overcrowding are contributing causes and thus in many instances the condition is responsive to improved management. It is more frequently encountered in housed animals than in extensively managed herds where there is more scope for the interplay of sexual activity among the sexes promoted by the senses of touch, sound, hearing and, more especially, the olfactory senses through the activity of pheromones. Missed heats are of short duration and/or of low expression and frequently occur at night when they would be missed by the livestockman. Lack of experience in detecting signs of heat are also contributing causes.

Diagnosis of silent heat rests to a large extent on rectal palpation to detect the degree and stage of ovarian activity (active corpus luteum and/or ripening follicle) and texture of the uterus. Such an examination assists in differentiating silent heat from anoestrus due to pathological conditions such as cystic ovary and retained corpus luteum. Treatment of silent heat includes attention to feed with adequate phosphorous, manganese and vitamin D supplementation (Chapter 6). Although selection among individuals may assist in reducing the number of females subject to this condition many producers resort to crossbreeding in which the hybrids are more sexually active. A heat-expectation chart can also be prepared in order to forecast when individual animal heats are due. For the pathological conditions of the ovaries preventive measures by selection, crossbreeding, nutrition and hygiene under tropical conditions are more desirable than treatment. Hormonal and other treatments are used, however, for valuable stock and in other situations considered to warrant their use.

Herd infertility

Conditions affecting the whole herd include:

  venereal infertility due to viral, bacterial and protozoal infections;
  infectious abortions;
  infections causing repeat breeding of females in the herd;
  infections occurring during and soon after pregnancy; and
  infections causing neo- and post-natal calf mortality close to and soon after calving.

Venereal infertility is caused by infectious agents for the most part transmitted during natural mating or as a result of artificial insemination. The genital tract of both sexes is the area most affected. The protozoan parasite *Trichomonas foetus* is one of the most common causes of venereal disease in beef cattle, symptoms in cows being frequent return to service, vaginal discharge, inflammation of the uterus and sometimes abortions. Treatment of the females is best achieved with hormones; in the bull (the main target of treatment) thorough washing of the prepuce coupled with medicaments administered by mouth have had some success.

Another major problem among the venereal diseases is the viral infection known as coital exanthema, affecting mainly the bull and known worldwide as IBR–IPV. In addition to respiratory infection, particularly in feedlot cattle, breeding problems include shortened oestrus cycles and lowered conception rates. Where the disease has not been eradicated by testing and slaughter, annual vaccination from 3 months of age is practised.

The problem of repeat breeding of the female is often the fault of the sub-fertile or infertile bull and male buffalo. In the female infection of the uterus soon after calving (post-partum metritis) has worldwide distribution, including the tropics, and is often, though not always, associated with a history of retained placenta, difficulty in calving and unhygienic calving conditions. Treatment and prevention lies chiefly in culling of susceptible females, provision of clean calving facilities for intensively managed herds and vaccination against the enzootic abortions described below. Hormonal treatment may be used where indicated.

The infectious abortions have in the past caused the greatest reproductive losses, among which brucellosis or Bang's disease, causing abortions in cattle and severe systemic disorders in man, is one of the best known. Brucellosis, in contrast to the venereal diseases mentioned earlier, is transmitted *per os*, that is, by ingestion of infected material. In the female the ingested infective agent, *Brucella abortus*, localises in the foetal and maternal placenta resulting in abortions which characteristically occur somewhere between 6 and 8 months. A 'wave' of abortions during this period assists in diagnosis.

Abortions do occur in cattle affected with severe tsetse-transmitted trypanosomiasis. Likewise, abortions may be expected to occur in other febrile diseases. The disease caused by *Brucella abortus* has been eradicated in those countries where a rigid programme of testing and slaughter of infected animals has been operated. In endemic areas, as in much of the tropics, a vaccination programme is adopted by what is termed 'calfhood vaccination' at 3 to 6 months of age with live attenuated *B. abortus* strain 19 vaccine and sexually mature females with two successive vaccinations 6 weeks apart with inactivated 45/20 *B. abortus* vaccine.

Artificial insemination

The technique of artificial insemination (AI) involves the collection of semen which is ejaculated by the bull into an artificial vagina, its dilution and storage and subsequent use by ejecting the semen by a special syringe through the recipient cow's vagina into the cervix (fig. 4.2). The special syringe consists of a long glass or metal tube which is guided into place by the inseminator's hand via the rectal wall which lies parallel to and immediately above the vagina and cervix (fig. 4.2). The method most used for collecting semen from the bull is to bring him up behind and slightly alongside a standing cow or 'teaser' so that when he 'jumps', that is, mounts the cow, his penis is deflected by the hand of the assistant into the artificial vagina. The bull may also be made to ejaculate by massaging the ampullae or wall of the vas deferens through the wall of the rectum, or by an electrical vibrator via the rectum, although the latter methods are generally less satisfactory than using a teaser cow.

The number of cows that can be impregnated by any one bull can be greatly increased by the use of AI. If a bull produces on an average 5 ml of semen, up to 200 cows can be inseminated after appropriate dilution and consequent increase in volume of the semen. Diluents consist of mixtures of egg yolk and phosphate or citrate buffer solution, or skim milk, coconut milk, or other diluents. Antibiotics are also added to eliminate contaminants. Storage of diluted semen at the carbon dioxide (dry ice) temperature of −79 °C or in liquid nitrogen at −196 °C makes it possible to keep selected bull's semen for considerable periods and allows it to be transported in suitable containers over long distances. Bulls selected for use in AI centres have their semen collected and examined for the presence of abnormal shapes or large numbers of inactive sperm which could reduce fertility, and bulls showing such abnormal features should not be used for AI purposes. They are also checked for such infectious reproductive diseases as brucellosis, vibriosis, pustular vulvo-vaginitis and other infectious conditions which could be transmitted to cows.

The anatomy of the buffalo reproductive organs and the general physiology of reproduction in buffalo are much the same as in cattle so that the same basic techniques of artificial insemination can be used in buffalo. The introduction of AI is fairly recent but has been used more especially in India, where it is practised on a considerable scale. The buffalo bull is reportedly quieter and easier to handle than temperate-type *Bos taurus* bulls and is less concerned as to whether or not a teaser cow is on heat at the time he is brought to her for mounting and semen collection. By contrast, the Zebu bull tends to be lethargic at semen collection and does not demonstrate the same degree of libido he does with natural service.

Artificial insemination in cattle and, more recently, in the buffalo, has had greatest application in the dairy industry. In cattle it has been used extensively for upgrading local dairy-type breeds, for example, in eastern Asia, East Africa, Central and South America and in the Caribbean. An estimated 48.4 million cattle and water buffalo were inseminated throughout the world in 1960. However, during that period, only 1 per cent of beef cows out of a total of 18.7 million head of dairy cattle, taking the USA as an example, were bred by artificial insemination. This indicates, even though great progress has been made during the past two decades, that AI in advanced beef producing countries still has a long way to go due to the expertise and technicalities necessary for its satisfactory usage and the difficulties in detecting heat in females within beef cattle management systems, especially those on extensive management.

Examples of such problems include the short duration of the heat period of many Zebu breeds, also the short and 'silent' heats that often occur in exotic cattle breeds managed in the tropics.

Embryo transfer

Methods have now been developed for the recovery by non-surgical means of fertilised ova from 'donor' cows and their transfer for subsequent development in the uteri of 'recipient' cows. Donor cows are caused to superovulate, that is, to produce large numbers of ova so that up to about 10 embryos may be recovered. Superovulation is brought about by hormonal injections in the donor cow with serum gonadotrophins on or about the tenth day of the oestrus cycle, followed by prostaglandin injections. By this method several fertilised ova from one donor cow can each be developed in nondescript foster cows. Some 50 000 embryo transfer calves are born annually throughout the world and as techniques are improved this number will increase. Although embryo transfer is currently confined to countries with the more developed animal industries one of its most effective and economical uses in the tropics could lie in the introduction of new cattle and possibly buffalo breeds from one country or continent to another. A specific example would be the embryo transfer of trypano-tolerant cattle breeds from West to East Africa. This has recently been accomplished by the implantation of N'dama embryos into Boran cows in Kenya.

Further reading

Abhi, H,. L., Nagpa, M. P., Sharma, T. L. and **Grewall, A. S.** (1973). A study on the breeding behaviour of Murrah buffaloes and their breeding efficiency through artificial insemination under farm conditions. *Indian J. of Dairy Sci.* **26** (2), 107–113.

Arora, R. C. and **Pandey, R. S.** (1982). Current research status of buffalo endocrinology. *Wld. Rev. Anim. Prod.*, **18** (2), 15–23.

Branton, C. (1970). Fertility. In *Cattle production in the tropics*, Vol. 1, **ed. W. J. A. Payne.** Longman: London. 263–325.

Cockrill, W. Ross (ed.) (1974). *The husbandry and health of the domestic buffalo.* FAO: Rome.

El-wishy, A. B., Abdou, M. S. S. and **El Sawaf, S. A.** (1971). Reproduction in buffaloes in Egypt. II: Fertility of buffaloes served at varying times after calving. *Vet. Med. J. UAR*, **19**, 123–130.

Fahimuddin, M. (1975). *Domestic water buffalo*. Oxford and IBH Publ. Co.: New Delhi.

Pant, H. C. and **Roy, A.** (1972) In *Improvement of livestock in warm climates*, ed. **R. E. McDowell**. W. H. Freeman and Co.: San Francisco. 563–600.

Vandeplassche, M. (1982). *Reproductive efficiency in cattle: a guideline for projects in developing countries*. FAO Anim. Prod. and Health Paper no. 25. FAO:Rome.

Williamson, G. and **Payne, W. J. A.** (1978). *An introduction to animal husbandry in the tropics*. 3rd edn. Longman: London.

Yeates, N. T. M., Edey, T. V. and **Hill, H. K.** (1975). *Animal science: reproduction, climate, meat, wool*. Pergamon Press: Polts Point, NSW, Aust.

5 Breeding and selection

The basis of inheritance

All body tissues – muscle, fat, nerve, bone and others – consist of individual cells which vary in size and shape according to their function. Bone cells, for example, are extremely hard, the cells of ligaments by nature of their shape and grouping and required function are somewhat elastic while fat cells, by extreme contrast, are soft and with such delicate cell membranes as to be almost invisible under the microscope except as faint lines. All cells contain protoplasm, consisting of cytoplasm surrounded by the cell membrane and enclosing a nucleus and centrosome. Cells are able to metabolise nutrients and carry out other bodily functions such as the carriage of oxygen by the red blood cells and to grow and multiply.

The cell nucleus, which might be considered as its functional headquarters, contains one or more smaller bodies known as nucleoli and adjacent to these are large numbers of smaller particles known as chromatic granules. At a certain stage of activity during cell division these granules take on the appearance of thread-like structures which are known as chromosomes. These chromosomes occur in pairs, the total number of which varies with species of animal. For example, cattle and buffalo have 50 and 48 pairs respectively.

Chromosomes multiply by division at the same time as the cell is dividing and, like the cell, retain their individual characteristics. The chromosomes are of primary importance because they carry what has been called the coded messages or genes that are responsible for transmitting inherited characteristics from one generation to another. All body functions are basically biochemical reactions which are under the control of catalysts known as enzymes. Enzymes are made up of proteins, the latter consisting of a number of polypeptide chains, each chain being composed of a number of amino acid units. Each gene controls the synthesis of one polypeptide chain and consequently genes control the synthesis of enzymes which themselves control all body reactions. It has been shown by research workers in Cambridge that the active substance in the gene can be described as two chains of nucleotide molecules twisted around one another in a spiral known as a 'double helix'. The sequence of nucleotide molecules in this spiral structure is considered to determine the genetic information carried in the gene. Since the total possible combination of nucleotide molecules is very large the quantity of stored genetic information (i.e. heritable characters) is very great indeed.

The following is the way in which cell division and multiplication are considered to take place. First, there are two clearly differentiated cell types in the body. These are:

1 somatic cells or those that make up all body structures and most functions; and
2 germ cells or those concerned essentially with the reproduction of the new generation.

When somatic cells multiply (divide) the daughter cells are replicas of the mother cell. However, when germ cells multiply the number of chromosomes is reduced to half the species number. The somatic cells are termed diploid, containing 2n chromosomes and the germ cells haploid, as they only contain n chromosomes or half the number in the somatic cells. Somatic cell division is called mitosis. In mitotic division each daughter cell receives the same number of chromosomes as is possessed by the mother cell. This is a continuous process by which worn-out cells replace one another and is particularly active in the young, growing animal. Germ cell division, called meiosis, occurs in the reproductive cells of both males and females. There are differences between chromosome pairs within the same species and in particular between the sex chromosomes that determine the sex of the individual animal. There are certain useful sex-linked characters in domestic animals that are due to genes carried on the sex-chromosome itself, such as feather patterns in chickens, in which a particular feather colour may be shown in one or the other sex immediately after hatching, thus enabling instantaneous identification of a chick's sex without additional handling. This is not the same as sex-influenced characteristics in which certain traits, e.g. milk production, are only exhibited by the one sex. The other chromosomes in the cell that are not related to sex characteristics, are known as autosomes. The autosomes control other characteristics such as coat colour and polledness.

The process of meiosis takes place with the development of the spermatozoa in the testicle of the male, and eggs or ova in the ovary of the female. The two processes are basically the same except that in the male four spermatozoa are produced from a single primordial spermatogonium while only one functional ovum is produced from the oogonium. This applies in all animals, whether they be moniparous, producing normally one offspring like cattle and the buffalo, or multiparous like sheep and goats, producing two or more offspring.

When the spermatozoon and ovum combine in fertilisation the now fertile ovum contains the full complement or diploid number of chromosomes, half from each parent and representative of the species. By this means meiosis retains constancy in the chromosome number and ensures that both the male and female parent contribute genes to their offspring that are representative of, though not identical to their own characteristics and those of their species. One of the mechanisms by which variations in inheritance occur takes place at a stage in meiosis known as synapsis, in which there is some interchange of genes.

The inheritance of characteristics

Genetics, or that branch of science that deals with the basis of inheritance, first came into prominence with the discoveries of the Augustinian monk, Gregor Mendel in 1866, when he published his observations on the inheritance of various characteristics in garden peas. This pioneering work in the field of genetics was later substantiated by other scientists at the turn of the century. This is not to say that animal breeding and selection in one way or another had not been practised before Mendel's scientific observations. Robert Bakewell in England had already begun to produce improved cattle breeds in the eighteenth century; the Arab horse was already famous and such people as the pastor-

alists of Africa had for centuries selected their cattle for such physical features as distinctive coat colour and size and shape of horns. Similar selection had likewise gone on among cattle breeds in Asia. Mendel's work, on the other hand, was an attempt to explain the laws of inheritance on a scientific basis.

The Mendelian basis of inheritance

The basic principles are that:

1 Inheritance is through units known as genes.
2 Genes are present in pairs, one member of each coming from each parent via the spermatozoon and ovum, respectively.
3 At the time an individual forms germ cells, the paired genes of maternal and paternal origin separate without having influenced each other and go into different germ cells. This sequence of events is known as the 'Law of Segregation'.
4 Each gene maintains its identity for generation after generation and does not blend with other genes to form a new kind of hereditary substance.

The parent gives to each offspring only a sample half of its own inheritance and the laws of chance govern this sampling, subject to the restriction that each sample must contain one gene of every pair. The members of a pair of such genes are called alleles. Some alleles are dominant and others are recessive. An individual's genetic make-up or constitution is called its genotype, which describes the individual's genetic formula and the way he or she breeds. The physical appearance of an animal, on the other hand, is referred to as its phenotype. When the members of a given pair of alleles are alike, the individual is described as being homozygous for that particular pair of alleles. When a particular pair of alleles are unalike, the individual is called heterozygous for that particular pair. The horned and hornless conditions in cattle are examples of the homozygous and heterozygous condition and may be represented as follows where:

PP – polled (hornless)
Pp – polled
pp – horned

In this example the polled character (P) is truly dominant over the horned condition (p). This means that the phenotype of both the homozygous and heterozygous animal carrying the gene for the polled condition will be polled and only the homozygous recessive animal will be horned. The polled condition, characteristic of the well known Aberdeen Angus temperate climate beef breed, is also sometimes found in such breeds as the humpless N'dama of West Africa, the Caracul of Brazil, and the Sinu of Colombia.

Any individual contains a large number of gene pairs controlling different characters. The members of the different pairs of alleles sort independently of one another when the germ cells are produced. This is the principle of independent assortment. An example is given in fig. 5.1, involving two allelic gene pairs in which a polled black bull (both dominant characteristics) is bred to a horned red cow and the heterozygous progeny in the F_1 generation then bred together. To return to the single pair of alleles, in which only three kinds of zygote or fertilised ovum are possible, namely, the homozygous dominant, the heterozygotes and the homozygous recessive. With one pair of alleles and using combinations of the three kinds of zygote, there are six types of mating possible. These six fundamental types of mating, involving only one pair of alleles, are termed mono-hybrid or single-cross matings and include:

Homozygous dominant × Homozygous dominant
Homozygous dominant × Heterozygote
Homozygous dominant × Homozygous recessive
Heterozygote   × Heterozygote
Heterozygote   × Homozygote recessive
Homozygous recessive × Homozygous recessive

A descriptive account of the six fundamental types of breeding of livestock, including various combinations of crossings between animals with homozygous and heterozygous dominant and recessive characters, will be found in the recommended reading at the end of this chapter.

Qualitative and quantitative traits

Qualitative traits, which are either present or absent in an animal, include such characteristics as coat colour and horned or polled conditions in cattle. Such traits are controlled by a single, or by a small number of genes and are easy to recognise. Mendel, when he worked with garden peas, dealt also with single gene characteristics which were of high heritability. In livestock breeding, however,

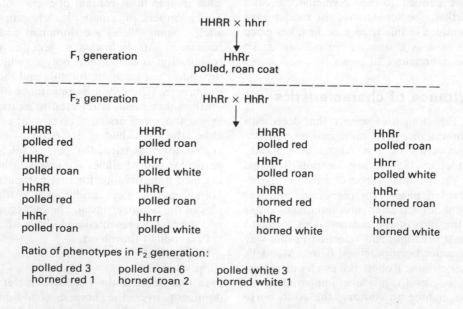

HHRR × hhrr

F₁ generation → HhRr
polled, roan coat

F₂ generation → HhRr × HhRr

HHRR polled red	HHRr polled roan	HhRR polled red	HhRr polled roan
HHRr polled roan	HHrr polled white	HhRr polled roan	Hhrr polled white
HhRR polled red	HhRr polled roan	hhRR horned red	hhRr horned roan
HhRr polled roan	Hhrr polled white	hhRr horned white	hhrr horned white

Ratio of phenotypes in F₂ generation:

polled red 3   polled roan 6   polled white 3
horned red 1   horned roan 2   horned white 1

fig. 5.1 Illustration of the principle of independent assortment the geneticist is working with a wide variety of characteristics, known as quantitative characteristics which are dependent on large numbers of genes whose individual expression is also markedly affected by modifications or differences in the environment. Such traits are also referred to as polygenic characters. Take, for example, selection for a character such as liveweight for age, in which there might be a wide range of differences in a particular group of animals. Weight for age is a quantitative character and shows continuous variation. Differences in weights between individual cattle, say, at $2\frac{1}{2}$ years of age, are determined by both genetic and environmental factors. To decide which might be the best animals in this particular group to retain for future breeding purposes it is therefore necessary to identify and to take into account any environmental factors in order to assess their genetic worth. Factors which may be termed environmental also include the sex of the calf, the age of the dam and the number of calves she has previously produced. These factors may influence the calf's growth; a Zebu cow in her third or fourth lactation may produce considerably more milk than in her first lactation, so that her third or fourth calf might be expected to make better liveweight gains to weaning than the dam's previous calves. Such differences would be due, at least in part, to environmental factors and not necessarily to any genetic factor. The breed of calf also influences growth, so that comparisons of liveweight gains within the same breed should be used. There are, however, usually environmental factors that cannot be identified and so it is necessary, as far as is possible, to standardise the management for the group from which selection for breeding stock is being made.

There may be positive as well as negative differences in liveweight of the individuals under selection, that is, some individuals may be heavier and others lighter than the average for the group. After correction for any factors considered due to environment, the difference may be attributable to genetic factors. Not all of these, however, will respond, at least observably, to selection. That proportion of the difference between the individuals that is due to additive (quantitative) gene action and which may respond to selection

procedures is called the heritability of the trait(s) in question.

The degree of heritability of a trait can be calculated by a number of means and is usually expressed by the symbol h^2. Quantitative characters are referred to as 'additive' or 'discontinuous', being traits for which there can be extreme variation between animals. In dealing with such quantitative traits animal breeders are concerned with what is known as population genetics. A detailed discussion of this subject is available in publications in the recommended reading list at the end of the chapter.

The basic equation that describes heritability is:

$$P = G + E$$

where P is the phenotypic variation, G the genetic variation and E variation due to the environment.

Heritability can be measured in a number of ways: from the relationship between parent and offspring; from an actual response to selection and from comparisons using twins. Traits with h^2 above 0.25 may be expected to respond to some of the selection procedures described below. It must be remembered also that estimates of heritability of a particular trait may vary from place to place. Some of these differences may be due to real differences between herds, or to errors' in sampling, or to differences in environment and management.

Table 5.1 provides some heritability estimates of important characteristics of beef cattle. Some traits

Table 5.1 Heritability estimates of some important characteristics of beef and dual purpose cattle

Characteristic	Heritability (h^2)
Birth weight	0.40; 0.25 ± 0.125; 0.19 ± 0.15; 0.31
Weaning weight	0.35; 0.28 ± 0.32; 0.32; 0.30
Weight at 18 months	0.40; 0.42
Mature weight	0.70
Calving interval	0.05
Weight for age	0.07 ± 0.21
Gain in feed lot	0.45
Efficiency of gain	0.40

The alternative estimates derive from different studies (see acknowledgement of sources)

have much higher heritabilities than others. It will be noted that traits that are developed at an early stage in life, such as carcass traits, are generally of quite a high heritability; traits such as fertility and viability (not listed in Table 5.1) are of lower heritability.

From the practical standpoint, the breeder should be made aware, as far as is possible, of the heritability of the trait or traits for which he intends to select. Genetic progress for those traits with low heritabilities will be slow. Improvement in such traits as fertility and calving interval can for the most part be brought about more quickly by improvements in feeding and management and/or by crossbreeding.

Gene interactions

The only interaction of genes so far considered is that of a dominant over a recessive character. However, many genes will also interact with each other where one of the genes in an allelic pair may be acting to cause the development of a certain characteristic in one way, while the other gene of the allelic pair may be acting to cause the development of the characteristic in a different way. What will be the outcome depends upon how strong the dominance may be. The dominance may be very strong, as occurs in what is called overdominance, or there may be complete dominance, incomplete dominance and finally, lack of dominance. Such variations in the degree of dominance occur in coat colour inheritance and other characters. An example of incomplete dominance in cattle is where the heterozygous animal resembles the normal homozygous one, although it is shorter legged and much smaller, while the homozygous recessive animal is called a monster or 'bulldog' calf that dies before birth.

An example of where dominance is lacking in alleles occurs in the mating of red hair-coat (RR) Shorthorn cattle and white hair-coat (rr) Shorthorn cattle. All of the F_1 offspring are red-roan (Rr) in colour, that is with white and red hairs evenly intermixed.

Epistatic genes are those which may cover up the proper expression of characteristics by other genes to which they are not allelic and so modify the phenotype, but not the genotype. A good example of this is the albino gene, which is epistatic to all colours. In such a case, although the albino offspring may possess many colour genes, the presence of the albino gene makes it a white animal, with pink eyes.

Genotype/environmental interactions

As mentioned earlier, phenotypic differences between animals are determined by genetic factors contained within the chromosomes, and by factors resident outside the chromosomes. But in addition to this, phenotypic differences may also occur as a result of interactions between the genotype and the environment. Such interactions have been defined as the differential response of a specific genotype in different environments. These interactions may arise between the genotype and the location, and between genotype and age or generation of the animal. Some genotype–environment interactions are advantageous to the individual animal under a given set of circumstances, whereas others are not. Some cattle, for example, when transferred to a tropical environment, shed their coat hairs more rapidly and tolerate the heat better than others in the same herd. On the other hand, some improved temperate-type breeds may perform far below their capacity under tropical conditions.

There are certain physical characteristics of livestock in the tropics, such as size at maturity which, although the reasons for it are not fully understood, suggest a marked influence of the environment on genotype. In general, cattle, sheep and goats in the humid tropics are smaller than their counterparts in the drier savannas, or in more temperate zones. The dwarf sheep and goats and the Shorthorn cattle of humid West Africa are examples, being very small in comparison to the large Zebus and long-legged sheep and goats of the drier, northern guinea savanna and Sahel zones. There appears, also in tropical Africa, to be some relationship between size and trypanotolerance, the cattle, sheep and goats living in tsetse-challenge areas being either of the dwarf or semi-dwarf varieties or breeds. To what extent the small size of these animals is related to an interaction between some genetic resistance to trypanosomiasis, or between the hot, humid environment, or to both, is not at present understood.

If, therefore, it is accepted that growth rate is one of the major determinants of productivity in meat animals, it is also necessary to consider this characteristic in relation to the environment in which the animal is to perform. It may be that growth rate is the expression of the same characteristics under conditions favourable for growth, but this would not appear to be the case under most tropical conditions.

Experiments were conducted in Queensland, Australia, in which Brahman, Brahman × Hereford crosses and fourth generation Hereford × Shorthorn crosses, were managed under varying conditions of stress. The low stress group were allowed free access to lucerne chaff, housed in shaded pens and kept free of ticks, worms and, as far as possible, protected from such diseases as bovine infectious keratoconjunctivitis (pink eye), which is a disease of the eye and eyelids affecting range cattle in tropical Australia and elsewhere. For the high level stress groups the cattle were put under free-range grazing conditions and exposed to ticks, worms and infectious diseases. In addition this group was subjected, according to the time of the year, to varying levels in the quantity and quality of feed available. The middle group was also exposed to free grazing conditions, but with lower environmental stresses than the high stress group. The Brahmans made the highest gains and the improved Hereford × Shorthorn crosses the lowest under conditions of high stress. On the other hand, under low stress, the opposite occurred. Thus, although the Hereford × Shorthorn crossbred cattle had the highest growth-rate potential they did less well than the tropically adapted Brahman breed under the same high stress conditions, although their performance exceeded that of the Brahmans in the low stress situation. The Brahman × Hereford × Shorthorn crosses, as one might have expected, performed half way between the other two groups. Although the Brahmans were better able to accommodate to changes in levels of stress, all three groups responded positively to improvements in conditions and, likewise, all responded adversely, with lowered growth rates, under high stress conditions.

Therefore, although an animal's maximum growth rate is determined by its growth potential, it is its level of adaptation to environmental stresses such as feed quality and availability, climate and disease, that will determine what proportion of the potential growth can be achieved under field conditions. Where selection is carried out under field conditions varying from high to low stress, as may happen between seasons, years and locations, growth potential and level of adaptability will be alternatively favoured. Under these conditions any long term improvements in growth rate would be expected to be low.

This raises important considerations in selection procedures. Take, for example, selection of breeding stock for growth rate that are to be exposed to the high stresses of free-range management under tropical conditions, entailing exposure to endo- and ecto-parasites, high solar radiation and seasonal scarcity of feed. Selection would be for the more heat tolerant Brahman, even though other breeds might have a better growth potential under low stress conditions. However, adaptation to the environment varies not only between breeds, but also among individuals within the same breed or herd, so that individual selection still continues to be an important tool in the selection process. It is because of differences between breeds, or individual animals within breeds or herds in their growth potential and level of adaptation that genotype/environment interactions occur. Such differences also have an important bearing on the outcome of any attempt to improve growth rate by selection for growth rate itself. It may be, that because of the antagonisms which appear to exist between some of the components of adaptation and production, it will not be possible to develop breeds capable of expressing the best of both of these qualities under all conditions.

The outcome of genetic/environmental interactions is thus varied and it is possible that genes affecting a particular trait in an animal may not affect that trait in the same way when the animal is exposed to two contrasting environments. For instance, gene mutations in cattle affecting coat hair colour and texture, coat shedding, sweat gland size and shape and possible genetic resistance to trypanosomiasis are examples of genotype/ environmental interactions that are beneficial under a given set of circumstances. Some cattle, even in the same herd, will adapt more quickly than others to a new environment. Easy coat shedding, for example, may be advantageous in the hot, humid, lowland tropics, but an animal with this characteristic might be at a disadvantage in tropical highland areas, where the climate may be far more temperate in character. The breeder may thus need to pay as much attention during his selection procedures to genetic/environmental interactions in such animals, as to hereditary factors.

Genetic improvement

The genetic composition of a beef or buffalo herd is made up of the genotypes of the many individuals in the herd. The aim of the breeder is to increase the proportion of genes that are likely to increase production above that of the average herd and, at the same time, reduce the number of less productive genes. He may achieve this by the process known as selection. Having selected his breeding stock the method or system of breeding he adopts will also affect the genetic composition of the herd.

Selection
Selection is of two kinds, natural and artificial. Natural selection takes place continuously in populations of animals and is attributable to the action of natural forces. It produces, by random mating, changes in gene frequency which allow survival and reproduction of the fittest. Random mating occurs rarely in cattle except on open rangeland and, for example, in feral buffalo. Artificial selection, on the other hand, is controlled by man and includes four forms of non-random mating which will be described later. In practice, the breeder chooses, on the basis of whatever evidence he may have on their performance, the better male and female animals as breeding stock and disposes of the rest, for fattening or for other purposes.

Selection can be directed towards dominant or recessive gene traits, multiple allele or additive gene action, or towards epistasis or overdominance. Selection for a qualitative dominant characteristic such as the polled condition described earlier, and

for some qualitative recessives, is a comparatively straightforward procedure.

It is much more difficult to improve by selection characteristics of economic importance such as milk yield and carcass quality, which are associated with many polygenes (gene pairs) acting additively. The extent to which polygenes are expressed in the phenotype varies from trait to trait and from environment to environment. To make the greatest possible progress in milk and beef production, therefore, it is necessary to adopt selection and mating procedures appropriate to each trait and to each environment. In practical terms the breeder should ensure that the traits for which he is selecting are measurable, heritable and of economic importance.

Factors controlling genetic improvement
Heritability As referred to earlier, heritability is the term used to describe the strength of inheritance of a character, that is, whether it is likely to be passed on to the next generation, or not. Dalton defines it as follows: 'For a given trait heritability is the amount of superiority of the parents above their contemporaries which on average is passed on to the offspring'.

It is measured by: (1) the degree of relationship between parents; (2) the actual response to selection; and (3) comparisons among twins (i.e. monozygous or identical twins and dizygous or non-identical twins).

The selection differential This is a measure of how good the parents chosen to produce the next generation will be. It is the average superiority of the selected parents over the mean of the population in which they were born. Very simply, to calculate the selection differential within a selected group for a trait such as kg/day gain, the following calculations are made:

Mean of selected bulls 1.50 kg/day gain
Overall herd gain   0.80 kg/day gain
Selection differential   1.50–0.80 = 0.70 kg/day

If the selection differential for a group of cows in the herd was 0.80 kg/day, then the average for the two selection differentials would be:

$$\frac{0.70 + 0.80}{2} = 0.75 \text{ kg/day}$$

Were there no component of selected cows the product would be halved because the selected bulls would contribute 50 per cent of the genes of the progeny i.e.

$$\frac{0.70 + 0}{2} = 0.35 \ \text{kg/day}$$

The generation interval The generation interval is a further factor which influences progress made from selection. It is usually measured in a population as the average age of the parents when offspring are born. The length of the generation interval is influenced by the age at first service of the bull, age at first calving of the cow and the average reproductive life of the population in question. In the tropics, where generation intervals are longer under traditional systems of management, efforts to improve environment, particularly nutrition, can reduce age at first service and consequently, age at first calving. Other factors which may change the genetic structure of a population, albeit only to a very limited and often undefinable extent, include gene mutations, which may be harmful or beneficial. The laws of chance operating at the time of gene segregation could also determine gene frequency.

The three components outlined above, heritability, selection differential (SD) and generation interval (GI) can be put together to give an estimate of genetic gain as follows:

for a generation: $h^2 \times SD$

and for a year : $\dfrac{h^2 \times SD}{GI}$

Aids to selection of breeding stock

Individual and mass selection This form of selection is practised by the breeder without consideration for pedigree or collateral relatives (family selection). The selection of animals on the basis of their individual performance is referred to as performance testing. Genetic progress through performance testing will result only for those traits which are highly heritable and can be measured in the live animal and where applicable, in both sexes. It is therefore a commonly used method in both beef and buffalo meat production systems. Performance testing is practised largely in developed beef producing countries and in those coun-

tries in the tropics such as Brazil, Kenya and Botswana, where there is an export meat trade. The tests involve selecting the best individual from within a similar age group (i.e. comparison of contemporaries) that have been treated in the same way. They are carried out, either on individual farms, or at testing stations, where variations which may be caused by environment can be better controlled. Growth rate to 18 months of age is a good indicator of final liveweight, has a relatively high heritability (Table 5.1) and is one of the more important characteristics in beef cattle and in buffalo bred for meat production. When the 18 month liveweight of a group of animals has been adjusted for any effects due to environment, selection of the heaviest ones as future sires will achieve genetic progress for this particular trait.

The results of an individual performance test can, to ascertain their value and accuracy, be compared with those obtained from a subsequent progeny test. To select the best individual the breeder has one single performance test record of each animal's performance so that an estimate of the breeding value (BV) for a given trait is calculated as:

BV = heritability (h^2) of the trait × (average of the individual under test − average of contemporaries), or

BV = h^2 (individual variation)

Lifetime performance records provide the breeder with more than the single record of an individual referred to above. Their chief value is in respect of female records, for example, in lactation yield and calving performance, indicating level of productivity achieved over a lifetime and genetic ability to perform in a given environment. The correlation between such lifetime records is referred to in statistical terms as repeatability. Repeatability tells how an animal will repeat a trait during its lifetime and is measured, as described earlier for heritability, on the scale of 0 to 1.0 or 0 to 100 per cent. A disadvantage to the use of lifetime performance is that having to wait for a completed lifetime record before using it in selection, increases the generation interval. In practice, however, where repeatabilities are reasonably high, e.g. between first and second lactations, selection of an individual can be done without waiting for the full lifetime performance.

How may such repeatability records be used as an adjunct to calculate the breeding value (BV) estimate outlined above? For this the BV is obtained by multiplying the animal's average deviation from records of contemporaries by a formula (a confidence factor). In arriving at the value of the confidence factor represented by the formula

$$\frac{kh^2}{1 - (k - 1)t}$$

the following need to be known:
k (the number of records), h^2 (the heritability of the trait) and t (the repeatability of the trait).

Using the above formula the BV may be calculated as follows:

$$BV = \frac{kh^2}{1 + (k - 1)t} \times \text{(average deviation of the dam's records from her contemporaries)}$$

Table 5.2 Breeding value calculation in three cows

Example	Cow A	Cow B	Cow C
Deviation (kg) at			
calving 1	−20	+60	−10
2		+24	+15
3		+30	+20
4			+10
Total deviation (kg)	−20	+144	+35
Mean deviation (kg)	−20	+38	+8.8
Breeding values (kg)	0.300 × (−20)	0.474 × (+38)	0.511 × (+8.8)
BV	−6	+18	+4.5

Table 5.3 Confidence factors based on number of records

No. of records	Factor	No. of records	Factor
1	0.300	6	0.544
2	0.418	7	0.568
3	0.474	8	0.578
4	0.511	9	0.587
5	0.536	10	0.594

Suppose in a beef herd, selection of dams was being carried out on the basis of calf weaning weight. For this calculation all calves would be age corrected for weaning weight and the number of calvings taken into account. The breeding values involved for three beef cows with one, three and four calvings, calculated as outlined above, are shown in Table 5.2. Note that the confidence factor (Table 5.3) increases with the number of calvings and that in this particular case cow B had the most promising breeding value in terms of her calves' weaning weights.

Pedigree selection The pedigree represents the performance of the ancestors of an animal. Pedigree records are today used principally as a guide by breeders seeking to avoid inbreeding in their herds. It is also of some use when there is no other information available on stock being purchased, or otherwise intended for breeding purposes. At one time, selection by pedigree was widely practised especially in dairy cattle, but it now has very little use due to the development of progeny and performance testing. The pedigree might be used, for example, in the case of a newly acquired breeding bull of known pedigree from which it might be able to ascertain how well – if at all – his sire or dam, or other close relatives, including collateral ones such as cousins, had performed. A reliable pedigree must, therefore, contain the records of all close relatives – both good and bad – so that a truer picture of the bull's ancestry can be presented. Depending upon the detail and accuracy of a pedigree, it might be assumed that at least some of the good or the bad genes had been passed on to the individual in question.

Progeny tests By this method an individual is evaluated on the basis of performance of its progeny. It is the most accurate way to determine the breeding value of an animal, particularly where the heritability of a trait is low, where it cannot be measured in the live animal or where it can only be measured after slaughter. Progeny testing has been greatly increased in effectiveness through the use of artificial insemination (AI) in dairy cattle and increasingly so with beef cattle, in which the semen from a single bull can be used on a large number of cows. For the test, the aim should be to use as many sires as possible, producing as many progeny as possible from randomly selected dams. No progeny should be culled until the end of the test.

Choosing a selection method

The breeder now needs to choose a specific selection method.

Tandem selection This is the method most commonly used. The breeder selects for and improves one character until he is satisfied with it, whereupon he selects for another character and so on for a third. Where the characteristics are independent of one another, each one remaining stable while the other is dealt with, progress would be fairly steady. However, where there is some genetic correlation or antagonism between the individual traits, progress will be slower, in what is termed a 'see-saw' or up and down manner.

Independent culling levels This involves setting a required standard of performance for a particular trait and culling those animals that do not succeed in achieving it. The system may be of use where major decisions have to be taken, say, during periods of drought or food shortage. A major disadvantage is that one may cull an animal for not achieving the required standard for one particular trait, while at the same time it may have other desirable traits.

Index selection This amounts to giving a score to a number of individual traits and combining these into a total or index. It has an advantage over independent culling in that a high score for one trait, in many circumstances, can make up for deficiencies in another. The following information is necessary to construct a selection index:

1 the heritabilities of the relevant traits;
2 the genetic and phenotypic correlations among them; and
3 the economic value of each trait.

The figures in the index do not always remain constant. For example, the economic values of traits will require periodical checking by the breeder. A number of selection indices have been developed for beef cattle which differ mainly from each other in the estimates of genetic variance and co-variance. Where there is a high genetic correlation between two traits, such as weaning and birth weights, very little is gained by adding the second trait to the index. Weaning weights and liveweight gain are the most desirable traits for inclusion in a beef cattle selection index. Sleekness of coat hairs in tropical cattle breeds is another trait. It was observed during the development of the Jamaica Red breed that selection for sleek coats led to rapid change in coat type accompanied by improvement in both growth rate and fertility. This is another example of desirable production characteristics that are both strongly inherited and closely correlated. Whether or not selection is directed at separate characteristics or at general average performance, the tendency would be for merit in one characteristic to be offset by below average standard in another. This emphasises the need to aim at selecting for only those characteristics that are most important in economical terms. Such characteristics as size and shape of ears and horns and coat colour, sometimes sought after by breeders' associations in the past, though they may be attractive, bear little or no relation to meat quality and productivity.

Artificial insemination as an aid in selection Artificial insemination (see also Chapter 4) allows for the impregnation of a large number of cows with the semen from a comparatively small number of chosen bulls. AI has enabled very considerable selection pressures to be used, especially in dairy cattle, to achieve maximum genetic improvement. The benefits generally accepted to be derived from AI are that it allows maximum exploitation of the best sires and fullest and most economical use of selected ones. In New Zealand most gain (70 per cent) is reported to come from selection among a group of young bulls which are bred from about 2.5 per cent of the best dams in the population followed by selection of bull mothers.

In tropical Africa, Kenya had the distinction of being the second country in the world to start (in 1935) an AI service for farmers. The emphasis at that time was on the eradication of diseases associated with breeding, but is currently on genetic improvement. AI in Kenya also spares the smallholder the cost of maintaining breeding bulls and makes available to him the semen of genetically superior sires. The original breeding programme for beef cattle was based on upgrading local cattle with an exotic breed, but this has now changed in the direction of crossbreeding between two or more breeds. This is aimed at making use of additive and non-additive gene action and also at what are termed 'position effects', the latter, for the most part, entailing the use of semen from a large-sized exotic beef breed on small, but locally adapted, breeding females.

The Kenya Central Artificial Insemination Station (CAIS) had an impressive record, the total number of semen doses issued per year to dairy, beef and dual purpose farmers rising from 80 000 in 1964 to 718 000 in 1973. During 1973, 23 000 (3 per cent) semen doses were for beef and dual purpose cattle breeding, the sires being of the Charolais, Hereford, Boran, Aberdeen Angus, Galloway, Sussex, Sahiwal, Simmental, Brown Swiss and Red Poll breeds. Attention has also been given to the synchronisation of oestrus with progestin and prostaglandin, with particular reference to those regions where the climate calls for a seasonal breeding routine. However, Kenya's AI service has more recently retrogressed.

To summarise, AI may be used in beef herds to facilitate:

1 the importation of new gene material into breeding herds;
2 crossbreeding in areas unsuitable for maintaining high fertility levels of the exotic bull, but where the performance of crossbreds is superior to that of the local breeds;
3 crossbreeding programmes entailing the use of two or more breeds and the accompanying problems and expense of managing bulls of different breeds on the same premises; and
4 operating an economic beef production programme in which a high premium is paid, either locally, or for export purposes, for feedlot performance and carcass quality.

In general terms AI allows for the rapid identification of the most suitable genotype and breeding system for a given environment. After this, and to avoid the many managerial problems associated with AI, the breeder may return to a programme of natural service, using bulls from some local and approved nucleus bull herd.

It is of some interest to note that not all AI programmes in the tropics are living up to their early promise and in many cases a return to increasing use of the bull in natural service is being considered by local authorities. There are also dangers inherent in the misuse of AI in tropical areas. There are many situations where indiscriminate upgrading with exotic breeds has led to lowered performance in the crossbred progeny, despite marked success in the first crosses. This applies, more especially, to dairy cattle. The main application for AI in beef cattle production, provided adequate management procedures are available, would appear to be in systematic crossbreeding in the exotic beef breeds in the more temperate climates of the tropical montane uplands.

From the economic standpoint, the annual cost of using homebred or bought-in Zebu bulls under Kenya ranching conditions would be cheaper than the costs for AI. On the other hand, provided management was of a standard to maintain high levels of herd fertility, AI with exotic bull semen is considered a cheaper procedure than to maintain the bulls themselves under ranching conditions, due to higher capital and operating costs.

Breeding methods

The aim so far has been to discuss how the breeder might go about selecting parent stock in his herds for the next generation. He will then need to decide how to breed them, that is, what type of method or system to adopt in mating them together. In the present context breeding method is intended to indicate the mating programme only and does not include, as already discussed, aids to selection and selection procedures.

The two main breeding methods are closebreeding and outbreeding. Closebreeding is the term used to describe the mating of individuals that are more closely related by descent than would be the progeny of randomly chosen mates. Put in another way, it is the mating of animals that are more closely related to each other than the average of the population, i.e. those with one or more ancestors in common. Outbreeding is the opposite to closebreeding, in which animals are mated that are less closely related to the average of the population from which they came.

Table 5.4 Breeding methods

Close breeding (Mating relations)	Outbreeding (Mating non-relations)
Inbreeding	Crossbreeding
Linebreeding	Outcrossing
	Backcrossing
	Topcrossing
	Grading up
	Mating likes
	Mating unlikes

Both closebreeding and outbreeding are sometimes included under the general heading of inbreeding and crossbreeding, respectively, but as indicated in Table 5.4 the last two may be considered as a specific approach to an aspect of the first two.

Throughout the breeding programme the breeder may find it necessary to switch from one method to another since the breeding policy may, as time passes, be affected by economic, environmental or other factors.

Closebreeding
Inbreeding has been most used in cattle breeding in England over the past two centuries in the development of new breeds. The Shorthorn is an example with coefficients of inbreeding rising from zero in 1790 to 0.26 by 1920. Most modern breeds of cattle have very low, 1 per cent or less, coefficients of inbreeding, although higher levels have been practised in the tropics in individual herds.

Closebreeding is generally considered as brother × sister (full-sib), or sire × daughter mating; half-brother × half-sister (half-sib) is also fairly close inbreeding and mating of cousins, mild inbreeding. The degree of inbreeding of an animal can be measured from its relationship to its ancestors on both sides of the pedigree. As with heritability, both relationship and degree of inbreeding can be measured mathematically, the degree of inbreeding of an individual being called the inbreeding coefficient or coefficient of inbreeding, represented by the symbol F_x. For example, the inbreeding coefficient of a calf born of a bull × his daughter mating would be 25 per cent or $F_x = 0.25$. In cattle this would be very close inbreeding.

Linebreeding is also a form of inbreeding which is still generally practised and is the term used to describe the mating of individuals in such a way as to keep their descendants closely related to some outstanding animal. In this way the superior qualities of the best of the progeny tested sires in a herd may be handed down to subsequent generations without the undesirable effects that will arise from what is termed 'close-inbreeding'. Examples of

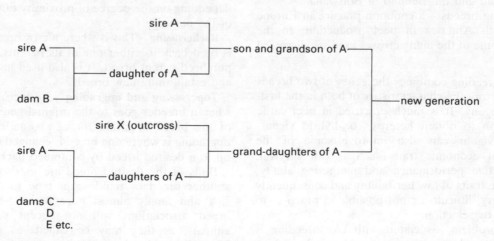

fig. 5.2 A linebreeding programme to ensure the transmission of the desired traits of an outstanding bull (sire A) to his descendants

71

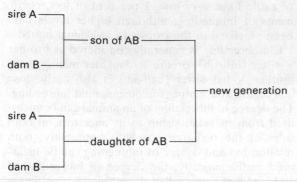

(a) Full-sib mating
(brother and sister)

sire A ——┐
          ├—— son of AB ——┐
dam B ——┘   │
                          ├—— new generation
sire A ——┐   │
          ├—— daughter of AB ——┘
dam B ——┘

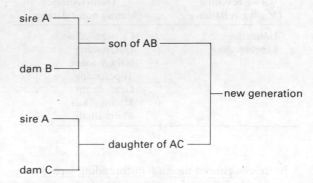

(b) Half-sib mating
half-brother and half-sister)

sire A ——┐
          ├—— son of AB ——┐
dam B ——┘   │
                          ├—— new generation
sire A ——┐   │
          ├—— daughter of AC ——┘
dam C ——┘

This is also the format of a bracket pedigree, which can be extended 'backwards' to include grandparents and great-grandparents, cousins, etc.

fig. 5.3 Examples of inbreeding

linebreeding and inbreeding are given in fig. 5.2 and fig. 5.3.

Outbreeding

Crossbreeding Crosses can be made between species, breeds, strains or lines, including inbred lines. The sire breed in crossbreeding terminology is written first.

1 Crossing species – examples are the Cattalo (Cattle × Bison) of North America, the Buffalypso of Trinidad and the Beefalo of Botswana.
2 Crossing breeds – a common practice in Europe and North America in beef production; in the tropics some of the many crosses used are discussed later.

Crossbreeding combines the genes of two breeds and therefore the characteristics of both in the first-cross progeny. It is much practised in beef cattle production to obtain heterosis or hybrid vigour. Hybrid vigour can also improve some of the important economic traits such as calf survival, reproductive performance and mothering ability, which are traits of low heritability and consequently either very difficult, or not possible in practice, to improve by selection.

One problem associated with crossbreeding is that the breeder cannot go on indefinitely making first-crosses from his purebred parent breeds to

benefit from the hybrid vigour of the F_1 generation. He must therefore make a decision as to how to mate those crossbreds which he maintains in his herd as replacements for breeding purposes. He has several alternatives, depending upon his objectives. Generally speaking, his aim will be to improve performance in a local breed. This he may try to do by using the following mating procedures.

Outcrossing This is usually done by a breeder bringing in a new sire, often referred to as bringing in new blood. The outcross may be mild or severe, depending on the degree of proximity of the source of the new sire.

Backcrossing This is where a crossbred offspring is bred back to either one of its parents, or to the purebred parent breed. It is also used in upgrading and establishing new breeds.

Topcrossing and upgrading A topcross is made when a breeder goes to the original genetic source of the breed or strain for new genetic material; upgrading is where one breed is changed by grading up to a desired breed by continued backcrossing.

Bulls of the desired breed are used on cows of another breed or nondescript type to produce $\frac{1}{2}$, $\frac{3}{4}$, $\frac{7}{8}$ and finally almost pure breeds. Sometimes breed associations will not accept such grade animals, as they may be called, as purebreds. Upgrading of local cows with purebred exotic bulls of improved breeds may fail to achieve the desired results since the hybrid vigour of the early generations, as well as the hardiness of the local foundation cows, may be lost during the upgrading process. There are, nevertheless, many exceptions to this in which more carefully planned upgrading regimes have been used in many of the more developed beef producing areas. In the humid tropical zone of West Africa the grading up of mixed types of intermediate sized cattle by humpless N'dama bulls has produced grade offspring after two to three backcrosses closely resembling the N'dama, both in beef conformation and improved trypano-tolerance.

Great advantage is gained from crossbreeding in producing calves from crossbred cows in which hybrid vigour expresses itself most in those traits related to female productivity and survivability of the young in early life. Crossbred cows should thus have a decided advantage in the raising of calves. Furthermore, continuous rotational mating of crossbred cows with the bulls least related to them will result in the expression of hybrid vigour in both cow productivity and calf growth rate. The methods used in this process may include upgrading, back-crossing and crisscrossing, as illustrated in figs. 5.4, 5.5 and 5.6.

Generation	Mating pattern	
	bull ×	cow
	N'dama [N]	Keteku [K]
	%	%
Parental	100[N]	100[K]
F_1	100[N]	50[K] : 50[N]
F_2	100[N]	25[K] : 75[N]
F_3	100[N]	12.5[K] : 87.5[N]
F_4	100[N]	6.25[K] : 93.75[N]

fig. 5.4 An example of the upgrading of Keteku cows using N'dama bulls

Generation	Male		Female
	A	×	B
F_1	A	×	AB (50A : 50B)
F_2	B	×	AAB (75A : 25B)
F_3	A	×	AABB (37½A : 62½B)
		etc	

The genetic composition of F_3 females will be the same as F_1.

fig. 5.5 An example of backcrossing using two types of sire, one from each of breeds A and B

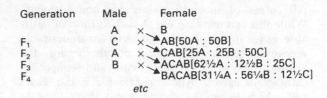

Generation	Male		Female
	A	×	B
F_1	C	×	AB[50A : 50B]
F_2	A	×	CAB[25A : 25B : 50C]
F_3	B	×	ACAB[62½A : 12½B : 25C]
F_4			BACAB[31¼A : 56¼B : 12½C]
		etc	

fig. 5.6 An example of crisscross breeding using sires of three breeds (A, B and C)

Mating like and unlike The former, sometimes called assorted mating, is no longer considered an efficient way to alter gene frequency compared to other methods of selection and mating. The same applies to mating unlike.

Special breeding programmes
Purebreeding The purebred breeder is one who has chosen to work with one particular breed of cattle or buffalo. The commercial breeder may chose to breed purebred stock for sale as breeding animals. The pastoralist, on the other hand, may have other reasons for keeping to one breed. He may admire and select his chosen breed for their colour, horn size, suitability to the environment, milk production, working capacity, or for a combination of these or other characters.

The purebred breeder may practise any of the mating systems described above, from assortive mating, to inbreeding and outbreeding, in attempting to achieve his goal. Purebred selection procedures need time and care in their operation and considerable wastage occurs from culling and other causes. Consequently, when breeding stock of known genetic worth are sold on the commercial market, the price paid for them is greater than that which would be paid for the same animals in terms only of carcass or liveweight value.

Where the breeder resorts to inbreeding, this entails the practice of mating related animals in which the progeny will be more inbred than those born of randomly chosen parents. It was a method used much more in the past by cattle breeders when developing new and improved breeds. Any selection programme involves some degree of restriction of the number of parents used in each generation. As selection intensity increases animals within the herd tend to become more related to one another.

All forms of inbreeding increase homozygosity. While this can increase the chance fixation of desirable genes it can also do the same for undesirable recessive genes. Examples of these are the achondroplastic or bulldog calf and congenital cataract in calves. Another example is the dwarf calf which began to appear some years back in some of the improved beef breeds in North America, such as the Hereford.

Other effects of inbreeding include decrease in body size, vigour, fertility, as well as lowered productivity and increased mortality. While the disadvantages of inbreeding are recognised by most breeders, inbreeding is still sometimes practised, for example, in progeny testing where a bull may be mated back to his daughters to test for the presence of undesirable genes.

Systematic crossbreeding This is carried out by the retention and use of sires of the pure parent breeds in rotation. The sire of one breed is used during one generation and of the other breed during the next generation. The crossing of two breeds in rotation is referred to as crisscrossing. Triple or tri-hybrid crossing is a term sometimes used where three breeds are used. The procedures are illustrated in figs. 5.5 and 5.6. The value of systematic crossbreeding arises from the maximum use of the resulting hybrid vigour.

Developing a new breed This involves the use of two or more breeds or types in a limited crossing, or backcrossing programme, followed by selection among the resulting progeny. The breeder may stop using the introduced breed at the F_1 cross, or after one or more generations of backcrossing to the introduced bulls. After this, the backcrosses are selected and bred amongst themselves (*inter se* crossing) in order to fix the desired type.

Choosing a breeding system for a tropical environment

The beef cattle producer in the tropics may, in first establishing his ranch or other production system, select his foundation stock on a phenotypic basis for such characteristics as breed or type, coat colour, adaptability to local conditions and general hardiness and to manage these under the best conditions he can provide. It is a well known feature of trade cattle on the hoof and many local breeds selected on sight and at random that they respond extremely well to improved feeding. Beyond a certain point, however, genetic improvement can only be achieved by selection for specific traits or for a combination of these.

The livestock breeder has three major choices: selection and use of local (i.e. indigenous) breeds; the replacement of local breeds by more productive exotic breeds; and crossbreeding, including crosses between local breeds, back-crossing with selected local or exotic breeds and the evolution of new breeds.

The use of local breeds The main advantages are that:

1 they are readily available in large numbers;
2 they are acclimatised to the local environment and adapted to traditional husbandry methods; and
3 they probably possess desirable genetic traits associated with acclimatisation.

The main disadvantages are that:

1 natural selection in the past has probably been for survival, probably at the expense of production traits such as fast maturity or milk production; and
2 because of an initial low level of production characteristics, improvement by selection is a slow process.

The use and selection of indigenous livestock would appear to be most useful where:

1 the socio–agro–economic situation is such that more refined breeding or management programmes could not immediately be envisaged and where the emphasis would still continue to be placed on improved nutrition and management, e.g. in many semi-arid regions of Africa and under the circumstances previously mentioned relating to pastoralist peoples;
2 the environmental stress on local stock is very severe and genotype–environment interactions are highly significant; and
3 the indigenous breeds possess some specific adaptive or resistant trait such as trypanotolerance in the dwarf West African cattle breeds and the adaptability of the water buffalo to the flood conditions of the Amazon Valley in South America.

The value of some of the indigenous breeds is becoming increasingly evident to many livestock breeders and many international and local government livestock organisations are now giving special attention to ways and means of expanding the numbers and distribution of certain indigenous breeds that could be of increasing economic importance. Attention is also being given to the preservation of those particular breeds or types of cattle that are in danger of disappearing because of indiscriminate interbreeding with other local breeds. Examples of this are the West African Shorthorn and the Latin American Criollo, the latter breed at a time when it is being found that the Criollo × Zebu are superior to many other crosses with the Zebu under local conditions. There is a similar danger of losing certain indigenous breeds on account of excessive use of upgrading programmes that are conducted without sufficient note being taken of the various attributes of the two parent stocks.

Examples of where the utilisation and improvement of indigenous breeds is justifiable are:

1 the N'dama and West African Shorthorn breeds of West Africa;
2 Zebu breeds such as the Boran in East Africa and the Wadara in West Africa for meat production in upland and semi-arid areas;
3 the Ngaundere and other Adamawa types of the montane uplands of West Africa;
4 the Caracul of Brazil, and the Criollo of Venezuela and certain countries in Central America;
5 Sanga breeds such as the Mashona, Tuli and Africander in Central and southern Africa;
6 Bos (Bibos) spp. breeds such as the Bali for work and meat production in the humid areas of Southeast Asia;
7 the Shuwa Arab cattle of Chad and other Sahel areas of West Africa, and many other local breeds owned by pastoralists which are highly important also as pack animals; and
8 water buffalo for work and meat production in the humid areas of South and Southeast Asia and in South America, especially in the Amazon Valley.

The above are listed with the major emphasis on meat production and work. If one introduces the other feature of milk production of Zebu cattle, with its high fat or energy content, then the list of examples could be appreciably longer in order to indicate all the inherent values of many of the indigenous breeds.

An outline of some of the more extensive breeding programmes in tropical Latin America, tropical Africa and Australia will be provided at the end of this section.

The importation and use of exotic breeds To a considerable extent, the breeding of livestock for a specific purpose and environment is of comparatively recent origin, although the nomadic pastoralist has developed, over the centuries, a long-legged and rangy beast ideally suited to the semi-arid tropics, as well as a heavier and shorter-legged animal suitable for tropical montane uplands.

Whatever the origin today, however, the term 'exotic', from the standpoint of the beef cattle producer or the producer of other classes of livestock in the tropics, is generally accepted to mean improved beef breeds brought into a tropical environment from more temperate climate areas. Examples of such breeds are the British Shorthorn and South Devon, or the French Charolais. But these introductions may not necessarily, in all cases, be temperate climate breeds. In Australia, for example, the American Brahman was introduced to tropical Queensland for crossbreeding with the British Shorthorn. The Santa Gertrudis breed of southern Texas has also been introduced. In the Australian context these two breeds may be referred to as exotic. Similarly, the Indian Sahiwal introduced to Mali, and to East Africa, to improve milk production by crossing with the local Zebu may also be referred to as exotic. Broadly speaking, therefore, breeds introduced to a country for improvement purposes from other continents may be regarded as exotic.

The main aim of importing exotic stock is to achieve rapid improvements in productivity as compared with local breeds. This may be achieved if suitable exotic breeds are found possessing desirable genes for production that are not otherwise available in local stock. This also assumes that the local environment can be improved or modified sufficiently for such desirable traits to be demonstrated in the imported stock. The two major disadvantages are, firstly, the expense of importing exotic stock and the small number that can be imported and secondly, the acclimatisation of the imported stock may be time consuming as well as expensive. The last mentioned difficulty would not apply where AI facilities are available. The importation of exotic beef breeds is likely to be most useful where:

1 few or no indigenous breeds are available to exploit the beef production potential of a specific tropical environment; and
2 climatic, disease and nutritional stresses are moderate, such as on tropical oceanic islands and tropical highlands.

The importation and use of exotic breeds of cattle and buffalo is, or could be, of more economic importance in relation to milk production than to beef production. This is because the environment is more readily influenced or controlled in dairy herd management than is the case for beef cattle. Importation of exotic stock for beef production could be beneficial:

1 where dairy projects allow for slaughter of veal calves or where conditions are available for intensive rearing of beef;
2 in tropical montane upland areas that allow for the use of pure exotic breeds in the absence of undue disease or other stress;
3 for improved Zebu breeds in some regions of Southeast Asia where the indigenous stock are poor and unproductive; and
4 for further introductions of improved Zebu breeds, for example to Australia and parts of Central and South America.

Crossbreeding and upgrading of indigenous breeds The relative merits and demerits of crossbreeding for improved beef production have been mentioned earlier. Whereas the particular advantage of crossbreeding is that obtained from hybrid vigour or heterosis, the major practical problem from the commercial standpoint is that at least two distinct breeds must be maintained to ensure the continued production of half-crosses showing the desired hybrid characteristics. This requires quite large-scale operations and a highly organised management. One of the more obvious procedures

would be the use of imported semen, as practised in India for buffalo and dairy cattle breeding and in Kenya for dairying, but this is less practicable and often impossible, in beef production systems. However, both crossbreeding as well as the grading up of indigenous breeds, either by the use of imported exotic stock or their semen, or by the grading up of one indigenous breed by another, provide a challenging and possible solution for more rapid and economical beef production in the tropics. Some of the programmes already in practice are:

1 The upgrading of local beef-type Zebu of the montane uplands of West Africa using the South Devon beef breed – producing encouraging growth rates but concurrent disease problems such as an increased susceptibility to skin diseases (Chapter 8).
2 Di-hybrid Criollo × Zebu and tri-hybrid crosses such as Criollo × Zebu × Charolais cattle in Central and South America.
3 Upgrading of Southeast Asian indigenous cattle with American Brahman and the possibility of crossing the *Bos (Bibos)* spp. breeds such as the Bali with European-type Red Poll or other beef breeds.
4 Grading up of the more nondescript but for the most part more trypanotolerant semi-dwarf intermediate type Borgou or Keteku cattle of West Africa to the pure N'dama trypanotolerant breed.

Introducing new breeds for crossbreeding Where crossbreeding with local breeds is planned, the breeder must determine whether improved performance may be obtained by:

1 grading up the local animals by continued back-crossing to the introduced breed;
2 using heterosis in a systematic breeding programme by retaining both the introduced and local breeds; or
3 developing a new breed by selection and *inter se* mating among first, or after one or more backcross generations.

Two basic differences may be considered in the rationale for introducing new or exotic blood to improve production. On the one hand, as in tropical Australia, the Zebu has been introduced for crossing with traditional British or other European beef breeds in order to improve the heat tolerance of the latter breeds, as well as their resistance to disease and to tick infestation. The aim here is to infuse sufficient Zebu blood to obtain added heat tolerance and disease resistance without, at the same time, lowering unduly the beef producing characteristic of the improved beef breeds. On the other hand, for example in tropical Africa, the aim is to improve the beef producing characteristic of the local breeds by the introduction of improved exotic stock, while at the same time maintaining much of the heat tolerance and disease resistance of the local breeds. A clear understanding of the aims and associated problems is required in both of the above cases and it will depend upon the skill and judgement of the breeder to achieve a suitable compromise. Examples of such a compromise include the Santa Gertrudis, Brangus and Charbray breeds of the USA and the Droughtmaster of Australia (Chapter 3). At the same time, with the improvement of local breeds by one means or another, there will also be the need for improved management techniques. The advantage of an upgrading programme is that although improvement in indigenous stock by this means is comparatively slow, there is also opportunity for management systems to be improved at the same time and in line with the requirements of the upgraded stock. Exotic breeds have considerable potential for improving the beef conformation and growth rate of local breeds under good management on improved, intensive grazing systems such as the

fig. 5.7 N'dama × Brown Swiss

N'dama of West Africa crossed with the German-type Brown Swiss cattle in Togo and Nigeria (fig. 5.7).

Introduction of exotic breeds to a country may not be a simple and straightforward matter. There are, for example, restrictions on importing improved Zebu breeds such as the Boran of East Africa to West Africa because of the danger of introducing the tick-borne East Coast Fever (Chapter 8); quarantine regulations for such epizootic diseases as foot and mouth disease also restrict inter-continental or inter-regional shipments and exchange of cattle for improving breeding programmes. Due cognisance needs to be taken at all times of statutory animal disease control regulations before embarking on any programme involving the introduction of exotic stock.

Some breeding programmes in the tropics

Crossbreeding in Botswana

A study in Botswana of pure breed performance and that of crosses with the indigenous Tswana cow is being carried out to assess the performance of the various crosses under extensive management conditions, when compared to that of the indigenous cows. The programme is planned to cover the following three main areas;

1 evaluation through performance testing of the major beef cattle types to determine their qualities;
2 continued performance testing of superior types for long term improvement; and
3 exploitation of the effects of hybrid vigour through crossbreeding.

The Tswana is the indigenous breed being tested. Four other breeds, the Brahman, Tuli, Bonsmara and Africander are also being evaluated as pure breeds suited to extensive production. Detailed evaluation of crossbreeding programmes, already initiated by government for a number of years both through sale of bulls and AI, is also in progress using Africander, Tuli, Brahman and Simmental bulls on Tswana cows. Some preliminary crossbreeding trials have also been carried out with South Devon, Italian beef breeds and the American bison (*Bison bison*).

The crossbred calves sired by Simmental bulls were significantly heavier than calves of all the other breed crosses at birth, weaning and 18 months of age. The Tuli × Tswana crosses showed little improvement, probably because the Tuli originates from cattle closely related to the indigenous Tswana. The calves from crossing of widely dissimilar breeds such as the Simmental and Brahman × Tswana in most cases showed a marked degree of hybrid vigour. The Tswana is evidently well suited to production under local conditions; likewise, the Tuli has very good reproductive performance. Both these local breeds, therefore, appear highly suitable dams for use in a crossbreeding programme.

The Beefalo in Botswana In addition to the efforts of beef breeders to improve productivity by crosses between local cattle breeds and between improved *Bos taurus* and *Bos indicus*, interest was shown as early as 1914, in Canada, in the possibility of an advantageous hybrid crossing between the North American bison (*Bison bison*) and domestic cattle. The idea was to combine the traits of hardiness and size of the bison with the growth rate and carcass quality of beef cattle. The resultant progeny in Canada were called 'Cattalo' which contained less than half bison parentage. Markedly lowered fertility in both the male and female hybrids led to the decision to abandon the programme in 1966. Only a few years later, in 1970, considerable interest was aroused in California, USA in the merits claimed for a hybrid called the Beefalo ($\frac{3}{8}$ bison × $\frac{5}{8}$ Charolais and Hereford). While some of the results ascribed to the Beefalo were suspect, in particular as to growth on high forage feeds, it was decided in Botswana to assess the productivity of Beefalo crosses with Tswana cows. Semen from Beefalo bulls was used to artificially inseminate Tswana cows. In the same experiment, Tswana cows, managed under extensive grazing conditions, and supplemented with bonemeal, salt and phosphate, were inseminated using Chianina, Romagnola, Marchigiana, Brahman and Simmental semen.

It was concluded that although the data was limited to one calf crop sired by only two Beefalo bulls, breeding with the Beefalo bull in Botswana, without recourse to the problems involved with AI, has no advantage over crossing with continental breeds of beef cattle.

Sahiwal crossbreds in Kenya
The Sahiwal has been used in Kenya to improve both meat and milk production in pastoralist, ranch and farm herds. Of all *Bos indicus* breeds the Sahiwal has the best potential for milk production, it has good mothering ability and its adaptability to the local environment is of somewhat the same order as that of the indigenous Zebu breeds.

The Sahiwal has been used to improve milk production in pastoralist herds, particularly those of the Maasai, by introducing Sahiwal bulls. In dry montane areas $\frac{2}{3}$ Ayrshire × $\frac{1}{3}$ Sahiwal crossbreds have been used for milk production and $\frac{3}{8}$ to $\frac{5}{8}$ Sahiwal × $\frac{5}{8}$ to $\frac{3}{8}$ Ayrshire for meat production. Sahiwal crossbreds have also been used in the semi-humid coastal zone.

Crossbreeding programmes in Latin America
During the last two decades an extensive series of beef cattle crossbreeding experiments have been carried out in various parts of tropical Latin America, including Bolivia, Costa Rica, Colombia and Venezuela. The Criollo breed (Chapter 3) is rapidly being replaced by upgrading it with various Zebu breeds or by importing purebred Zebu cattle to the extent that it may disappear altogether.

Despite the popularity of the Zebu its production levels have, for the most part, been unsatisfactory and this, coupled with the danger of losing the Criollo, has prompted crossbreeding programmes with these two and with other breeds at many livestock experiment stations.

The following breed combinations have been tried:

1 Criollo × *Bos indicus* breeds
2 Criollo × Santa Gertrudis
3 Criollo × *Bos indicus* × Charolais
4 *Bos indicus* breeds × European-type *Bos taurus* breeds
5 *Bos indicus* breeds × American Brahman

The results obtained from these studies involving many thousands of observations, have been summarised by Plasse. Some salient features are:

1 Criollo × *Bos indicus* crossbreds showed considerable heterosis and also superiority over purebred Zebus for all traits, including growth, carcass characteristics, reproductive efficiency and weaning weight produced per cow bred.

2 Upgrading Criollo to Zebu was successful only up to the second generation, the performance of higher grades being below that of the Zebu.

3 *Inter-se* mating of the F_1 Zebu × Criollo crosses showed good results in the first generation, also for a gene pool combining Criollo, Zebu and Charolais genes.

4 The average of three generations of rotational crossbreeding so far studied showed a better performance of the crossbreeds over the purebred Zebu.

5 Crossing American Brahman with other Zebu breeds had no effect on growth traits.

6 When European-type *Bos taurus* bulls were used on Brahman cows, growth rate of F_1 calves was better than that of the Brahmans but reproductive efficiency of F_1 cows was poorer.

In Brazil three breeds of Indian origin have been used for crossbreeding purposes; the Nellore, Guzerat and Gir. The Indu-Brasil breed has been established from a mixture of crossbreds of these breeds and others. Data on the growth performance of the Indu-Brasil and the three breeds of Indian origin are provided in Table 5.5. The Canchim is a stabilised crossbred developed in Brazil with some ⅝ Charolais and ⅜ Zebu blood. Work on this breed was initiated at the Fazenda de Criacao de Sao Carlos, Sao Paulo State in 1940. The foundation herd of 300 Zebu cows was crossed with Charolais bulls. Data on purebred and crossbred animals was collected and compared over a period of 25 years, during which time various crossbreeding programmes were tested to obtain ⅝ Charolais × ⅜ Zebu and ⅝ Zebu × ⅜ Charolais crossbreds (Table 5.6). The ⅝ Charolais crosses were found to be the best in terms of beef conformation and dressing percentage when managed under range conditions. The ⅝ Zebu crossbreds, although hardy, were less precocious, leggy and lacked body capacity and spread of ribs.

Table 5.5 Liveweights at different ages for four breeds of cattle in Brazil

Breed	12 months		24 months		30 months	
	Males	Females	Males	Females	Males	Females
Indu-Brasil	227	202	377	297	536	335
Nellore	201	176	381	275	495	322
Guzerat	230	198	420	304	515	353
Gir	189	165	329	259	423	294

Table 5.6 Average liveweight at 24 months and daily gains from birth in Charolais and their crosses with Zebu cattle, Fazenda Sao Carlos, Sao Paulo State

Levels of blood	Mean live weight at 24 mths and SE of mean (kg)		Mean daily gain from birth to 24 mths and SE of mean (kg)	
	Males	Females	Males	Females
Charolais	489 ± 6.3	409 ± 3.9	0.610 ± 0.020	0.518 ± 0.015
½ Charolais-Zebu	366 ± 4.6	377 ± 2.6	0.468 + 0.020	0.471 ± 0.015
¾ Charolais-Zebu	473 ± 14.3	333 ± 3.7	0.597	0.430 ± 0.015
⅝ Charolais-Zebu	434 ± 8.1	385 ± 4.6	0.561 ± 0.020	0.488 ± 0.015
¾ Zebu-Charolais	433 ± 43.7	369 ± 2.6	0.542	0.476 ± 0.015
⅝ Zebu-Charolais	419 ± 11.2	363 ± 3.4	0.548 ± 0.020	0.468 ± 0.015
Bi-Crossbred				
⅝ Charolais-Zebu [canchim]	445 ± 14.5	376 ± 14.9	0.559	0.468

They were also light in the round producing a lower proportion of valuable cuts. The Canchim was considered as an excellent sire for crossing with local (Criollo-type) cows.

Crossbreds in the Caribbean
In the Caribbean the Jamaica Red and Jamaica Black are recognised breeds resulting from crosses of *Bos taurus* with *Bos indicus* breeds; the Nelthropp of the Virgin Islands is of some interest in that the humpless foundation stock were the N'dama cattle of West Africa, most probably a legacy from the slave trade era.

Improvement of buffalo
In comparison with cattle very little attention has been given to the improvement of the buffalo by the accepted methods of animal breeding. This may be due, to a large extent, to the various prohibitions and prejudices, whether for economic, social or religious reasons, against the buffalo, in spite of its key role in the economies of so many countries in the tropics. There are wide variations in size and weight of different types, breeds and individuals that provide considerable opportunities for the selection of breeding stock for meat production. Some research on selection in this direction has been initiated over the past few decades, e.g. in Egypt, India, Bulgaria, Thailand, the Philippines and Australia. For the most part, however, studies have related mostly to milk production, the view of many breeders being that more immediate improvement in growth of the buffalo will come from better feeding and management. Nevertheless, there are increasing numbers of proposals coming forward for more intensive research towards a better understanding of the greater potential of the buffalo.

In India and Pakistan breeders follow local, traditional systems of breeding and selection which entails a minimum milk yield and selection of breeding stock on the basis of dam performance and type. Conformation is also an important factor in selection of animals for work. Herd recording is carried out only at large government farms, military stations and universities. Selection is assisted by culling of low milk producing cows. There is a growing awareness of the need for progeny testing and bull selection. Most of the research on coat colour and horn shape has been done in India, Thailand, Malaysia, Pakistan, and the Philippines. Crossbreeding of river and swamp buffalo with the object of inducing hybrid vigour, milk yield and draught qualities in the crosses has been done in the Philippines, Thailand, Malaysia and Indonesia. Brazil is among the first countries in the tropics to establish a breed society, the Buffalo Breeders Association – which has defined breed standards for registration purposes and is now recognised by the government. Some attention has been given to establish colour types in the swamp buffalo, namely the Rosilho (roan) and Pietro (black). A shorthorn type has been developed by frequent crossing with imported buffalo from Italy, commonly referred to as the 'Mediterranean type', which in colour and conformation resembles the buffalo of Greece, Bulgaria, Italy and other countries in Europe. Proposals have also been made for the establishment of a breed society in Nepal by the Nepal Livestock Development Mission (FAO) to develop pure Murrah breeding herds.

Work has been in progress over the past thirty or so years in Trinidad on establishing a new breed of buffalo specifically suitable for meat production. This new breed, now universally recognised as the 'Buffalypso', has been developed by comparatively indiscriminate crossing of various breeds of buffalo imported from India to Trinidad, mainly the Murrah, Surti, Jafarabadi, Nili and Bhadawari, all pure breeds that have now virtually disappeared from the scene in Trinidad. The development of the Buffalypso is due mainly to the work of Dr S. P. Bennet, while he was working at a local sugar company. He described the main features of the breed as: a reddish-brown or copper coloured coat with a white star on the forehead being permitted; thick and taut skin; a broad head with horns growing backwards and curving upwards; prominent and intelligent-looking eyes. The body (fig. 5.8) is short-legged and compact with straight topline standing on well turned thighs and buttocks with muscle well down the inside of the legs. A comparison of growth and carcass characteristics of the buffalo with Zebu cattle and local buffalo is provided in Chapter 8.

fig. 5.8 Buffalypso

Although the swamp buffalo will interbreed with the river buffalo, attempts at hybridisation with other bovine species have not been successful. Water buffalo will not interbreed with either Zebu or *Bos taurus* cattle, nor with the bison or the African buffalo. There is, however, sexual activity demonstrated between buffalo and cattle where herds are seen together. Buffalo males will serve cows and conversely, bulls will serve buffalo females, but such unions are sterile. It is believed that these sterile unions are due to the high dissimilarity of karyotypes between the species which inhibits zygote formation. The 'Cattalo' is a fertile hybrid cross between the North American buffalo (*Bison bison*) and cattle.

Improvement of those characteristics with low heritabilities, such as age at first calving, service period, conception rate and calving interval, that do not respond to selection requires attention to management, nutrition and hygiene. Hybrid vigour may also be exploited. On the other hand, heritabilities are high for birth weight and for body weight at given ages and rates of gain between these ages. Such traits are measurable in breeding stock of both sexes so that progeny testing for selection among them is not necessary where comparisons are to be made. Management conditions, however, must be the same for all animals.

Further reading

APRU (1980). *Beef production and range management in Botswana*. Animal Production Research Unit, Min. of Agriculture: Gaborone, Botswana.

Arora, R. C. and **Pandey, R. S.** (1982). Current research status of buffalo endocrinology. *Wld. Rev. Anim. Prod.*, **18** (2), 15–23

Dalton, D. C. (1981). *An introduction to practical animal breeding*. Granada: London.

Faulkner, D. E. and **Brown, J. D.** (1953). *The improvement of cattle in British colonial territories in Africa*. Colonial Advisory Council of Agric. Anim. Health and Forestry Publ. no. 3. HMSO: London.

Hill, D. H. (1967) Cattle breeding in Brazil (with a note on the buffalo): a review. *Anim. Breeding Abstr.*, **35** (4), 545–564.

Plasse, D. (1976). The possibility of genetic improvement of beef cattle in developing countries with particular reference to Latin America. In *Beef cattle production in developing countries*, **ed. A. J. Smith.** Edinburgh. Univ. Press: Edinburgh.

Sheridan, A. K. (1981). Crossbreeding and heterosis. *Anim. Breeding Abstr.*, **49**, 131.

Trail, J. C. M. (1980). Merits and demerits of importing exotic animals compared with the improvement of local breeds. *Brit. Soc. Anim. Prod. Occ. Publ. no. 4. London.*

Turton, J. D. (1981). Crossbreeding of dairy cattle – a selective review. *Anim. Breeding Abstr.*, **49**, 293.

6 Nutrition and growth (by the late Martin Butterworth)

Introduction

Cattle and water buffalo are ruminants; i.e. they possess a complex stomach consisting of four parts: the rumen, reticulum, omasum and abomasum. In the adult ruminant, the first two of these form a large compartment and together account for more than 85 per cent of the total size of the stomach and have a capacity of some 200 l. This reticulo-rumen maintains a constant temperature (about 39 to 40 °C), a more or less constant pH (between 4.5 and 7.0 but more usually about 6.0), and this is maintained by the buffering effect of the saliva which is added to the rumen contents in large quantities. The rumen is anaerobic (i.e. contains little or no oxygen), nutrients are added to it at regular intervals, both by the ingestion of food and from the saliva (inorganic nutrients) while the particle size of the food is reduced by rumination. The constant muscular movement of the reticulo-rumen ensures that the rumen contents are always mixed while the filtering of smaller particles to the more distal parts of the alimentary canal through the reticulo-omasal orifice ensures separation of fine from coarse particles. Concentrations of volatile fatty acids and other dissolved compounds are maintained at a constant level by continuing absorption. It thus provides the ideal environment for large numbers of many types of micro-organisms, both bacteria and protozoa, and it is these that give the ruminant its unique nutritional characteristics. Fungi are important in the digestion of cell walls. These characteristics include the ability to digest cellulose, the ability to use non-protein nitrogen (e.g. urea) as a raw material for protein synthesis and the ability to exist without dietary sources of B-complex vitamins. Cattle and water buffalo can thus make use of low protein, high roughage materials which would not otherwise be generally useful as livestock feeds.

Essential nutrients

Nutrients are components of food which may be utilised by the animal after digestion and absorption has taken place. They comprise: proteins, carbohydrates, fats, vitamins, minerals and water.

Proteins

Proteins are composed of aminoacids which are used in the body to form muscular tissue, enzymes and hormones. They also play a part in detoxification reactions and may be used as a source of energy.

Because of their role in tissue building, proteins are of particular importance in the nutrition of the young growing animal but they are also critical in reproduction as they are concerned with the correct functioning of the hormonal system leading to reconception as well as being required for the growth of the foetus, the foetal membranes, the uterus, mammary tissues, etc. Subsequently, a significantly increased requirement for proteins is caused by lactation.

In non-ruminant animals, it is important that rations should be balanced for the so-called essential aminoacids. These are aminoacids which are not synthesised in sufficient quantities to maintain the productive functions of the body. Because of the activities of the rumen micro-organisms previously referred to, cattle and buffalo are more independent of dietary sources of these essential aminoacids. However, the aminoacid composition of protein that escapes fermentation in the rumen is important.

Some micro-organisms ferment protein to give energy with the evolution of ammonia. Part of this ammonia is re-incorporated into protein by bacterial enzymes; the digestion of dietary protein by bacterial proteinases also results in free aminoacids. These are quickly re-assimilated by other microbes to form protein. The quantity of free amino acids in the rumen at any one time is therefore small; the absorption of free aminoacids from the rumen is negligible.

The ability of microbes to incorporate ammonia into protein enables the ruminant to use non-protein nitrogen (NPN). Microbial protein passes to the duodenum and is digested by intestinal enzymes similar to those of the non-ruminant.

The minimum amount of ammonia in rumen liquor to sustain the well-being of the microbial population appears to be about 5–10 mg/100 ml although levels of more than 30 mg/100 ml may be used for protein synthesis. Excess amounts are absorbed into the bloodstream and detoxified to urea in the liver. Although the greater part of this urea is excreted in the urine, part of it may be secreted in the saliva and recirculated to the rumen. This enables an animal fed a low protein diet to economise on nitrogen.

Cases of toxicity occur when quantities of ammonia in the bloodstream are too great for the liver to detoxify. It is important to mix feeds carefully so that the animal does not ingest too much urea at one time.

About two-thirds of the protein which reaches the duodenum is microbial in origin. However, this protein on its own is often not enough to sustain maximum levels of production. Protein which escapes degradation in the rumen but arrives intact in the duodenum is also required. This is sometimes known as by-pass or escape protein. It appears that the aminoacid composition of this protein complements that from bacteria.

Some indication of protein in this by-pass role may be given by its solubility. Soluble proteins are more easily degraded than insoluble ones. Heating or treatment with formaldehyde reduces solubility and can lead to increased value of the supplement. However, if this treatment is too severe, Maillard condensation reactions occur between proteins and carbohydrates. Compounds formed in this way are not available to the animal as they cannot be digested in the posterior tract. They can be measured by the determination of acid detergent insoluble nitrogen (ADIN).

Some aminoacids may be metabolised to glucose after absorption (they are glucogenic) and may be used in this way if insufficient undegraded carbohydrate is present in the duodenum (see below). The various pathways involved in protein digestion in the rumen and duodenum are shown in fig. 6.1.

Carbohydrates
Carbohydrates eaten by ruminants may be loosely classified into structural and storage carbohydrates. The former are those commonly found in the cell

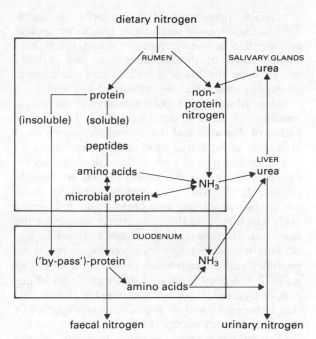

fig. 6.1 Nitrogen metabolism in the ruminant

walls of the plant and comprise celluloses and hemicelluloses while the latter are simpler sugars and starches.

In the traditional system of analysis, the structural carbohydrates were grouped under 'crude fibre' while the soluble carbohydrates were grouped under 'nitrogen free extractives'. It was originally thought that the crude fibre fraction was indigestible while that of nitrogen free extractives was digestible. However, while this was generally true for monogastric animals, subsequent investigation showed that this was not the case for ruminants. In fact, in tropical forages, the crude fibre fraction is often more digestible than the nitrogen free extractive.

Newer methods of analysis have recognised this problem and have attempted to differentiate the forage plant into fractions which are more closely related to digestibility and intake.

Lignin is indigestible and is the principal substance which limits the ability of the rumen micro-organisms to digest the cellulose carbohydrates in the cell wall. It thus accounts for an

83

appreciable percentage of the variability in digestibility. Lignification tends to be greater in tropical grasses than in their temperate counterparts at a similar stage of development and this partially accounts for the lower digestibility of the former. Silica also lowers the digestibility of cell walls.

Plant cell walls have been measured by the determination of neutral detergent fibre. The combination of this with acid detergent fibre gives a good indication of both true fibre and hemicelluloses.

The greater part of carbohydrate digestion occurs in the rumen where the main products are volatile fatty acids (VFAs). The most important of these are acetic, propionic and butyric and it is these acids which provide the main energy source for the ruminant. Branched chain volatile fatty acids (e.g. iso-butyric, iso-valeric) are required by some microbes and are important in the digestion of cell walls. It has been estimated that from 75 to 90 per cent of ingested starch is digested in the rumen, and that between 42 and 68 per cent of all digestion of energy-rich feeds occurs there.

Carbohydrates may escape digestion in the rumen either by being carried through to the small intestine without having been attacked by the micro-organisms or by being assimilated and incorporated into a micro-organism. For example, large amounts of starch are assimilated into protozoa.

On reaching the small intestine, digestion is similar to that of the non-ruminant. Amylase is secreted into the small intestine by the pancreas while the intestine itself secretes maltase.

The importance of these 'by-pass' carbohydrates (i.e. those which reach the small intestine without having been digested) should be noted. Although the ruminant obtains the greater part of its energy requirements from the VFAs produced in the rumen, there are still processes which require glucose. These include the oxidative metabolism of the kidney medulla, the brain and red blood cells. Glucose is also required for tissue synthesis. It is important therefore that glucose precursors reach the small intestine unchanged. These include not only carbohydrates but also certain glucogenic aminoacids.

Carbohydrates are the main (but not the only) source of energy to the ruminant and so it is convenient at this point to describe some of the methods which have been developed for describing the energy value of a feed. Although the two methods which will be used in this book are metabolisable energy (ME) and total digestible nutrients (TDN), several other systems will be described as these are still widely used elsewhere.

Digestible energy This represents the gross energy of the feed from which has been subtracted the loss of energy which is not digested and which leaves the intestine in the faeces.

Metabolisable energy (ME) This is the digestible energy, less the energy lost in the urine and as methane, which is produced by fermentation in the rumen; about 20 per cent of digestible energy. Table 6.1 shows some values for the metabolisable energy content of tropical grasses. Although these have been estimated from digestible energy values, they are indicative of what is to be expected.

Net energy There is a further loss of energy associated with ingestion of feed and this is known as the specific dynamic effect of the food or the heat increment. When this is deducted from the metabolisable energy we are left with the net energy. This is the energy available to the animal for maintenance, growth, milk production, etc. Net energy has been used for the development of various feeding systems. One of these which is commonly used, particularly in the UK, is the Starch Equivalent. This relates the energy value of a feed to that of starch in terms of efficiency for the fattening of a bullock. Similar systems have been based on barley (The Scandinavian Feed Unit). Current usage in the USA is the use of net energy for either maintenance (NE_m) or gain (NE_g). The efficiency with which the energy is used varies for the two processes.

Total digestible nutrients (TDN) The calculation of TDN is an arbitrary system based on the determination of the digestibility coefficients of the various nutrients, as determined by proximate feed analysis. It is calculated as follows:

TDN = digestible crude protein + digestible crude fibre + digestible nitrogen free extractives + 2.25 × digestible ether extract.

It thus takes into account that the ether extract has a higher energy value than the other compo-

Table 6.1 The nutritive value of some tropical grasses

Grass	Stage of growth	Crude protein (%)	Digestible crude protein (%)	Total digestible nutrients (%)	Digestible energy (KJ/kg)	Metabolisable energy[1] (KJ/kg)
Digitaria decumbens (Pangola)	immature	14.9	71.5	60.7	11.9	9.9
D. decumbens	pre-flowering	13.7	66.0	59.1	11.1	9.2
D. decumbens	flowering	8.2	60.6	64.0	11.9	9.9
D. decumbens	post-flowering	3.2	17.5	65.9	12.7	10.5
Cynodon dactylon (Star)	immature	12.2	68.4	56.9	11.1	9.2
C. dactylon	mature	8.8	57.9	52.8	10.1	8.4
Hyperrhenia rufa (Jaragua)	mature	5.7	31.8	51.0	9.4	7.8
Brachiaria decumbens (Kenya sheep grass)	flowering	7.8	33.5	60.3	12.3	10.2
Setaria sphacelata (Kazungula)	mature	7.0	51.5	61.4	11.2	9.3
Tripsacum laxum (Guatemala)	mature	7.8	50.5	61.9	12.2	10.1
Brachiaria mutica (Para)	post-flowering	4.5	31.6	57.2	11.6	9.6
Paspalum dilatatum (Dallis)	in flower	9.9	54.1	57.2	11.1	9.2
Pennisetum purpureum (Napier, Elephant)	pre-flowering	9.2	51.6	51.7	10.1	8.4
Oryza sativa (rice)	regrowth	9.0	58.0	55.7	10.7	8.9
Saccharum officinarum (sugar cane)	tops	6.3	50.6	59.3	11.1	9.2

[1] calculated by multiplying digestible energy by 0.83.

nents of the feed. The levels of TDN in some tropical grasses are provided in Table 6.1.

Disadvantages of the various systems The main disadvantage of systems based on net energy is that few studies have been carried out on tropical and subtropical feeds. This is also true of the determination of metabolisable energy which requires sophisticated and expensive equipment in order to estimate the energy losses as methane. Some values are available for the digestible energy content of tropical grasses (Table 6.1) but both this system and metabolisable energy suffer from the disadvantage that they do not reflect the efficiency with which feeds are used for maintenance or for production. The use of TDN is based on hypotheses which are generally unacceptable for ruminant animals, and the additional value given to the ether extract fraction is not warranted in the case of tropical forages because this fraction largely consists of pigments and waxes which are not utilised. Nevertheless, despite these disadvantages, a large amount of data is available for tropical and subtropical grasses and other feeds.

Lipids

These are determined as ether extract in the proximate feed analysis. They comprise glycerides, i.e. esters of fatty acids with glycerol, free fatty acids, cholesterol and other steroids; lecithin, chlorophyll, etc.

In general, tropical forages contain relatively small amounts of ether extract (less than 3.0 per cent of dry matter) and much of this is not available to the animal as it consists of pigments, waxes, etc.

However, lipids are found in other feeds which are commonly used both as supplements and in the formulation of feedlot rations. These include oil seeds and oil seed meals, meat and fish meals and bone meal as well as cereals and cereal by-products.

The content of lipids in any given feed depends a great deal on the manner in which it has been processed. Oil seeds which have been solvent extracted contain less than those which have been extracted using the expeller method and special steamed bonemeal is relatively free of ether extract (less than 1 per cent) while raw bone meal may contain 4 per cent or more.

Most of the digestion of lipids occurs in the rumen. Esterified fatty acids are released by hydrolysis and unsaturated fatty acids are hydrogenated to become saturated. The glycerol and galactose liberated from the lipids are fermented to yield short chain fatty acids.

Lipids are also synthesised in the rumen as they form part of the structural components of bacteria and protozoa. Sometimes more lipid leaves the rumen than enters it; if this escapes digestion in the lower gut, then a negative digestibility coefficient results.

Only a fraction of the free long chain fatty acids is assimilated in the rumen. The fatty acids which originate in the diet together with those from the microbial lipids are absorbed as micelles in the presence of bile and converted into chylomicron triglycerides in the intestinal mucosa.

The depot fats of ruminants are more saturated than those of non-ruminants and characterised by a high content of stearic acid. This is because the dietary fatty acids are hydrogenated in the rumen and thus only saturated acids are incorporated into the chylomicrons for subsequent absorption and deposition.

Lipids also contain 'essential fatty acids' i.e. linoleic and arachidonic acids. These are only of importance in the nutrition of the pre-ruminant animal which received adequate quantities in the colostrum and milk, as well as in body reserves acquired prior to birth.

Minerals

These may conveniently be divided into two groups; those which are required by the body in relatively large quantities, major or macro elements, and those which are only required in small quantities, micro or trace elements. The first group comprises: calcium and phosphorus, sodium and chlorine, potassium, magnesium and sulphur. The second group comprises: cobalt, copper, fluorine, iodine, manganese, selenium, molybdenum and zinc. Iron is required in larger quantities than most trace elements, but is usually grouped with them.

Minerals have many functions in the body. These may be arbitrarily divided into three types; structural, physico-chemical and biochemical.

The physico-chemical functions are largely regulatory. Sodium as sodium bicarbonate in the saliva buffers the contents of the rumen and maintains its pH within acceptable limits, while the chlorine in hydrochloric acid provides the acidity of the true stomach.

Minerals play a biochemical role in metabolic reactions. Thus, phosphorus in adenosine di- and tri-phosphate and phosphocreatinine takes part in the energy transfer reactions of the body while haemoglobin, containing iron, is important in the transport of oxygen. Some minerals form part of enzymes or act as co-enzymes while iodine forms part of the molecule of the hormone thyroxine.

Although all the elements must be present in sufficient quantities in the diet of the animal, some are particularly critical in that they are frequently deficient in the pastures grazed by the beef animal. More emphasis will be given to these in the following discussion.

Calcium and phosphorus Both calcium and phosphorus are important in the formation of strong, healthy bone in the growing animal. Bone acts as a reservoir for both elements during times of shortage and thus short term deficiencies may not be serious. However, in the long term, deficiencies cause bone debility which may lead to fractures.

Phosphorus deficiency, which is relatively common, as will be seen later, causes reduced growth rate and appetite, reduced milk yield in the lactating cow and consequent decreased growth rate of the calf prior to weaning. It was previously thought that a phosphorus deficiency was associated with low levels of fertility but it now seems that there is little evidence to support this belief.

Livestock which have been deprived of phosphorus for some time manifest a characteristic depraved appetite or 'pica', when they are likely to eat soil and chew dry bones. It was this latter tendency which caused outbreaks of botulism ('lamseikte') by the ingestion of the organism *Clostridium botulinum* from rotting meat attached to bone. It was the investigation of this disease in southern Africa which drew attention to the other functions of phosphorus in animal production and which led to the elucidation of much of the subsequent work on this element and on other minerals.

Calcium deficiencies are less common in the

grazing ruminant and cause similar symptoms of bone malformations as those of phosphorus. The two may be differentiated, however, by the levels of the two elements in the blood. When calcium is deficient phosphorus tends to be higher and vice versa.

Levels of both calcium and phosphorus are dependent upon the level of vitamin D in the diet. However, this is not normally a problem in tropical and subtropical climates as levels of radiation from the sunlight are sufficient to ensure that sufficient vitamin D is produced by the animal itself. This takes place by the irradiation of the compound 7-dehydrocholesterol in the coat of the animal.

It is not only the absolute levels of calcium and phosphorus in the diet which are of importance but also the ratio of one to another. In some areas, excesses of calcium interfere with the absorption of phosphorus.

Sodium and chlorine Deficiencies of both these elements are conveniently remedied by supplementation with salt and this should normally be fed free choice to grazing animals or at the rate of 0.1 per cent of dietary dry matter. Lack of salt gives rise to slow growth, impaired appetite and unthriftiness. The consumption of salt commonly varies with soil salinity and the succulence of the forage. More is consumed with succulent than with dry feed.

Salt may be fed either loose or in rock form; although consumption is higher with the former, adequate intakes are maintained with the latter. It is common to use salt as a carrier for other minerals, the use of iodised salt being almost universal and salt is frequently used to increase the palatability of bone meal.

Salt may also be used to limit the consumption of protein supplements where it may constitute from 10 to 40 per cent of the mixture. The exact proportions depend on local conditions and a suitable mixture must be arrived at as a result of experience.

Potassium, magnesium and sulphur Adequate levels of both potassium and magnesium occur in most feeds for beef production in tropical and subtropical areas, although it is possible that excesses of potassium in molasses in some countries could precipitate magnesium deficiencies. Similarly, the provision of sulphur is rarely a problem

although it has been implicated in low methionine synthesis in cases of rations high in NPN and is essential for rumen fungi.

Cobalt Cobalt is important to the ruminant because of its role in the synthesis of vitamin B_{12} by the micro-organisms of the rumen. This vitamin takes part in many reactions in the body including those leading to the formation of red blood cells. It is also implicated in the metabolism of propionic acid which is one of the main products of carbohydrate breakdown in the rumen.

Deficiencies of cobalt have been observed in several tropical and subtropical countries. It has been stated that, next to phosphorus, and possibly copper, it is the mineral which most frequently presents deficiencies in the grazing animal.

Deficiencies have been reported from tropical Africa, Asia and Latin America. Symptoms include loss of appetite and body weight, rapid muscular wasting, depraved appetite and severe anaemia which may result in death. Sub-clinical deficiencies may be diagnosed by levels of the element or of vitamin B_{12} in the liver.

Deficiencies of cobalt may be remedied in several ways. One of the most popular is the use of the cobalt bullet. This is a mixture of cobalt oxide and a hard-setting clay. Because of its high density, the bullet lodges in the rumen or reticulum after oral administration and may remain there for several years. Minute quantities of cobalt oxide are released, sufficient for the needs of the rumen micro-organisms. The efficiency of this release is increased by giving the animal a steel screw or 'grinder' at the same time as the bullet. This grinder removes the layer of calcium phosphate which tends to form round the bullet, inhibiting release. In animals which are given a mineral supplement, cobalt may also be added in the form of oxide or sulphate.

Cobalt is the element which is required in the smallest amount of all the trace elements. The requirement is only between 0.05 and 0.10 mg per kg of dietary dry matter. If a 450 kg steer requires 7 kg dry matter per day, its requirement of cobalt is less than 1 mg.

Copper Copper is present in one of the enzymes involved in respiration (cytochrome oxidase) and also plays a role in haemoglobin synthesis. It is involved in the formation of the dark pigment (melanin) in hair and in the formation of wool protein (keratin).

Deficiencies of this element, while not so common as those of phosphorus, have been observed in many tropical and subtropical countries of Africa, Asia and Latin America as well as Australia. Deficiencies are accompanied by changes in bone structure which cause fragility, by anaemia and by defective pigmentation. In extreme cases, it may cause death ('falling disease' or 'sudden death') and may play a role in infertility. As with cobalt, sub-clinical deficiencies may be indicated by levels of the element in the liver. The only method of diagnosing a deficiency which is entirely reliable, however, is to see whether the animal responds to supplementation.

Deficiencies may be corrected by the addition of copper sulphate at a level of 0.5 per cent to the common salt which is generally fed free choice. Some doubts have been expressed as to the effectiveness of copper sulphate, however, and it may be that copper is more effectively administered as an injection of copper glycinate or edtate.

The requirement for the element is 4 mg per kg of dietary dry matter. However, this may be increased in the presence of high levels of molybdenum or sulphate as these substances inhibit absorption. The use of excessive copper is dangerous as this accumulates in the liver and may be toxic.

Fluorine A definite level of fluorine for beef cattle has not been established. It is more important, however, to avoid an excess than to worry about a deficiency. Fluorine is toxic, causing abnormalities of bones and teeth and it also accumulates in the body. It is often present in rock phosphates and in superphosphate fertiliser and care must be taken that it is removed if these are to be fed to cattle, particularly to breeding stock. Levels of 100 mg and 40 mg per kg of dietary dry matter for finishing and feeding cattle respectively should not be exceeded.

Iodine Iodine is an important constituent of the hormone thyroxine which is produced in the thyroid glands and helps to regulate metabolism. Deficiencies of iodine cause an enlargement of the thyroid glands, known as goitre, which is readily identified by a swelling on the neck. Breeding cows which are deficient in iodine give birth to weak and unthrifty calves which may die soon after birth.

Although little work has been done on iodine in tropical and subtropical countries, it is likely that deficiencies are very widely distributed. Iodine deficiencies occur in the human population of every continent, in almost every country, and it is likely that deficiencies in the cattle population follow a similar distribution.

Despite this wide distribution however, clinical symptoms of deficiencies rarely occur because of the widespread practice of offering iodised common salt free choice. If this is not available, salt may be iodised by the addition of sodium or potassium iodide or of sodium iodate. A quantity of 0.05 per cent potassium iodide has been shown to be sufficient to prevent the appearance of clinical symptoms of iodine deficiency. Iodine may also be administered to animals in their drinking water. A suitable quantity is one tablespoonful per day of a solution of 1.5 g potassium iodide in 1 litre of water.

Salt which has been iodised should not be exposed to strong sunshine as this will reduce the iodine level.

Goitre is not only produced in the case of a deficiency of iodine but also by certain plants which contain goitrogens. These include most members of the *Brassica* family, such as kale, cabbage, rape, etc., but these are not commonly fed to cattle in tropical areas. However, groundnuts also contain these compounds and may cause goitre when fed at high levels of the diet.

Zinc Zinc forms part of several enzymes which are essential for both digestion and cellular metabolism. A deficiency in beef cattle causes a condition known as parakeratosis which is recognised by skin lesions. Although deficiencies of this element were described only recently, it is likely that they are more widespread than had originally been supposed.

The requirement of zinc in beef cattle amounts to some 20 to 30 mg per kg of dietary dry matter. Deficiencies may be remedied by the incorporation of zinc sulphate into the common salt.

Molybdenum, manganese and selenium Although it is likely that molybdenum, manganese and selenium are essential for beef cattle, it has not been conclusively demonstrated that deficiencies of these occur in practice and they are not therefore dealt with in detail here.

Iron Although the importance of this element as part of the haemoglobin molecule is well known, tropical soils and forages seem to be relatively rich in iron and the only occasion where a deficiency has been conclusively demonstrated is in subtropical Florida.

Vitamins

Vitamin A Apart from its part in the processes of vision, the role of vitamin A in metabolism has still not been fully clarified. Nevertheless, deficiencies of this vitamin are accompanied by a number of symptoms which may be serious. Milk deficiency of vitamin A results in reduced feed intake and rates of gain. More serious deficiencies result in night blindness, staggering gait and muscular seizures, excessive weeping and keratinisation of the cornea of the eye. Further deficiencies in fattening cattle may cause severe diarrhoea.

In breeding cattle, bulls suffering from vitamin A deficiency lose their sexual activity. Sperm production is decreased and the number of abnormal sperm in the ejaculate increases. Although oestrus in the breeding cow does not appear to be affected, deficient cows become pregnant less easily.

Vitamin A is supplied to the grazing animal from pigments known as carotenoids which are converted into vitamin A in the walls of the intestine and in the liver. The efficiency with which this transformation takes place depends on the type of carotenoid and the animal concerned but may be reduced by stress conditions brought on by high temperatures or disease.

Both vitamin A and its precursors may be stored in the liver for periods of several months and this reserve is usually sufficient to tide the animal over periods of deficiency provided that these are not too long.

The precursors are present in sufficient quantities for the grazing animal when abundant green grass is available but the level diminishes as grasses dry out after the rains. Rations based on such ingredients as maize stover, sugar cane bagasse and cotton seed products may also give rise to deficiencies.

Levels also decrease when feeds are subjected to high temperatures or sunlight for long periods and when feeds are processed by steam, etc. The presence of minerals also catalyses the destruction of vitamin A.

Deficiencies of vitamin A may be corrected by the intramuscular injection of esters of vitamin A, or by the intra-rumenal administration of some vitamin A rich substance such as shark liver oil. Suitable quantities are 0.5, 1.0 and 2.0 million units for calves, fattening cattle and cows respectively.

Vitamin D Vitamin D is closely concerned with the absorption and metabolism of calcium and phosphorus and its deficiency gives rise to rickets as well as decreased feed intake and growth rate. The vitamin is formed by the irradiation of cholecalciferol in the presence of sunlight. For this reason, deficiencies are rare in tropical and subtropical climates where the sun's radiation is not a limiting factor. Vitamin D is also plentiful in sun-cured roughages because of the irradiation of ergocalciferol.

Beef cattle require 275 IU per kg of dry diet.

Vitamin E Vitamin E is an anti-oxidant and is concerned with the absorption and storage of vitamin A. As vitamin E is normally present in adequate amounts in green forages, it is unlikely that deficiencies will be encountered in cattle grazing in tropical and subtropical areas. Deficiencies of this vitamin cause symptoms similar to those caused by lack of selenium. However, although deficiencies of this mineral have been reported from some regions of the tropics and subtropics, it is unlikely that they are as important as those of the other trace minerals already dealt with. Requirements of vitamin E range from 15 to 60 IU (mg) of β-tocopherol per kg of dietary dry matter.

Vitamin K This vitamin is associated with blood clotting and is normally synthesised in the rumen in adequate amounts. In temperate climates, deficiencies are precipitated by the consumption of mouldy clover hays which contain substances called dicoumarins. However, the author has not encountered reports of this occurring in tropical areas.

Vitamin B complex In an animal with a functioning rumen, the vitamins of the B complex are normally synthesised in adequate amounts by the micro-organisms. In the pre-ruminant calf, they are supplied in the milk of the dam.

Exceptions in the adult animal are vitamin B_{12} (cyanocobalamin) which is not synthesised in the absence of cobalt as mentioned earlier. It has also been shown that a deficiency of thiamine (vitamin B_1) can occur in young cattle fed high energy rations. This causes a condition known as polioencephalomalacia (cerebro-cortical necrosis) which is characterised by uncoordinated movement and depression of ruminal activity accompanied by increased levels of blood pyruvate and lactate, thiamine being a co-enzyme in carbohydrate metabolism. This condition can be treated by large doses of thiamine as well as by reducing the concentrate and increasing the roughage proportions in the ration.

Differences in digestive efficiency between cattle and buffalo

Although it has been a traditional belief that buffalo are more efficient than cattle in the digestion of feeds, there is little to support this belief. The structures of the four compartments of the stomach of the two species are basically the same and little difference in digestive ability would be expected.

The few studies that have been carried out indicate that differences between the two species are small, the difference between species being often less than the difference between animals of the same species, in so far as the production of both ammonia and volatile fatty acids in the rumen is concerned. There is some evidence that indicates that the count of micro-organisms in the buffalo is greater than that in cattle but the lack of basic information as to rumen volume, rate of passage, etc., render this comparison of little value. The evidence that buffalo digest fibre better is equivocal but they probably utilise fat more efficiently.

It is certain that a great deal more work must be carried out on the digestive physiology of the buffalo before valid comparisons can be made and firm conclusions be drawn.

The supply of nutrients

The majority of cattle and buffalo in the tropics and subtropics feed on grass which provides their main source of nutrients. This section will deal with the problems of quantity and quality of tropical grasses. Other feeds will be dealt with later when intensive feeding systems are discussed.

Quantity

Grass production in the tropics is characterised by periods of luxurious growth followed by periods of dormancy. The grass becomes dormant either because of lower temperatures, lack of soil moisture or because of a combination of the two. The length of these dormant seasons varies from place to place but in general ranges from four to eight months. There may also be a season of secondary rains which provide a subsidiary peak of production. This variability of supply causes difficulties in herd management. If numbers are suited to dry season availability, the grass will be wasted during the wet season and if stocking rates are adjusted to wet season production, then there is not enough forage during the dry season. In other parts of the world, seasonal surpluses of forage may be utilised by fattening store cattle but in developing countries, the market is rarely sophisticated enough for this to be feasible.

The other method of overcoming seasonal variations is that of forage conservation. This is not the place for an exhaustive treatment of this subject, but the basic methods will be mentioned.

Silage is made by the anaerobic fermentation of grass. This fermentation results in the formation of lactic, acetic and propionic acids which preserve the material in a palatable form. Silage may be made from either natural or cultivated grass and on a small or large scale. Silage has the advantage that it can be made independent of weather conditions. It can be made in simply constructed silos above ground, in pits or even in heaps on the ground. As it is important to exclude oxygen, silage must be well packed and covered by some air-proof material.

Hay is grass which has been dried by exposure to air and sunlight. It may be made from some of the fine-stemmed grasses. *Digitaria* spp., *Cynodon* spp. and *Chloris gayana* make good hay. It must be made when the quality of the grass is still good, i.e. before it has become too mature (see following discussion) and this is often while the weather is rainy; drying is difficult and moulds develop, making the hay unpalatable. If the grass is cut and then left until the weather is drier, there is a leaching of nutrients. Thus, although good quality hay can be made in the tropics, the timing often presents difficulties.

The third, and most common way of conserving forage is as standing hay or forage. In this method, the grass is protected from cattle until it is required for grazing during the dry season. Although this is a good practice with grasses which 'hay' well such as many in the western USA, it is not generally so successful with tropical grasses because they lose nutritive quality quickly as they mature. However, the practice is widely carried out and provides low quality roughage which may be supplemented by protein and other nutrients.

Composition

As tropical grasses mature, their composition changes and the nutritive value declines.

Carbohydrates In general, tropical grasses contain more structural carbohydrates than their temperate equivalents. As the grass matures so these cell wall components increase, as do crude fibre, detergent fibre, lignin, etc. The lignin has a tendency to be further increased by high temperatures on account of the repeated wilting to which grasses in tropical climates are subjected.

Crude protein The percentage of protein in the grass becomes progressively less with increasing maturity. This is because the cell wall fraction increases and that of cell content, which contains most of the protein, decreases. When the plant is dormant metabolic activity is minimal and protein declines. Regrowth of *Cynodon plectostachyus* (star grass), for example, contained 14.7, 12.8 and 7.9 per cent crude protein at 3, 4 and 5 weeks of age respectively. The protein content of mature grasses frequently falls below 2 per cent.

Phosphorus The decline in phosphorus level is similar to that of crude protein. For example, the phosphorus level of *Pennisetum purpureum* (elephant grass) dropped from 0.78 to 0.39 per cent as the grass matured from 30 to 50 days and at 70 days, it contained only 0.23 per cent. Grasses which contain less than 0.14 per cent are generally considered to be deficient but values of 0.05 per cent are frequently encountered.

Carotene As the grass dries out with maturity, the carotene content decreases. This is paralleled by a decrease in ether extract. Grasses which have dried out to a pale straw-like colour are deficient in this precursor of vitamin A.

Digestibility

The decline in the level of the various nutrients mentioned above is also accompanied by a decline in their utilisation or digestibility.

Carbohydrate The energy available from carbohydrate is reduced by an increase of lignin. This is indigestible and is the component which is responsible for protecting the cell contents. Acid detergent fibre contains such fractions as lignin, cutin and tannin-protein complexes and is also negatively correlated with dry matter digestibility.

As digestibility declines so does intake. This is attributable to a decrease in the digestibility of the cell wall fraction. Low protein levels also affect digestion of dry matter adversely. This is probably because the branched chain fatty acids produced by the de-amination of certain aminoacids, are required by the micro-organisms responsible for cellulose breakdown.

Protein As the level of crude protein in a forage decreases, so does its digestibility. This relationship is logarithmic and the values to be expected are shown in Table 6.2. It will be seen that at a protein level of about 2 per cent (the actual value is 2.2 per cent), the digestibility of the protein is zero and below this it becomes negative. This is possible

Table 6.2 Expected digestibility of crude protein at various levels

Crude protein (%)	Digestibility (%)	Digestible crude protein[1] (%)
2	−4.0	–
4	23.7	0.9
6	39.8	2.4
8	51.3	4.1
10	60.2	6.0
12	67.4	8.1
14	73.6	10.3
16	78.9	12.6

[1] % digestible crude protein = % crude protein x % digestibility.

because the body continually excretes protein even though the diet contains low levels of protein or even no protein at all. This endogenous protein originates from undigested residues of digestive enzymes and from cell walls.

The digestibility referred to in Table 6.2 is apparent digestibility; i.e. no correction has been made for the endogenous fraction of the crude protein. When this is done, the corresponding value is the true digestibility coefficient. The level of acid detergent fibre is also highly negatively correlated with digestibility of crude protein. That of crude fibre, on the other hand, is not.

As the level of protein in a forage declines with maturity therefore, so does its digestibility and negative values for digestible crude protein are commonly encountered. This effect is aggravated by simultaneous increases in the fibre fraction of the grass.

Phosphorus It has been shown that the availability (this term is normally used rather than digestibility in the case of minerals) of phosphorus decreases as does the level of this element in the forage. The relationship is logarithmic and is similar to that which occurs with crude protein.

Intake

Another important aspect which must be considered in connection with the supply of nutrients is the amount of forage which the animal will voluntarily consume. This is affected by various factors.

Intake depends on the quantity of herbage on offer. Cattle consume more when forage is dense and bite size is larger than when plants are widely distributed and the animal must spend a longer time in harvesting. Intake is also dependent upon length of time spent grazing. If cattle must seek shade during the hotter times of day or if they are not allowed access to pasture, where night paddocking is practised for example, then intake is naturally diminished. High temperatures *per se* also have a depressant effect on intake as do inadequate supplies of water.

Low intake is associated with low digestibility which is also associated with slower rates of passage through the gut. This occurs with increasing cell wall content of feeds.

Low intakes are also associated with low protein levels, possibly because of a reduction in the rate of cellulose digestion as mentioned previously.

It is apparent that many factors associated with mature grasses in the tropical environment lead to decreased forage intake. Although less emphasis has been given to this aspect of nutrient supply than to digestibility, intake probably plays a more important overall role. However, so many factors intervene in regulating intake that investigation is difficult. It is also difficult to generalise as to what affects intake under any particular set of circumstances.

Other effects

Several other effects accompany increasing maturity. These include:

1 the total production of volatile fatty acids (VFAs) decreases;
2 the number of micro-organisms, both bacteria and protozoa, in the rumen decreases; and
3 the rate of passage of feed through the alimentary tract decreases.

Increasing maturity of forage then is associated with a number of changes, all of which decrease its nutritive value.

Requirements for nutrients

The nutrient requirements of a beef animal depend on its physiological state, whether it is maintaining, losing or gaining weight, whether it is pregnant or barren, and whether it is dry or lactating. Various factors influence requirements within these various categories.

In this section the nutrient requirements for maintenance, reproduction, lactation and growth will be considered.

Maintenance

Requirements for maintenance are affected by weight, activity, ambient temperature, age, and nutritional state.

The heavier an animal is, the greater its nutrient requirements. It has been shown that this does not vary directly with the weight of an animal, but that a small animal has a relatively higher requirement for nutrients than a large one. This is because of its greater surface area per unit weight. This is related to the body weight to the power of 0.75, otherwise known as the metabolic weight. An example will make this clear. An animal of 200 kg has a metabolic body weight of 53 kg and a requirement for metabolisable energy (ME) of 28 MJ whereas an animal whose weight is 400 kg has a metabolic body weight of 89 kg and a requirement for ME of 48 MJ; i.e. its requirement is not twice but only 1.7 times as great.

Maintenance reflects the fasting metabolism of the animal (i.e. the energy expended in the essential activities of the body, e.g. breathing, circulation). However, the activity of the animal in harvesting its food, watering, etc., must also be included. This is difficult to estimate as it depends on the distance the animal has to travel.

When forage is readily available and the animal can obtain its requirements from a small area, the activity increment is small. However, as forage becomes scarce and the area required to harvest its requirements increases, so does the activity increment. In some cases this increased demand for forage can exacerbate overstocking, leading to overgrazing. If this is continued, deterioration of the sward occurs, herbage production is diminished and a vicious circle starts, the animal needing an even greater area to harvest its forage.

A young animal has higher requirements for maintenance than an older one because it is normally more active.

A further factor which affects the maintenance requirement is the ambient temperature. Beef animals are homeothermic; that is, they must maintain their body temperatures within a relatively narrow range, although some cattle, e.g. *Bos indicus* breeds can tolerate a wider range than others. This means that in cold temperatures, they must expend heat in order to maintain their body temperature. This is not important in the tropics, but it should be remembered that energy must be spent to dissipate heat. Thus heat dissipating mechanisms – panting, sweating, etc. – require expenditure of energy. This is not taken into account in the elaboration of feeding standards, but it is of practical importance in animal feeding. This is one reason why feeding becomes less efficient at higher temperatures.

Maintenance requirement is reduced after the animal remains at the same liveweight for some time. Steers of various weights and breeds in Kenya required on average 40 per cent less food than expected after remaining at the same weight for 24 weeks. When restored to normal levels of nutrition, compensatory growth occurs (see below). This has important implications for animals in tropical and subtropical situations which may frequently be exposed to feed shortages.

It is worthwhile noting that an animal which is only maintaining itself is, by definition, not producing. A corollary of this is that a high producer uses a lower percentage of its nutrients for maintenance than a low producer. This is made clear by the data in Table 6.3. As the steer gains increasingly more weight the percentage of the particular nutrient (in this case energy) required for maintenance, decreases.

Reproduction

Two aspects of reproduction must be considered in relation to nutrient requirement. The first important period is when the animal is mated (or joined)

Table 6.3 Requirement for maintenance and growth at different rates of gain

Expected weight gain (g per day)	Requirements for maintenance (MJ per day)	Total requirements (MJ per day)	Maintenance requirements as % of total
0	29.4	29.4	100
500	29.4	50.8	58
700	29.4	54.6	54
900	29.4	55.9	53
1100	29.4	59.2	50

and the second is the last third of gestation when the foetus and related tissues require significant quantities of nutrients.

The requirement for additional nutrients at breeding time is reflected in the feeding standards. However, it is well known that when a number of cows are put to the bull, those that are heavier or in best condition are the most likely to conceive or reconceive. Hence the importance of having cows in good breeding condition before joining. Practical farm management indicates that cows which are in poor condition may be given additional feed at this time. Additional feed also frequently has the effect of bringing hitherto anoestrus cows into heat and tends to reduce the spread of the calving season. Adequate protein is of great importance.

It is also important for the bull to be in good condition at the start of the breeding season to ensure that sperm production is adequate and that abnormal spermatozoa are at a minimum.

Additional nutrients are also required during the last 3 to 4 months before parturition. The foetus grows slowly for the first 5 to 6 months of pregnancy and although nutrients are required, they may be supplied without difficulty from the cow's daily intake or reserves. However, during the last third of pregnancy, the weight gain due to the products of conception is approximately 0.4 kg per day, or some 35 to 40 kg over the last 90 days. This includes not only the contribution of the foetus, but the associated membranes and tissues, the placenta and also the increased mammary development which occurs before parturition. As a rough rule of thumb, additional weight gain during pregnancy should be about twice the birth weight of the calf.

Particular nutrients which are important during pregnancy include protein, calcium and phosphorus. A deficiency of iodine may lead to the birth of a goitrous calf. Other elements are not so critical. A deficiency of iron in the cow is not passed on to the calf which appears to behave as a parasite for this element, though an iron deficiency may become critical later because of low iron levels in the milk.

A deficiency of vitamin A in the diet of the mother may cause deficiencies in the calf and therefore this vitamin is important during pregnancy.

Detailed requirements of the buffalo cow during gestation have not been calculated. However, the gestation period of buffalo is longer than that of cattle (about 278 and 280–290 days or more respectively) while the birth weight of the buffalo calf is about 28 ($\pm$ 5.7) kg and 23 ($\pm$ 3.9) kg for males and females respectively which are larger than those for many tropical breeds of cattle. It would be expected therefore that the requirements of the buffalo cow may be somewhat higher than those of the Zebu cow. However, there is some evidence from Papua New Guinea that buffalo cows are better able to withstand a lower level of nutrition during lactation than cattle and still reconceive. Buffalo also responded more favourably to supplementation during lactation than did the cows. In total, the calf crop from the buffalo was some 50 per cent higher than that of the cows during the three years of the trial despite the fact that the gestation period of the cow is shorter.

Lactation

The importance of the drain of nutrients caused by lactation is readily appreciated by scoring a herd of breeding cows for physical condition after weaning. In such an appraisal, of a commercial herd in Malawi, the only cows to be classified as 'fat' (when judged as fat, medium and compound) were those which had not reared a calf.

Several factors influence nutrient requirements for lactation including the following: quantity of milk produced, stage of lactation and milk composition. Relatively little work on the lactation of the beef or buffalo cow has been carried out but the following points are of importance.

The milk production of a cow increases as the cow matures from first calving to 6 to 8 years of age and thereafter declines, although the second lactation may be lower than the first because of poor management or environmental stress. The milk yield is also influenced by the size of the calf as it is, in part, a response to suckling. The lactation curve tends to reach its peak rather later than does that of the dairy cow.

The quantity of milk is dependent on the breed of the animal; normally Zebu breeds produce less than European beef breeds and so-called dual purpose breeds produce more. The Simmental, for example, may produce so much milk under good conditions of management that the calf is not able to consume it all and the cow must be milked or used for multiple suckling. The persistence of the beef cow is not generally as great as that of the dairy cow (particularly in the case of the Zebu breeds) so that little is to be gained by weaning the calf after 205 days.

A beef cow of a European breed produces from 5 to 10 kg of milk per day and a calf requires about 5 to 6 kg of milk per kg of liveweight gain. This would be equivalent to approximately 1 000 kg of milk in a standard 205 day lactation. The additional daily requirements for protein due to lactation at this level is some 450 g per day. If feeding standards for dairy cattle are compared, this is equivalent to a daily production of about 6 kg of milk with a butterfat percentage of 3.5 per cent. Recent feeding standards have differentiated between high and moderate yielding cows in terms of nutrient requirements and it is interesting that not only is more protein required for the high yielding cow, but that the protein concentration of the diet has also been increased from 9.2 to 10.8 per cent.

It is the function of a beef cow to give birth to a calf each year and to wean it at the highest weaning weight with as little additional feed as possible. This means that creep feeding (giving additional feed to the calf before weaning) is a practice that cannot be recommended in management systems based on grazing. Creep feeding has the additional disadvantage that it obscures the effect of the milk yield of the dam on the weaning weight of the calf and makes selection of the cow herd on calf weaning weights impossible.

The nutrient requirements for milk production vary with the composition of the milk. The butterfat component is particularly important in this respect. Although the requirements have not been worked out in detail for beef cows, the following requirements for dairy cattle may be of interest.

It should be noted from Table 6.4 that as butterfat increases, not only do the requirements for energy increase, but so too do those for protein. This is a reflection of the increased metabolic activity. Milk composition varies during the lactation, values for butterfat and protein being somewhat higher at the beginning and end of the lactation while lactose exhibits the opposite trend.

The breed of the cow also affects milk composition. As in the case of dairy animals, some breeds give consistently higher levels of butterfat than others.

In general, the breeds that give least milk give a higher level of butterfat. Zebu and Sanga cattle give low yields of milk with high butterfat, often more than 5 per cent.

Diet may also influence milk composition. When new spring grass is available, the grass contains low levels of fibre and the rumen fermentation results in low levels of acetic acid. This in its turn may result in low levels of butterfat because acetic acid is an important precursor of this fraction. The buffalo cow has often been shown to produce 1 700–2 200 kg of milk in a lactation with good management and yields of up to 4 500 kg have been reported. However, the figure of 500 kg/lactation is used by the Government of India to predict the

Table 6.4 The requirements for nutrients of milk with varying butterfat content

Butterfat (%)	Protein (g per l)	Metabolisable energy (KJ per l)	Calcium (g per l)	Phosphorus (g per l)
2.5	66	3.8	2.4	1.7
3.0	70	4.2	2.5	1.8
3.5	74	4.4	2.6	1.9
4.0	78	4.8	2.7	2.0
4.5	82	5.1	2.8	2.1
5.0	86	5.4	2.9	2.2
5.5	90	5.7	3.0	2.3
6.0	94	6.0	3.1	2.4

yield of peasant-owned buffalo over the whole of this sector.

The milk production of unselected buffalo cows may be slightly higher than equivalent beef cows but weaning weights obtained for buffalo calves indicate similar yields and persistence of lactation. On the other hand, buffalo milk is much higher in butterfat than cow's milk (Table 6.5).

Total feed requirements of the herd

Table 6.6 shows the actual feed requirements of the beef cow according to the various physiological states throughout the year. Values have been calculated for both high and low producing animals. It is interesting that in both cases, the feed required for maintenance accounts for by far the greatest proportion of the total. A barren cow needs more than three-quarters of the feed required by a cow that rears and weans a calf of 200 kg or more.

The table shows that a productive cow needs approximately 3 mt of feed dry matter per year. This is important to bear in mind when assessing stocking rate in terms of pasture productivity.

Table 6.7 Factors for converting various age groups of cattle into livestock units

Mature cow with calf	1.0
Mature bull	1.25
Two year old	0.9
Yearling	0.5
Weaned calf	0.2

In an integrated beef herd, mother cows are not the only stock to be fed. Provision must also be made for the requirements of followers. Total forage requirements may be calculated as follows. Stock in the herd are converted to livestock units (LSUs) by the use of factors which allow conversion from one kind or class of animal to another. Generally accepted factors are given in Table 6.7.

The requirements of a herd of cattle comprising various age groups may be calculated by the use of the appropriate factors. The example given in Table 6.8 will make this clear. The total feed requirements for the herd for one year are therefore $218 \times 2\,916$ kg, or approximately 635 mt.

Table 6.5 Composition of buffalo milk and cow's milk (percentage by weight)

Type of milk	Butterfat	Protein	Lactose	Total solids	Water
Buffalo	7.64	4.36	4.83	17.96	82.40
Bos taurus cow	3.90	3.47	4.75	12.82	87.18
Bos indicus (Zebu) cow	4.97	3.18	4.59	13.45	86.55

Table 6.6 Requirements of the beef cow according to physiological state

Physiological state	Days	Requirement of dry matter (kg per day)	Total dry matter (kg)	Percentage of requirement Low yielding	Percentage of requirement High yielding
Maintenance	365	6.1	2226.5	86	76
Gestation	90	1.4	126.0	5	4
Lactation (5 l per day)	90	2.7	243.0	9	–
Lactation (10 l per day)	120	4.7	564.0	–	19
Total					
(5 l per day)			2595.5		
(10 l per day)			2916.5		

Table 6.8 Conversion of a herd into livestock units

	Number	Conversion factor	Livestock units
Mature cows	100	1.00	100.0
Bulls	4	1.25	5.0
Two year olds	58	0.90	52.2
Yearlings	62	0.70	43.4
Weaned calves	68[1]	0.60	17.0
Total	292		218

[1] Five months only because weaned at 7 months.

Incidentally, the above example is based on the actual number of animals expected in a herd when the following assumptions are made: calving percentage 75 per cent; mortality 5 to 10 per cent; replacement rate of cows 15 per cent per annum; replacement rate of bulls 25 per cent per annum; age at first calving 3 years; and age at slaughter 3 years. These are fairly typical for a well managed operation where young stock are farm fattened to slaughter. Total herd requirements in this system are therefore rather more than double the require-

ments of the cows alone. An alternative system would be to sell all the weaners except those required for replacements. This would enable more mother cows to be kept.

There are many alternative systems but the type of operation to be carried out must be based on the total feed resources available.

Management of the breeding herd

The individual nutrients and the requirements of the cow during pregnancy and lactation have been

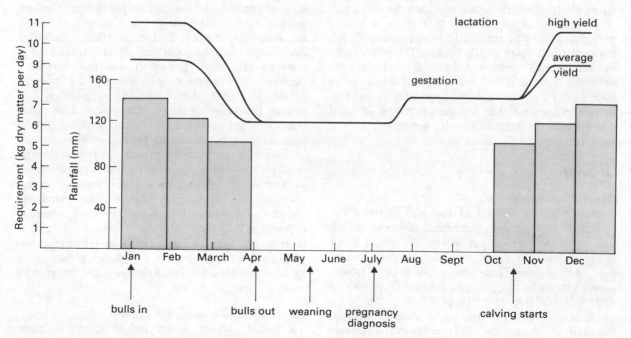

fig. 6.2 Management of the breeding herd according to requirement and rainfall (750 mm over 6 months)

97

considered, as have the nutritional characteristics of tropical forages. A management calendar which enables periods of maximum requirement to co-incide with seasons of maximum forage availability may now be constructed. An example is shown in fig. 6.2.

For purposes of this model, it has been assumed that the rainy season starts in October and ends in March and that the period of maximum forage availability will thus be about December. The requirements of the breeding cow (as in Table 6.6) are shown graphically and it may be seen that the nutritional requirement is highest soon after the birth of the calf. As the calf grows and its require-ments for milk increase, more forage becomes avail-able. The main stimulus for milk production in the beef cow comes from the suckling action of the calf which is at its maximum between one and two months after birth. If the breeding season starts in December, therefore, the cows should be in good condition and calving will take place before the period of maximum forage availability so that this coincides with the maximum requirements of the cow. The figure also shows other periods of nu-tritional stress, during late gestation for example, when additional supplementation of protein and phosphorus may be required to compensate for the poor nutritive value of the forage. The other dates in the management calendar depend on the breeding season. It will be seen that the weaning date comes early enough for there still to be suf-ficient forage available for the calf to be in good condition at the start of the dry season.

Growth

General considerations
Growth may be defined as the sum of those co-ordinated biological and chemical processes which start with the fertilisation of the ovum and finish when the body size and physiological functions of the adult animal have been attained. Growth consists basically of cell multiplication (hyperplasis) and cell enlargement (hypertrophy) but also involves storage of nutrients in excess of those required for maintenance. True growth is irrever-sible as opposed to storage which may represent a temporary phase after which stored nutrients may be utilised by the animal during times of need.

Growth takes place according to an orderly sequence, or gradient. Growth of skeletal and nervous tissue has precedence over all other growth while the head has precedence over the body. At birth, cattle have large heads, long legs and shallow bodies. As the animal matures, the round and loin grow at a faster rate than the head and extremities as these have already almost attained their adult size at birth. Growth is not only an increase in body weight therefore, but is accompanied by a change in form and proportion.

Growth occurs in two phases; the self-accelerating phase and the self-inhibiting phase. The in-flection of the growth curve (i.e. the linkage of these two phases) represents the time of maximum velocity of growth and occurs in cattle at about six months of age, i.e. just before weaning in the normal beef animal.

Growth is under the control of various hormones. These include the growth hormone or somatotropin from the anterior pituitary, the thyroid hormone, the gonadal hormones and hormones from the adrenal cortex. The androgenic hormones from the gonads have a stimulating effect on growth while the oestrogens have a depressant effect. Similarly, deoxycorticosterone from the adrenal cortex stimu-lates growth while hydrocortisone and cortisone depress it. Thyroxine is necessary for normal growth but either hypo- or hyper-thyroidism can disturb the growth pattern. The effect of all these hormones is integrated and factors which augment growth do so by increasing protein synthesis.

Growth is an anabolic process and is character-ised in the young animal by the deposition of protein in the muscular tissue and of minerals in the skeleton. As the animal matures, this emphasis changes to the deposition of fat. However, some fat deposition does occur during the first phase and it is probable that 10 per cent of the gains of the young animal represent fat. It is difficult, therefore, to draw an accurate dividing line between growth and fattening.

Nutrient requirements for growth
The main factors which influence the nutrient requirements for growth are rate of gain and live-

Table 6.9 Nutrient requirements for growing-finishing calves and yearlings of two weights with different daily gains (nutrient concentration in diet dry matter)

Weight (kg)	Daily gain (kg)	Roughage (%)	Total protein (%)	Metabolisable energy (MJ per kg)	Total digestible nutrients (%)	Calcium (%)	Phosphorus (%)
100	0	100	8.7	8.4	55	0.18	0.18
	0.5	70–80	12.4	9.2	62	0.48	0.38
	0.7	50–60	14.8	10.5	70	0.70	0.48
	0.9	25–30	16.4	11.8	77	0.86	0.57
	1.1	15	18.2	13.0	86	1.04	0.70
400	0	100	8.5	8.4	55	0.18	0.18
	1.0	45–55	9.4	10.9	72	0.22	0.21
	1.2	20–25	10.2	11.8	80	0.27	0.25
	1.3	15	10.4	13.0	86	0.29	0.26
	1.4	15	10.5	13.0	86	0.29	0.26

weight for age. The higher the rate of gain which is expected, the higher the level of any particular nutrient which is required. This is shown clearly in Table 6.9.

The concentration of protein required by a growing–finishing steer calf or yearling weighing 100 kg from not gaining weight to gaining 1.1 kg per day, increases from 8.7 per cent to 18.2 per cent, or more than twofold. The increases for calcium and phosphorus are even more dramatic, being sixfold and fourfold respectively.

The effect of nutrients on liveweight is also demonstrated by Table 6.9. While the maintenance requirement for protein in the older and heavier animal is similar to that of the younger animal, the concentration required for the maximum rate of gain is only 10.5 per cent. This is also shown clearly by the values for calcium and phosphorus where the levels required at the maximum rate of gain are only about 150 per cent of those required for maintenance alone. These values indicate that the emphasis has changed from the deposition of muscle and skeletal tissue to the accumulation of fat. This is of practical importance because fat, having a high energy value, is more expensive to deposit when high-energy concentrates are in short supply.

Weight gain and carcass composition

There is a wide range in daily liveweight gains of beef cattle on tropical and subtropical grasslands. Gains are affected by the type of grass, breed of animal, management system, amount of rainfall and many other factors. However, it seems likely that daily gains to be expected under reasonable circumstances would range between 700 and 800 g per day. This is consistent with the nutritive content of the grasses and the requirements of the growing animal. It is recognised that much higher values have been achieved on grass/legume pastures and highly fertilised swards but it is considered that these growth rates are exceptional.

There are far fewer data for buffalo. Few valid trials have been carried out which compare the growth rate of buffalo with beef cattle under similar conditions. Some growth rates are shown in Table 6.10. It seems likely from inspection of the data that growth rates of buffalo would be similar to that of beef cattle. It would also be expected that selection would rapidly increase potential growth rates. There is a large variation among animals and very little selection for growth rate has been carried out to date.

The carcass composition of beef animals under tropical conditions has not received much attention, probably because of the cost and labour required for this type of investigation. However, excellent data for Boran cattle are available from Kenya. Cattle were killed at various ages and carcass dissections carried out. Some of the results are

Table 6.10 Comparative weight gains of buffalo and cattle found in specific studies

Species and breed	Weight gain (g per day)	Remarks
Buffalo (Russian)	1123	Buffalo more efficient than cattle; 93 days on feed
Local Russian cattle	680	
Buffalo (Egyptian)	630	Semi-intensive feeding to 18-months
Native Egyptian cattle	420	
Russian buffalo	933–1140	Intensive fattening
Yugoslavian buffalo	810–1500 (mean: 1097)	Intensive feeding; 5% worse performance than cattle 105 days on feed
Buffalo, Northern Territory, Australia	560	All hay fed
	670	All pellets
	640	¾ hay, ¼ pellets
	740	¾ pellets, ¼ hay
Angus steers	720	
Friesian steers	880	All concentrate ration
Hereford steers	1080	
Murrah buffalo	360	Grazed on limited *Brachiaria brizantha* pastures
Local buffalo (Sri Lanka)	370	
Sinhala	270	
Red Sindhi	300	
Friesian	130	
Buffalo, Trinidad	617	Grazed on medium quality *Digitaria decumbens* pastures
Jamaica Red	477	
Brahman	295	
Buffalo, Trinidad	667	Grazing good *Digitaria decumbens* pastures
Buffalo, Trinidad (Buffalypso)	512	Grazing *Digitaria decumbens* pastures
Buffalo, Pakistan	500	Males
Sahiwal	400	
Red Sindhi	300	
Thari	400	

shown in Table 6.11. It is clear that as the animals get older, the proportion of fat deposited increases while that of lean decreases. Later work carried out in Kenya showed that of 88 Boran and crossbred steers to be dissected, 49 (or 56 per cent) had a carcass fat content of over 20 per cent. These values for African Zebu cattle are in close agreement with values of 26.1 per cent separable fat in Zebu carcasses dissected in the southern USA. Comparable values for British beef breeds were 32.8 per cent. It has been shown that the per-

Table 6.11 Fat and lean in carcasses of Boran steers killed at different ages

Age at slaughter (years)	Lean (% cold carcass wt)	Fat (% cold carcass wt)
1.5	64.4	17.6
2.5	64.9	17.9
3.5	59.4	26.6
4.0	55.6	33.2
5.0	54.3	34.6

centage of fat in a beef carcass also depends on the rate of fattening as well as the age of the animal. To put this another way, rapid fattening leads to the same level of fatness being reached at lower carcass weights. This means that with the current demand for a carcass with less fat, rations using more roughage may be used.

Less information is available for the buffalo. It was shown in Australia that when some British breeds of cattle were compared with buffalo after fattening, the carcass fat content was much lower in the buffalo. This data is shown in Table 6.12. Not only did the buffalo go on feed with less carcass fat, they also put on far less fat during the period spent in the feedlot (131 days).

Table 6.12 Proportion of fat in the carcass on entry to the feedlot and at slaughter of buffalo steers compared with three British breeds

Breed	Fat as a percentage of carcass weight	
	Entry	Slaughter
Angus	23.3	39.4
Friesian	21.5	23.3
Hereford	21.6	35.7
Buffalo	8.7	12.0

Further studies carried out by the same workers showed that the type of diet fed (i.e. ratio of concentrates to roughages) had little effect on the total quantity of fat to be deposited and also that it was extremely difficult for the buffalo to put on high levels of fat. Levels of more than 20 per cent dissectable fat were only reached after more than 260 days or about 8.5 months in the feedlot. The above results are similar to those obtained in Bulgaria with three different breeds of buffalo. After a fattening period of 130 days, total dissectable fat in the carcass was only about 10 per cent.

It is fairly clear then, that buffalo, however fattened, produce a carcass with a lower percentage of fat in it than beef cattle fattened under similar circumstances. This finding has several practical implications. Buffalo do not require rations high in concentrates; this is important in the tropics where concentrates are expensive and may be needed for human food. The buffalo produces a carcass with a low fat content which is popular with the modern consumer. Thirdly, since fat is the body tissue with the highest energy content, gain in weight in buffalo should be more economical than a similar gain in beef cattle. Although, again, little evidence is available on this point, there are some indications that the growing buffalo uses food slightly more efficiently than beef animals. This is also supported by evidence from the Northern Territory of Australia where buffalo have survived and cattle have not.

Compensatory growth

The growth of an animal usually takes place at a more rapid rate than normal after periods of undernutrition. This phenomenon is known as compensatory growth. The extent of this ability to recover from undernutrition depends on various factors. These include the nature, severity and duration of the period of undernutrition and the pattern of subsequent feeding.

The recovery of weight appears to be because of both a lengthening of the growth period and an increase in the rate of weight gain. This latter factor appears to be a result of various interacting mechanisms. These include an enhanced efficiency of utilisation of feed and increased appetite.

Some indications of the extent of this improved efficiency have been obtained by the work on Boran steers already referred to in the section on maintenance requirements. It has been suggested that the increased efficiency accompanying reduced feeding (i.e. some 40 per cent) persists, in steadily decreasing degrees, for up to 15 weeks after the start of realimentation.

The phenomenon of compensatory growth has several important implications in beef cattle production in the tropics. It has already been pointed out that growth is often restricted by insufficient pasture of poor quality. However, this is generally followed by periods when good quality pasture is available in large quantities. Compensatory growth occurs and usually this is sufficient to outweigh any transient advantage to be obtained by supplementation during periods of scarcity. Thus the usual post-weaning check encountered in beef calves may generally be ignored provided the calves enter the dry season in reasonable condition.

The other aspect of compensatory growth which has considerable commercial application is that of realimentation of adult animals off poor range. Economically attractive gains in weight and in carcass quality can be obtained by feeding such animals on relatively inexpensive rations. The most usual length of such fattening periods is about 100 days, corresponding closely with the period of increased efficiency mentioned earlier.

Intensive feeding

Management of the intensively-fed animal is different from that of the grazing animal in several respects. The most important of these is that while the grazing animal enjoys considerable liberty to select its own diet, the stall-fed animal is entirely dependent on the feeder for its supply of nutrients. It is therefore extremely important that all nutrients are supplied in the ration.

Because of the confined nature of the stall feeding or feedlot operation, it is important that strict attention is paid to disease control. Once established a disease can spread extremely rapidly.

Similarly, initial processing is important. Cattle must be vaccinated against diseases prevalent in the area and dipped to ensure that they are tick-free when they enter the lot. Growth stimulants, e.g. stilboestrol, resorcylic acid lactone, etc. and injections of vitamin A are also given at this time.

Once the animals are in the feedlot, care must be taken to ensure that they do not suffer from digestive upsets while becoming accustomed to the concentrate ration. Good quality hay, molasses and salt may be fed free choice for several days. Clean water must always be available. Concentrates may then be introduced and slowly increased until the animals are on full feed after two or three weeks.

Some breeds are not suited to feedlot fattening and suffer from 'laminitis' or lameness induced by excessive consumption of concentrates.

The proportion of concentrate is usually increased as the animal finishes until it constitutes 50 per cent or more of the ration. However, in some feedlot operations in tropical and subtropical climates, cattle do not attain the same level of finish as would be expected in a temperate climate and lower levels of concentrate can be used. Similarly, shorter feeding periods may be indicated for some tropical breeds of cattle, and for mature animals which are brought into the feedlot after periods of relative feed scarcity on range.

The appropriate slaughter weight for any particular breed must also be considered; if an attempt is made to take an animal to a final weight which is too high for the breed, rate of gain will decrease and feed conversion efficiency (the quantity of feed eaten per unit of gain in liveweight) will increase.

A number of systems which have been effectively used in the tropics and subtropics will be briefly mentioned below in order to give some indication of possible feeding regimes.

Maize silage and maize grain
This is the typical traditional system in the USA and elsewhere. The roughage part of the ration is derived from maize silage and the concentrate from flaked or rolled maize together with a protein supplement normally composed of an appropriate oil seed meal. It has been difficult to implement in developing countries because of the widespread dependence on maize grain as a human staple and because of competition for land with reasonably high rainfall which is required for the production of maize silage. Feedlot operations in South Africa and Zimbabwe and experimental feedlots in Kenya have used this system effectively.

Sorghum silage and agricultural by-products
After trials were made on a wide range of forage sorghums in Kenya, it was found that some of these could out-yield maize by more than 100 per cent. Sorghum also requires less rainfall than maize and can therefore be grown in areas that are marginal for cultivation of food crops. In Kenya, sorghum silage has been fed to complement maize germ and bran meal (hominy, which is a by-product of maize milling for human consumption), molasses and urea and pyrethrum marc. The latter is the residue from the pyrethrum plant after the insecticide has been extracted. However, for a variety of reasons there is no longer a viable feedlot industry in Kenya.

Grass silage Grass silage has the advantage that it may be made at any time of year and that grass production often exceeds the animals' capacity to eat it. Grass silage has been effectively used in stall-feeding programmes in Malawi where it has been fed with crop residues such as groundnut tops as well as maize bran or *madea*. Successful use of grass silage has also been made in Swaziland where veld grass silage has been fed with urea/molasses and whole cotton seed.

Molasses Molasses provides the major source of energy for fattening cattle in Cuba and elsewhere. Molasses with urea (2.5 per cent dissolved in water) is fed free choice with a restricted quantity of fresh cut forage (10 to 15 kg). This ration is limiting in 'by-pass' protein and is supplemented with fishmeal containing protein of low solubility at the rate of 300 to 500 g per day.

Sugar cane Because it is a highly efficient producer of readily available energy compared with other crops, sugar cane has been fed as the main component of fattening rations in various parts of the world. It was originally thought that it was necessary to remove the hard outer rind of the cane before feeding to cattle but utilisation is not impaired if the cane is chopped using either a machete or forage harvester.

Bagasse This is the highly lignified (20 per cent) residue left after the extraction of sugar from cane. Although most of it is used for fuel or for the production of paper and other materials, the pith or short fibres may be used in feedlot rations, where roughage is in short supply. In Mexico, bagasse pith has been substituted for maize stover up to a level of 27.5 per cent of the ration before efficiency was impaired. It is worth noting that although vitamin A levels in the rations of feedlot animals must always be carefully adjusted, rations based on bagasse and maize stover tend to be particularly deficient. Bagasse is also useful as a carrier for molasses. This increases both its nutritive value and palatability. Ratios of bagasse to molasses which have been used successfully in commercial mixtures range from 1:2.5 to 1:6.

Crop residues Many crop residues may be used in intensive feeding. A flourishing smallholder fattening scheme has been built up in Malawi based on the use of maize stover and *madea*. The latter is the maize germ and bran meal produced in the home by the use of the *mtondo* or pestle and mortar, and which the stall feeder obtains by bartering for salt. This may be supplemented with groundnut or bean haulm, sweet potato or cassava tops and fresh-cut green grass. A good market is available for the fattened animal, which is not normally more than six tooth at slaughter, and the smallholder makes a considerable margin.

Pineapple waste The processing of pineapples for canning is accompanied by large quantities of waste products. Although these were originally dried to produce a highly nutritive pineapple bran, this process is becoming less common because of the high moisture content of the waste and consequent high energy requirements for drying. An alternative has been developed in Malaysia which depends on the ensilage of the waste. Broiler poultry litter, oil palm waste and bakery waste/molasses are the principal additives. High margins are possible because use is made of waste resources of negligible commercial value. A further waste product derivable from the pineapple is the top, and although this is of relatively low nutritive value, it may be ensiled with molasses or pineapple cannery waste to make a useful roughage.

Cereal straws Cereal straws have generally been avoided in feeding operations because of their high lignin content which is sometimes combined with high levels of silica, the exception being maize stover. However, recent methods have improved the digestibility of these crop residues considerably by treatment with alkali and more lately, ammonia. This separates the uronic acids of the hemicelluloses from the lignin and thus allows them to be attacked by the enzymes of the rumen micro-organisms. The process originally involved soaking the straw in large volumes of liquid alkali. This has become unacceptable because it is highly labour intensive and water-polluting. However, a dry method has been developed which is more acceptable. Although little application has been made of this method in the tropics and subtropics, except in Sri Lanka, it might be promising because of the large quantities of highly lignified materials available. Ammoniated straw has also been successfully used in fattening programmes.

Citrus The use of citrus waste as cattle feed was pioneered in Florida but is now practised in most countries where a citrus canning industry exists. Cattle can be fed fresh waste citrus with no ill effects although these are better fed chopped so as to avoid the danger of them sticking in the oesophagus. Citrus waste, after processing, spoils readily and therefore is better ensiled. The waste can also be dried after adding lime to destroy the hydrophilic properties of the pectin. The dried citrus pulp or citrus meal is a good quality, high energy feed with an energy content only slightly lower than that of grain sorghum, and it may be used as the principal concentrate component of fattening rations. It should be pointed out, however, that although high in calcium, citrus pulp is low in phosphorus as well as protein and that care must be taken to ensure that vitamin supplementation is adequate. It is probable that, as with pineapple waste, increased energy costs would make ensiling a more attractive proposition than drying.

The above examples are not exhaustive but give some indication of methods which have been successfully used in developing countries. Intensive feeding has met with some criticism as being suitable only for capital intensive operations, catering to a luxury market, competing with humans for nutrients, etc. The previous examples have shown that intensive feeding may have an important role to play under specific conditions in some tropical countries. Further reference to this subject is made in Chapter 7.

Further reading

Butterworth, M. H. (1967). The digestibility of tropical grasses. *Nutrit. Abs. Revs.* **37**, 349–368.

Butterworth, M. H. (1985). *Beef cattle nutrition and tropical pastures*. Longman: London.

Chalmers, M. I. (1974). Nutrition. In *The husbandry and health of the domestic buffalo*, **ed. W. Ross Cockrill**. FAO: Rome.

Devendra, C. (1980). The potential value of grasses and crop by-products for feeding buffaloes in Asia. In *Buffalo production on small farms*, **ed. Tetangco Milagros.** Food and Fertiliser Technology Centre: Taiwan.

Göhl, B. I. (1975). *Tropical feeds; feeds information summaries and nutritive values*. FAO: Rome.

Ledger, H. P. and **Sayers, A. R.** (1977). The utilisation of dietary energy by steers during periods of restricted feed intake and subsequent realimentation. *J. Agric. Sci. (Camb.)* **88**, 11–26.

NRC (1981). *The water buffalo: new prospects for an underutilised animal*. National Research Council: Washington.

Van Soest, P. J. (1982). *Nutritional ecology of the ruminant*. O. and B. Books Inc.: Corvallis, Oregon.

7 Management systems

Beef cattle management systems in those countries where cattle industries have been highly developed may be divided into intensive and extensive systems. These may operate separately, or what is more general, with one system depending upon another in a process referred to as 'stratification'. In the very different socio-economic and agronomic situation in the tropics, however, traditional systems of livestock management relate to local farming practices. Varying degrees of intensive production may be found on mixed sedentary subsistence farms, while pastoralism in one form or another may exist in the drier areas.

With the exception of the pastoralist systems in Africa the majority of cattle in the tropics are managed in traditional systems of small-scale mixed farming or sedentary subsistence agriculture (Table 7.1).

Table 7.1 Distribution of cattle and buffalo by system in the tropics

System	Number of bovines (millions)	Bovines as % of total	Type of bovine reared
Nomadic herding	32	5	Cattle
Transhumance	63	10	Cattle
Commercial ranching	180	29	Cattle
Migratory shifting cultivation	6	1	Cattle
Sedentary shifting cultivation	30	5	Cattle and buffalo
Sedentary subsistence cultivation	290	46	Cattle and buffalo
Regulated ley farming	15	2	Cattle
Perennial crop cultivation	15	2	Cattle and buffalo

Pastoralism

Pastoralism is most important in the Sahelian zone of tropical Africa and in East Africa, north of the equator (fig. 7.1) from the west coast to Somalia. The Sahelian zone has a carrying capacity of over 33 million livestock units (LSU), equivalent to one-quarter of the livestock population of tropical Africa. This vast area is occupied by different pastoralist and agro-pastoralist groups. In West Africa, pastoralists include the Tuareg and Fulani of Mali and Niger and the Annakaza of Chad, the latter predominantly an arid zone camel-based people with high mobility and almost no links with agriculture. The Fulani of Burkina Faso and the Fulani and Tuareg of Niger are pastoral societies in which livestock are associated with a degree of rainfed dry land cropping, and some cultivation and exchange of manure for stubble grazing. Another distinctive sub-group of transhumant pastoralists are the Fulani of Mali. Their animal production practices include floodplains grazing and farming. Agro-pastoralists practise little mobility, cropping being the major component of their systems. Cattle are used mainly for milk production and sometimes for draught purposes.

In East Africa pastoralist groups include, among others, the Maasai, Suk and Turkana of Kenya, the Karamajong of Uganda, the Somali of Somalia, and the Borana of Ethiopia. All these have mixed herds and flocks of cattle, sheep and goats and some, such as the Turkana, the Borana and the Somali, also graze camels. The nomadic pastoralist occupies semi-arid and savanna lands, moving in response to the seasonal grazing and water needs of his herds and flocks. The perennial search for grazing and water places intense pressure upon him, especially during periods of drought; often he is forced, while in search of grazing, to take his stock into tsetse fly areas, risking infection from trypanosomiasis (see Chapter 8). Furthermore, in much of Africa his accustomed dry season pastures are being encroached upon by arable farmers.

Livestock in each selected area may be moved in rotation around the various watering points for

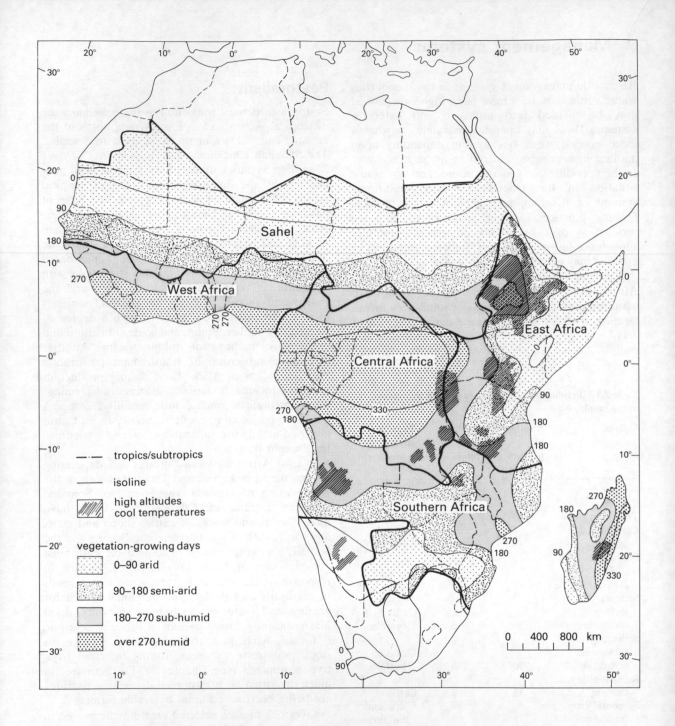

fig. 7.1 The regions and agro-climatic zones of tropical Africa following the FAO classification

fig. 7.2 Borana cattle at well head

distances of 10 to 20 km or more. Some groups, the Borana for instance, a semi-settled transhumant people, have a highly organised watering routine (fig. 7.2) in which their livestock are watered at three day intervals at traditional wells. These are virtually underground waterway systems whose historical origins are unknown and from which water is hoisted up to troughs above ground in camelskin containers by young men, poised at intervals on ladders leading down a shaft to the water. After three day periods without drinking cattle may consume a quantity of water up to 25 per cent of their body weight.

For the true nomad there can be no fixed abode. Cooking gear, basic furniture and camping gear are usually carried by bulls and/or camels. Women and children may ride on the pack animals. Milk, and in the case of the Maasai and some other non-Muslim peoples, blood obtained from bleeding the jugular vein, form a part of the diet. Meat is seldom eaten, except on special occasions such as marriage and other ceremonies and from animals slaughtered for salvage, or that have died. The Fulani, for example, will eat the carcass of an animal that has died of rinderpest.

Nomads have an intense affinity for their animals, knowing and naming each one, often by colour, size, parentage or month in which they were born. Their cattle respond to various commands and reprimands, either by voice or by tapping loudly on their walking sticks. The trick of commanding them to scatter when a cattle head tax collector appears on the scene and their re-call and re-mustering after his departure are good examples of this communication between the herdsman and his stock. Milking is done in the morning and calves are tethered or restricted in some other way at night, being allowed to suckle briefly before morning milking and again in the evening. Except in established and trained dairy herds Zebu cattle tend not to let down their milk in the absence of the calf. When a calf dies its skin may be put over another calf which is brought alongside the dam to achieve the same milk let down effect.

The system known as transhumance allows for a degree of permanent housing to be built in the wet season grazing areas. Some form of village community is developed and there is often active trading in milk in the wet season and purchase of consumer goods. At the end of the cropping season, where such transhumant communities are adjacent to arable farmers, particularly in West Africa, the pastoralist is allowed to graze his animals on crop stubble and in exchange the farmer is left with valuable manure.

Karamajong pastoralists of Uganda and the camp Fulani of parts of Nigeria adopt a system of more or less permanent settlement in the wet season grazing area. Fodder crops are grown to supplement dry season feeding. Camps may be moved after a period of years when overstocking and herbage shortage become a problem.

Strategies for the improvement of pastoral systems

Nomadism can no longer be considered as an aimless wandering of pastoral tribal people with their livestock. It represents a highly rational adaptation of human life to a severe and adverse arid environment. The pastoralist has successfully adapted to a marginal environment in which the ultimate goal is survival. The pastoralist's behaviour, in general, represents successful strategies for survival. In spite of wars, droughts, epidemics and accompanying famines, albeit with the tragic losses of both human lives and livestock, the pastoral system has survived.

However, most people think that the majority of pastoral systems are disintegrating under prevailing pressures. A large number of national and international projects have been established in an attempt to cope with the situation. In contrast to the subsistence systems outlined above, the aim of many of the livestock development schemes has been to maximise that part of the local food production system which can readily be transformed to other local systems and, where feasible, to integrate them into national and international markets. Success in such development schemes is often measured by economic indicators that are totally unrelated to the all important factor of production of food for the pastoralists.

Modern systems of cattle ranching aim to minimise labour input and to maximise animal productivity. The pastoralist, on the other hand, does not seek to minimise labour input; he is intimately connected with his animals and maintains continuous control over them to reduce losses from thieves, wild predators, disease and drought. It is a system where a comparatively large number of people depend for their livelihood on relatively small numbers of livestock and in which the potential for offtake is low. In the ranching system, on the other hand, a small number of people herd a large number of animals, seeking a high offtake and high productivity per person.

All in all, the conversion of forage under indigenous pastoral systems into blood and milk yields more calories of human food per forage calorie than are produced under the ranching system. Pastoralism is labour intensive, the whole social structure of the community being concerned, and uses about 25 times as much labour for the same number of livestock as is used on an African commercial ranch. From the national standpoint, however, since the bulk of the nation's meat supply may come from pastoral herds, aims to increase the offtake from these is a justifiable goal, provided such efforts do not endanger the food supplies of the pastoralists.

A traditional pastoral management system cannot be modified or manipulated intelligently until its traditional structure is fully understood. To achieve this end livestock projects are now being formulated through a systems study approach. Such studies entail an initial detailed survey of all the components of a system – household economics, animal disease, herd productivity characteristics such as calving rate, milk yield, growth rate, grazing management, supplementary feeding and many others. There are many interactions (fig. 7.3) between the components of the system under study. Various improvement innovations are then tested and cautiously tried within the system and their effects monitored over a period.

Strategies in tropical Africa

Pastoral development schemes in Kenya have been operating for a comparatively long time. They provide an opportunity to learn of the results from planned land use and will be presented later as a case study. With the coming of independence in 1963 a development plan was adopted that involved large resettlement schemes and a comprehensive range programme that took account of the terrain, traditional husbandry methods, previously established commercial systems, marketing potential and other factors. Part of this plan, formally established in 1968 as the Kenya Livestock Development Project, provided for the development of various ranching organisations and range management structures. They included cooperative societies and individual company ranches in what were already established as high potential range areas, and group ranches and grazing blocks in the traditional pastoral areas. In the latter, particular efforts were made to preserve the integrity of existing institutions while attempting to integrate them into more modern methods of production. In general, the Kenya plan has not achieved the success and objectives originally sought.

There are indications that the traditional attitude of suspicion among pastoralists of any form of arable farming is changing in some regions. Such change in attitude is largely due to the drastic shortage of food for both man and his livestock resulting from droughts. Two examples of this change in attitude and the measures adopted in response to it will be cited; the cases of the transhumant pastoralist Fulani in the sub-humid zone of Nigeria and the semi-nomadic Borana of the southern Ethiopian rangelands.

The transhumant pastoralist Fulani Dry season fodder for the Fulani is both scarce and poor in quality with the crude protein content of natural

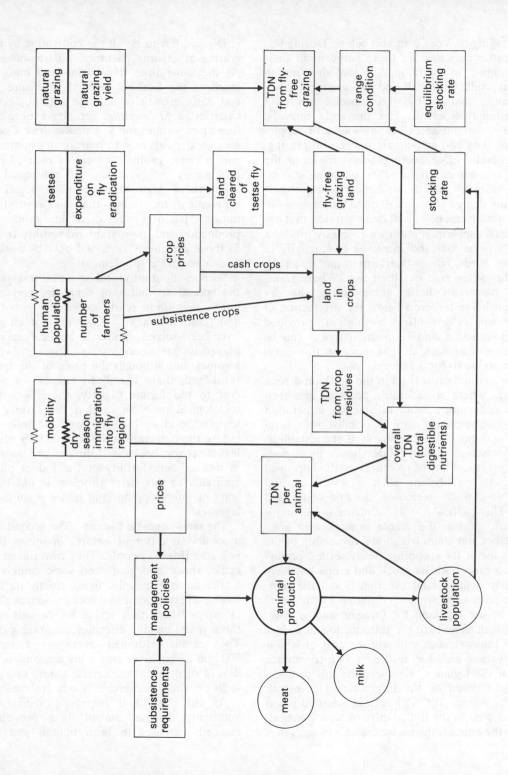

fig. 7.3 A model of traditional livestock production in the sub-humid zone of Nigeria, West Africa

109

grazing falling to 3 per cent and below. During this period cattle may lose up to 15 per cent of their body weight; in addition, as the dry season lengthens, milk yields fall and calf mortality rises. Furthermore, many cows fail to conceive as a result of nutritional anoestrus. For the truly nomadic pastoralist, without access to any source of supplemental feeding and inadequate dry season grazing, cows generally calve every other year. Even the herds of transhumant pastoralists coexisting in comparative harmony amid arable farmlands are subjected to some degree of malnutrition in the dry season.

In the past it has been well demonstrated that dry season feed supplementation with agro-by-products reduces weight loss and increases productivity in pastoralist herds, but costs, transport and uncertain availability often rule out their use. Where transhumant pastoralist herds graze during the dry season on harvested crop lands, the production of home-grown forages offers a solution, provided that various social and economic barriers can be overcome to make any developments in this direction acceptable to local farmers.

A case in question is cited in the sub-humid zone of Nigeria where considerable progress has been made in achieving a more satisfactory integration of the transhumant Fulani pastoralist into local farming systems. This has involved the establishment of what are called fodder banks by surface sowing up to 4 ha of pastures with improved legumes. In establishing such a system several barriers need to be overcome, the first being land tenure. This particular zone contains three major population groups: the arable farmers who keep few livestock but claim traditional ownership of the land and use it for cropping; newly settled pastoralists who raise both livestock and crops but have less clearly defined land use rights; and the transhumant pastoralist who is permitted by the local farmers to use the land for foraging and grazing. The major deterrents to the introduction of fodder banks to improve such land are the cost of labour for cultivation and for fertilisers before surface sowing of the legumes. To overcome this problem a method devised by the International Livestock Centre for Africa (ILCA) has been adopted based upon that used in the hill country of New Zealand, in which the animals themselves, under close super-vision, are left to do all the cultivating by intensive grazing of existing pastures and trampling of soil. At the same time their urine and dung provide much of the fertiliser needed to ensure vigorous and early growth of suitable legume seeds. Two varieties of *Stylosanthes* spp. have been used, *S. hamata* cv. varano and *S. guaianensis* cv. Cook which give good yields of 4 to 6 mt of dry matter per ha, with a crude protein content of over 13 per cent. Preliminary observations on controlled grazing using these high quality forage legumes as a supplement to, rather than as a substitute for natural pastures, resulted in gains in milk production and improved herd fertility comparable to those previously obtained only by using expensive concentrate supplements.

Such an input into local agro-pastoral systems has the special attributes of simplicity and economy, not to mention its ready acceptance by both farmer and pastoralist alike. However, not all problems have been solved; moderate applications of superphosphate are necessary to initiate growth of the legumes and although the price of the fertiliser is subsidised, there is still an element of additional cost to the farmer. Lastly, there is a potential sociological problem in that the farmer may be tempted to claim back his land for grain cropping before the pastoralist's stock have fully utilised the legume cover, because of the marked improvement in the soil and fertility of the fodder plots. One approach to this latter problem would be to find ways of intercropping land under grain crops with legumes.

The semi-nomadic Borana The second case is of a somewhat different nature, involving the semi-nomadic Borana people. They own mixed herds of cattle, sheep and goats and some camels and are a true pastoral people, living chiefly on milk and having a highly organised social structure. They live in camps where they reside for periods of two to three years, moving elsewhere as grazing demands. The terrain, although averaging a rainfall of 700 mm a year over two rainy seasons, is virtually devoid of dry season surface water, except at the wells or where handmade ponds are constructed.

As with the Fulani, improved medical care and veterinary disease control have brought about marked increases in both human and livestock populations with consequent severe competition between young cattle and the household for milk. Borana calves thus become deprived of an adequate milk intake. A few Borana are aware of the fact that home-grown cereals alleviate the critical dry season food situation and have planted maize. Efforts are now being made to introduce legumes into the system by intercropping cowpeas and maize, using the hitherto untouched heaps of manure around the camps.

Cattle ranching in East Africa

Commercial ranching systems started with European settlement in Kenya. With the coming of independence in 1963, Kenya had a background of long-term experience of local structures for both commercial and subsistence livestock production since within the period 1946–1963 government efforts to bring about development in range resources had already been made (fig. 7.4). Development projects have included sectional grazing

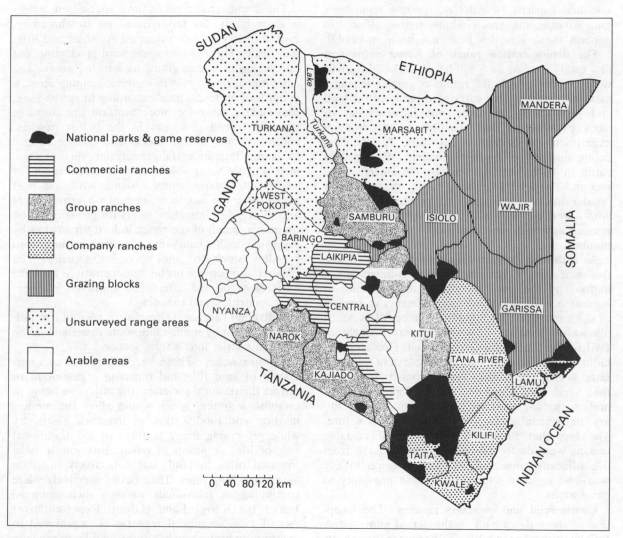

fig. 7.4 Ecological classifications of rangeland in Kenya

Legend:
- National parks & game reserves
- Commercial ranches
- Group ranches
- Company ranches
- Grazing blocks
- Unsurveyed range areas
- Arable areas

0 40 80 120 km

SUDAN
ETHIOPIA
Lake Turkana
TURKANA
MARSABIT
MANDERA
UGANDA
WEST POKOT
SAMBURU
ISIOLO
WAJIR
SOMALIA
BARINGO
LAIKIPIA
NYANZA
CENTRAL
GARISSA
NAROK
KITUI
TANA RIVER
KAJIADO
LAMU
TANZANIA
KILIFI
TAITA
KWALE
INDIAN OCEAN

schemes, a demonstration ranch at Konza, commercial and company ranches, individual ranches, group ranches, cooperative ranches and grazing block developments.

Sectional grazing schemes These are simple systems of grazing management, based on the traditional movement of livestock between wet and dry season areas. The schemes are administered by a government officer assisted by a grazing committee whose members are selected from the elders within the scheme. Such committee members have the dual capacity of enforcing grazing regulations and advising the ranch administrative officer. In general these schemes have not been successful.

The demonstration ranch at Konza This was first established as an 8 870 ha unit. The objectives were to demonstrate the results of grazing management in improving the carrying capacity of the land and productivity in cattle; the improvement of stock by breeding and selection; and to conduct experiments on pasture improvement. Ten families, comprising 90 persons and owning 1 400 head of cattle in 1949, were selected by the elders of the section. They were required to dip their cattle at regular intervals, to see that prophylactic inoculations were carried out, to follow a plan of rotational grazing and to restrict livestock to the prescribed number.

As with many government demonstration efforts, this was not a success, the programme being marred by the participating families refusing to honour one of the major commitments in respect of stock numbers; the statutory number of livestock almost doubled by 1954. The severe drought of 1961 forced the families to move out. However, the failure of the scheme was to some extent compensated for by the lessons learnt from it. It showed the need for adequate pre-development information, social, economic, agronomic and veterinary, before embarking on a project of this nature. The fact that thousands of metres of valuable fencing were destroyed by wild game animals from the adjacent rangeland was also a lesson to any would-be rancher setting up in close proximity to game areas.

Commercial and company ranches The inception of these dates back to the period immediately following the Second World War when British ex-soldiers were encouraged to take up farming in Kenya. High standards of animal husbandry and economy were achieved. Such ranches are productive enterprises in which land is leased by the government to a number of shareholders, with paid managers looking after the business. A compromise to this original structure was later organised in the form of a directed agricultural company. The articles of association give a place on the Board of Directors to the local range officer, who has a vote in all decision making.

The commercial ranches have specialised mainly in dairy herds, the latter based on crossbreeding, for the most part with imported Ayrshire and Friesian cattle. There is also some wool production and production of cereal grains in selected areas. The basic management system includes running animals in herds of up to 250 head according to age and sex, rotational grazing for more uniform utilisation of grass in fenced paddocks in the better ranches, control of bush encroachment and disease control measures. Despite certain constraints such as some members not being able to raise sufficient funds for share contributions before a loan is advanced, beef prices often too low to offset ranch overhead costs and shortage of immature steers for growing out on the ranch, much of the ranch industry flourishes by supplying high quality meat as well as improved breeding stock for the upcoming ranches. The ranches also provide useful demonstrations for local pastoralists on the effects of improved management, nutrition and breeding.

Individual ranches These were created for individual Maasai by subdividing some rangeland in the Kajiado district into 800 ha sections.

Group ranches These were introduced as a new system of land title and ranching organisation to attract the pastoral societies, the objective being to establish a system which would allow the modernisation and modification of livestock husbandry while preserving many features of the traditional way of life. A group of pastoralists jointly have freehold titles to land, but collectively maintain agreed stocking rates. They herd collectively while continuing as individuals to own their animals. Under the Kenya Land (Group Representative) Act of 1968 an official registrar is empowered to incorporate group ranches and generally to regulate the whole group movement. A committee of representatives undertakes management of the ranches, employing as necessary paid managers, assisted by government range extension staff.

A recent survey of Maasai herd structure in the group ranches indicated that the households were managing their herds for milk rather than for beef production. Stock numbers had increased over a period of some 12 years, more especially the sheep and goats. The ratio of cattle to small ruminants in the richer Maasai households was 1.2 : 1, declining to 1 : 1 in the poorer households. Meat cattle liveweights were: unimproved local Zebu

calves at 120 days weighing 48 kg (0.24 kg per day from birth) as against Sahiwal crosses at 53 kg. Total milk production rose from 3.2 l per day at 30 days to 3.6 l per day at 120 days post-calving, of which 20 per cent went for household consumption and 80 per cent for the calf. Disposal of animals took place through a variety of transactions – for sale, exchange for other animals, slaughter for home consumption and given or loaned to friends and relatives. Such emphasis on non-commercial means of offtake and acquisition are characteristic of most pastoral peoples. Sources of household income are illustrated in fig. 7.5.

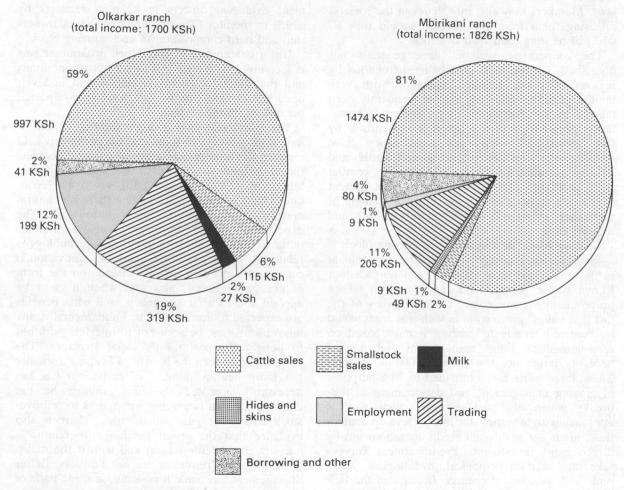

fig. 7.5 Sources of cash income for Maasai households in southeast Kenya, July 1981–June 1982

Cooperative Society ranches   These date back to the early 1960s and are run and managed according to the Cooperative Societies' by-laws, with government officers supervising the management, record keeping and accounts of the society. Members of the cooperative society are free to own and manage their individual herds under the overall supervision and within the broad policies of the elected ranch committee. In turn, the members pay to the cooperative fees for water, dipping and other improvements on a per livestock head basis, to enable loan repayments to be effected. The concept of these ranches has since been modified to enable them to operate under the cooperative society by-laws. Members may also buy shares in the society, releasing them from the burden, should they so wish, of herding their own livestock.

The cooperative societies have generally not flourished, for the most part being surrounded by regions of dense human population with very limited grazing land. Progress has frequently been marred by an invasion by illegal graziers, necessitating prosecution in a court of law. Reprisals by the culprits following such legal action have included theft of wire fencing and cattle and damage to watering facilities. Efforts to combat such problems are directed by a management committee responsible for the efficient running of the ranch through a hired ranch manager and support staff.

Grazing block development   A grazing block is a finite pastoral area determined by government in the more arid areas of north and northeastern Kenya where formal land tenure reform is not proposed in the immediate future. In view of the fact that animal production in such arid areas would be confined largely to grazing systems based on semi-nomadism, range management units are of necessity large: not less than 300 000 ha in area. These large units are subdivided for the purposes of grazing management and development of fire-breaks which are also used as roads and as approaches to watering facilities. Development of these areas is not through credit operations but by direct grant investment. Pre-investment surveys take into account ecological, hydrological, economic and sociological criteria. Because of the lack of any form of grouping between people and the land, the grazing block system, based upon rotational grazing overseen by a government grazing manager, was considered the most appropriate grazing system to develop.

To adapt to traditional grazing patterns, grazing lands are divided into four or five separate equal areas, depending on the system, with clearly defined boundaries or trace lines at about one km intervals.

On the grazing blocks milk production has been increased and stock mortality lowered. The producers have to some extent been reconciled to paying for the operation and maintenance of water facilities and to accepting the activities of government extension officers in keeping registers by which to monitor livestock numbers, stock ownership and herd composition in each grazing block.

Unfortunately the grazing block programme was not completed due to lack of development funds and the situation where developed and undeveloped blocks exist side by side has led to a partial breakdown in the system.

The pastoralist and group ranching   There is mounting evidence to show that the previously held view on the ultra-conservatism of pastoral peoples, their reluctance to adapt to or to accept new animal husbandry technologies and the social and economic changes taking place among their agricultural neighbours, is to some extent unfounded. The experience gained from the various systems outlined above is that wherever new technology is related to cattle and other livestock, innovation is cautiously welcomed. Much depends on the form of change proposed, how and when it is to be applied and to what age group, and what benefits are expected to accrue from it. Fundamentally, any innovations must be seen not to interfere with but to benefit the pastoralist's social structure. The pastoralist has seen the benefit of keeping a smaller but more healthy number of cattle but has not necessarily accepted the idea, though he has demonstrated an increasing willingness to sell livestock during the past two decades. There is also evidence that the group ranching programme is encouraging sedenterisation and with it the realisation that land resources are not limitless. Better management has made it possible, in some parts of the country, specifically on organised ranges, to improve milk yield by bringing in Sahiwal bulls for crossbreeding with local cows. Offtakes have much improved over the years, from less than 1 per cent in 1960 to 8 per cent from 1973 to 1977.

Rangeland project experience in Kenya In summary, national range development projects, some of which are outlined above, need the participation and confidence of the pastoralists for their success. The projects chosen after careful initial study of the project area, need to be suited to the conditions pertaining in a given location and at any given time. The establishment of group ranches for more technologically oriented farmers is most applicable in the high-potential grazing areas; the semi-nomad, by contrast, makes the most economic use of the poorest rangeland for the most part in semi-arid conditions. Any attempt to change pastoral societies into modern ranching communities requires staged inputs and modifications, carried out over what may be an unspecified period of time and geared to socio-economic and agricultural changes occurring on a national basis.

Ranching and range management

Rangeland carrying capacity and stocking rates

Stocking rate can be expressed in terms of number of livestock units (LSU) per hectare per year. In Botswana, for example, one LSU is defined as one mature animal with a liveweight of 450 kg. In general, this implies animals over 2 years of age, so that 1 to 2 year olds are equivalent to 0.5 LSU and calves to 0.1 LSU. Such values are arbitrary and may be altered according to the breed or type of animal and the system of management. In West Africa, the LSU for the much smaller, but mature trypanotolerant N'dama bull is calculated on the basis of about 300 kg liveweight. Provided the rancher has established what his LSU values are to be, he can estimate the stocking rates and thus the carrying capacity of his land by a process of trial and error.

There are wide variations on rangelands in yields of dry matter per hectare between years according to the amount of rainfall and its distribution. This can be illustrated in the case of northern Nigeria. Of a total of 17 million ha of land, upland savanna and alluvial areas comprise 58 per cent and 9 per cent respectively, while 30 per cent is cultivated or under fallow. This whole area may be divided into 14 rangeland types with forage production in the sparsely covered grasslands in the north yielding as little as 250 kg dry matter per ha in contrast to up to 4 000 kg dry matter per ha in the south. For estimates of carrying capacity, livestock units of 300 kg were used. To allow for inefficiency of use and wastage and to ensure the sustained productivity of rangeland, dry season usage of the total consumable herbage was set at 50 per cent and at 25 per cent in the wet season, in the latter case to allow for the fact that forage growth increases from near zero at the beginning of the rains, to maximum growth at the end of the rains. In those areas where there is cultivation of cereal crops carrying capacity per hectare will be increased accordingly to 2.5 ha/LSU, compared with 1.25 ha/LSU on the grasslands. These calculations were based on a daily consumption per animal of 7 kg of dry matter.

Management of natural grazing areas Grazing areas such as the veld and savannas of Africa and the campos and llanos of Central and South America that are used for ranching, whether they be open grassland, parkland or dense bush, are in a delicate state of balance. This is dependent upon such factors as rainfall, type of soil and bush fires, the latter in particular often preventing a grazing area from achieving its normal ecological climax. Bush – including smaller trees and shrubs – is in a constant state of competition for water and plant food. One factor may discourage the growth of grass but encourage bush growth and vice versa. Fire, for example, hinders the growth of bush and encourages the growth of grass. Fires early in the rains have a different effect on vegetation to fires occurring during the latter part of the dry season. Knowledge of such factors can help in planning a range management programme where regular burns are used to enhance grass growth at the expense of bush.

Perennial grasses, in making their normal wet season growth, build up carbohydrate reserves. After they have set seed these reserves are transferred to their root systems to keep them alive through the dry season months and supply them with energy for their initial growth when the early rains come. If the pastures are grazed heavily and continuously, especially in the latter part of their growing season, the grazing animals take into their own systems reserves which the grasses have built up for their maintenance. Consequently, the perennial grasses are starved out of existence.

The herbage then changes to a poor cover of annual grasses and weeds, sheet erosion sets in and the topsoil eventually becomes incapable of growing anything except the poorest, least useful types of vegetation. The scrub grows with the ascendant and sparse growth of grasses and weeds, but the grass is not enough to check the growth of bush which is the natural climax in much of the veld or savannas of Africa.

In order to achieve a balance of bush/pasture for stock raising in this type of environment skilled management is necessary. At first stock may do even better on the annual grasses, but gradually the bush encroaches at the expense of grass. The rancher must therefore aim to exploit the savanna but at the same time avoid bringing about a deterioration that will eventually rob him of his capital assets. He may decide that supplementation of feeds and the application of some fertilisers may be necessary for economic gains, but his main aim will be to rely, for the most part, on natural grazing and to do this he will need to limit as far as possible the stocking rate to the carrying capacity of the grazing areas. This is often very difficult to determine.

Overgrazing on tropical grasses during their growing season can do great damage and although there may be plenty of energy to be had by the grazing animal in the following winter months there may not be enough protein in the grass for the animal to make use of it. This leads to the inevitable dry season weight losses (figs 7.6, 7.7) if not actual death from starvation. Supplementation of their feed with protein concentrates or with urea, changes the whole picture in grazing animals, but to get through the dry season satisfactorily by one means or another does not mean that one should overgraze at any stage during the rainy season.

What is a safe stocking rate? The terms 'heavy' or 'light' grazing are comparative ones. For instance, in similar rainfall conditions, sandy soils can stand heavier grazing without deterioration than can the heavier soils. Where there is a three year grazing regime, with one year rest, the

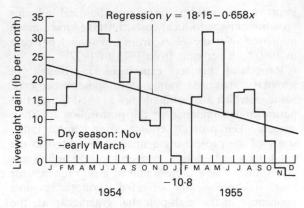

fig. 7.6 Mean monthly growth rate of N'dama cattle on range in the derived Guinea savanna (sub-humid zone) of Nigeria, West Africa

stocking rate may be said to be too intense if the pasture is evenly grazed down. At a correct stocking rate, on the other hand, although selective grazing is bound to occur and the range appear somewhat ragged, the stock will thrive and the natural grassland will not 'run out'.

Determination of the correct stocking rate requires:

1 a sound understanding of the basic principles involved;
2 acute observation of changes in the pasture and stock; and
3 an accumulation of experience over a period of several years.

A grazing plan Continuous light grazing has proved to be far less damaging to the grasses than any routine of heavy rotation grazing. However, there must be a periodic rest, without animals grazing throughout the whole of the summer, to allow the grasses to set seed and to build up their root reserves, which they cannot do if all their leaf has been eaten off while still green. This is known as the 'three herd, four paddock' system and it fills much of the basic requirements outlined above. In this way a particular paddock gets a full year's rest and with all the growth it can get out of a full rainy season to store reserves in the root system. This also provides fuel enough for what is known as a

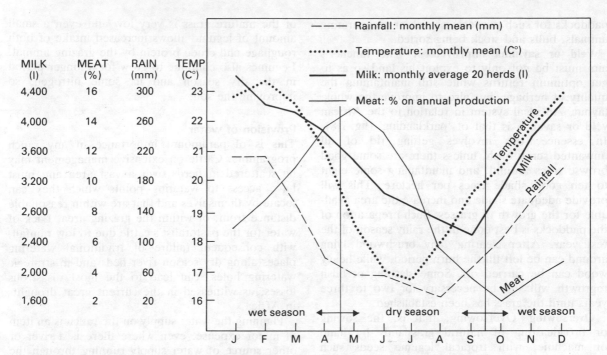

MILK (l)	MEAT (%)	RAIN (mm)	TEMP (C°)
4,400	16	300	23
4,000	14	260	22
3,600	12	220	21
3,200	10	180	20
2,600	8	140	19
2,400	6	100	18
2,000	4	60	17
1,600	2	20	16

- - - - Rainfall: monthly mean (mm)
.... Temperature: monthly mean (C°)
—— Milk: monthly average 20 herds (l)
—— Meat: % on annual production

fig. 7.7 Seasonal variation of milk and meat production in Central Brazil

'hot burn' that will set back the bush which has crept in during the previous three years of grazing.

Times to burn The effect of timing of the burn on subsequent pasture and bush growth will vary according to season, latitude, soil and vegetation type, etc.

It is important to note that if fire gets into a resting paddock in the dry season the crowns of the burned plants become exposed and the soil, unprotected by the forage, receives all the force of the wind and solar radiation, with consequent sheet erosion gradually developing between the stools or tussocks of grass. Also, where the soil is not moisture retentive, this early burn will encourage a shoot of green leaves which will shrivel and die in the absence of rain. This premature growth is also at the expense of root reserves which will also weaken the plant. Many of the transhumant and nomadic cattle owners of Africa practise early burning to get rid of coarse grass stems left over from the previous season and to obtain the coveted green shoots mentioned above to tide their cattle over before the advent of the rains proper. Where

overgrazing is inevitable, the consequent and progressive damage to and deterioration of the grazing areas can well be imagined.

Paddocking This is a more straightforward system on an arable-cum-beef dual purpose holding since it can be worked out according to water supplies available and other layout details. On an extensive ranching system this is a different matter. The economies governing such items as the correct sizes of paddocks will vary with circumstances. The first and major item is the available water supply and how it can be developed. For example, the heavy grazing rotational system involves the use of many more paddocks than the three herd, four paddock system mentioned earlier. Paddock size is related to the carrying capacity of the rangeland. For convenience a herd is limited to about 200 head of cattle. Assuming, say, 5 ha per beast with one in four paddocks resting, then paddock sizes of 1 000 ha would be adequate. On sparse grazing, however, 2 to 2½ times that area of paddock might be needed for groups of the same size. In addition to this it would also be necessary to create smaller

117

paddocks for such purposes as sick or recuperating animals, bulls and stock being sorted.

Veld or savanna improvement The rancher's aim must be not only to exploit his land so as to get optimum returns while still maintaining the quality of herbage, but also to improve the whole layout. An ideal system in relation to the African veld or savanna is that of 'parklanding' (fig. 7.8). In essence, this involves getting rid of all unwanted scrub bush, unless there are some good browse trees around, and maintaining some eight to ten good shade trees per hectare. This will provide adequate shade and increase the area available for the growth of grasses. Such preparation of the paddocks is best done in the rainy season of the rest year. After clearing, any brushwood lying around can be left till the burn period, while heavy wood can be carried off. Some slashing of bush regrowth will still be necessary for two to three years until the grass has been established.

Oversowing Oversowing, that is, the sowing or broadcasting of natural grasslands by hand or machine, with tropical legume seeds such as *Stylosanthes* spp., *Centrosema pubescens*, *Mucuna* spp., *Pueraria* spp., etc. has been successful in several countries, particularly where there is already a good grass cover. The best results in terms of production of beef in both the dry and humid tropics have been obtained where the legume is adequately fertilised. The added legume improves the quality of the feed, especially during the dry season, for at this time the protein content

fig. 7.8 Parkland grazing

of the mature grass is very low and even a small amount of legume allows increased intake of both roughage and crude protein by the grazing animal. Legumes also continue to grow for a longer period in the dry season and fix some nitrogen, so improving the soil.

Provision of water
This is of paramount importance in any ranch programme. Cattle on extensive management may be scattered in herds over a vast area and must have access to watering points which they can locate by themselves and that are within reasonable distance from, or within the grazing area. Lack of water for the pastoralist's cattle due to low rainfall, with consequent failure of traditional watering places along dry season river beds and in strategic watering holes, can lead to the most disastrous losses, as witnessed in the current great droughts in Africa.

Planning the water supply on the ranch is an item of major expense, even where there is a river or other source of water supply running through the establishment. When establishing a ranch the owner should plan to make optimum use of a natural water supply and determine the costs of water supply installations.

Distance of the watering point from the herd must be considered. Heavy in-calf cows may refuse to move more than about 1.6 km from the watering point, especially in hot weather, although under drought conditions they may often need to trek several times this distance. As a general rule, however, a distance of about 1.6 km from the nearest watering point serves as a suitable yardstick for positioning watering points for cattle.

Natural sources of water on a ranch include rivers, streams, rock holes, water holes, underground sources from shallow or deep wells, catchment sources such as runoffs from roofs and rocks, field tanks and dams.

Rivers Although an invaluable source of water, many rivers in semi-arid areas dry up. Where the bottom is sandy, sand river extraction pumps can be used to pump water from below the sand.

Dams Dams are filled by the runoff of rainwater. Dam sites should be chosen where possible in areas where the ground is least porous in nature.

They should be as deep as possible in relation to surface area to allow for evaporation. Fencing as a protection is preferable and ideally water should be conveyed by pumps to watering troughs.

Catchment areas differ from dams in that they are constructed in depressions that are filled by catchment water and cannot be washed away.

Dams can be quite simply constructed in stream beds. Depth is more important than surface area. Evaporation accounts for some 2 m of water in most places so that dams should be an additional 3 m in depth to account for both evaporation and seepage. The amount of seepage depends on soil permeability and the efficiency of the puddled core. A number of smaller, deep dams is better than a single shallower dam of greater surface area. More numerous and smaller dams also avoid over-stocking near the water source. The obvious disadvantages of the dam are:

1 standing water and mud around the edges can harbour parasite eggs; and
2 spillways tend to erode and must be carefully watched.

The ideal combination is to have a fenced dam with pipes, leading off to drinking troughs sited elsewhere. In low lying, sandy soils, sand dams are effective, the amount of water in them being dependent upon the sand grain size. Specially adapted sand pumps are used to pump the water. Reservoirs are used in very large establishments and their required volume capacity can be estimated on an average daily per head consumption of approximately 50 litres per mature beast.

Boreholes These are used extensively in semi-arid areas. Their depths vary from some 30 to 200 m according to the depth of the water table. Good borehole pumps will deliver 1 000 to 5 000 l

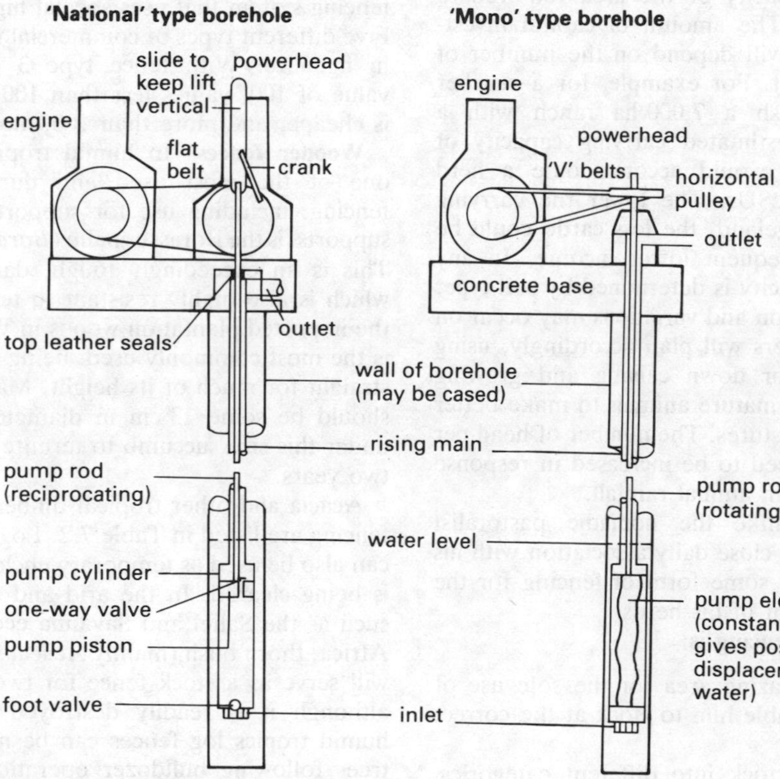

fig. 7.9 Principal working parts of 'National' and 'Mono' type boreholes

to the surface per hour. The number of cattle that can be watered at any one borehole will be determined by the yield of water and the layout of water troughs. If an average livestock unit consumes 30 l per day of water, a borehole pump yielding 5 000 l per hour and working for 8 hours will supply 40 000 l or enough for 1 300 mature cattle.

Pumps are worked by a diesel engine but where winds are a fairly constant feature borehole pumps can be worked by windmills. Examples of 'National' and 'Mono' type boreholes are given in fig. 7.9. As a rule 300 cattle may be watered at one point and the grazing area extended by piping to troughs at other watering points. When water availability is in excess of the carrying capacity of the land every effort should be made to avoid overgrazing.

Land enclosures and fencing

The value of land used for ranching is determined by the carrying capacity or the area required to support one LSU. The amount of capital investment in the ranch will depend on the number of cattle it will support. For example, for a rancher planning to establish a 7 000 ha ranch with a predetermined or estimated carrying capacity of 10 ha per LSU, it would accommodate a herd equivalent to 700 LSUs. The lower the carrying capacity of the rangeland, the less cattle could be managed with consequent lower income. In any event, carrying capacity is determined by soil type, rainfall and vegetation and variations may occur on a ranch. The ranchers will plan accordingly, using the wetter areas for down calving and growing stock, leaving more mature animals to make better use of the poorer pastures. The number of head per hectare may also need to be increased in response to marked changes in annual rainfall.

The rancher, unlike the nomadic pastoralist whose family live in close daily association with his stock, must rely on some form of fencing for the efficient management of his herds.

The purpose of fencing is:

1 to enclose the grazing area for the sole use of the rancher and enable him to stock at the correct rate;
2 to separate the stock into different categories, allowing for control of weaning and breeding herds;

3 to operate a rotational grazing system and conserve dry season grazing; and
4 to keep outside cattle off the ranch and preclude possible introduction of disease and indiscriminate breeding.

Fencing is costly and it should be used with the utmost efficiency, while allowing for the purposes outlined above. Considerable costs may be saved by using local timbers where these are available and suitable.

There is a wide variety of fencing used by cattle ranchers and their description and source may be obtained in the further reading provided at the end of this chapter. In brief, the conventional commercial cattle fence is a five strand wire fence using box-end anchors, standards at 15 m intervals and droppers at 3 m intervals between the standards. A modification to this type of fence that achieves greater economy in materials is the 'Suspension' fencing system that uses special high tension wires. Five different types of commercial fences are shown in fig. 7.10. With fence type 3 given a relative value of 100, values less than 100 mean the fence is cheaper and more than 100, more expensive.

Wooden fences In humid tropical West Africa one of the most used and durable woods for fencing, including use for support posts and gate supports, is the Borassus palm (*Borassus aethiopare*). This is an exceedingly tough, dark fibrous wood which is also highly resistant to termite attack. Of the imported plantation woods in West Africa, teak is the most commonly used, being fast growing and straight for much of its height. Main support posts should be some 13 cm in diameter because posts under this size succumb to termite attack in one to two years.

Acacia and other tropical timber trees useful for fencing are listed in Table 7.2. Log and bush fences can also be used as temporary enclosures when land is being cleared. In the arid and semi-arid tropics such as the Sahel and Savanna ecological zones of Africa, thorn bush (mainly *Acacia* spp.) laid in lines will serve as a stock fence for two to three years, although it is readily destroyed by fire. In the humid tropics log fences can be made from felled trees following bulldozer operations. Such fences can be stock-proof and last several years although

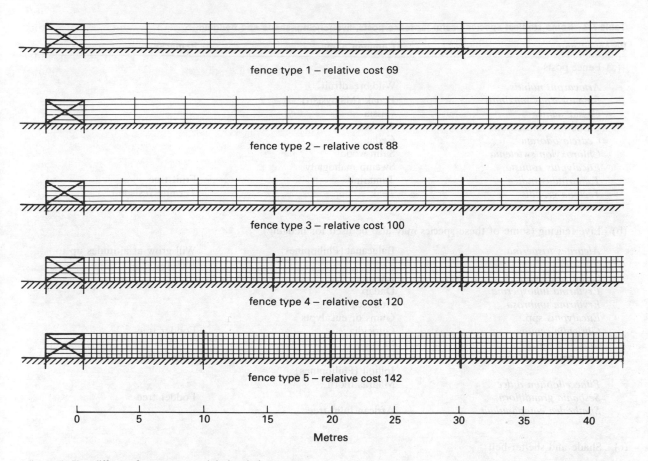

fence type 1 – relative cost 69

fence type 2 – relative cost 88

fence type 3 – relative cost 100

fence type 4 – relative cost 120

fence type 5 – relative cost 142

0 5 10 15 20 25 30 35 40

Metres

fig. 7.10 Five different fence types and their relative costs

valuable forest timber is unlikely to remain unused for any period of time.

Stone walls Although common in many stony upland areas of Europe and elsewhere, the stone wall enclosure is not frequently encountered in the tropics. They are, however, common in the West Indies and in Hawaii and may be found on government livestock stations in the stony Plateau area of Nigeria in West Africa. In Hawaii, dry stone walls are 0.9 to 1.2 m high and 0.9 to 1.2 m wide at the base. Their chief advantage is their durability and low maintenance cost. Some of the stock farm walls in Nigeria have stood for 30 to 40 years. However, initial costs of construction are high and skill is required in their construction. There is little doubt,

however, that where stone and labour are available and where basic principles of construction can be taught, the stone wall is a reliable method of enclosure.

Live fencing This is about the cheapest type of fence to erect because it can be obtained from locally grown trees and shrubs. It is, on the other hand, more expensive than other fences to maintain. Live fences are most easy to establish in humid areas, though in the drier savanna areas, some of the aloes and sisal are used. Some selected live fence trees and tropical hedge species are listed in Table 7.2. Once established live fences can also be used as main support as well as to supply some browse, and corner posts for wire fencing.

121

Table 7.2 Some tropical species useful for fence posts, live fencing, shade and hedging

Botanical name	Common name	Remarks
(a) Fence posts		
Artocarpus nobilis	Wild breadfruit	
Balanocarpus maximus	Penak (Malaysian)	
Cassia siamea	Cassia	
Casuarina equisetifolia	She-oak	
Cedrela odorata	Cedar	
Chloroxylon swietenia	Satin-wood	
Eucalyptus robusta	Swamp mahogany	
Tamarindus indica	Tamarind	Fruit tree
Tectona grandis	Teak	Termite resistant
(b) Live fencing (some of these species may also be used for hedging)		
Aleurites trisperma	Balucanat (Philippines)	Will grow at altitudes up to 1000 m
Ceiba pentandra	Kapok	
Erythrina lithosperma	Dadap	
Erythrina umbrosa	Ananaca	
Eucalyptus spp.	Gums or eucalypts	
Gliricidia sepium	Gliricidia	Fodder tree
Jatropha curcas	Physic nut	
Leucaena leucocephala	Wild tamarind Ipilipil (Philippines)	Fodder tree
Pithecellobium dulce	Madras thorn	
Sesbania grandiflora		Fodder tree
Spathodea companulata	African tulip tree	
(c) Shade and shelter-belt		
For drier areas		
Casuarina equisetifolia	She-oak	
Eucalyptus alba	White gum	
Eucalyptus citriodora	Lemon-scented gum	Will also grow on salty soils
Ficus benjamina	Java fig	
Mangifera indica	Mango	Fruit tree
Phoenix dactylifera	Date palm	Fruit tree
Pithecellobium saman	Saman	Produces sweet pods
Tamarindus indica	Tamarind	Fruit tree
For humid areas		
Anacardium occidentale	Cashew	Nut tree
Artocarpus altilis	Breadfruit	Fruit tree
Cocos nucifera	Coconut	Multi-purpose tree
For montane areas		
Acacia dealbata	Silver wattle	Thrives from 1500 to 2000 m; tannin extracted from bark
Acacia decurrens	Black wattle	

Table 7.2 Cont.

Botanical name	Common name	Remarks
Eugenia jambos	Rose apple	Fruit tree
Grevillea robusta	Silky oak	Thrives from 1200 to 2200 m
Tecoma leucoxylon	White cedar	
(d) Hedge species		
For drier areas		
Acacia modesta		
Agave spp.		
Carissa grandiflora	Natal plum	
Euphorbia tirucalli	Milk hedge	
Opuntia dillenii	Prickly pear	Edible fruit
Zizyphus spina-christi	Crown of thorns	
For more humid areas		
Duranta plumieri	Duranta	
Bougainvillea spp.	Bougainvillea	
For montane areas		
Aberia caffra	Kei apple	Thrives up to 2500 m
Berberis arista	Berberry	
Dodonea viscosa		Thrives up to 2000 m

Shade trees The importance of shade in the tropics has already been mentioned in Chapter 2. Shade trees, which are the natural and cheapest way of protecting animals from excess solar radiation, are important in both the dry and the wet tropics. All too often, in the establishment of a beef enterprise on new land, potential shade trees may be cut down indiscriminately in an effort to establish or promote improved pastures. Overall requirements for shade depend on the type or breed of cattle being used and the management system involved. On extensive management many indigenous shade trees also provide valuable dry season browse. Under more intensive management, in particular where this can be combined in the humid tropics with a tree cash crop economy, such as coconut, cashew and oil palm production, the trees provide in addition shade for the grazing livestock. Some details of useful shade trees are listed in Table 7.2.

Shelter belts These are protective belts of trees or shrubs to which cattle may retreat for shelter during storms and high winds and especially where there are sudden changes in temperature. Shelter belts are of most value in the more arid tropical areas and in the montane uplands. An ideal shelter belt consists of a central area of tall trees, surrounded by shorter species consisting of shrubs or very small trees. Tree belts should normally be planted at right angles to the prevailing winds, although freak storms may occasionally come in from a different direction. The species planted should preferably possess a dense evergreen foliage, a strong tough wood and be capable of natural regeneration from suckers. Suitable species are largely the same as those used for shade (see Table 7.2.).

Ranch design
The reader will realise that there are unlimited possibilities for design of ranch layout, depending on climate, terrain, availability of water, breed of stock used and many other factors. Under these circumstances it is only possible to discuss some simple, basic factors.

Number of paddocks Any ranch design usually

incorporates a perimeter fence and sub-division of the enclosed area into paddocks. The shape of the ranch is generally subject to the topography and natural features that determines the amount of fencing needed. For example, 20 km of fencing would enclose 3 180, 2 500 ha and 1 920 ha of circular, square, or triangular shaped ranches respectively. Square shaped ranches are more economic to enclose than long rectangular ones.

As already stated, in terms of initial capital outlay, ranch size should be such that the herd accommodated produces satisfactory sustained income and return on investment at the recommended stocking rate. The carrying capacity of the land will determine the size of the ranch necessary to achieve this. The number of paddocks depends upon:

1 *Grazing management* Whether or not some form or other of rotational grazing is adopted, grazing management should aim at applying as far as possible even grazing pressure to the whole ranch area. Watering points should be placed so as to achieve this. Areas may also need to be fenced off in order to conserve winter grazing and for purposes of periodic burning.

2 *Herd management* Facilities are necessary to allow calves to be weaned and to separate bulls from the breeding herd. Where a rotational breeding system is used two paddocks for the breeding herd during the breeding season will be required to operate the system. From the above a minimum of six paddocks is considered necessary. fig. 7.11 illustrates two such units, 'B' has one watering point and 'A' two points through recourse to reticulation. In general, the layout with two

watering points is preferable as it allows herds to be separated by a greater distance – a considerable advantage at weaning time – and helps to exclude bulls from the breeding herd.

Control handling facilities Such facilities should provide:

1 separate watering troughs for each paddock;
2 feeding troughs containing bonemeal, salt, or other mineral supplements;
3 a crush for administration of treatment and for hand spraying or dressing against ticks; and
4 a control sorting area.

Other facilities, depending on herd size, would include cattle dips or spray races and a weighbridge. Fig. 7.12 shows the control facility area to serve four separate paddocks. The same system can serve the six paddock set-up by interchanging the herds from paddocks 5 and 6 with adjacent paddocks 3 and 4, or 1 and 2.

Buildings and yards Buildings for both extensive and intensive management systems should be kept to a minimum practical level and the main emphasis placed on the handling yards, dips,

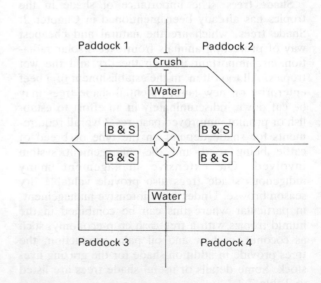

fig. 7.12 The plan of a kraal at the junction of four paddocks

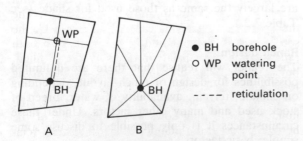

- BH borehole
- WP watering point
- - - - reticulation

fig. 7.11 Two possible six-paddock ranch designs

B & S bonemeal and salt

loading ramps and other structures essential to the enterprise. Large holdings will require a main central office building for the keeping of herd records, accounts, payrolls and other items, also adequate storage space and simple housing for any vehicles, tractors and maintenance facilities. There should also be a small store or section of the main store for drugs, dips and basic animal health equipment. Large establishments may have an office/laboratory for a resident veterinarian and/or auxiliary animal health personnel. It may also be necessary to have more than one dipping or spray-race point, placed at strategic positions on the ranch to avoid moving the individual herds too far at routine dipping times. Under pastoral conditions, dipping facilities may be difficult to provide, or they may be rejected, but on grazing reserves set aside for pastoralists, dips should be located at strategic points (fig. 7.13).

The establishment of a feedlot fattening yard is a specialised operation and is discussed later. Requirements for the intensive beef producer on improved pastures are little more than fencing, watering troughs and either available shade trees or simply constructed shelters. Paths from the paddocks should be arranged to allow easy access to and from dips or sprayraces, crushes and their accompanying yard structures such as loading ramps.

fig. 7.13 Cattle dip

Other equipment Where smaller ranches cannot afford the outlay for tractors and trailers, donkeys, mules, buffalo or oxen-driven vehicles can be used for carrying supplies and equipment within ranch boundaries.

Ranch labour Labour may be divided into managerial and general farm labour. The best manager is the owner himself, who will exercise, not unlike the pastoralist, personal interest in the ranch and in the stock. It must be admitted, however, that a good manager is sometimes a far better stockman than the owner himself. Where general farm labour is inexperienced, or more often disinterested due to poor housing and living conditions provided by the owners, management is of a low standard and productivity falls accordingly.

Cattle management practices on range

The aim of the commercial rancher is to produce the greatest possible amount of beef – acceptable to the market – as possible. To achieve this the ranch should be stocked at or approaching capacity. The situation outlined here is one in which the rancher is producing calves and growing them through to slaughter age. The breeding herd thus produces all the animals in the various age groups. The numbers produced by the breeding herd will be determined by:

1 the number of cows of breeding age;
2 the reproductive levels obtained; and
3 the mortality rates of young stock.

The significance of these factors is demonstrated in Table 7.3 in which herd structures are given at varying calving rates on ranches of 6 400 ha with carrying capacities of 16 and 12 ha per LSU. The first ranch has a carrying capacity of 400 LSU, the second 533 LSU. It should be noted that on both ranches the total capacity in terms of LSU is filled, but the size of the breeding herd varies according to calving rate.

When reproductive performance is low the number of breeding cows as a proportion of the herd is high and the number of growing stock relatively lower. For example, in Table 7.3 in the ranch with a carrying capacity of 16 ha per LSU and a

Table 7.3 Herd structures for a ranch of 6 400 ha at two carrying capacities and varying calving rates

	Animal type	LSU	50% Animals	50% LSU	60% Animals	60% LSU	70% Animals	70% LSU	80% Animals	80% LSU	90% Animals	90% LSU
Carrying Capacity 16:1	Breeding cow	1	230	230	210	210	190	190	176	176	163	163
	Bull	1	9	9	8	8	8	8	7	7	7	7
	Calf	0	106	–	115	–	122	–	130	–	135	–
	Heifer 1–2 yr	0.5	52	26	56	28	60	30	63	31.5	66	33
	Heifer 2–3 yr	1	51	51	55	55	59	59	62	62	65	65
	Heifer 3–4 yr	1	8	8	16	16	23	23	30	30	34	34
	Steer 1–2 yr	0.5	52	26	56	28	60	30	63	31.5	66	33
	Steer 2–3 yr	1	51	51	55	55	59	59	62	62	65	65
	Total			401		400		399		400		400
Carrying Capacity 12:1	Breeding cow	1	305	305	276	276	252	252	234	234	218	218
	Bull	1	12	12	11	11	10	10	9	9	9	9
	Calf	0	140	–	153	–	162	–	172	–	180	–
	Heifer 1–2 yr	0.5	69	34.5	75	37.5	80	40	84	42	88	44
	Heifer 2–3 yr	1	68	68	74	74	79	79	83	83	87	87
	Heifer 3–4 yr	1	11	11	22	22	31	31	39	39	46	46
	Steer 1–2 yr	0.5	69	34.5	75	37.5	80	40	84	42	88	44
	Steer 2–3 yr	1	68	68	74	74	79	79	83	83	87	87
	Total		533		532		531		532		535	

Note: LSU = livestock unit

calving rate of 50 per cent, cows constitute 57 per cent and heifers 28 per cent respectively, of the total LSUs. With high level reproductive performance and at the same carrying capacity a calving rate of 80 per cent results in cows constituting 41 per cent and heifers 33 per cent respectively of the total LSUs on the ranch.

All management practices in a beef herd are aimed at:

1 increasing the breeding cows' reproductive performance;
2 reducing overall herd mortality; and
3 attaining market weights at the earliest possible age.

In summary, these are best achieved by a rational breeding programme, breeding to suit the most favourable months of the year for calving, careful and economic culling of breeding cows and bulls, the provision of an adequate water supply, controlled grazing, supplementary dry season feeding, strict adherence to herd health procedures, controlled weaning procedures, correct timing for castration and grazing/feeding procedures that provide maximum daily liveweight gains for young stock under prevailing conditions.

Management of the breeding herd

In those regions of the tropics in which there is a distinct dry and wet season, it may be the practice to arrange for two separate calving times, i.e. the dry and wet seasons. It is usually essential, however, to feed supplements to the dry season calvers if the onset of the following rains is delayed. Dry season calving, on the other hand, probably favours the calf more than its dam since it may still need to suckle for a while and it will be of an age, with the approach of the wet season, to make full use of the whole of the grass growing season. Calving in the dry season also raises the annual calving percentage since some cows and first-calving heifers may not have picked up condition sufficiently in time to conceive for the next wet season calving. A further advantage to general herd management is that it reduces the number of essential but routine jobs to be done such as castrating, dehorning, earmarking and branding. Longer delays between dipping or spraying during the dry season are also an advantage. In general, under extensive management conditions, it is better to let the bulls run with the heifers so that they calve at the time best suited to themselves. Much depends, however, on the degree of supplementary feeding which can be practised.

On larger ranches a higher percentage of bulls per cow group is needed since the cow, which is only on heat for a few hours, may not have time to find a bull. Most stockmen allow no more than about 200 cows to a herd, requiring about 5 bulls, i.e. some 30 to 40 cows to a mature bull. Where two bulling seasons are practised, the number of bulls run with the herd can be reduced.

Bulls should enter the herd in good condition. If too lean, they should be fed in advance of bulling rather than trying to supplement their feed when they are actually working. Young bulls that are too lean should be given at least two weeks' rest before being put back with the breeding herd.

Bulling heifers are first bred on range on the basis of weight for age since they are generally considerably older than would be their sisters of similar weight under more intensive management conditions. In Zimbabwe, for example, locally bred and hardy range-type heifers are some 300 kg in weight and usually about $3\frac{3}{4}$ years old before being bred, that is about 4 years old at calving. These criteria are, of course, related to the breed in question; heifers of the N'dama breed of West Africa may be bred at liveweights below 220 kg, Criollo heifers in Colombia at 300–350 kg and Santa Gertrudis heifers in Texas at 350–400 kg liveweight.

Great improvements in herd economics are achieved through skill and thought in culling. Culling of aged breeding females is usually practised on understocked ranches, except for really poor heifers which would be culled immediately.

The objective is a herd of range cows which produce a calf every year, rear it to a good weaning weight and go on producing in this manner for as long as possible. This is the overriding consider-

ation for the rancher and it takes precedence over such details as conformation, evenness of type, colour, shape of ears and other fancy points.

Records of performance which can be clearly marked on a cow are most useful. For example, the last figure of the year in which a cow calves can be lightly branded on her hindquarter and the year of her birth on a distinctly numbered ear tag. Details of marking and methods of record keeping are provided at the end of this chapter.

Duration of mating This should be a compromise between the benefits obtained from a controlled breeding season and the need to get the highest numbers of females in-calf during the year.

In controlled breeding programmes, under conditions of good nutrition and mangement, allowance should be made for a breeding season of three complete oestrous cycles in order to minimise the possibility of the bulls missing any of the cows. In practice, this is a period of about 9 to 10 weeks. Where indicated, the mating period can be increased to 3 months, but low conception rates under more extended mating periods suggest either a bull problem or the need for a closer scrutiny and culling in the breeding herd. It is recommended, however, that where environmental conditions are precarious and variable, much longer breeding seasons be allowed in order to ensure optimum calving rates.

Pregnancy testing This is carried out by an experienced operator by rectal palpation in which the presence of the foetus can be detected by inserting the arm in the rectum and palpating the developing foetus and its membranes through the rectal and uterine walls.

Such procedures are used mainly in highly organised, more intensively controlled beef cattle units. One cannot deal with large herds on range in this way – in such cases the calving percentage is the overall indicator of pregnancy rates and those cows running without a calf at foot during the calving period are sufficient proof of barrenness. Under more intensive systems of management, however, the additional time and cost of pregnancy testing is adequately offset by savings through early detection of empty cows and their subsequent re-mating or culling. Under any circumstances, the barren cow is a passenger; she consumes feed that could be used by a pregnant animal and on this account should be culled and sold as a beef animal as soon as possible.

The cow

The reproductive rate of the cow, the growth rate of her calf to weaning and its efficiency of feed conversion are all important factors in herd management.

The most efficient measure of a beef cow's fertility is the number of calves per year of life. For example, a cow living to eight years of age and producing five calves would have a fertility efficiency of approximately 100 per cent, assuming that she was expected to calve down at three years of age and to produce one calf per annum for an expected lifetime productive period of eight years. This sort of calculation can be adapted to suit any local standards of reproductive efficiency. Beef heifers managed intensively will calve earlier than those managed under pastoral or ranching conditions.

Age at first calving

This will depend for the most part on breed and environment. The African pastoralist may expect his Zebu heifers to calve first at four to five years of age. On improved pastures in more humid zones and under optimum management and disease control conditions similar heifers may calve down at two and one-half to three years of age. Generally speaking, heifers of any breed managed under improved conditions in the tropics are expected to calve at this age. For example, using hand mating in Central America, first-calving heifers of the Charolais, Santa Gertrudis and Criollo breeds were 26, 28 and 33 months of age, respectively, whereas local Brahman heifers calved at 36 months.

A higher plane of nutrition will reduce the age of the heifer at puberty, but this may not always be desirable. The objective should be to breed heifers that are of optimal weight for the breed in order to avoid the possible complications of difficult parturition and to ensure adequate milk secretion at calving and general body stamina.

Calving rate

This may be conveniently defined as the number of live calves born for every 100 cows run with the bull. Most well-managed beef ranches aim at a 70 to 80 per cent or higher calving rate for optimum economic returns. Many Zebu-type herds in the tropics exhibit lower calving rates, depending on climatic and management conditions. Where management is good, however, breeds such as the N'dama of West Africa, the Caracul of Brazil and some Southeast Asian breeds attain 70–80 per cent calving rate under quite stringent range conditions. The West African Dwarf Shorthorn (Muturu) often referred to as a shy breeder, will also attain a calving rate of 70 to 80 per cent under optimum management conditions on improved pastures.

The cow at calving

The cow on range will separate itself from the rest of the herd and under normal circumstances calve down without assistance. Under any system of management the cow should be disturbed as little as possible and no interference or attempt to hurry the birth be made. Where practicable, however, and depending on the management system involved, she should be kept under observation, particularly if there is any real sign of delay and distress during calving. Examination with a well scrubbed and disinfected hand and arm may detect any abnormality such as a misplaced head or neck, or breech presentation, which will require veterinary attention.

The calf

Care of the calf at birth can pay big dividends and losses at this stage can be greatly reduced by sound management and an understanding of the needs of the newborn animal. Within minutes after birth the calf is dependent on itself for survival. It no longer gets nutrients, oxygen and warmth within the dam and it must get rid of its own waste products such as urine and faeces.

Colostrum It is important within one to two hours from birth that the calf should get up on its feet and commence to suckle, as the first or colostrum milk contains valuable nutrients which are essential for the calf. This colostrum also contains antibodies which help provide resistance to disease; more especially those which are local to the herd and to which the dam herself has already built up a considerable degree of resistance. The dam passes the antibodies to the calf in a passive manner (see Chapter 8) but the calf can only absorb them during the first 36 to 48 hours after birth. The vitamin content of colostrum is determined to some extent by the level and quality of feeding in the last few weeks of pregnancy. High quality green forage or hay or silage will raise the vitamin content of colostrum.

The following are basic guidelines to ensure the health of the pregnant cow and both the cow and her calf following its birth.

1 Always make sure the calf has access to colostrum. In the dry season, where possible, feed the breeding cow additional green fodder or well made hay or silage for some weeks before calving.
2 Make available good quality hay or other forage supplement to the calf in addition to the milk it is getting from the dam.
3 When shortages of vitamin A and/or D are suspected early in the calf's life, supply these as concentrated supplements.
4 Remember that a good early start in the health of both the dam and the calf helps to ensure the success of any beef production system.

Birth weight

Birth weight is obviously a breed characteristic of both exotic and indigenous beef cattle. Breeds such as the Charolais, Hereford and Brown Swiss produce calves with higher birth weights than do all types of tropical cattle. Comparative weaning weights are, on the other hand, more important for in general they indicate the milking potential of the dams. Male calves are usually heavier than females and it is generally accepted that twins are smaller than singles at birth. Exotic cattle tend to have a shorter gestation period than Zebu cattle.

Weaning

Weaning is a crucial time in the life of the calf for it represents both a nutritional and psychological change. For the first seven or eight months of life the calf on range has been constantly associated with its mother and has depended on her both for protection and food. Suddenly, under ranching conditions, it is cut off at weaning from both and

is naturally nervous and under stress until it learns to readjust to its new environment. The weaning process may also coincide with further stresses caused by vaccination, dehorning, castration and being conveyed to a livestock market or to a new management system and environment which is totally strange to it. Calves normally lose weight immediately following weaning. Their resistance is lowered, making them more susceptible to diseases, particularly the respiratory ones and the tick-borne diseases.

The age at which to wean beef calves depends upon the system of management and on social and climatic factors. In the tropics seasons have less influence on weaning programmes than in temperate zones unless systems of controlled seasonal mating are used to ensure a calf crop at a specific time so that calves may be weaned, for example, at the end of the dry or early in the wet season. In the northern hemisphere temperate climates range, calves born in winter and spring (December–April) are normally weaned some 6 to 9 months later, that is, in the early autumn or winter (October–November). As a general rule, however, irrespective of latitude, range-reared calves are weaned at 6 to 9 months of age, that is, they follow with their dams until rumen development is complete and they can feed themselves without recourse to the dam's milk.

The weaning process on range   Calves and cows should be separated at a considerable distance at weaning time to speed up the weaning process. To reduce the amount of bawling and the respiratory difficulties that may develop due to prolonged distress, calves should be out of sight and/or hearing of the cows. They should be divided into groups according to size and sex, depending on available space and fencing. During the first few days they should be confined to small shaded areas to reduce walking and consequent weight loss. Clean water and where possible palatable grazing should be available to encourage them to feed in the absence of their dams.

Where weaned calves are to be sold for intensive feedlot management a good practice is to bring the cows and calves into small paddocks of improved pastures at least 2 weeks prior to weaning. Feed should be placed in creeps where the calves can begin learning to eat concentrates and feeding in a confined area. The whole object of weaning management is to reduce stress from as many causes as possible in order to prepare the calf for a new mode of life.

By reducing the stress factors of poor management, inadequate nutrition and exposure to bad weather and parasites, the weight losses associated with weaning will be lowered, and there will be a smaller chance of the calves being injured, or developing respiratory or other diseases. This is especially so during the rainy season when sudden temperature changes can occur. In some ranching countries tranquillisers may be used to reduce anxiety and apprehension in calves that are in situations unfamiliar to them; however, the most important item in keeping nervous stress to a minimum is good management.

Climatic conditions can exert stress on livestock and predispose calves to disease, but proper and economic shelter can be provided to reduce unnecessary climatic stress during the weaning period.

Nutritional stresses are as common as climatic stresses on most ranches and are particularly important when calves and yearlings are on the move for long distances without stops for water and feed as, for example, in trade cattle on the hoof, or in road or rail trucks.

Another type of environmental factor creating stress is the host–parasite relationship. Heavy infestation of stomach worms makes calves easy prey for respiratory and other infectious agents. The anaemia caused by hookworms also lowers the calf's resistance to other diseases.

Weight losses at weaning   Under most conditions calves lose weight immediately following weaning and it takes from 2 to 3 weeks or more for them to regain this weight. If they are shipped immediately to distant market or feedlots this will take longer.

Many factors influence the amount of weight loss in calves during weaning. A calf whose dam has been a good milker is less likely to have learned to eat grass or creep feed to the same degree as the calf whose dam was a poor milker or the calf that was forced to find more of its own feed supply early in life. The calf fed well by its dam will be in better flesh condition and more subject to weight loss than calves weaned in a thinner condition. Calves that

have been trained to eat creep feed prior to weaning are less likely to suffer weight loss than non-creep-fed calves. Furthermore, if calves are dehorned, castrated, vaccinated and soon after transported for long distances, they will suffer greater weight, disease and/or death losses than those which are not subject to these ordeals.

Selection at weaning   Under moderate range conditions the dam's milk yield is dwindling rapidly 6 months after parturition. It therefore becomes practicable to wean the calf sometime from this period onwards. Early weaning at 6 to 7 months of age allows the calves to graze the better paddocks without competition from their dams. The weaners can be herded off onto separate pastures. Under optimum pasture conditions and where the fat vealer calf is being produced weaning can be delayed for 8 to 9 months. This applies especially in the wet tropics where the rainy season may extend for eight to nine months of the year. Where selective breeding programmes are practised, calves can be weighed at weaning and potential breeding stock selected at this stage.

Culling

Weaning is also a most suitable stage at which to cull unwanted cows and the poorest of the heifer weaners. Unwanted cows may be culled on the following basis:

1 if found non-pregnant at the test;
2 if of a pre-determined age, say 10 years, at which the cows in question no longer equal the average production for the herd;
3 if the cow weans a calf below the average weight for the herd or generally inferior to its herd-mates; or
4 if the cow has defects such as damaged teats, or faults such as being very wild and breaking fences.

The best criterion for culling, provided such data is routinely collected, is calf performance since, after all, whatever other defects a dam may appear to have, if she weans a good calf she is still an economic asset. One further aspect – it is pointless to cull too drastically if there are insufficient replacement heifers coming up to maintain breeding herd level. This is especially so with Zebu cattle. Many an old Zebu cow marked for culling has been returned to the herd to produce another three to four calves when nutrition and management conditions have been adjusted to suit the individual circumstances.

Pre-conditioning calves

Pre-conditioning is the process of preparing the calf to better withstand the stresses of leaving its mother. The calf destined for the feedlot has to learn to eat new kinds of feed and to pass through the various channels of trade until it reaches its destination. Pre-conditioning is a relatively new idea prompted by the need to cut costs due to death losses, weight losses, veterinary medical expenses and long recovery periods.

Pre-conditioning may be considered as a means of quality control. To the rancher–producer, pre-conditioning means a combination of ways of handling calves before, during and after weaning and during marketing to improve their health and vigour and to assist them to adapt to their new surroundings as feeder cattle. To a feeder, a pre-conditioned calf means one that is in good health, has already been introduced to feed and water troughs, has been immunised against the common diseases, treated for parasites and is ready to start eating and gaining as soon as it arrives at the feedlot. The reader may consider how such criteria might apply to, or be adapted to suit his own local conditions.

Backgrounding

This is a practice used by some feedlot operators to get calves acquainted with their new environment before they are actually placed in the feedlot. This may be done by placing the calves in small paddocks of up to 1 ha which are maintained in good grass and which have manger space at one end. This amounts to an over-size drylot type of pen with a pasture in it. The feed used is the same as the calves will receive later in the feeding pens. This provides the calves with a good clean place in which to recuperate from their journey from the market or the ranch. Such a procedure is well suited to humid and semi-humid conditions where paddocks of good grass/legume mixtures can be combined with feedlot facilities.

If the backgrounding is done on the ranch where the calves were produced, the weaning and pre-conditioning diets can be similar. This will minimise problems associated with the rations and will tend to alleviate any possible stress of changing diets. Rations will necessarily vary with areas and locally available feeds. Experience indicates that there is probably little reason for high-priced, high-protein supplemental feeds. A simple mixture of highly palatable ingredients will suffice (see Chapter 6).

Post-calving routines

Under extensive ranch management conditions, about mid-way through the new mating period and at which time the last calf crop will be about 10 to 12 weeks old, the routine programme of branding and/or ear marking, castration, dehorning and vaccination of calves can be carried out. The vaccination routine at this stage must of necessity be selective in order to fit in with local disease problems and statutory regulations for age at vaccination.

Systems of restraint and handling vary considerably according to circumstances. N'dama cattle of West Africa are notoriously agile and difficult to handle when managed under ranching conditions although when reared under pastoralist or settled mixed farming conditions they are comparatively docile. In fact, most ranched cattle are more difficult to handle than the cattle owned by pastoralists or mixed farmers. Handling procedures vary therefore according to the form of management. Individual restraint by hand or by roping and casting is practised on many ranches. The most suitable way to handle calves, especially in large numbers, is to draught them off from the dams and run them through a chute or race at the end of which a calf cradle or crate has been placed. This avoids undue excitement when the calf is handled and in the dry season it helps to keep down the dust. When environmental conditions are very hot, dusty or generally not up to adequate hygienic standards, the more traumatic operations of dehorning and castration can best be left until last.

Dehorning and tipping There are many advantages in dehorning beef cattle; they are less dangerous to themselves during fighting or when being handled together in large numbers and they are, of course, less dangerous to those persons mounted on horseback or on foot handling them. It may be argued – and with some grounds for agreement under extensive management conditions – that the intact horn enables the animal to protect itself from intruders and predators of both human and animal form; also against fly worry, but these advantages must be weighed against the disadvantages already mentioned. Social factors must also be considered. Many pastoralists in tropical Africa attach great importance to horn shape and size and even when persuaded to adopt or participate in improved pastoral management or commercial ranching enterprises this admiration for and desire to retain the horn still remains.

Except in dairy-beef units or intensive schemes, the dehorning of very young calves is not normally relevant in beef herds. Dehorning, in actual fact disbudding, is related to the early growth of the horn buds. In the first one to two weeks of life, when the horn buds are soft, they can be rubbed off comparatively easily with a caustic soda stick.

Another method, recommended by Yeates and Schmidt in Australia, and used up to nine days of age, is to paint a mixture of antimony trichloride, salicylic acid and flexible collodion in the proportions 28:7:65 onto the horn buds after first snipping away the nearby hair (fig. 7.14). There is no need to tie the calf up and the method involves little pain.

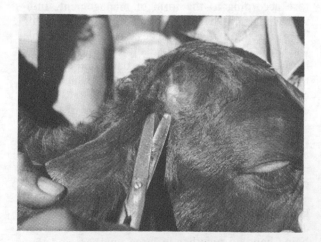

fig. 7.14 Dehorning (disbudding)

At about three weeks of age, when the horn is still quite small but becoming hard, a special shearing iron with hollowed-out end will dehorn very effectively. The iron, heated either electrically or by fire to a bright red colour, is placed over the horn, pressed onto the skin and rotated. This sears a complete ring around the horn base, so that the blood circulation is destroyed and the horn bud eventually drops off.

From about three weeks to two months, that is before the horn becomes firmly fixed to the skull by the horn core, removal of each developing horn with a sharp knife is possible. A little surrounding skin should also be removed to ensure completeness. A scooped gouging tool may also be used very effectively.

The question of dehorning cattle older than about three months of age must be considered. The practice is common enough, but not perhaps advisable after six months of age. The horn core commences to grow out from the skull at about three months and by six months it is substantial in size with a cavity continuous with that of the frontal sinus extending into it. Removal of the horn exposes this sinus and though the cavity generally closes over within a few weeks, infection is a risk. After about six months the blood supply to the horn becomes much more developed, so that dehorning is accompanied by considerable bleeding. In adult cattle the bleeding includes the spurting of arterial blood and occasionally ligation or pulling of the arteries may be necessary to arrest bleeding.

If cattle aged from 6 to 12 months of age are to be dehorned, a larger pair of scoop dehorners than those used for younger calves should be used. Also, as such animals would be too large for a calf cradle, they would need to be restrained either by roping on the ground or in a cattle crush (fig. 7.15). For cattle more than one year of age large, guillotine-type dehorners are required. The animal is secured in a dehorning bail, with its head tied firmly to one side with nose tongues, so as to provide adequate restraint on the animal and unimpeded access for the person cutting the horn. When one horn has been cut off, the animal's head is tied on the other side and the operation repeated.

Because of the exposure of the frontal sinus, and the risk of infection and profuse bleeding, as well

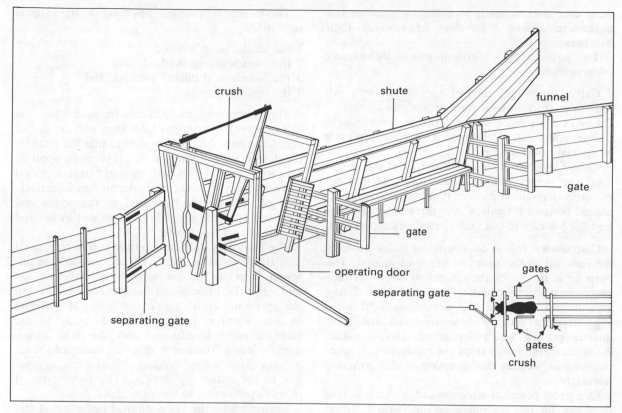

crush

shute

funnel

gate

gate

operating door

gates

separating gate

gates

crush

separating gate

fig. 7.15 Plan for funnel, shute, crush and separating gate

as the general trauma and unpleasant nature of this operation, the dehorning of adult cattle is not recommended. Instead, the policy of routinely dehorning calves at branding time is preferred. Alternatives are the 'tipping' of adult cattle horns, or a breeding programme that introduces the polled characteristic into the herd (see Chapter 4).

Tipping is a far less severe operation than dehorning of older cattle. Sawing or using the guillotine to cut off some 5 to 7 cm only from the end of the horn (fig. 7.16) does not usually penetrate the sensitive part of the horn core. Some bleeding may occur from the small terminal part of the horn artery if more than 5 to 7 cm of horn is cut, but bleeding can be stopped easily with a dry cotton plug applied with zinc oxide non-elastic plaster and painted over with stockholm tar. Tipping does expose a little of the more sensitive quick of the

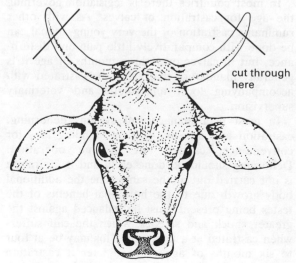

cut through here

fig. 7.16 Tipping the horn

133

horn core and so tends to make the animals less aggressive among themselves or towards their handlers.

To summarise recommended dehorning programmes:

1 Calves up to nine days of age: disbud with collodium mixture, caustic soda or hot iron cautery.
2 Calves from three weeks to two to three months of age: gouge out the horn core using a sharp knife or special gouging iron.
3 Calves three to six months and over: use guillotine, saw, or dehorning wire. Note that in some countries legislation dictates that a local anaesthetic should be used for calves over three months of age and the job carried out under veterinary supervision.

Castration This is an operation which involves the removal of the testes of the male animal. The purpose is to render the animal sterile, to reduce aggressiveness, to promote fat deposition during growth and to avoid the development of male characteristics such as excessive crest and forequarter growth which depreciates carcass value. Removal of the testes stops the production of spermatozoa as well as the secretion of the hormone testosterone.

One great practical advantage of castrates is that they can be run on range or otherwise fattened along with heifer calves and older females.

In most countries there is legislation governing the age for castration of calves. As with other ruminants castration of the very young animal can be done with comparatively little pain and disturbance, but in calves over three months of age it is generally mandatory that calves be castrated with accompanying local anaesthetic and veterinary supervision.

In most beef management systems dehorning, castration and any marking or branding are, for convenience, carried out in one operation. Dehorning should be done early and if castration is not carried out at the same time the additional body growth due to the hormonal benefits of the testes being present must be balanced against the greater shock and setback which the calf suffers when castrated at a later age. This may be at four to six months of age or even later if castration coincides with the round-up and weaning.

There are four main approaches to surgical castration:

1 the elastic band method;
2 the bloodless ring method;
3 the bloodless Burdizzo method; and
4 the open technique.

The rubber ring method can be used when the calf is a week old and no later than two months of age. Care must be taken to ensure that the testicles are descended and that the ring is properly applied. The ring must be checked regularly over a period of two weeks to make sure that it has effectively shut off the blood circulation to the testes and scrotum. The scrotum and the testes will wither and dry up after a few weeks.

The bloodless Burdizzo method is now in general use. Burdizzo pliers (fig. 7.17) are provided in different sizes to use on animals of different age and size. The principle of the Burdizzo is to crush the spermatic cord so that the testes shrivel and become inactive, while the blood supply to the scrotum remains effective and the skin consequently intact. To achieve this only one cord should be crushed at a time holding this as close as possible to the outer lipped edge. The latter type of pliers is preferable to the non-lipped type.

Castration by the open surgical operation is still preferred by some but is losing favour except for use in older animals where the Burdizzo is not effective. The obvious disadvantage to its use is

fig. 7.17 Burdizzo pliers

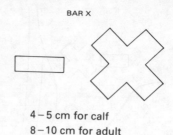

BAR X

4 – 5 cm for calf
8 – 10 cm for adult

fig. 7.19 Cattle brands

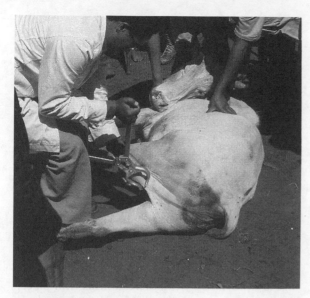

fig. 7.18 Bull cast for castration

that the open wound will attract flies and this can be a considerable nuisance, especially in 'blow-fly' areas. Some ranchers castrate out of the fly season in order to avoid this problem.

Where it may be necessary to castrate older animals such as culled bulls they may be cast (fig. 7.18), a procedure that requires sedation and careful handling, or castrated in a crush in the standing position. The operation is a hazardous one needing the specialised attention of the veterinarian and an experienced ranch hand. In many tropical countries the meat of a mature bull has special chewing value and in such circumstances castration and subsequent tenderising before slaughter is of little practical importance.

Branding The main purpose of branding is to identify the ownership of the cattle concerned and to assist in immediate identification from a distance of individuals in a herd for breeding and other purposes. Branding may also be used to establish the origin of migrant herds and trade cattle on the stock route. In parts of Africa, for example, cattle may be branded on the cheek to indicate that they have come from a bovine contagious pleuro-pneumonia-affected area. Branding may be a personal matter, in which an owner identifies his own

ranch or neighbourhood, or a statutory regulation in which only prescribed brands can be used. An example of a specific brand is given in fig. 7.19. The following branding methods may be adopted:

1 temporary identification by the use of paints;
2 hot iron branding; and
3 cryo or freeze branding.

When calves of only about 10 weeks old are being branded small (4 to 5 cm) branding irons should be used both to minimise the size of the wound and to avoid too large a brand which is unsightly and incurs excess hide damage when the skin expands during the subsequent growth of the animal.

The branding iron should be heated to a dull red colour but not beyond that point. If there is a thick hair coat on the branding site it is good practice to brush the hot iron lightly back and forth across the area to burn away the excess hair. The brand is then firmly pressed onto the skin for sufficient time to make a shallow imprint into (but not right through) the hide. The resulting brand should be permanent, though hair will generally grow across it and except in short-coated animals, clipping may be necessary in future years to read the brand.

Numerals indicating the year of birth or the individual identification number of particular animals are sometimes also fire-branded on some other position such as the mid-side, but these have no official status in the matter of ownership; they are purely for convenience in stock management. An alternative way of affixing identification numbers is to use freeze branding, as the resulting different colour of the hair allows the numbers to be read at a distance and without clipping.

135

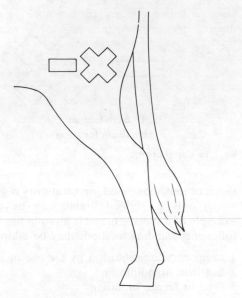

fig. 7.20 Branding over the 'gaskin' area

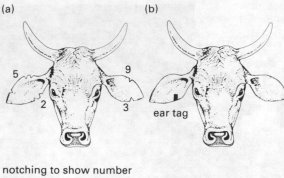

notching to show number
5239

fig. 7.21 The use of notching and eartags for identification

The site chosen for branding should be on an area of the body which will cause least destruction of the saleable hide while at the same time enabling easy identification of individuals in the group. The sites most commonly used are the rump, just below the tailhead, in line with the pinbone, or in the 'gaskin' area of the hind leg in line with the stifle joint (fig. 7.20).

The following are additional management hints at branding time:

1 Use more than one branding iron to save time.
2 Allow two seconds' contact with the skin using a red hot iron.
3 Where hair branding only is needed as, e.g. for cattle show purposes, light pressure only is required with the red hot iron. The hair brand lasts for about one month. Some countries allow a bonus on the hide for no brand marks and hence the value of cheek or neck branding. If calves are branded on the cheek, a smaller iron is needed.

Ear marking This can be used as a sole identification feature for cattle or it may be used as an adjunct for breeding purposes and/or for routine vaccinations of public health importance as, for example, in tuberculosis and brucellosis control.

Ear marking can be done by 'notching' and/or by the use of metal or plastic ear tags (fig. 7.21). Ear tags are provided by commercial firms with pincers or punches to insert them. Many ranchers devise their own tags. A simple one is a triangle of plastic containing an identification number or other particulars which is inserted by a punch. The long-used system of ear notching, while it avoids the use and possible loss of plastic or metal tags, has the disadvantage that higher identification numbers, requiring a greater number of notches, may mutilate an ear to such an extent that the ear itself becomes torn or even partially removed when the animal is exposed to severe fly worry combined with *Acacia* thorn or other thorny scrub undergrowth on range.

The buffalo on range

It has been demonstrated in Australia, Brazil, Borneo, Sri Lanka and elsewhere that buffalo, with attention to certain of their special requirements, can be adapted to range management systems. This applies also to buffalo which have become feral or semi-feral.

Borneo

In Borneo there are areas where the buffalo is being reared as a meat animal. In Sabah for example, the Banjou people maintain mixed herds of cattle and buffalo under ranching conditions in what is classified as well watered open forest

136

country. The buffalo at 5 years of age are rounded up on separate days to the cattle, either for training or for sale as live or slaughter animals. Those for sale as meat are shot, while those for training or sale on foot are lassoed with a loop of rope on a bamboo pole, or driven into a corral. Most of the animals are owned on a family or cooperative basis and kept as a form of capital investment, to be sold only when cash is required.

Australia

Perhaps the best example of ranch rearing of the swamp buffalo is to be found in the tropical areas of Australia's Northern Territory, that is between latitudes 11 to 14°S and longitudes 130 to 134°E. Small groups of swamp buffalo were brought to this area from 1826 onwards, the first groups coming from Timor and from Kissa Island, in what is now Indonesia.

Although these early introductions proved in general unsuccessful and in most cases controlled breeding programmes were finally abandoned, the imported buffalo spread and multiplied as feral animals. This occurred to such an extent that a peak population was reported in 1964 of 150 000 head of feral buffalo. These animals settled mainly in the floodplains of the Northern Territory where the climate is monsoonal, with a heavy rainfall period of some 1 000 to 1 500 mm from September/October to March/April, followed by a dry season, virtually without rain. In this part of tropical Australia temperatures are high, with maximum humidity occurring during the rainy season.

The vegetation of the terrain is characteristically that associated with swamp country, with spear grass (*Imperata* spp.) and indigenous sorghums on the ridges; on the plains there are mainly freshwater mangroves with eucalyptus trees on the ridges and on the periphery. The terrain is not at first sight attractive for any form of range management, but it has proved to be suitable for the thousands of feral buffalo that have established themselves to such an extent that there are good prospects of their management on a commercial ranching basis.

Behavioural studies have been carried out on these feral buffalo. In particular, the phenomenon of site attachment has been noted. This is, that even under the most inclement conditions such as intense drought, buffalo may refuse to move to another site or grazing area, even if food is scarce and yet available in an alternative site. Wallowing areas have also been observed to be important for feral buffalo on range and it has been shown that those animals with access to wallowing graze longer over a 24 hour period than those without wallows. Extra grazing time means increased liveweight gains and consequently increased productivity per hectare. Adequate shade and an abundance of drinking water also enhances growth rate. Water buffalo depend not only on dry land grazing and browsing, but also on what they can gather under the water. Buffalo can submerge themselves and graze quite effectively for a brief period under water.

The system of domestication of feral stock for establishing a ranch is reportedly simple. Captured young calves appear to give little trouble although older males and cows are tethered to trees for periods of up to 6 days following capture. The older animals tend to spill the drinking water brought to them and scatter their feed for about 4 days after capture but once they have been overcome by hunger and thirst they settle down satisfactorily to the new environment. After about 10 days they can be handled with ease. This involves walking them around in an enclosure and handling them physically, but with patience and gentleness. As might be expected, cows with calves at foot and older bulls take the longest time to settle down to new conditions of management. Basically, however, and in the family subsistence farming system, the buffalo is the most docile of animals.

Many small properties in the Northern Territory of Australia now contain domesticated buffalo and the animal is to a considerable extent no longer regarded as feral. It is estimated that there may be over 200 000 head and legislation has been introduced recognising them as having the status of commercial livestock and thus eligible for branding, earmarking and slaughter at abattoirs which are licensed for export.

A small meat industry was established in the Northern Territory in 1959, during which period some 2 500 head of feral buffalo were slaughtered.

By 1971–72, some 17 000 were slaughtered during the year and local meat works were expanded to cope with this increase in meat production, used both for human consumption and, where not acceptable, for manufacturing into feeds for domestic pets. Slaughterhouse exports in 1982 were approximately 33 000 head.

Much of the Northern Territory buffalo slaughter is on a system of harvesting, not dissimilar to that adopted in parts of East and southern Africa for the seasonal harvesting of wild game animals. The buffalo are hunted, usually from a four-wheel-drive vehicle and special permits are given to protect herd numbers; for example, only bulls three years of age and over may be slaughtered. The shooter and assistant(s) travel around looking for prey; the buffalo is selected and shot, bled immediately and then winched onto a truck for transport back to the abattoir as quickly as possible.

Various methods of handling and capturing feral buffalo for slaughter have been tested and improved over the years. At some abattoirs, animals are caught and brought alive to the abattoir, unloaded into yards and sprayed with water, which has been found to have a very calming effect on them, prior to being shot and bled. Such catching procedures, however, still require handling of the individual animal and at some stations, such as Woolner and Munmarlary, it has been found relatively easy to drive the buffalo from the main herd into fenced enclosures. A further development has been the design of portable traps capable of

holding some 70 head of buffalo at a time. The trap is built of 5 cm diameter steel tubes, some 55 m long, with extended wings 45 to 90 m long and forming a funnel-like chute 275 m across at the widest end into which the buffalo are driven and so along the trap into the loading vehicle. Another refinement, using permanent traps, is to drive the buffalo into the traps by means of a low-flying helicopter used as a sort of airborne drover.

Buffalo slaughtered in the early killing season, that is, during the early rains, usually give the best carcasses, averaging 230 to 250 kg of meat for animals in good flesh, although those in poor condition may yield as little as 160 to 180 kg. Buffalo in optimum condition have yielded as much as 280 to 290 kg of boned-out meat. Buffalo meat is now being exported from Australia to other countries for sampling on the commercial market and buffalo steak is served in many Australian hotels and restaurants. Although the industry is still in the developmental stage, buffalo producers have established the 'Buffalo Owners and Breeders Association of Australia', and there is every reason to believe that buffalo will be accepted and managed as commercial meat animals in the same way as cattle. Growth rate of the Brazilian buffalo and carcass characteristics of the Egyptian buffalo are given in Tables 7.4 and 7.5.

The Americas

Buffalo were introduced to several areas of Brazil over the past century, but it is generally considered

Table 7.4 Daily weight gains of buffalo in Brazil

No. of animals	Age in days	Wt. at commencement of tests	Wt. gain at end of 140 days (kg)	Weight gain per day (kg)
1	499	459.7	182.0	1.300
2	479	500.0	165.3	1.180
3	476	522.7	169.0	1.207
4	475	343.0	142.0	1.014
5	473	456.0	147.3	1.052
6	473	382.0	156.0	1.114
7	472	431.3	173.3	1.237
9	467	446.0	165.3	1.180
13	423	463.3	162.0	1.157
76	463	462.0	204.0	1.457

Table 7.5 Weight of different ages, dressing percentage and proportions of lean meat, fat and bone in Egyptian buffalo calves: 4 groups of 42 calves

Initial weight (kg)	Age	Weight after 6 mths (kg)	SE per kg weight gain	Weight after 12 mths (kg)	2 bulls slaughtered at	Weight (kg)	Dressing (%)
43.3	1 wk	137.6	2.901	266.2	12 mths	363	51.52
103.0	6 mths	236.9	4.137	289.6	18 mths	400	57.30
160.1	12 mths	332.5	4.495	474.5	24 mths	480	54.17
233.6	18 mths	408.9	5.107	–			

Proportions of lean meat, fat and bone in right side carcass:
  at 12 months – 71.44, 8.56, and 20.15%;
  at 18 months – 69.37, 12.17 and 17.46%;
  at 24 months – 73.46, 8.96 and 17.58%
Meat–fat–bone ratios for these same ages are:
  3.6, 0.4:1; 3.8, 0.7:1 and 4.2, 0.5:1.

that the true potential of this animal in the country's agricultural economy was not fully appreciated until the early 1930s, after the establishment of a herd at Belem by the Instituto Agronomico del Norte. It was soon realised that the Amazon Valley was ideally suited to the water buffalo and estimates indicate that there is an annual increase in their numbers in this area of 3 to 10 per cent. The breeds are of the Pieto (Black) or Mediterranean type, maintained for the most part on the island of Marajo, which is the largest inland waterway island in the world. There are also large herds of purebred Murrah and Jafarabadi and their crosses in the State of Sao Paulo, where the climate is mainly subtropical and agriculture is more highly developed. Although milk is the primary product of these herds, large numbers of calves are reared and the meat is of growing importance and highly acceptable to the consumer.

Systems of management of the buffalo in Brazil, except on more specialised private or government farms and experiment stations are, for the most part, haphazard. In the Amazon Valley about one-third of the farms keep buffalo as well as local Criollo cattle, excepting in the more low-lying areas, where only buffalo can be kept. A small number of buffalo are feral but they do not constitute an economic potential as they do in Australia.

The main breeds introduced to the Caribbean, originally for work on the sugar plantations, are the Murrah, Jafarabadi, Nagpuri, Surti and Ravi. Measurement of liveweight gains was initiated in 1964. Preliminary results for animals at different ages gave a range of approximately 0.5 to 0.7 kg gain per day for animals grazed on Pangola grass (*Digitaria decumbens*) at a stocking rate in two successive seasons of 2 to 3 animals per hectare. These were considered encouraging results and were it not for the need to dispel existing prejudices against the consumption of buffalo meat, supplies from this animal could rapidly augment the existing short supply of meat, necessitating at present costly imports from other countries.

Studies in Trinidad, based on a projected herd life for buffalo females of eight years, a calving rate of 75 per cent and a calf mortality of 12 per cent, indicated that with a foundation herd of 1 200 breeding females subsequent progeny could satisfy that country's meat requirements by the turn of the century, taking into account the annual increase in human population during the same period. The importance of the breeding and research programme in Trinidad and Tobago on the buffalo is now recognised elsewhere in the Americas. Exports of small numbers of calves and young male and female stock of breeding age have already been allowed to neighbouring countries such as Venezuela and Colombia.

Other countries in Latin America, such as Bolivia and Peru, have so far shown little interest in the buffalo as a source of meat due, perhaps in part, to the fact that many of the rural folk are cattle oriented, or, as in Peru, accustomed to other domestic ruminants such as the llama. More recently, however, the Universidad de la Amazona Perunana Iquitis in Peru has initiated imports of a small number of breeding buffalo from Brazil for experimental purposes and there are plans for further imports from elsewhere. Preliminary studies show that there are considerable possibilities for the buffalo in the Peruvian Amazon Valley where huge areas of natural grasslands provide unlimited supplies of forage. The *selva* lowlands of the Amazon Valley, though subject to seasonal flooding, are also considered ideally suited to the water buffalo. Indeed, the valleys of this great river would seem to offer great prospects for utilising the buffalo to improve the much needed supply of animal protein in some countries in the Americas.

Buffalo management

Management of the water buffalo in the traditional sector is much the same as that for cattle except for certain features relating to differences in grazing and breeding behaviour and water requirements. Husbandry practices are largely influenced, according to the country and agro-climatic conditions in which buffalo are found, by the breed or type and their economic uses. The standard of animal husbandry by local farmers who follow traditional systems of management and breeding is generally very low.

Swamp buffalo husbandry in Southeast Asia
The swamp buffalo has been described as a semi-domesticated nocturnal animal that resists all attempts to keep it under stall-fed conditions. It is a most versatile ruminant ideally suited to the cultivation of paddy. Nonetheless, swamp buffalo are generally undernourished and managed under somewhat primitive conditions. Calves run with their dams, usually with a cord around their necks to keep them under control, until, by two years of age, the noses of both males and females are pierced and ringed in preparation for their use as draught animals. Castration at a young age is not favoured by farmers, in order to retain the large hump and heavy shoulders desirable for work in the entire male. Buffalo bulls not achieving this

physical character, along with old work animals, are sold for slaughter. The swamp buffalo, whatever its working assignments, whether for traction in paddy cultivation, lumber hauling, working of water wheels or 'puddling' of clay for bricks, or as a source of power for sugar cane crushing, performs all such tasks with great endurance and docility.

The main differences in the river buffalo from the swamp type are that they are more docile in habit and can be herded and managed much like cattle. Their chief use is as dairy animals, although in the hilly and forested areas of the Indian subcontinent, they are used for draught purposes. Meat and work may be considered as the by-products of buffalo dairying in many developing countries. Under the stimulus of dairy development and particularly to meet the demand for both meat and milk products for urban communities much larger numbers of buffalo are being kept by farmers under new and improved systems of husbandry. These farmers include the small milk producer, the larger privately owned buffalo dairy farm, the rural milk production units, the large rural dairy farms and the milk colonies in India. The main aim of the last mentioned is to remove milking buffalo from the more congested areas in the bigger cities and townships to more hygienic surroundings with adequate facilities for water, housing and feeding. In addition there are organised buffalo dairy farms owned by agricultural companies and government and military livestock centres and it is in these that breed and managerial improvements have mainly occurred.

Stabling at night on dry ground will improve breeding efficiency and also helps to avoid parasitic diseases and constitutional defects in the calves. The swamp buffalo, after a day's work in cultivation for about 5 hours, or timber hauling for about 10 hours is left to graze and wallow. Buffalo in the village will gather into one herd by noon and take to the swamp until late afternoon, each individual selecting its own wallow, or sometimes the whole village herd uses a communal wallow. By the late afternoon they emerge from the wallow to graze on reeds or other aquatic herbage till late in the evening, after which they move to rest on dry ground until daybreak. Their main activity, including breeding, sparring with their horns among the males and activity of the calves, occurs at night.

At the end of the main three month working season swamp buffalo may be driven into the forest to remain there until the end of the harvest season. Farmers in Southeast Asian countries usually keep two to three animals per family, one of these being a bull, as a source of power. In Thailand, the average is 2.1 buffalo per farm, starting work at about three to four years of age and working for an average of 13.9 years. Well managed draught buffalo used for timber haulage work for 10 hours per day and move a dead weight of up to 1 tonne.

Recent survey studies on small farms in the Polonnaruwa and Matara districts of Sri Lanka on buffalo management show the average farm in the highlands to be 1.6 ha with 1.0 ha of paddy land. Such a farm unit averages 4 head of cattle and 20 local buffalo used for milk and draught. Buffalo have free grazing on natural pastures in the paddy fields and adjacent jungle and on roadside waste grassland. There is no cultivation of improved pastures. Cows produce about one litre of milk per day; ploughing is, with males and, when necessary done with non-pregnant dry cows, although the preference is for bulls for both ploughing and puddling, a pair managing to plough 0.2 ha and puddle 0.05–0.1 ha. The genuine dual purpose draught/milk-type of local buffalo is found in the Anuradhapura district and no difference is reported between the draught output of male and both milking and dry buffalo cows. The emphasis is on a low cost/input basis, that is, with no concentrate feeding. Profitability analysis studies have highlighted the economic advantage of dual purpose herds.

The buffalo cow

On smallholdings in India women and girls look after the animals, while the men and boys work them. Management of the female buffalo on smallholdings will vary according to the season and the sequence described here is one found in India. In the Indian summer from March to mid-June, grazing and the use of some sort of shade are regulated according to the degree of solar radiation and the ambient temperature. Shelters are simple buildings, either half or full-walled with adequate door and window openings for ventilation. Water and roughage are provided in the shed. During the heat of early March animals are kept in the shed from 10 to 17 hours with grazing in late evening and early morning. From early April it is essential to protect the animals from the hot sun and winds by covering the openings to the shed with canvas, straw or whatever else is available for this purpose. Light is reduced as much as possible, reduced light being related, it is believed, to the onset of heat in the female. The window and door coverings are raised in the early morning and late evening to allow in fresh, cooler air. The animals at this stage, having spent from 7 to 19 hours in the shed, are then allowed access to all-night grazing. If there is no wallow, care is taken to splash the buffalo with water at regular intervals. Cut green grass is fed *ad lib* together with legume hay. 0.5 g of copper sulphate a day is said to induce oestrus in lactating and dry buffalo. Vasectomised bulls are commonly used for the detection of heat. They are brought to the shed three times a day and cows on heat can be given AI or put to selected local bulls. It is customary for the cow to be served twice within one hour. Selected herd bulls are often raddled and left with the females during night grazing.

The villagers therefore lay particular emphasis on management and type of housing or shelter according to temperature, radiant energy, rainfall and wind velocity. The system of housing in the arid or humid tropical zones is related to both economic and practical considerations, such as the size of the holding, size of herd and type of farming system. Housing on smallholdings is much the same as that for Zebu cattle, except for the additional need for water both for drinking purposes and for splashing by hand. Swamp buffalo are more casually maintained than the river buffalo, being kept near to the farm house in stalls without a roof, or under trees, or in the rice store near the house for security reasons. After the paddy harvest, large numbers of swamp buffalo are managed under natural conditions in the forest for much of the year. This also applies to the more nondescript types of river buffalo in the more forested and hilly parts of India. After work, or grazing in the forest during the day, the animals are herded near the farm house for safety, often taking shelter under the thatch projecting from the house roof. In South India, many buffalo at night are herded into a *tucl* which is a round enclosure made of stones. There is no roof. The calves are kept separately.

The buffalo calf
In South and western Asia the rearing of buffalo is much neglected. This may be intentional, as in India and Pakistan, where the buffalo dairy farmers rear mainly heifer calves and allow male calves literally to starve to death. Such a situation is mainly due to the fact that there is little or no demand for buffalo calf meat, nor are they needed later, except in the hilly tracts of India, for work which is for the most part done by draught bullocks. However, where buffalo are maintained almost exclusively for work, as in Sabah, Taiwan and in the Philippines, calves are allowed to suckle freely up to the age of 12 months and often beyond this until the cow goes dry. In Egypt, male calves, other than those reserved for breeding, are allowed to suckle for about six weeks and then slaughtered for veal. With the gradual change in feeding habits in India and Pakistan and the increased demand for meat, it is anticipated that the rearing of male buffalo calves will be encouraged. On smallholdings in Indonesia both male and female calves are reared, both sexes, including cows over three years of age, being used for work. Bulls are generally sold for slaughter when the owner needs money.

It is common practice, as with the Zebu calf under traditional systems of management, for the buffalo calf to be at foot while the cow is being milked. Calves most frequently suckle from the rear and this often leads to hypertrophy of the buffalo cow's hindquarters. The buffalo calf can be switched over to pail-feeding more easily than the Zebu and in well managed buffalo dairy herds, the calf is removed from the dam as soon as colostrum secretion has ceased and bucket fed until weaning at around 8 to 10 months of age. In Iraq, calves are allowed to suckle up to 6 months of age during which time the two quarters reserved for this purpose are alternated at intervals.

In eastern and Southeast Asia swamp and draught-type river buffalo calves are not weaned. When the farmer wishes to get milk for the household the buffalo cow is usually caught and milked, after being suckled briefly by the calf which has been kept away from the dam overnight. In the dairy situation, calves are kept separately and brought near to their dams to stimulate let-down at milking time. The cow is milked first, leaving last strippings for the calf. Variations in management do occur, however, and in many Muslim communities special attention is given to the young animals which have first claim to the dam's milk. For the most part, however, in traditional management systems, buffalo calves are undernourished with consequent slow growth and delayed maturity. Buffalo calves are highly susceptible to neglect and to injury and disease during the first six months of their life, losses of up to 80 per cent being recorded. A recent small farm survey in Sri Lanka cited calf mortality losses of 20 to 40 per cent.

Intensive systems of cattle management
Management systems in beef cattle raising are broadly classified as extensive and intensive. Extensive systems are applicable to pastoralism and ranching; intensive systems to more confined management on improved pastures or in feedlots (see Chapter 6). In the above context, both systems refer to the feeding management regime. However, the term 'intensification' may also be applied with reference to a breeding programme, such as heifer management and controlled breeding on a ranch. The management system may also relate to a particular category of farming, cattle reared by sedentary subsistence farmers being, for the most part, considered as managed intensively. There are two major methods of intensive production. The first is to rear and fatten cattle on pasture and/or fodder; the second is to manage them, either from birth, or during some other stage of their lives, in confinement. The terms semi-extensive or semi-intensive are sometimes used and this may be considered as a period of confinement combined with limited periods of grazing.

In the past it was considered that there was no place in the tropics for intensive cattle fattening systems, the reasons being the high cost of feed, the cereals in any event being required for human consumption, high fixed overhead costs and lack of technological skills. For those and other reasons feeding cattle on pasture in the humid tropics is still considered the cheapest feed resource, despite the perennial constraint of wide variations in pasture productivity between the rainy and dry seasons. However, there is now increasing evidence from work being carried out in Central America and in Nigeria, Niger, Ethiopia and Kenya in tropical Africa that there are intensive feeding systems suited to local conditions and available feeding stuffs that are economically feasible.

Management of more intensive production systems does, however, require the availability of suitable technology, together with back-up agricultural policies with regard to land tenure, taxation, credit and trade policies and input–output prices. Developed countries have available both capital and technology for improved livestock productivity, combined with a shortage of labour, whereas in the less developed livestock producing countries of the tropics, the opposite generally prevails.

In general, more intensive management systems require some degree of expertise, both as regards

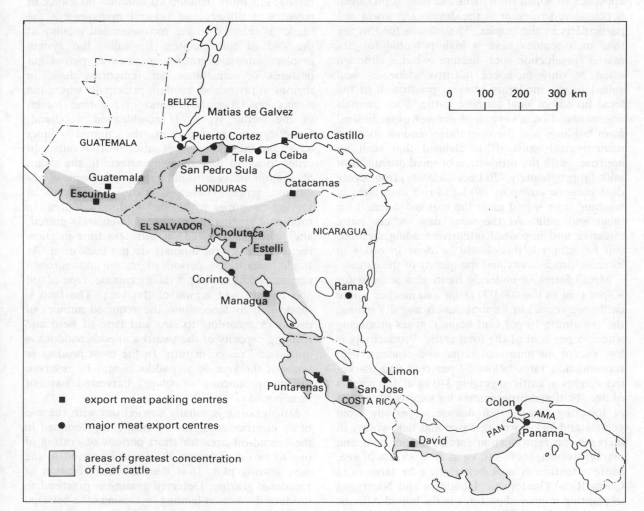

fig. 7.22 Major centres for the production, packing and export of beef from Central America and Panama

health and feeding of livestock, and in management of improved pastures or feedlot regimes. In addition the entrepreneur in developing countries has additional problems such as the high cost of transport and by-product feeds together with poor marketing facilities.

In Mexico, for example, major constraints to intensive production are the high cost of feed, high interest rates on livestock loans and shortage of high quality technology for the management and operation of the more sophisticated production systems. Despite these constraints the dual purpose approach in which both meat and milk is produced is considered relevant in the developing world and particularly in the tropics. The reasons for this are that such regions have a high potential for dry matter production per hectare which, although often of only mediocre nutritive value, is well suited to the moderate rates of production of the local breeds of dual purpose cattle. Such animals are managed on a very large number of traditional farm holdings and the operations require no great technological skills. It is claimed that such an approach with the production of small quantities of milk (approximately 720 l per lactation) from every dual purpose cow plus 180 kg of calf liveweight at weaning time would meet the national demand for meat and milk. At the same time, where more effective and improved intensive feeding methods can be adopted, this should be done in order to increase productivity and the quality of the carcass.

Mixed farms of under 50 ha in area account for 90 per cent of the 400 000 farms and ranches where cattle are reared in Central America and Panama, the remaining 10 per cent being ranches producing some 65 per cent of the total cattle. Productivity is low except on improved farms and ranches, with reproduction rates below 50 per cent and market liveweights of cattle averaging 340 kg at 4 to 5 years of age. National programmes for improvement aim at lowering losses from disease, especially from genital and tick-borne diseases and tick worry, to increase the reproduction rate to 80 per cent and market liveweights to 410 kg at $2\frac{1}{2}$ to 3 years of age. More attention is now being given by farmers in Costa Rica, Guatemala, Honduras and Nicaragua to planting improved pastures in the humid Atlantic Slope region (fig. 7.22), an area previously considered unsuitable for cattle because of danger from ticks, disease and sunburn. With adequate care and management, including routine vaccinations and dipping, it is now considered that there will be no greater problems than those currently met with on farms on the Pacific Slope side. With these various inputs it is estimated that local demand in meat will be met and meat exports increased by 10 per cent.

Year-round grazing

The principles involved in the management of cultivated pastures used in this system are discussed briefly. For more detailed information on choice of pastures, fertilisers and general management the reader is referred to the recommended reading at the end of this chapter. Basically, the system involves intensive grazing on sown or permanent pastures or sometimes on temporary leys, in regions of favourable rainfall, principally where the climax vegetation is lowland or highland forest, or the wetter types of broad-leaved woodland. Grass/legume mixtures in the humid tropics have produced some of the best results. In order to avoid the damaging effects to the sward of continuous year-round grazing, systems of rotational, strip or deferred grazing by animals of varying categories within the herd are adopted. In rotational grazing the pasture is intensively grazed, after which it is rested for sufficient time to allow regrowth before the animals are put back on it. As would be expected, periods of grazing and regrowth vary according to the prevailing climate, type of soil and pasture and season of the year. The land is subdivided by fences into the required number of paddocks according to size and type of herd and carrying capacity of the sward and each paddock is grazed and rested in turn. In the most productive times of the year some paddocks may be reserved for the production of silage, harvested hay, or standing hay.

Strip grazing is usually carried out with the use of an electric fence, the animals being confined in the fenced-off area for short periods of grazing of one to two days before the fence is moved to the next grazing plot. It is thus an intensification of rotational grazing. Deferred grazing is practised to produce dry season feeding by closing off a selected paddock early in the rains and allowing the grass to mature for grazing as standing hay in the dry season. Alternatively, after grazing is stopped before the end of the rains, a nitrogenous fertiliser is applied and the pasture rested to produce relatively young grass for early dry season grazing.

General operating procedures are relatively simple and overhead costs, other than those for initial clearing, planting, fencing, watering and dipping or spray-race facilities, are low. Fencing, the extent of which will depend upon the system of grazing, whether strip, rotational or continuous, can be of simple design, using three or four strands of barbed wire and hardwood uprights, or concrete uprights with metal droppers. (See pages 120 and 121.) Electric fencing becomes too expensive when large numbers of animals are grazed in separate groups. Watering can be carried out quite simply with plastic pipes from a supply source to some simple type of drinking trough inside the paddocks. Mixed mineral salt licks are made available in wooden troughs. Pasture in the humid tropics can stand heavy grazing and last 5 to 10 years and longer without need for ploughing up and re-planting, or putting under crops in a mixed animal/crops farming system.

Some degree of stratification within this system may be practised as regards herd management. Quite a large percentage of the herd, including non-working bulls and cows with heavy unweaned calves at foot, utilise feed for maintenance rather than for production purposes. Fattening steers and young heifers and bulls, on the other hand, are more efficient at utilising their feed for growth purposes so that it is good management practice to allow them access to the best pastures.

The problem with any production system based on pastures, be it extensive or intensive, is the seasonality of grass production that causes variations in both the quality and quantity of animal feed. This applies particularly in those areas, however productive they may be during the rains, that have a well defined dry season. The effect of this dry season check on growth rate during the dry season is illustrated in fig. 7.6, page 116. As production is intensified it is necessary to make the most efficient use out of the nutritional resources available to the animal by such measures as reducing stocking rate, manipulation of rotation

procedures and the use of alternative sources of feed. Some general approaches to the problems of dry season feeding are as follows:

1 transfer of stock to more humid areas for grass production during the dry season and efficient use of the forage produced;
2 irrigation of part of the pastures during the dry season, though this is often not feasible for both economic and practical reasons;
3 conservation of surplus forage produced during the flush stage of growth at the beginning of the rainy season – this requires some technological skills, also handling and transport;
4 reservation of selected areas of standing hay or deferred grazing;
5 production of supplementary crops for dry season feeding – this requires additional labour input and time;
6 feeding of supplementary feeds based on locally available crops or crop by-products.

Intensive grazing on improved pastures Mention has already been made of extensive production of beef from natural grasslands. Enterprises of this nature, except on highly improved natural grasslands, where a cow-and-calf programme can be taken right through to the finishing stages, depend for the most part on the method used for finishing the beef animals. This may be either on a ranch with adjacent feedlots for intensive feeding with forages, oil seed by-products or other concentrate sources, or at feedlots situated elsewhere. In contrast to these more costly enterprises, involving considerable capital input, there is increasing evidence to show that intensive production of beef on improved grass or grass/legume pastures, even without excessively high levels of fertiliser, shows great potential for semi-subsistence farmers in the tropics.

Intensive grazing techniques can be used for:

1 an intensive cow-and-calf programme;
2 the finishing of store cattle off range;
3 as part of a mixed farm regime; and
4 the fattening of surplus dairy calves.

With the exception of technique (1) which is more of a specialised programme, both techniques (2) and (3) can be incorporated into a semi-subsistence farming programme. Fattening of surplus dairy calves on pasture is confined in much of tropical Africa to government and other institutional dairies. Beef/milk production, on the other hand, is a common practice on ranches in Central America. In Colombia 46 per cent of the milk entering the commercial market came from beef herds in 1976 and better productivity in terms of milk, meat and reproduction performance is being aimed at by national efforts to encourage pasture improvement under the Beef Production Systems Programme organised by the International Centre for Tropical Agriculture (CIAT).

While many of the problems of seasonal setbacks in year-round grazing regimes need to be resolved, a number of grazing trials in the humid tropics have demonstrated that by improved husbandry and nutrition Zebu cattle on good grass/legume pastures can reach slaughter weights of 500 kg in 3 to 3½ years, or an average of 0.45 kg daily liveweight gain throughout life. For export purposes in Kenya, as an example, top quality beef should attain this weight at just under three years of age, when such an animal may be classified as in prime condition, that is, with the desired amount of lean meat.

Experiments carried out in East and West Africa, Brazil, Jamaica, Colombia, Mexico and Puerto Rico have nonetheless shown that the output from different grasses is highly variable and depends on the interaction of a number of factors, such as density of sward, age of herbage, soil fertility, amount of fertiliser applied, soil moisture, ambient temperature, type, age and health of animals stocking rate, and grazing and animal management.

Grazing trials conducted in Brazil to measure stocking rates and liveweight gains on different grass species receiving various fertiliser levels have shown, for example, that the addition of 200 kg/ha of nitrogen fertiliser to Guinea grass (*Panicum maximum*) pastures more than doubles liveweight gains. In Nigeria grazing trials in the humid tropical part of the country, with improved pastures and fertiliser at moderate levels, but using a high stocking rate for intensive grazing over 64-day periods, produced total liveweight production for the test period ranging from 341.8 to 490.7 kg/ha and average liveweight gains of 0.37 to 0.53 kg/day (Table 7.6). Similarly, in a very simple exercise, using a rotation system based on three separate 0.44 ha paddocks of grass/legume (*Cynodon plectostachyus/Centrosema pubescens*) pastures, three yearling White Fulani (Bunaji) Zebu bulls attained average liveweights of 444.4 kg at three years of age. Other examples of intensive beef production on improved pastures on high fertiliser rates in Puerto Rico and Brazil are shown in Table 7.7. As stated earlier, methods of grazing, such as continuous or rotational sytems, can greatly influence total liveweight production as well as the stocking rate. Examples of grazing trials from experiments in Colombia are given in Table 7.8. Such intensive grazing management procedures may be aimed at reducing, as far as possible, the dry season check and sometimes losses in weight of range cattle which can occur on year-round grazing programmes on native pastures, as shown in figs 7.6 and 7.7, on pages 116 and 117 respectively.

It has been shown that intensive beef production can be geared to seasonal operations.

Table 7.6 Liveweight and lean meat production on pasture subjected to varying levels of fertiliser treatment including trace minerals at Ibadan, Nigeria, during 64 days of grazing

	Treatments[1]							
	I	II	III	IV	V	VI	VII	VIII
Stocking rate (head/ha)	14.4	14.4	14.4	14.4	14.4	14.4	14.4	14.4
Total liveweight gain (kg/ha) (64 days)	454.3	490.7	410.4	453.9	341.8	428.1	379.1	462.7
Mean liveweight gain (g/head/day)	492.2	531.3	445.3	492.2	370.3	464.1	410.9	501.6
Meat produced (kg/ha)[2]	240.8	260.1	217.5	240.6	181.2	226.9	200.9	245.2

[1] I No fertiliser   II 502.11 kg super/ha   III 502.11 kg super + 251 kg S.A./ha   IV Treatment III + Mg + Cu + Mo + Zn + B
V Treatment IV minus B   VI Treatment V minus Zn   VII Treatment VI minus Mo   VIII Treatment VII minus Cu
[2] Based on dressing percentage of 53%

Table 7.7 Animal production from various grass species in Puerto Rico and Brazil

Grass species	Carrying capacity (animals per ha)	Liveweight gains	
		Daily gain per head (kg)	Yearly gain per ha (kg)
Puerto Rico[1]			
Panicum maximum	6.50	0.59	1325
Digitaria decumbens	6.00	0.57	1140
Pennisetum purpureum	5.75	0.57	1125
Bachiaria mutica	4.50	0.48	790
Brazil[2]			
P. maximum cv. Coloniao	2.30	0.44	330
P. maximum cv. Tanganyika	1.75	0.39	296
Hyparrhenia rufa	2.00	0.48	320
D. decumbens	2.30	0.38	330
Cynodon dactylon cv. Coastal	1.3	0.26	140
Melinis minutiflora	0.9	0.36	120

[1] Averages of several intensively managed grazing trials on steep slopes, receiving 2.5 tons/ha annually of 14-4-10 fertiliser.
[2] Averages of hot and cool seasons in the state of Sao Paulo; carrying capacities varying with season and thus approximated.

Table 7.8 Animal output with different systems of pasture management in Columbia

Pasture management system[1]	Stocking rate (animals per ha)	Liveweight gain	
		Daily gain per head (kg)	Yearly gain per ha (kg)
Continuous grazing on natural pastures	1.4	0.40	205
Continuous grazing, weed control	1.9	0.40	275
Alternate grazing two paddocks, weed control	2.5	0.52	475
Alternate grazing, nitrogen fertilisation	3.0	0.50	550
Rotational grazing	3.4	0.49	610
Rotational grazing, nitrogen fertilisation	5.1	0.47	875

[1] Averages from 25 regional trials, with native pastures of naturalised grasses and improved species such as *Brachiaria decumbens*, *B. Mutica*, *Dichanthum aristatum*, *Digitaria decumbens*, *Hyparrhenia rufa*, *Panicum maximum*, *Paspalum notatum*, using steers and heifers of native races, Zebu, and native x Zebu weighing from 200 to 350 kg initially.

It is claimed by workers in Australia that, given equivalent operational opportunities, seasonally oriented intensive systems of cattle production, based on grazing and with minimal conservation of feed, provide greater yields of animal protein per unit area of land and capital involved than feedlot operations that are highly geared to the feeding of grains, oil seed supplements and conserved forages. As described in the following section, also, seasonal production can be the key to more efficient integration of intensive with extensive systems of management.

Estimated levels of annual beef production in tropical Australia using comparatively low levels of nitrogenous fertiliser in the monsoonal and humid zones are provided in Table 7.8. The highest liveweight gains recorded in the tropics were on pangola (*Digitaria decumbens*) pastures at Parada, north Queensland. Over a three year period the highest mean annual liveweight gain of 2760 kg/ha was produced at a stocking rate of 12.4 animals/ha on pastures receiving 673 kg/ha/year nitrogenous fertiliser. Liveweight gains per head ranged from 0.58 to 0.71 kg/day.

Table 7.9 Estimated annual beef production on nitrogen fertilised pastures in monsoonal and humid tropical environments in Australia

| Rainfall (mm) | Liveweight gain (kg per ha per year) | |
	Monsoonal (6 months dry)	Humid tropics (long growing season)
750–1000	150–250	300–400
1000–1500	250–400	400–700
1500–2000	350–550	1000–1500
over 2000	450–600	1300–1600
Irrigated	1600–2000	

Fertiliser application was 200–300 kg of nitrogen per ha.

fig. 7.23 Cattle feeding on bagasse and molasses

Fattening under a system of semi-confinement

This system is recommended where the aim is to establish a feedlot fattening regime used only during the dry season with fulltime grazing on natural or improved pastures during the wet season. It involves intensive feeding on agro-by-products during the dry season combined with a limited period of restricted grazing. Restricted grazing for three to five hours daily should provide some 20 per cent of total digestive nutrient (TDN) requirements, the remainder coming from whatever available supplements are being fed in the confinement yard. Since confinement occurs only during the dry season a simple enclosure for the cattle will suffice.

Full confinement

This is basically the feedlot system in which there is no outside grazing, either during the dry or the wet seasons, the animals being fed entirely in confinement from locally grown feeds, or feed from other sources such as agro-byproducts. Where confinement occurs under wet tropical conditions, some degree of shelter is needed and partially slatted floors for removal of manure in liquid form are the most appropriate.

Use of the feedlot in a system of stratification

As referred to earlier, stratification can include finishing range or dual purpose cattle on superior natural or improved pastures or in feedlots either under a 'green-lot' system in which the green crop is harvested and fed to the cattle in yards, or the 'dry-lot' system, using grains or agro-byproducts. Some spectacular liveweight gains are reported from this system: in Australia gains in yearling steers off-range of up to 1.4 kg/day were obtained in feedlots using simple rations of sorghum and roughage. In much of tropical Africa, where the majority of beef cattle originate from pastoralist-owned herds, feedlot finishing has its greatest potential in fattening units situated near cattle trade routes and adjacent to some type of agro-processing factory. An example of a state organised fattening scheme is located at Mokwa in northern Nigeria where trade cattle are selected from groups trekking to the southern markets and held for fattening for periods of up to two to three months. The ration consists of bagasse and molasses from the nearby sugar refining factory at Bachita (fig. 7.23).

Despite the many constraints to feedlot systems in tropical Africa there are recent claims to economically viable trials using Zebu trade cattle fattened intensively in the sub-humid sorghum and maize producing areas of West Africa. The cattle used were Sokoto Gudali and Bunaji from northern Nigeria. Average daily weight gains (ADG) were 0.91 kg during 11 weeks of fattening and a feed conversion efficiency of 1:6. Individual total weight gain was about 36 per cent of the initial weight. These results compare favourably with similar exercises using Boran cattle in Kenya fed a ration of molasses/urea, maize milling by-products

Table 7.10 Cost of weight gain for varying periods on feedlot in Nigeria

Period on feedlot (days)	Cost of feed per kg gained (Naira)	(US $)	Profit per animal (Naira)	(US $)	Profit per unit capacity (Naira)	(US $)
0–48	0.90	1.67	18.36	34.15	85.9	159.77
0–62	0.88	1.64	32.14	59.78	127.5	237.15
0–76	0.89	1.66	43.12	80.20	148.5	276.21
0–90	0.99	1.84	39.30	73.10	119.5	222.27

and less than 5 per cent protein supplement. Cut stoloniferous grasses were fed as roughage. The ADG of the Sokoto Gudali was marginally but not significantly superior to that of the Bunaji. Since the Bunaji generally fetch a slightly higher price at the market, this small difference was considered to be of no economic importance. Profit per animal and per unit capacity were calculated (Table 7.10) assuming that they were disposed of for slaughter after varying periods in the feedlot. From this data it appeared that the optimum time for disposal of fattened animals was 10 to 11 weeks after commencement of fattening. During this trial it was observed that for animals at the same initial weight, those in poorer condition gained faster than those in good condition which supports the concept of compensatory growth (see Chapter 6). Since feed efficiency of animals that have suffered an initial period of feed deprivation is greater than those on unrestricted diets during the period of realimentation (i.e. return to full-feeding) it was postulated that there may be an advantage in terms of reduced feed costs if animals in comparatively poor condition were purchased for feedlot operations.

Some may criticise this trial on account of the use of sorghum or maize in the rations. However, this work was carried out in a cereal grain producing area where it is also an established practice for northern Hausa farmers and householders to purchase pastoralist livestock for backyard feeding of cattle, sheep and goats, on cereal grains, groundnut, hay and haulm, corn stover and other roughage in preparation for slaughter at Muslim festivals.

The average size of holdings varies considerably from a minimum of 2.5 ha in much of Africa, to 10 ha in Trinidad and 20 to 30 ha under development planning in India. In Latin America, as in parts of East and northeast Africa, areas of land previously in private hands have been allocated to land reform programmes. In Central America and Panama some 90 per cent of the farms are of a subsistence nature and less than 50 ha in size – a large holding by many standards – from which a small number of cattle are sold. The majority of beef animals in this area, however, are produced under extensive management conditions on ranges on the Western Pacific Slope. The chief obstacles to intensive beef production on grass in the tropics are the overhead costs for planting improved pastures and fencing, including at least four paddocks for adequate rotational grazing, and housing and feeding facilities in the case of grass feeding in feedlots. Where zero grazing or a cut and carry system is practised, the cost of labour runs away with profit unless family labour is employed. It is not unusual in Ghana, West Africa, for instance, for children to cut grasses and shrubs at strategic times before morning school, during the lunch break and again in the evenings.

Some outstanding results in liveweight gains of grass-reared cattle finished under feedlot conditions in Brazil, Cuba and Kenya are provided in Table 7.11. It should be noted that under these management conditions, the crossbred progeny of Charolais,

Table 7.11 Breed differences in daily liveweight gain of Zebu and crossbred cattle under feedlot conditions in tropical countries

Country	Ration	Liveweight gain (kg per day) Zebu	Crossbred	Percentage difference
Brazil	Sugar cane	0.865	1.128	30
Cuba	Earmaize	0.880	1.138	29
Cuba	Molasses	0.797	0.934	17
Kenya	Maize silage	0.883	1.060	20

149

Friesian or Brown Swiss bulls on local Zebu cows were superior in performance to the pure Zebus.

There have also been encouraging results in some areas, such as in Kenya, where it has been demonstrated that harvesting maize at the end of the wet season is one way of ensuring feed for the dry season. Supplemented with molasses, urea, maize milling by-products and milling cereals (of a quality not suitable for human consumption) and minimal amounts of protein supplement (less than 5 per cent) maize silage can produce economic feedlot gains. However, as previously stated and for a variety of reasons there are no longer operational feedlots in Kenya. The best grasses to feed as roughage with molasses were for example, *Pangola* spp. or African star grass (*Cynodon* spp.).

Intensive production of beef calves

Intensive management for beef production starts with the calf. This type of production has received far less attention in the tropics than dairy cattle in which the interactions between breed, nutrition and environment are somewhat better understood. The dairy industry in many other parts of the world, however, now provides large numbers of surplus calves for veal or for rearing as beef animals.

Early weaning of beef calves, as distinct from weaning dairy calves from liquid milk at 12 to 16 weeks of age or earlier, or beef calves following their dams on range for six to eight months, requires special care in feeding and management in order to obtain good growth rates and to avoid disease hazards predisposed by digestive disturbances. For the sake of economy, early weaning to avoid consumption of too much whole-milk, is practised at ages of three to five weeks, by which time calves can be weaned onto replacer concentrate feeding. Such calves may be slaughtered early for veal, or reared for beef at selected market ages in feedlots.

Two kinds of operation are usually involved:

1 Rearing of surplus bull-calves on dairy farms and selling these as early as possible for subsequent intensive fattening at beef feedlots.
2 Purchase of approximately one week old calves by the specialist who rears them for a period for subsequent sale to the feedlot.

In temperate climates there are a number of systems by which beef calves are intensively reared, but all use varying quantities of cereal grains. However, cereal grains cannot be considered for intensive fattening schemes on a commercial basis in the tropics. In fact, many countries in the tropics are forecast to double and even quadruple the demand for cereal grains for human consumption within the next few years. Thus cereal grains can play little part in mixed farming, dual purpose livestock feeding systems. Preston in Mexico defined a way of achieving a dual purpose cow system in which the objective is to finish the weaned calf in the shortest time possible within the limits imposed by available foodstuffs. The basis of the system assumes that a calf will be weaned at 180 kg at about 200 days of age, plus an average of 4 l of milk daily, for sale or for the household over a 180 day lactation.

Feeding management of calves

The natural instinct of the calf is to suckle. Suckling can be from either a foster-mother or from milk buckets with rubber teat adaptors. More commonly, however, the calf is taught to drink from the bucket. In all cases of artificial feeding the milk should be warmed to blood heat and utensils kept clean and sterilised.

It is essential to give colostrum at least during the first 36 hours after birth. Colostrum intake from the dam at birth is the greatest safeguard against disease and gives optimum initial growth. This also means that some form of liquid diet is necessary for the first three to five weeks of age to obtain the best growth rate and general health. The dairyman is in a position to use whole-milk for a limited period before weaning onto solid feed; the non-dairy specialist intensive beef-calf rearer, however, depends more on a milk replacer at weaning. The type of replacer used will depend on local prices for milk substitutes and other factors. Milk replacers must contain highly digestible ingredients. The best replacer is one containing 22 to 30 per cent milk proteins and approximately 19 per cent milk fat, to which the fat soluble vitamins A, D and E have been added. The use of rubber nipples for milk containers is recommended provided hygienic methods are adopted; these include washing in cold water followed by hot water and then drying. Best results are obtained using individual calf housing.

The energy in the dry feeds is provided mainly by cereal grains. Intensively reared calves rapidly become accustomed to utilising dry feeds, even at three weeks of age. The major problem is in persuading them at first to eat. The method of weaning, either abruptly or gradually, at three to six weeks of age is thought to have little or no effect on calf losses.

Palatability of the feed is essential to initiate the sense of taste. This is aided by allowing calves free access to water when solid feed is first provided. Contrary to some opinions, access to hay with the calf on concentrate feed does not improve the growth rate, although it does so in older cattle. It should be emphasised, however, that for the calf destined to eat a considerable quantity of roughage later in life, roughage feeding before weaning prepares the forestomachs for this type of feed. The inclusion of molasses enhances feed intake.

Feeding management principles The following three principles should be kept in mind when feeding young calves:

1 The rumen activity which develops in early life as a result of a specific feeding routine, e.g. all-concentrate, or concentrate plus roughage, can affect the animal's later growth performance.
2 Calves reared on high cereal all-concentrate rations without adequate roughage to slaughter age may be more prone to rumen disorders and liver abscesses than roughage supplemented calves.
3 Calves reared on whole-milk or milk replacers may be less able to utilise high urea-containing feeds at about three months of age than those reared on pasture or with additional roughage feed.

It is recalled that the rumen or first stomach of the growing suckling or milk-fed calf is not fully developed until the animal is over six months of age. The principle of intensive baby beef production, as with any early weaning system, is thus to get the calf to eat solid feed as early in life as possible. All management and feeding methods therefore aim at stimulating rumen and at the same time, reticulum and omasum stomach development and function as soon as possible.

Methods of achieving this vary, but the feeding and management procedures are basically the same, namely:

1 The calves are bottle-fed for the first two feeds after weaning from the dam at $2\frac{1}{2}$ days of age. This encourages them to drink at a more regulated rate and avoids too rapid drinking of milk and consequent digestive upsets when they start feeding from the bucket.
2 Dry food is introduced *ad lib* at the same time as bucket milk feeding. Some calves may start to ruminate at about one week of age. West African Zebu calves have been observed to start chewing the cud at 10 to 14 days of age. Weaning from bucket milk depends upon the time at which a calf will start chewing the cud. As a guide, however, no calf is weaned from the bucket until it has been chewing the cud for $2\frac{1}{2}$ to 3 weeks and on an average for a total of 4 to 5 hours in a day. Failure to observe this principle may result in severe digestive disturbances.
3 Daily routine should include a long rest period during the night followed by three distinct feeding periods during the day. Between feeds the calf may play, groom itself, or rest, depending on its mood and the environmental temperature. The growth pattern in fast-maturing calves on a high plane of nutrition is fairly uniform. Reports on the growth of Friesian cattle, however, indicate a marked bone growth at months 7 to 9 and 9 to 10, followed by a final rapid muscle and fat development for 6 to 10 weeks to produce a good carcass.

Multiple-suckling of calves

Where conditions permit it is a sound economic practice to raise more than one calf on a beef type nurse-cow. Assume, for example, that a mediocre Zebu cow produces 700 kg of milk in a lactation if regularly milked. A calf may consume only 225 to 275 kg of this and the cow tends, unless milked by hand, not to secrete the maximum amount of milk since she is not being 'milked out' by the calf at each suckling.

Multiple suckling consists of putting orphan male calves to a foster-mother. In dairying countries this is from dairies where the majority of unselected male calves are not wanted. A batch of these calves can be weaned, say, at 3 to 4 months of age and a further batch put onto the dam.

Such a practice, although it sounds comparatively simple, needs some skill in management. New calves must be introduced to the dam carefully, for example, while she is suckling her own calf, so that she will not notice it. Rubbing the new calf with the dam's faeces, or with those of her own calf may help. The age-old practice of many nomadic cattlemen of placing the skin of a dead calf over the back of an orphan calf to persuade the dam of the dead one to adopt the orphan is well known.

Opportunities sometimes arise, as in West Africa, where the bulk of cattle sold come from pastoral communities, for the purchase of orphan calves during periods of heavy demand for meat. When cattle owners need money for urgent purposes, or during droughts when overstocking occurs, pregnant females frequently calve down when they reach the market and before the dam is sold as a meat animal. Such calves are too young to be considered as edible meat by the local consumers. They are bought at low cost and reared as orphans, either on a foster-dam, or on bucket feed. They must be carefully checked to avoid introduction of disease to the herd. Body temperatures are taken twice a day, blood and faecal samples examined in the laboratory and the animal kept in isolation with the foster dam for a month. Some calves are often very weak on arrival. A useful practice is to give them small feeds from a bottle of 5–10 per cent glucose in water before putting them onto milk. This gives them a little energy and a chance to settle down to the new environment and helps the digestive system to prepare for the first milk feed after what may well have been one to two days without any feed from birth.

The calf that suckles its dam and is reared to weaning on whole-milk is generally the healthiest and most vigorous calf and will produce at slaughter the best beef carcass, if subsequently properly fed and managed.

Further reading

APRU (1980). *Beef production and range management in Botswana*. Animal Production Research Unit, Min. of Agriculture: Gaborone, Botswana.

Heady, H. F. and **Heady, E. B.** (1982). *Range and wildlife management in the tropics*. ITAS, Longman: London.

Hill, D. H. and **Upton, M.** (1964). Growth performance of range reared N'dama and Keteku cattle and their crosses in the derived Guinea savanna zone, Western Nigeria. *Trop. Agric.*, **41** (2), 121–128.

ILCA (1979). *Trypanotolerant livestock in West and Central Africa*. Vol. 1: *General study*. Vol. 2: *Country studies*. ILCA Monograph no. 2. International Livestock Centre for Africa: Addis Ababa.

ILCA (1980). *The design and implementation of pastoral development projects in tropical Africa*. ILCA Working Doc. no. 4. International Livestock Centre for Africa: Addis Ababa.

Le Houerou, H. H. (ed.) (1980). *Browse in Africa – the current state of knowledge*. International Livestock Centre for Africa: Addis Ababa.

Monod, T. (ed.) (1975). *Pastoralism in tropical Africa*. OUP: London.

Okorie, I. I., Hill, D. H. and **McIlroy, R. J.** (1964). The productivity and nutrition value of tropical grass/legume pastures rotationally grazed by N'Dama cattle at Ibadan, Nigeria. *J. Agric. Sci.*, **64**, 235–245.

Olayiwole, M. B., Buvanendran, V., Fulani, I. J. and **Ikhatua, J. U.** (1981). Intensive fattening of indigenous breeds of cattle in Nigeria. *Wld. Rev. Anim. Prod.*, **27** (2), 71–77.

Pratt, D. J. and **Gwynne, M. D.** (1977). *Rangeland management and ecology in East Africa*. Hodder and Stoughton: London.

8 Herd health management

Introduction

As the diseases and parasites affecting livestock in the tropics have been described comprehensively in another book in this series, *Diseases and Parasites of Livestock in the Tropics*, only the more relevant aspects of herd health management and disease control will be considered in this chapter.

Much of what has been discussed in the preceding chapter relates, albeit indirectly, to health as well as to production and associated management systems. Examples of this are proper management of the breeding cow, or the calf at calving time and at weaning. Efficient and economic animal husbandry is dependent upon the health of the herd since poor health and management lower production. Fatal disease will obviously end production for the individual animal, while such devastating infections now confined to the tropics as the virus disease, rinderpest, will bring about a catastrophic halt to the overall production of a herd. Less spectacular, but of considerable importance in reducing overall herd efficiency, are the chronic or sometimes intermittent diseases such as tuberculosis or mastitis in cattle. The livestock producer in the commercial sphere must maintain constant vigilance over herd health to ensure optimum production. Recovery after illness is not the sole criterion; a beef breeding cow that recovers from mastitis, but at the same time loses the function of three-quarters of her udder so that she can no longer adequately suckle her calf, is of no more use in the breeding herd, although she could be sold as a meat animal on the local market, or for salvage slaughter.

Profitable animal production, therefore, demands the efficient management of healthy animals. Disease is one of the most important limiting factors to profit in many livestock enterprises in the tropics, requiring constant vigilance and veterinary disease control measures, both in the private management sector and as part of statutory government disease control regulations. Such control measures are not only concerned with diseases caused by infectious agents such as the ultra-microscopic viruses, the bacteria, fungi, protozoa and ecto- and endoparasites, but also with such stress factors as climate, low planes of nutrition, mineral and trace element deficiencies, metabolic disorders and losses from plant poisons and other toxic factors.

The relationship between climate and disease

The various combinations and seasonal fluctuations of climate have a marked effect on the progress and incidence of many cattle and buffalo diseases in the tropics. Tropical climates may be arid or semi-arid and very hot, often with extremes of day and night temperatures, or they may be hot and humid, either almost all the year round, or only during one or more rainy seasons. Cattle and buffalo may be subjected to various climatic stresses such as sudden changes in temperature due to storms, making the young animal, in particular, more susceptible to chills and to possible pneumonia, or the infectious agents themselves may be more prevalent under certain climatic conditions. An example of the latter is the seasonal buildup of helminth or worm parasites in pastures during hot, humid weather. This, coupled with the rapid growth of succulent pastures at this time, exposes the cow or buffalo to heavy infection following grazing. Conversely, during the dry season, although feed supply from the pastures may be lower, the larval stages of the helminth parasite will also be less prevalent and consequently there is less exposure of the grazing animal to infection.

Natural vegetation in the tropics

This varies greatly, not only with season, but also with latitude and altitude. Variations in temperature, rainfall, humidity and altitude have a marked influence on vegetation. This influence of the climate on the growth of different types of vegetation in the tropics also regulates the presence or absence of numerous pathogenic organisms and more especially the arthropod or insect vectors of many livestock diseases, for example, ticks which transmit the protozoan diseases such as East Coast Fever (ECF) of cattle in East Africa, and the tsetse fly, the vector of trypanosomiasis. Some tsetse flies prefer the open savannas of tropical Africa, others more riverine or high forest areas. The life cycles and habitats, therefore, as well as the behaviour and pathogenicity of these parasites, coupled with climatic factors, have a profound effect on livestock practices and management.

The cause and nature of disease

Certain pathogenic organisms and other disease-causing agents will bring about the damage, degeneration and possible death of various body cells. When too great a number of the body cells of one or more organs of the body are damaged and can no longer perform their particular function, the animal will show signs or symptoms of these dysfunctions. That is, they show symptoms of disease or ill health. For example, when the blood-stream is attacked by certain protozoan parasites and there is invasion of the red blood corpuscles as in babesiosis or tick-borne fever of cattle, there are symptoms of anaemia including listlessness. Where bacteria invade the respiratory system and the lungs are severely involved, there may be distressed breathing and other more severe symptoms indicating pneumonia. The animal may recover by various natural defence mechanisms, or it may be treated and recover or, if too many body cells die so that the organ or organs concerned can no longer function adequately, the animal will die.

Not all living organisms that invade the body are pathogenic or cause disease. Some are symbiotic, that is, they live in harmony with the animal host cells, while others are positively helpful and synergistic as is the case with the rumen microflora that synthesise certain nutrients and vitamins (see Chapter 6).

The non-living agents that can cause disease include: heat, for example burns from solar radiation and damage from the short wavelength ultra-violet portion of the solar spectrum; excessive cold causing, as in burns, cell destruction and possible sloughing of dead or necrotic tissues from the body; mechanical injuries such as cuts, bruises and fracture of bones; plant and other poisons; and nutritional deficiencies of protein, mineral and trace elements.

A group of disease conditions characterised by the presence of tumours or swellings also occur in cattle and the buffalo as well as in other domestic animals and man. Although their cause in some cases has been ascribed to viruses, this is not always so and the causes still remain obscure. There are two kinds of tumour, the benign or non-malignant type and the malignant type commonly referred to as cancer. The malignant type is much more harmful, is usually difficult or impossible to treat and either causes death of the animal or necessitates its slaughter for salvage purposes. One of the commonest malignant tumours is the so-called eye-cancer of Hereford cattle. Many benign tumours, on the other hand, can be treated or removed surgically.

Predisposing factors

There are times when disease-causing organisms may invade the animal body but not actually cause disease. Many such organisms may already be within the body but have no harmful effects in the absence of some other factor or factors which will trigger off the disease itself by providing a suitable environment for the pathogen to develop and multiply. These other factors are known as the predisposing causes of disease that are within or/and around the animal and they are of considerable importance in livestock husbandry. Extremes of heat or sudden drops in temperature can be mentioned in this context; severe stress during transport and the presence of one disease stimulating the development of another latent pathogen are further examples. In the latter case this occurs when cattle babesiosis or tick-borne fever may be accompanied by clinical symptoms of trypanosomiasis which had hitherto been suppressed, or the onset of gastritis in the young calf due to too rapid feeding and/or inadequately warmed milk.

Management has therefore a most important part to play in the prevention of disease through reduction or elimination of the predisposing factors. Sound husbandry practices such as good hygiene and nutrition will go a long way to doing this, although there are some infections, especially viral diseases such as rinderpest, which have no respect for the condition of the animal and, provided the host cattle are susceptible and the virus gains entry to the herd, cause severe outbreaks of the disease.

The pathogenic or disease-causing organisms

The disease-causing organisms or pathogens are classified into six major categories: viruses, bacteria, rickettsias, fungi, protozoa and metazoa. The viruses are the smallest ranging from about 0.23 to 0.30 microns (1 micron or $\mu = 0.001$ mm) and visible only with the electron microscope; bacteria are larger, ranging from about 0.8 to 10.0 μ and together with the fungi and protozoa visible with the ordinary microscope. The metazoa include the larger pathogens such as the helminth or worm parasites.

The viruses are minute transmissible particles that can be carried in the air, in droplets of moisture, body secretions and excretions and in intermediate hosts. When they invade the final host, they multiply within the body cells. During multiplication they may damage the cell to cause disease and because of their intracellular nature are very difficult to treat.

The bacteria, which are single-celled organisms of the plant kingdom, are found throughout nature. The majority are saprophytic and many play useful roles in nature such as the bacteria of the rumen. Others are disease-causing pathogens although, as previously mentioned, they may not cause disease unless predisposing factors are also present. Some, such as the anthrax bacillus, form spores and may survive in the soil for years. Some of the infectious diseases of cattle and buffalo that may be encountered under both extensive and intensive management are listed in Tables 8.1 and 8.2.

The rickettsias are a group of micro-organisms which resemble bacteria in many respects and viruses in others. They are smaller than bacteria with sizes from 0.3 to 2.0 microns in length and 0.4 microns in width. Most but not all are transmitted by arthropod vectors. They are obligate intracellular parasites and grow only in living tissue. Most rickettsias can survive only briefly outside the living cell. They die quickly when exposed to chemical disinfectants, drying and heat, and their growth is inhibited by antibiotics such as tetracyclines. Rickettsial infections are transmitted by lice, fleas, mites

or ticks, and one at least is apparently carried by flies.

The pathogenic fungi, including the yeasts and moulds, also belong to the plant kingdom but differ from the bacteria in that the vegetative body, or mycelium, which is composed of filaments or hyphae, often contains many branch-like structures, characteristic even to the naked eye in some of the larger fungi. Spores are also produced for reproduction and propagation and, like some of the bacterial spores, they are very resistant to many chemicals, as well as to heat and drying. A common fungal disease, both of animals and man, is ringworm.

The protozoal diseases are of special importance in the tropics. Protozoa are unicellular organisms having no rigid cell walls, with a nucleus and associated structures. Many possess organs of locomotion such as flagellae – a whip-like process seen in many pathogenic trypanosomes. Others move with an amoeboid action using pseudopodia or, literally, false legs and envelop their prey during feeding. In man and the chicken a typical example of a protozoan parasite is the one causing malaria, which penetrates the red blood cells. In cattle and many other domestic ruminants, tsetse-borne trypanosomiasis and the world-wide distribution of the babesioses or tick-borne fevers are examples of protozoan diseases that cause immense economic losses. The metazoa are multicellular organisms, as distinct from unicellular bacteria and protozoa, and are members of the animal kingdom. As with some of the bacteria and protozoa, not all metazoa are disease-causing pathogens. Some live within or on the host in a state of mutual benefit or symbiosis, but for the purposes of this discussion reference will be made to only a few of the more important disease conditions of cattle and the buffalo caused or transmitted by ectoparasites such as ticks, flies, fleas and mites and endoparasites such as helminth or worm parasites.

The ectoparasites belong to the Phylum *Arthropoda*. This Phylum includes all the parasitic insects in the Class *Insecta*, an example being the tsetse fly, and the Class *Arachnida*, which includes the spider-like parasites such as ticks and mites. The endoparasites belong to two Phyla, namely the *Platyhelminthes* with two Classes – the *Cestoda* or

Table 8.1 Selected information on some infectious diseases of cattle and buffalo

Disease	Transmission	Incubation period	First symptoms	Animals affected	Preventive measures
1 Viral diseases					
Foot-and-mouth disease (FMD)	Direct contact or contact with material contaminated with the discharge from lesions; carried by birds mechanically; also wind-borne	3 to 8 days	Salivation, blisters on tongue and feet, high fever, lameness	Cattle, buffalo; all other domestic ruminants; pigs	Segregation, isolation of premises, strict sanitation; vaccination of valuable stock
Rinderpest (cattle plague)	Direct contact or contact with material contaminated with discharge from lesions	3 to 15 days	High fever, blood-stained diarrhoea, severe erosive mouth lesions; acute outbreak affecting many animals	Cattle, buffalo; occasionally small ruminants	Vaccination as calves and 12 months later or as mandated
2 Rickettsial diseases					
Heartwater	Infective ticks	9 to 28 days	High fever, nervous signs, convulsions; may be sudden death without symptoms	Cattle and small ruminants	Tick control and elimination
Anaplasmosis	Infective ticks, biting flies, contaminated blood on knives, etc.	3 to 4 weeks or more	High fever, jaundice, distressed breathing, unsteady gait; varies from acute to mild and chronic	Cattle, especially newly imported susceptible stock; most severe in older animals	Chemotherapy in early stages; vaccination for control
3 Bacterial diseases					
Anthrax	Water and food contaminated with blood and excretions or by wound infections; possibly certain flies	A few hours to 1 to 2 weeks	Sudden death in per acute form; or high temperature; swellings, abortions, diarrhoea	Cattle and buffalo; also small ruminants and other domestic animals	Annual vaccination
Haemorrhagic septicaemia (HS)	Food, water, etc., nasal secretions and saliva	24 hours upwards	Sudden death or respiratory signs; doughy swellings around larynx and brisket	Buffalo (very severe) and cattle	Sanitary; segregation; chemotherapy; vaccination 1 to 2 annually

Table 8.1 Cont.

Disease	Transmission	Incubation period	First symptoms	Animals affected	Preventive measures
Blackquarter	Water and food contaminated with blood and excretions or by wound infection	2 to 5 days	Typically 'gas gangrene' with crackly sounds under pressed skin; or sudden death without symptoms	Cattle and small ruminants	Annual vaccination
Contagious bovine pleuropneu-monia (CBPP)	Close contact with infected animals, and inhalation of disease organisms	14 days to several months	Frequent painful cough; stands with elbows out, often gasping and thick mucus discharge from mouth and nose; acute cases die 1 to 3 weeks, or more protracted	Cattle	Annual vaccination; slaughter and compensation as determined by local legislation
Dermatophilosis (originally streptothricosis)	Bacterium *D. congolensis*; Predisposed by onset of rains and high humidity; trauma from tick and fly bites and thornscrub scratches; other unknown relationships, i.e. intercurrent disease	Not known under natural conditions, but appears within weeks after onset of rains	Extensive pustules of skin followed by diffuse coalescing and spreading of scaly lesions with skin folding and thickening on dorsal and lower body, especially limbs in West Africa	Very severe in cattle in West Africa, cause of major losses in exotic beef types destined for cross-breeding including Brahman, Santa Gertrudis and Charolais; recently identified in Nigeria (humid zone) in imported water buffalo	Chemotherapy with massive doses of antibiotics, etc. in sheltered herds but of little use (economically and logistically) with cattle on the range; regular dipping is of some value

4 Protozoan diseases

Disease	Transmission	Incubation period	First symptoms	Animals affected	Preventive measures
East Coast Fever (ECF)	Infective ticks (ECF confined to much of East and parts of Central Africa)	1 to 4 weeks	High fever, unthriftiness, weakness, exudates mouth and nose; enlarged lymph nodes; diarrhoea, death in 5 days to 1 month	Young Zebu cattle but adults more resistant; exotic breeds very susceptible; also buffalo	Tick control and elimination; in some areas injection of calves with infective material followed by antibiotic therapy on first-time reaction
Piroplasmosis (babesiosis or redwater)	Infective ticks	1 to 4 weeks	Fever, sometimes reddish urine; progressive weakness	Cattle, buffalo and other livestock	Tick control and elimination; chemoprophylaxis (immunisation)

Table 8.1 Cont.

Disease	Transmission	Incubation period	First symptoms	Animals affected	Preventive measures
Trypanosomiasis (nagana, etc.)	Tsetse fly	Few days to some weeks	Intermittent fever; listlessness; unthriftiness; progressive emaciation; lowered productivity and death	Cattle, buffalo and other livestock	Fly eradication and chemoprophylaxis; use of trypanotolerant breeds
Surra	Blood-sucking flies mainly	Few days to 2 weeks	Fever, emaciation; progressive unthriftiness; sometimes death in early stages	Mainly camel and horses but sometimes cattle and buffalo	Chemotherapy; prophylaxis; sanitation

Table 8.2 Some health problems associated with intensive management systems

Condition	Cause	Symptoms	Treatment	Prevention	Remarks
The enterotoxaemiacs	*Clostridium perfringes* (bacteria)	Severe dysentery in calves 7 to 10 days or up to 10 weeks old; abdominal pain and some nervous symptoms; frequent deaths	Hyperimmune serum and broad spectrum antibiotics	Vaccination of young animals and dams before calving in enzootic area	Pre-calving vaccination of dams where calf fattening programme planned
Blackquarter (blackleg, quarter-ill)	Other *Clostridium* spp.	(See Table 8.1)	—	—	—
Footrot	*Fusiformis nodosus* and other bacteria	Lameness; swollen, hot, painful feet; cracking between hoofs; ulceration; may invade joint	Clean wound; antiseptic dressings; systemic treatment with sulphonamides and antibiotics	Hygiene and avoid muddy yards; keep down flies; footbath with copper sulphate or formalin	Other organisms associated with cause; also predisposed by ticks and some nematode larvae
Pink eye (infectious kerato-conjunctivitis)	*Moraxella bovis* (bacteria)	Lacrimation with profuse tears in early stages; conjunctivitis and photophobia	10% solution; zinc sulphate or antibiotic solutions (eye wash)	Some success with vaccine; keep down dust and flies where possible	Where vision affected assist in feeding and watering
Internal parasites	(see text)	(see text)	(see text)	Regular check and appropriate treatment; hygiene	Check incoming new stock

Table 8.2 Cont.

Condition	Cause	Symptoms	Treatment	Prevention	Remarks
Ringworm	*Trichophyton* spp.; *Microsporum* spp. (fungi)	Coat hairs snap and exudate forms, spreading circular crusts up to 3 cm to coalesce with others	Brush and wash lesions with fungicide; corticosteroid supporting therapy; oral antibiotic; griseofulvin effective but costly	Effective fungicide in cleaning housing; 2 to 5% phenol or 2% formaldehyde and 1% caustic soda	Pre-disposed by poor condition so improve diet
Respiratory diseases	(i) Many bacteria, viruses and other agents, including physical and chemical	Severe depression; distressed breathing, coughing; may be associated with other malaise such as diarrhoea	Sulphonamides and antibiotics	Vaccines of limited value	Hygiene and avoid stress
	(ii) Pneumonic pasteurellosis, *P. multocida* and *P. haemolytica* (bacteria)	Short incubation, up to 24 hours; high fever, depression, off feed, distressed breathing and coughing; may be diarrhoea after some days; sudden death in acute cases	Sulphonamides and antibiotics	Vaccination some two weeks before climatic changes, such as onset of monsoon, also before transport, especially buffalo	—
Laminitis	An allergic systemic disturbance; pre-disposed by overfeeding on grains	Acute or sometimes delayed onset with severe pain, usually in all four feet; heat and swelling at 'coronet' above hoof; sweating; difficulty in moving; in chronic cases hoof may separate from coronet	Early administration of antihistamines and corticosteroids; analgesics to relieve pain	Care in management and avoid overfeeding with grains	Calves $4\frac{1}{2}$ to 6 months in feed-lot most susceptible
Acidosis	A metabolic disorder associated with over-feeding with grains	Increased urination; unease; distressed breathing; dehydration	Replace fluids (intravenously) and oral sodium bicarbonate (15–30 gm)	Feeding and management care	—

Table 8.2 Cont.

Condition	Cause	Symptoms	Treatment	Prevention	Remarks
Bloat (ruminal tympany)	(i) Primary – due to complex reactions in rumen ingesta, resulting in foaming or belching frothy bloat (ii) Secondary – due to other diseases	Marked distension of rumen on left side of the animal; lack of eructation and disturbed breathing	For primary bloat pass stomach tube and give oils to reduce frothing; in extreme cases to save death from asphyxia puncture rumen to release gas	Avoid sudden heavy feeding on lush pasture or cut-and-carry fodder	Commercial feed additives against bloat are costly
Grass tetany (staggers)	Predisposed by sudden exposure to lush pasture especially if low in magnesium; also association with low calcium	Most characteristic – unsteady gait, anxious expression, twitching of facial muscles, especially of eye and ears; may collapse and die	Administer calcium and magnesium solutions and supplement feed; top dressing of intensively managed pastures with calcium magnesite	Care in putting out to intensive grazing after dry-season feed shortage	Common in lactating cows, but also seen in fattening steers
Urea poisoning	Over-feeding on, or accidental access to urea fed as a cheap protein supplement; results in production of excessive quantities of ammonia	Severe abdominal pain; muscle tremors; unsteady gait; distressed breathing; bloat and sometimes bellowing	Often to no avail, but several pints weak acid such as vinegar may help, also calcium borogluconate	Management care, and keep urea supplement down to 3% maximum of concentrate supplement	Excess feeding of soya bean meal may facilitate breakdown of urea to ammonia
Calf scours (diarrhoea)	*Salmonella dublin* and *S. typhimurium*; also *Escherichia coli* (bacteria)	Often acute onset, foul smelling faeces, dehydration, debility; off feed; dry muzzle; often death	Allow colostrum wherever possible; prophylactic treatment with sulphonamides and antibiotics	Some vaccines are useful	Hygiene and emphasis on preventive measures

160

Table 8.2 Cont.

Condition	Cause	Symptoms	Treatment	Prevention	Remarks
Other calf diarrhoeas	*Coccidia* spp. (protozoa)	Diarrhoea which is sometimes bloody; lack of appetite and severe weight loss; may be confused with classical calf scours	Sulphonamide drugs effective provided supportive treatment given, avoid dehydration	Allow access of calves to separate drinking areas	Early detection and differential diagnosis important; hygiene essential

tapeworms, and the *Nemathelminthes* which includes the roundworms. Not all insects or worms, such as the honey bee or earth worm, are parasites. Nevertheless, a vast number of them are and the livestockman in the tropics needs to keep constant vigilance to protect as far as possible his livestock from them. This applies in particular to the introduction of new and exotic stock which are more susceptible to many parasites which the local stock have learned to tolerate.

The defence mechanisms of the body against disease

The study of the defence mechanisms of the animal's body and its reactions to invasion by pathogenic organisms constitutes the science of immunology. The body has two major systems of defence: primary defences such as the skin, and linings or mucous membranes, as in the nose and intestines; and secondary defences, including cellular responses of the body, such as the white blood cells which phagocytose or devour invading micro-organisms. Furthermore, the white corpuscles and other blood cells which form part of the immune system of the body produce what are termed humoral antibodies which react against or neutralise the antigen of the invading pathogenic bacteria or viruses and their toxic products. These body defences and the speed with which they can be brought into action are most important, both in resistance to and recovery from disease.

The animal body is invaded most frequently via natural orifices such as the mouth, nose or genital organs, through broken skin or from the bites of external vectors such as ticks and flies. Such insect vectors become infected with micro-organisms when they feed on the blood of other infected animals and transmit them when they feed again on another host animal. Infectious micro-organisms (i.e. the antigens) introduced by one means or another stimulate the host to produce specific antibodies to combat them. These defences may be so effective that the antigen is overcome immediately, or there may be a longer period of time before this may happen. The antigenic response of the host animal is not always successful and, in checking the onset of symptoms of a specific disease, if other treatments fail, it will die. Symptoms of disease are not present in the early incubation stage when the micro-organisms are multiplying in the body, but appear when they have overcome the body defences and are the outward or clinical signs of the damage they have done to the body tissues. If the antigenic response is successful the host animal is said to be immune to that particular organism.

The situation just described refers to immunity acquired through natural active infection with the pathogenic micro-organisms and is referred to as a naturally acquired active immunity. Another form of acquired immunity is where a calf receives antibodies contained in its dam's colostrum (see Chapter 7) so that it starts life protected to some extent from those diseases which the dam herself has had. This protects the calf until it is old enough to begin to produce its own antibodies and is referred to as a naturally acquired passive immunity.

The ability of the body to react to invasion of pathogens in the way described above is the basis of protection provided by vaccines and other biological products. Vaccines generate an immunity

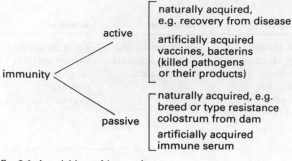

immunity

active
- naturally acquired, e.g. recovery from disease
- artificially acquired vaccines, bacterins (killed pathogens or their products)

passive
- naturally acquired, e.g. breed or type resistance colostrum from dam
- artificially acquired immune serum

fig. 8.1 Acquisition of immunity

by artificial means as distinct from immunity arising from natural infection. The types of immunity are summarised in fig. 8.1.

Vaccines against specific diseases are made from the causative viruses, bacteria or their products, and some helminth or worm parasites. They may be live or attenuated (i.e. reduced in virulence) vaccines or they may be killed or inactivated vaccines (i.e. killed by heat or formalin, etc.). Live vaccines give a longer period of immunity than inactivated ones. Immune serum for passive immunisation is collected from an animal which has recovered from a natural infection, or it may be manufactured commercially from an animal hyperimmunised artificially by repeated and increasing doses of the pathogen to produce sufficient of its own immune serum for use in other animals. Immune serum protects for only a short period when compared with active immunisation by vaccines and is therefore used more as a temporary protective measure.

How animals combat disease

Animals may inherit a specific immunity to a disease, or receive it positively through the dam's colostrum, acquire it either as a result of success-fully overcoming natural infection or as a result of the administration of a biological substance such as a vaccine or a bacterin. Vaccination may produce active and continuing immunity to a disease although this is not always completely successful since animals differ in their response to vaccination. Some vaccines produce mild reactions to the specific organism or other substances contained in the vaccine and the animal may have a slight

temperature rise and be off its feed. Within a period of some one to three weeks from the time of vaccination the animal will have produced enough antibodies against the antigen of the vaccine to resist natural infection. This latent period of immunity varies with different disease-causing agents and two factors are important for the livestockman to bear in mind. First, an animal is not protected from a specific disease immediately after vaccination against it and secondly, vacci-nation of an animal during the incubation period of a naturally contracted disease may not protect it. Sometimes, on account of these factors a vaccine may be blamed by the livestock owner for not having protected an animal, or even for having caused the disease. Such misunderstandings need not occur if the principles involved are fully under-stood. The use of immune serum, however, may prevent a disease from developing even during its incubation stage, although such passive immunity rarely lasts for more than two to four weeks.

Hypersensitivity

This occurs where the animal develops something resembling an antigen–antibody reaction to certain proteins and chemicals which develops slowly in the body cells after initial exposure to the foreign substance. It is subsequently expressed as a severe allergic reaction in which the toxic products involved may cause smooth muscle spasms with symptoms of itching, coughing, lacrimation and other secretions and oedematous, fluid-filled subcu-taneous swellings. Such symptoms may pass off rapidly, or they may even cause death, especially after repeated exposure to the sensitising antigen. Susceptibility to hypersensitivity varies among indi-vidual animals and although it is much more common in man than in his domestic animals it may be a cause of unthriftiness in cattle. A type of sensitisation in cattle which may be confused with that just described is known as photosensitisation in which certain chemicals contained in plants, drugs or insecticides will react within the animal's body under the influence of solar radiation. Some drugs, e.g. phenothiazine, used against intestinal worms, contain these substances and in these cases it is necessary to keep cattle out of direct sunlight for a period after oral treatment.

Methods of disease control

Despite the fact that many of the great panzootic diseases that swept through the tropics, devastating not only cattle and other domestic ruminant herds, but also wild ruminants, have been kept under control, there are still outbreaks of these, e.g. contagious bovine pleuropneumonia in Africa and parts of western Asia and foot-and-mouth disease in Africa, Asia and Central America. They present a constant threat to other tropical areas from where they have been eliminated.

Protection against infectious disease lies primarily in avoiding contact with the infected animal or with material infected by them. The following are recommended basic sanitation principles for resident herd management, the acquisition of new stock and outgoing stock.

Resident herd management

1 Divide the herd into as many independent units as is economically and practically feasible and in each unit avoid overcrowding. This applies not only to cattle on feedlot or other intensive systems, but also to overcrowding in night paddocks or holding yards where there is greater opportunity for transmission of contagious disease and helminth parasite buildup.

2 Divide each unit where possible into equal age and sex groups, e.g. yearling heifers and yearling bulls.

3 Maintain strict adherence to vaccination schedules according to age groups and relevant statutory regulations for vaccine use.

4 Keep a constant look-out for any signs of infectious or other disease and report as quickly and as accurately as possible symptoms and case history to a veterinarian or other designated local animal health authority.

5 Isolate suspected infected animals from healthy animals, either by moving the healthy stock to uncontaminated ground or by removing the sick animal(s) from the healthy herd. The decision to move animals one way or the other depends upon the management system involved, the land or enclosure space available, the type of disease and the number of animals infected. It would be pointless to move a whole herd or feedlot unit to new ground because one or two animals were sick, but there would be good reason to move all healthy animals to new ground because individual cases of sickness were due to the previous area being highly contaminated with pathogenic organisms.

6 The segregated healthy animals that have been in contact with the sick animals should be held in quarantine over the maximum period for incubation of the disease or suspected disease in question. No newly purchased stock or other acquisitions should be added to this quarantine group until after the end of the prescribed incubation period.

7 Where considered necessary and in accordance with veterinary advice and statutory animal health regulations, sick animals should be slaughtered and carcasses disposed of after completion of postmortem and other diagnostic procedures.

8 Where salvage slaughter is permitted in such cases as old age and non-productivity, non-infectious conditions of no public health importance, or in cases of fractures or other traumatic conditions, the carcass may be sold, depending on its condition and local regulations, for such purposes as for human consumption, processing into animal feed protein supplements or processing as fertiliser.

9 Use chemical disinfectants to destroy microorganisms, burn carcasses and contaminated material or bury carcasses in quicklime. Steam is useful for sterilising contaminated equipment and feed utensils, especially if incorporated with a detergent, but is of little use in most buildings, where inaccessible cracks and crevices may protect microorganisms and other parasites.

10 Make sure there is adequate and proper disposal of manure under more intensive management systems and the use of disinfectants or insecticides around damp disposal areas to keep down fly larvae is essential.

Purchase of new stock

One of the most common mistakes made by the livestockman is to introduce new animals to his otherwise healthy herd without taking full precautions to prevent the entry of disease by way of the new stock. Assuming that there is a possibility of a disease being introduced through the newly purchased stock, there are three phases of the disease during which it can be attacked.

1 The pathogenic organism in question may be prevented from entering an area by putting the new animals in quarantine.

2 If the pathogen does invade the herd it may be forced to deal with an unfavourable condition or habitat, for example, by the use of more resistant or tolerant local cattle breeds, or by the control of insect vectors of the disease by adequate insecticide spraying.

3 By the use of vaccines, bacterins or, for short-term protection, antisera.

Outgoing stock

The commercial rancher or intensive or semi-intensive producer must be equally concerned with the proper health management of his saleable stock, either for local meat markets or for sale as breeding stock, as the veterinarian. The breeding stock may be inspected by government before shipment to a local market or for export purposes to breeding farms or other organisations. They may be shipped long distances by rail, on-the-hoof, or they may be transported privately with little or no formal pre-shipment examination. Whatever the situation, there are certain basic requirements for outgoing commercial stock. These are:

1 They should be of the approved age or body weight for shipment elsewhere, either for fattening, or for breeding purposes.

2 The conditions by which they proceed on foot, rail or by road must be in accordance with local and/or statutory regulations.

3 Appropriate vaccination, anti-serum or other preventative treatments should be administered prior to shipment, and the necessary documentary coverage provided for each animal. Where animals trek long distances overland on foot or by road transport, such documentary evidence is inspected along with the animals concerned at strategically placed government livestock inspection posts. Animals that do not pass the tests are removed from the shipment and either sold for local slaughter or otherwise disposed of.

The control of endoparasites

It is generally accepted that protozoan and metazoan parasites constitute one of the major obstacles to the development of livestock industries in the tropics. This is more so in the hot humid tropics where the survival and rate of development outside the final host of many of these parasites is improved by increasing temperature and moisture, whereas extreme desiccation usually destroys them. However, even in the drier zones, pastoralists have learned that continued movement to new pastures results in healthier livestock.

The following selected and routine procedures are essential to control parasitic diseases of cattle and buffalo in both extensive and more intensive management systems. Certain diseases of public health importance are also mentioned.

The tapeworms or cestodes

Cysticercus bovis of cattle and buffalo is of major economic importance. It is the intermediate stage of the adult tapeworm of man. *Taenia saginata*, and cattle become infected by accidentally ingesting with pasture segments of the mature worm passed in human faeces. They develop in the bovine species as about 1.0 cm milky-white, bladder-like cysts and invade the muscles. Man can then become infected by eating raw or inadequately cooked meat of an infected carcass.

Treatment and control The intermediate cyst stage found in the musculature of cattle cannot be treated although the mature worm can be treated in man. The only effective methods of control are:

1 by preventing people defaecating on pastures or around yards and feedlots, calves being highly susceptible to infection;
2 by avoiding the use of untreated human faeces and sewage as fertiliser;
3 by ensuring adequate cooking of meat; and
4 by establishing adequate meat inspection facilities at local abattoirs.

Adult tapeworms found in cattle such as *Moniezia* and *Avittelina* spp. are usually transmitted through intermediate hosts such as beetles and mites ingested during grazing. They are not particularly harmful except in very heavy infestations or where there is undue stress, when they will cause unthriftiness, anaemia, rough coats and other general signs of debility. Treatment was at one time difficult but it has now been greatly facilitated by modern proprietary drugs containing the active principle niclosamide.

Roundworms or nematodes

There exists a formidable list of roundworms affecting cattle in the tropics, the majority of which also occur in more temperate zones but which, in a tropical environment, find conditions ideal for their development at all stages of their reproductive cycle. The two broad groups affecting the gastro-intestinal tract are the strongyle worms and the ascarids or larger roundworms.

In general the common feature of the life cycle of the strongyle worms is that they develop in the faecal mass to the highly active, infective free-larval stage and are then deposited on the herbage where they are likely to be ingested. Oxygen, warmth and moisture encourage their development and survival, whereas severe dryness and desiccation soon kills them at both the pre-infective and larval stages. Two species, *Bunostomum phlebotomum*, the hookworm of cattle and the ascarid worm of calves, *Neoascaris vitulorum*, can be contracted from the dam by the neonate calf across the placenta or through the dam's colostrum. *Bunostomum* spp. can also gain access through the skin.

The symptoms of infection vary with the causative parasite, the degree of infection and the age of the host. Young animals are in general the worst affected; in some cases such as neoascaris infection in calves, the mature worm is seen only in the young calf and is self-limiting by the time the calf is about six weeks of age. In most strongyle infections animals show a progressive loss of condition, with or without diarrhoea and productive efficiency is impaired, through loss in appetite and body weight. In more chronic stages there may be oedematous swellings under the skin and in the tissues, especially under the jaw and along the brisket. In severe hookworm infection, symptoms of anaemia, including pale mucous membranes and extreme listlessness, are most prominent. Death follows in most cases. In some animals the infection may be sub-clinical and simply manifested in unthriftiness, while others may recover with increasing age and resistance. Major economic losses occur through retarded growth and lowered production.

Treatment and control Since severe symptoms of helminthiasis develop generally as a result of an excessive rate of intake of infective larvae in a susceptible animal, so that it has no time to build up any natural resistance to the parasite(s) concerned, the rationale in control measures is best directed to reducing the infective stage of the parasite so that the cattle host has time to slowly build up a state of natural resistance. Although feasible, keeping an animal parasite-free is neither practical nor economical except in very special circumstances.

The management approach is to combine attempts at control of infection rate with anthelmintic treatment. The livestockman will need to consult an animal health adviser as to the most suitable method to employ since the epizootiology of the different parasites varies between species and genera and in different environments. This approach requires the following:

1 A programme of pasture rotation to avoid overgrazing with concomitant excessive parasite build up.
2 The use of a six week pasture rotation schedule to allow reduction of strongyle larval stages as practised in some temperate regions is less effective in the tropics because of the much longer survival time of the larvae. A rest period for the pasture during the dry season of at least two months in the humid or sub-humid tropics allows the best chance for strongyle larval stages to die off.
3 Since young animals are more susceptible to worm infestation than older stock they should be drenched (i.e. treated) and separated from the main herd at weaning.
4 Combining treatment with pasture management depends upon a sound understanding of the life cycles of the prevailing parasites and the measures required to break such cycles. If this is known the following type of programme can be introduced:

(a) treatment of all stock before the end of the rainy season;
(b) resting of pastures during the dry season;
(c) treatment of all stock in the middle of the dry season and before the beginning of the rainy season;
(d) treatment early in the rains, at mid-rains and again towards the end of the rains; and

(e) since dams approaching and immediately after parturition build up a heavy worm egg burden which reaches its peak some weeks after the calf is born, cows should be given anthelmintic treatment shortly before, or immediately after calving. Where possible young stock should be separated from the main herd as soon as they are weaned.

Treatment does not clear stock of all worms and for this reason repeat treatments are necessary. Where rainy seasons are very prolonged the number of treatments required may be totally uneconomic and under such conditions a reduced stocking rate may be the only answer.

General considerations in the treatment and prevention of helminthiasis

Choice of anthelmintic Anthelmintics are chemicals which are used either to treat animals that are heavily infected and showing symptoms of worm infestation or they may be used prophylactically. Prophylactic treatment prevents potentially dangerous numbers of worm eggs or larvae reaching the ground, thereby reducing the number of parasites voided by infected animals, which could cause a continuation of the cycle after ingestion by other susceptible animals. There is no anthelmintic, however, capable of eliminating all roundworms of ruminants. One of the chief properties of modern anthelmintics is that they will kill not only the adult stages of the worms, but also many (though not all) of the younger, immature stages of their development. Most anthelmintics used today thus have 'broad spectrum' activity, in that they act not only on several worm species, but also on some of their immature stages. Only a few of these are listed below as their correct use and administration must depend upon detailed consultation between the livestock owner and the veterinarian.

Neoascaris infection of calves, once a severe problem in the tropics, can now be treated effectively with piperazine, as adipate citrate or dihydrochloride salt at a dose rate of 200–400 mg per kg liveweight. The special advantage of this drug is that it is relatively non-toxic and can be used on the very young calf, in fact, during the first one to two weeks of its life. This is important since neo-

ascaris are most harmful up to the age of six to eight weeks.

Strongyle infection can be treated effectively with a wide range of modern anthelmintics, although some of them may have more effect on one particular strongyle species than on others. Only the active principles of the drug are mentioned here since they are manufactured under a wide variety of international trade names.

Phenothiazine is one of the most important anthelmintics that has been discovered and although in use for several decades it is still quite effective and cheap, especially for use against roundworms of intermediate size. Dosage is as a drench at 200–400 mg per kg liveweight. It can also be added to cattle feed or salt mixtures for daily consumption in small amounts. One danger of the drug is that maximum doses can cause photosensitisation (mentioned earlier) if animals are exposed to strong sunlight soon after drenching. For this reason most manufacturers recommend full treatments, as distinct from low-level prophylactic doses, in the late afternoon so that animals are not exposed to strong sunlight for some 12 to 18 hours after treatment.

Other drugs include thiabendazole, which is highly effective when administered as a drench against most roundworms at the rate of 50 mg per kg body weight, the organo-phosphorus compounds at the rate of 55 to 110 mg per kg liveweight (handlers should avoid undue contamination of their skin with this compound since it is toxic) and bephenium hydroxynaphthoate at the rate of 250 mg per kg body weight. The latter is very effective against the strongyle hookworms such as *Bunostomum* spp. Tetramisole/levamisole at the rate of 7.8 mg per kg liveweight and pyrantel tartrate at 25 mg per kg body weight are also very effective against strongyles such as *Ostertagia* spp. and *Cooperia* spp.

A considerable advance in the prevention and control of some of the ruminant roundworms was made some years ago by veterinary scientists at Glasgow University in Scotland. They discovered that by subjecting the larval stage of certain pathogenic nematodes (in this case lungworm *Dictyocaulus* spp.) to X-irradiation, the larvae could no longer multiply and become pathogenic but would act as an antigen, or vaccine, and so stimulate an antibody reaction in the host cattle without causing any symptoms of helminthiasis. It is probable that other vaccines against roundworms may soon be available for commercial use. The anthelmintic methyridine can be administered by subcutaneous injection and is therefore very useful for the treatment of sick, pregnant or excitable animals.

Flukes or trematodes

Among the flatworms the Class Trematoda or flukes, particularly in many parts of the tropics including Africa, the Indian subcontinent, Southeast Asia and many of the Pacific Islands, cause immense losses in domestic ruminants. The main culprit is the tropical liver fluke, *Fasciola gigantica*, although the smaller *Fasciola hepatica* of temperate countries is also found in parts of the tropics where it is confined to the cooler, higher altitude areas. *F. gigantica* also requires a water snail as an intermediate host and infection of stock results from cattle drinking at water holes, wells and other wet areas which have become populated by snails infected from the faeces of other cattle. Such a buildup of parasites of one kind or another is one of the problems of fixed water holes and wells since infected stock congregate around them at regular intervals and soon contaminate the soil. Other flukes, including the rumen fluke, also occur, but the giant liver fluke causes the most serious losses in cattle, with poor condition and often deaths in advanced cases. Control measures include:

1 prevention of access of cattle to infected snail areas;
2 adequate drainage of areas around wells and drinking holes so that the intermediate fluke stage, the *metacercaria* cannot survive long enough to infect the snails;
3 where possible the use of proper watering troughs sited on dry and quick-draining ground;
4 destruction of snails by molluscicides, the most used one being copper sulphate at the rate of 1 part to 100 000 parts of water, using two treatments three months apart;
5 treatment of individual animals with drugs containing hexachlorethane or more recent drugs such as nitroxynil in 20 per cent solution which is injected subcutaneously at the rate of 1 ml per kg body weight.

Since infection may cause severe debilitating effects in cattle the important approach is to prevent infection by proper hygiene and management.

Diseases caused by arthropod parasites

These include insects such as flies, mosquitoes, lice and fleas and the acarine or spider-like mites and ticks. They are all ectoparasites and impair productivity, not only by the intense mechanical worry and surface injury they can cause, but also through the ability of many of them to transmit viral, bacterial, fungal, protozoan and other diseases. Others cause loss of condition and damage to hides because of the migratory routes that they take during their development stages.

The arthropods may act, in the transmission of disease, purely as mechanical carriers on their mouth parts of micro-organisms while they feed on one infected animal and then bite another susceptible one. Or they may be involved in an essential part of the life cycle of an infectious protozoan or metazoan parasite. Examples of simple mechanical transmission of disease are numerous; in cattle, African trypanosomiasis can be transmitted mechanically on the mouth parts of biting flies such as the *Stomoxys* species of stable fly and the *Tabanid* species of horse or deer flies. Anthrax may also be transmitted in this way. At the same time, the tsetse fly of Africa provides the intermediate host stage for the trypanosome parasite to develop cyclically before it is transmitted through the fly's saliva to infect the cattle or buffalo host with trypanosomiasis.

Other flies that are a particular nuisance as irritants or as disease-transmitting agents include: the midges or *Simulium* spp. and *Culicoides* spp.; stable flies, *Stomoxys* spp.; horn flies, *Haematobia* spp.; buffalo flies, *Lyperosia* spp.; tropical warble flies, *Dermatobia* spp.; warble flies, *Hypoderma* spp.; and the tsetse fly *Glossina* spp.

The tsetse fly (fig. 8.2) assumes major importance in Africa because of its role in the transmission of tsetse-borne trypanosomiasis (*Nagana*

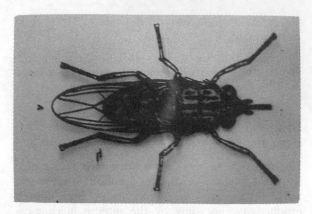
fig. 8.2 Tsetse fly

or *Sannare*) of cattle and small ruminants. The camel and domestic buffalo are also susceptible. It is estimated that some 11.7 million km^2 of Africa, and more especially Central Africa, are infested by this fly and in many cases whole areas are closed to cattle production because of the perennial infestation with the fly (see fig. 3.1 on page 18). Livestock distribution depends also on distribution of tsetse fly species as there are coastal or high forest, riverine and savanna species. Certain of the riverine species, such as *Glossina palpalis*, are present in the vicinity of streams and rivers throughout the year and can live not only on warm blooded animals such as small wild game and on domestic animals, including ruminants, but also, in the absence of warm blooded animals, on cold blooded creatures such as lizards and other reptiles. They do not travel very far, they require shade and have generally low infection rates with trypanosomes, but they are present throughout the year and present a constant though often low-grade challenge to domestic livestock. Another riverine tsetse, *G. tachinoides*, has a much higher infection rate but its distribution is more restricted. It is in such areas that, over the centuries, small trypanotolerant cattle breeds such as the N'dama and West African Shorthorn and other dwarf ruminants have developed. The tsetse of the more open savanna areas of Africa, *G. morsitans*, prefers to live on wild game, which are resistant to trypanosomiasis and on cattle if game are not available. It is a fly which

can cover quite wide areas and, although to survive it must feed within a few days after emerging from the pupal stage, it frequently carries a high trypanosome intermediate stage infection rate and is a constant threat to the cattle of the pastoralist, forcing him to move his cattle to drier and more tsetse-free areas during the rainy season.

Control of the tsetse fly and trypanosomiasis

Eradication of the vector Eradication of the tsetse fly remains the basic approach to eliminate trypanosomiasis but many of the methods available are costly and require skilled personnel and constant checking of areas where the fly has been eradicated in order to avoid re-infection. Methods of control or eradication have included killing out wild game to eliminate the reservoir hosts of trypanosomiasis – a method now no longer in use; clearing of bush to form areas or belts too wide for the savanna tsetse to travel across in search of food; clearing of riverside bush to reduce shelter and deprive riverine tsetse of breeding grounds; the use of insecticides applied by hand or by aerial spraying – both methods much in use today; and the laboratory breeding of large numbers of male tsetse which have been sterilised by irradiation and their release into tsetse infested areas. This biological control method, which has been used successfully in some other tropical and subtropical areas to eliminate the screw-worm (*Callitroga* spp.) is in the experimental stage but may have some potential, at least in certain areas, for eliminating the tsetse fly. There is no doubt that in some areas of Africa where population buildup is occurring at a rapid rate – in some countries at a rate of 2.5 per cent increase per annum – and where increasing land areas are coming under more intensive farming systems, the consequent clearing of the land for cultivation and the building of settlements is automatically rendering the environment unsuitable for tsetse. This forces the tsetse to move elsewhere in search of food or, in some cases, eliminates them.

Drug treatment and prophylaxis A wide range of drugs has been used since the turn of the century, those most used today being the phenanthridinium and quinapyramine compounds and diminazine aceturate. The last named has mainly therapeutic or treatment properties against the trypanosome, and the first two are used for both treatment and prophylactic or preventive purposes. The prophylactic drugs are compounded in the more insoluble salt forms and so have a longer action due to their slower absorption from depots in the muscles where they have been injected. The use of trypanocidal drugs in livestock is under strict statutory control by the governments using them.

The following procedures may be adopted in establishing a beef cattle enterprise where challenge from tsetse fly and trypanosomiasis is a problem:

1 In light challenge areas where infection rate is low and the particular trypanosome strain not very pathogenic, maintenance of the herd in a state of premunition, i.e. with infection present but not serious unless resistance is broken down due to unusual stresses such as pulling the plough or other traction work. Zebu animals can be managed under such circumstances, with occasional treatments with trypano-chemotherapeutic drug administration if and when necessary.
2 Under heavy fly challenge maintenance of a susceptible herd, either exotic or indigenous, by the use of trypano-chemoprophylactic drugs every two to four months. Care has to be taken to avoid the development of drug-resistant trypanosome strains; the correct and regular dosage is necessary, with periodical changes of the type of drug used. This procedure requires careful veterinary supervision.
3 The use of indigenous trypanotolerant breeds. Occasionally, and under stress, or through change of environment and exposure to a different strain of trypanosome, such breeds will need treatment, but this is the exception rather than the rule.

It is important to bear in mind that an animal classed among the trypanotolerant breeds of cattle is not, by virtue of this fact, automatically immune to trypanosome challenge. Stress may cause a breakdown and, more especially, exposure to tsetse challenge of young or newly purchased stock that have been reared in an area free from tsetse and without challenge from trypanosomiasis. Where newly purchased trypanotolerant breeds are being moved to new areas, they may be given a trypano-chemoprophylactic drug to acclimatise them to the new environment.

Although the term trypanotolerant is generally accepted for the small breeds of cattle, sheep and goats able to survive under perennial tsetse challenge, such animals can succumb as stated above to clinical trypanosomiasis, with accompanying lowered productivity and even death under severe or unaccustomed stress. Experimental work in the Gambia indicates that the trypanotolerant nature of the N'dama reflects the quantitative rather than the absolute nature of the trypanotolerance. In other words, the degree of illness, length of recovery period, or possibly death, are conditioned by the weight of challenge with the infecting trypanosomes. For this reason it is important to know, from the standpoint of land use and development, the level of trypanosomiasis infection likely to occur in livestock being introduced to a given area. This level of infection depends on several factors including density of the fly infestation, the species of tsetse, as some species are more effective transmitters of the trypanosome than others, the infection rate in the flies, the density of potential hosts in the area and climatic conditions. An additional hazard mentioned earlier is that other biting flies may transmit the disease mechanically on their mouth parts (i.e. without cyclic development of the trypanosome within the fly). The term trypanosomiasis 'risk' has thus been recommended by researchers in the field rather than the more commonly used 'tsetse challenge'. Where an area is being chosen, say, for ranching, information on the possible trypanosomiasis risk can be obtained by fly trapping, counting and identification of the species of tsetse, dissection of the fly to establish the infection rate and, finally, periodical checking of blood from a sample of newly introduced cattle for the presence and number of trypanosomes. High, medium, or low parasite counts are indicative of the degree of infection.

Although the N'dama (fig. 8.3), West African Shorthorn (fig. 8.4), Borgu (fig. 8.5) and Keteku (fig. 8.6) are considered major trypanotolerant breeds, there are also Zebu breeds that have developed some degree of tolerance to infection; for example, the small Zebu cattle found around the shores of Lake Victoria where there is considerable challenge from tsetse. Among the many West African Zebu breeds, the White Fulani (fig. 8.7) is considered to have a greater tolerance to infection

fig. 8.3 N'dama

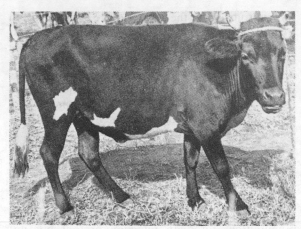

fig. 8.4 West African Shorthorn

fig. 8.5 Borgu

fig. 8.6 Keteku

than the other breeds, particularly where physical stress is minimal and nutrition adequate.

Under such conditions many animals remain productive while in a state of low-grade infection, that is, they harbour the trypanosome in their bloodstreams at low levels which do not cause clinical symptoms of the disease, unless these are precipitated by undue stress. This is not unlike a situation in which man, adapted to his environment, may live in an endemic malarial area in a similar state of balance with the invading parasite.

Doubts have been expressed for many years as to the productivity of the much smaller trypano-tolerant breeds of cattle when compared to the larger Zebu breeds and humpless Sanga and other crossbred types from the mainly tsetse-free areas. Although the trypanotolerant breeds were imported to Central Africa for the commercial ranchers and small farmers with considerable success as long ago as 1904, it is only during the last two decades that much wider interest has been given to their econ-omic possibilities. To the present time, no

170

fig. 8.7 White Fulani

successful vaccine has been produced against trypanosomiasis. Furthermore, the limitations of present methods of control of the vector and chemotherapy and chemoprophylaxis have stimulated the desire and emphasised the need for new strategies that might lead to more efficient land usage of the vast areas of Africa currently made inaccessible to livestock by the tsetse fly.

As a result of this increased interest in trypanotolerant cattle breeds, as producers of meat in tsetse infested areas, research over the past few years has been directed towards assessing their productivity when compared to the larger Zebu and humpless Sanga cattle. The emphasis has been on comparisons of breeds and types in a given environment. Comparisons have been based on major production traits, namely reproductive performance, cow and calf viability, milk production, growth and cow body weight, each of which has been evaluated to establish a 'productivity index'. The indices were derived under two management systems, in villages and on ranches or livestock stations, with four levels of trypanosomiasis risk designated as zero, low, medium and high. The procedures used in calculating a productivity index are shown in Table 8.3 while the values obtained for the different breeds in different situations are provided in Tables 8.4 and 8.5. The data in Table 8.5 indicate little or no difference between trypanotolerant and Zebu groups for the major index of productivity (per 100 kg of cow maintained per year). The data for feedlot performance indicate that while the Zebu was superior to the N'dama in

Table 8.3 Steps in the calculation of productivity indices

Parameter	Code	Calculation
Cow mortality during year (%)	A	
Calving percentage (%)	B	
Calf mortality to 1 year (%)	C	
Calves reaching 1 year (%)	D	$B(100 - C) \div 100$
Calf weight at 1 year (kg)	E	
Annual milked-out lactation yield (kg)	F	
Cows completing a lactation[1] (%)	G	$100 - (C\frac{1}{2})$
Total liveweight equivalent of milked-out yield (kg)	H	$F(G \div 100) \div 9$
Total weight of 1-year-old calf produced per cow (kg)	I	$E(D \div 100)$
Weight of 1-year-old calf plus liveweight equivalent of milk produced per cow maintained[2] (kg)	J	$(I + H) \div [100 - (A \div 2) \div 100]$
Average cow bodyweight (kg)	K	
Weight of 1-year-old calf plus liveweight equivalent of milk produced per 100 kg of cow maintained annually (kg)		$J \times 100 \div K$

[1] A cow whose calf dies during the lactation period is considered on average to have actually produced milk during half the period.
[2] Cows dying during the year are considered on average to have been maintained for half a year.

Table 8.4 Productivity of trypanotolerant and Zebu × trypanotolerant cattle on two ranches under medium trypanosomiasis challenge

Parameter	Nigeria		Benin	
	N'dama	Keteku	Shorthorn	Borgu
Cow viability (%)	99	99	95	88
Calving percentage (%)	58	57	58	33
Calf viability to 1 year (%)	95	95	76	72
Calf weight at 1 year (kg)	156	142	85	119
Productivity index[1] per cow weight (kg)	86.4	77.3	38.4	30.1
	260	260	152	226
Productivity index[1] per 100 kg of cow maintained per year (kg)	32.2	29.7	25.3	13.3

[1] Total weight of 1-year-old calf plus liveweight equivalent of milk produced.

terms of absolute daily gain, the daily liveweight gains per 100 kg body weight maintained were virtually the same. In practical field management the off-take of meat per hectare of pasture could be increased by a higher stocking rate with the smaller trypanotolerant breed.

Ticks

Ticks are found in all parts of the world and transmit many of the bacterial, viral, protozoal and other diseases of livestock in the tropics. Apart from the diseases they transmit, ticks engorge themselves with blood of the host, about 1 ml per engorged female, and in large numbers cause severe anaemia and debility. All ticks cause damage to hides and skins through their piercing mouth parts, resulting in secondary invasion by other parasites, and some species secrete toxic substances that cause necrosis or death of skin around the penetrated area. Others produce a toxic substance that in cattle causes a condition known as tick paralysis.

The buildup of a tick population on range or in intensive pasture management systems can be considerable, particularly in the wet season. It is essential for the livestockman to have an under-

Table 8.5 Productivity of trypanotolerant and Zebu cattle in three locations under zero, light and medium trypanosomiasis risk

Parameter	Nigeria (zero risk, station management)			Ivory Coast (low risk, village management)		Central African Republic (medium risk, village management)	
	N'dama	Shorthorn	Zebu	Shorthorn	Zebu	Shorthorn	Zebu
Cow viability (%)	100	100	100	98	96	96	95
Calving %	100	96	91	70	72	68	63
Calf viability to 1 year %	97	95	100	55	60	80	65
Calf weight at 1 year (kg)	131	101	200	75	90	90	120
Annual milked-out yield (kg)	–	–	–	70	144	–	71
Productivity index[1] per cow per year (kg)	128.0	92.0	181.0	37	55	50	58
Cow weight (kg)	266	183	343	200	270	190	320
Productivity index[1] per 100 kg cow maintained per year (kg)	48.1	50.2	52.8	18.5	20.5	26.3	18.2

[1] Total weight of 1-year-old calf plus liveweight equivalent of milk produced.

 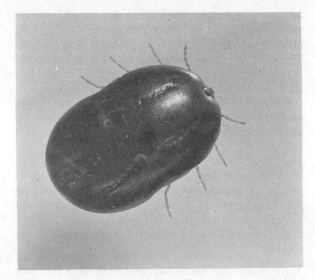

fig 8.8 Engorged female ticks: blue tick (left) and cattle tick (right)

standing of the basic principles of the life cycles of the main species and the way in which these relate to control measures. Ticks transmit disease by moving from one host to another between blood meals, as in two- and three-host ticks, or by the disease itself passing through the ovarian stage of the female tick and thus ensuring its survival and possible transmission to other livestock in the infective larval stage. There are two main families, the *Ixodidae* or hard ticks and the *Argasidae* or soft ticks. The hard ticks have a hard dorsal plate or shield, the scutum, which is very prominent in the male and in some species spectacularly coloured, whereas in the female it is less prominent and hardly visible even in the fully engorged female (fig. 8.8). The soft ticks are mainly parasites of birds and are of no importance in cattle or buffalo production.

The life cycle of ticks Certain ticks are one-host ticks which spend their full feeding time on one individual animal. After the larval tick has reached the animal from the pasture it feeds and becomes a nymph, feeds again to become an adult and the females again engorge and drop to the ground to lay their eggs. The parasite stage from larva to adult takes about three weeks, all of which is spent on the host. An example of this tick is *Boophilus*

decoloratus, the blue tick which transmits the protozoan diseases, babesiosis or red-water fever and anaplasmosis or gall sickness and is widespread in Australia, Central and South America, the West Indies and Africa. The situation is different with the two-host tick in which the larvae and nymphs spend two weeks or more on one host; the nymphs then drop off, moult to become adults and seek a second host on which they remain for five or six days or more. The tendency is for the larval and nymphal stages to be spent on small ground game animals and the final stage on cattle. An example is *Rhipicephalus appendiculatus*, the brown ear tick, which transmits one of the most serious diseases of cattle in East Africa – East Coast Fever. In the three-host tick each stage drops to the ground after a feeding period which may last as little as three days. An example of this tick is *Amblyomma variegatum* the bont or variegated tick characterised by its radially striped legs and multi-coloured shield, which transmits a disease of cattle and other ruminants known as heartwater.

Engorged female ticks lay their eggs on the ground in sheltered places in a single cluster of thousands of eggs. The female dies after the eggs are laid and if the conditions are right the eggs hatch after a period of weeks or months as larvae or seed ticks which then climb blades of grass or shrubs and await to attach themselves to a passing host. Ticks may survive in pastures and shrubs, provided the conditions are moist and otherwise favourable, for as long as one to two years, but they cannot survive in dry conditions.

Control of ticks This means prevention of the diseases of cattle which they carry. This can be approached in two ways, firstly control off the host by such methods as grass-burning, cultivation and starvation through long periods of de-stocking and secondly their destruction on the host by the application of acaricides. either by dipping or spraying the cattle, which is still the most practical and effective approach (figs. 8.9 and 8.10).

Requirements for a standard dipping tank are as follows:

1 It should be sited on well-drained land with ample space for mustering and yarding the cattle; the water supply should be clean and preferably piped.

2 The swim-bath, excluding the ramp at both ends for entry and exit, should be at least 4.6 m to 7.3 m long with a minimum depth at the tank's centre of 185 cm to allow for total submergence when the animal dives into the tank. The lower length limits are suitable for the smaller breeds. The foot bath should be at least 4 m long and 0.2 m deep.

3 The dipping tank should be roofed.

4 The drainage should be such that much of the dip that drains off the cattle flows back into the tank.

5 The dip should be regularly checked using standardised methods for the type of acaricide used.

The spray race In principle this involves passing the animal through a tunnel of constant acaricide spray which is forced through nozzles by a machine pump. It resembles, therefore, the ordinary hand spray or pump (fig. 8.11) but enables the animal to be sprayed all over the body at one and the same time. The design of a spray race is given in fig. 8.9. Basically it consists of a system of pipes, the tunnel through which the animal passes, fitted with spray

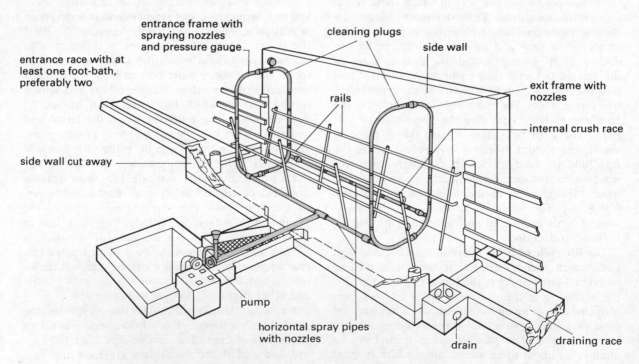

fig. 8.9 The essential features of a good cattle spray race

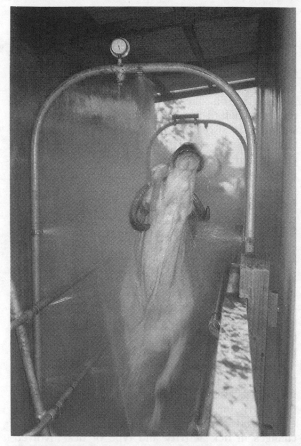

fig. 8.10 Spraying cattle

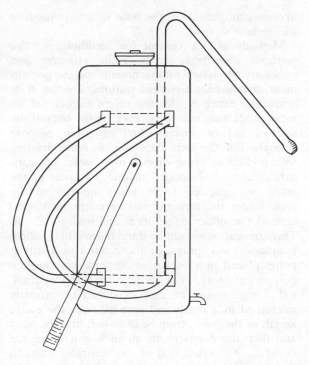

fig. 8.11 Hand pump spray

nozzles so placed as to spray the animal over all body surfaces. The acaracide is drawn from a sump and forced through the nozzles by a centrifugal pump which can be driven by a tractor power take-off belt, or by an electric or petrol motor. Foot baths should be provided as for dipping tanks. This removes much of the organic matter, such as mud and faeces, from the animal's hooves before they enter the spray race; if they are treated with 5 per cent copper sulphate or 1 to 3 per cent formalin, the foot bath also protects against footrot. The two functions are not carried out simultaneously. A side gate can be used when the foot bath is used as footrot control, so that animals do not have to go through the spray race. The drainage should be efficient so that the major part of the spray that drains off the cattle returns to the sump.

The spray race is an efficient, economical and safe method of applying an acaricide and offers less danger for valuable exotic or other breeding stock, for cows in calf and for young stock. As with the dipping tank, cattle may take some time to get accustomed to the herding and driving through the race. This can best be achieved by having a few old timers lead the novices to get them used to the procedure.

Excessive shouting or beating of the animals should be avoided, although some decisive prodding at strategic moments is necessary to keep the cattle moving through at an even rate. One danger for cattle unused to the system, especially young range cattle, is that they will try to jump over the spray from the nozzles at the race entry point. This may lead to slipping or placing of legs over the lateral horizontal bars of the race. Strong wire mesh attached behind the bars will prevent this;

likewise, roughening of the floor surface in the race will reduce slipping.

Methods of tick control for smallholders The methods described above, while effective and necessary for larger establishments, or for government animal health control stations, are too elaborate and expensive for the mixed farmer, whose meat production enterprise may consist only of the sale of old or surplus dual or triple purpose animals. For the individual animal, hand dressing with a cloth or brush dipped in a bucket of acaricide mixture and applied in selected areas of the body, will suffice. These areas are behind the ears, under the forearm and between the thighs, around the udder or scrotum and under the tail. This application should be done thoroughly. Simple knapsack hand sprays, or those fitted to a stirrup pump placed in a bucket of acaricide solution are quite satisfactory. A systematic approach is essential. Large groups of animals should be properly restrained in a crush and sprayed over the entire length of the back, from head to tail; first the head and then the flanks in an up-and-down or zig-zag direction, to ensure that as the acaricide drains to the ground it covers the whole body surface in the process.

A simple and economic dip for medium-sized holdings is the Machakos dip used in Kenya. This consists of a concrete bath holding some 2 250 l so that animals when entering the bath are standing up to their chests and flanks in the acaricide solution. The acaricide is also poured over the head, back and rump to ensure complete body coverage. Great care should be taken to avoid leaving the cattle, which are head yoked for restraint, for too long in the dip. About 15 to 30 seconds will suffice since many of the acaricides are highly toxic and if absorbed through the skin in excessive quantities will cause severe nervous symptoms such as trembling, and ear and eyelid twitching, diarrhoea and other symptoms. Advanced cases die in convulsions. Treatment should be applied as soon as symptoms appear. The cattleman should immediately wash off all residual dip from the animal's skin with clean water to prevent further absorption and obtain the assistance of a veterinarian.

Acaricides used for tick control The early chemicals used included arsenic trioxide which proved effective for many years until certain ticks became resistant to it. The chlorinated hydrocarbons, benzene hexachloride (BHC) and toxaphene (chlorinated camphene) were then extensively used, especially toxaphene, which has a longer residual action due to its resinous nature which makes it stick to the skin and coat hair, even in wet weather. It also resists breakdown in the dipping tank far better than BHC. The other well known chlorinated hydrocarbon internationally known as DDT is also an effective insecticide but the development of resistance to it and its cumulative and toxic effect in body tissues, as also with BHC, has resulted in many governments forbidding their use. The organo-phosphorous compounds, such as chlorfenvinphos, coumaphos and trichlorphon, are now largely replacing the chlorinated hydrocarbons and are effective and safe to use in that they do not have any residual effect in the body tissues. They are, however, highly toxic if used in incorrect proportions and cattlemen and dip attendants should wear protective clothing to avoid getting excess quantities on their hands or other parts of the body.

Timing of dipping and spraying This is referred to as the dipping interval or number of days between acaricide treatments. It should be decided upon early on the advice of a veterinarian and may be altered from time to time due to seasonal changes in tick activity and type of tick involved. In general, the following regime should be followed:

1 for two-host ticks and three-host ticks dipping every five to seven days, with a good residual effect acaricide such as toxaphene, against East Coast Fever; and
2 for a one-host tick e.g. in the control of babesiosis or redwater carried by *Boophilus* ticks, dipping every 7–14 days, depending on the degree of challenge.

There is a tendency in some areas, during the dry season, to extend dipping intervals to three weeks. The safety of this procedure depends very much on the degree and type of tick challenge.

Control of other insects

Lice, mites, fleas and other ectoparasites are a constant threat to cattle and buffalo health and productivity, both by the worry and irritation they cause, as well as from the diseases many of them may transmit. Regular dipping helps to control lice and fleas, also the skin surface inhabiting mange mite. Acaricides, with the exception of 1 per cent DDT, have little effect on flies, including stable flies and horn flies. Reduction in their numbers can best be attempted around buildings and installations through proper sanitation. Black flies or *Simulids* can occur in vast numbers around cattle and buffalo and can be partly reduced in number by treatment of their breeding areas in streams by DDT, which kills the larval stage. Midges can also be controlled to some extent by spraying swamps with DDT or diesel oil, but care should be taken to keep range cattle out of such treated areas. The myiasis-causing flies of cattle, particularly the *Dermatobia hominis* fly of tropical America, penetrates cattle skin and the developing larvae cause swellings and discharges with often secondary bacterial infections. Dipping helps to control infection to some extent, but systemic application by absorption through the skin or by mouth in the feed with organo-phosphorous compounds has also proved an effective control method. Control of the blow flies and screw-worm flies such as the *Chrysomyia* involves not only attempting to keep down fly numbers by proper disposal of carcasses and other rotting materials, but also attacking the larval forms of the fly which are scavengers in animal wounds, especially following routine procedures such as castration and dehorning. Where hand-dressing of the individual animal's wound is not practicable, regular dipping kills the larvae. In the Caribbean the technique of releasing sterilised male flies, mentioned earlier, as a control method, has been used effectively to reduce American screw-worm (*Callitroga*) fly numbers.

Disinfection and sterilisation

Physical conditions, such as heat and radiation, and chemical substances that destroy pathogenic organisms, are the two major groups of agencies used for sterilisation and disinfection. The terms disinfection and sterilisation tend to be used somewhat loosely and for similar purposes. In practice, however, the destruction of pathogens is often sufficient to control infection and in this case the term disinfection is mostly used, especially when it refers to the surfaces of equipment, or the interior of buildings, concrete floors of yards and other surface areas. An antiseptic agent is one that destroys pathogens on the skin. Sterilisation refers to the complete destruction of all pathogens and non-pathogenic organisms and is achieved by heat, e.g. by burning or boiling and by steam under pressure (autoclaving) for more resistant organisms. The term is sometimes used when certain therapeutic drugs are used to completely eliminate a pathogen from the host's body.

The use of heat
Heat may be used in the following ways:

1 For disinfection of buildings, clear away all bedding and other litter which might catch fire. Apply a blowtorch to floors, walls, doors and equipment, taking care not to ignite wooden equipment.
2 Boiling water can be used for floors and if mixed with 1–5 per cent caustic soda (sodium hydroxide) is especially effective against worm parasite eggs. Instruments such as castrating knives and scissors can be sterilised by boiling in water for 30 minutes.

Burying
Holes dug for burying carcasses must be deep enough, say down to 2.0 m, to completely cover the carcass with sufficient soil so that wild predators and dogs do not dig it up again.

Where carcasses are burned, especially after infection with a disease such as anthrax in which the bacterial spores can remain viable for years, a deep 2.2 m trench should be dug to receive the infected carcass which should then be covered with quicklime (calcic oxide) before burying. Where burying is not possible the carcasses should be burned over a crossed slit-trench 2 m long and 0.5 m wide, with bars across to support cut wood, then the carcass and more wood on top of the carcass, then additional wood, dried grass and kerosene in sufficient quantities to completely burn the carcass. Smaller carcasses can be burned over a bed of burning wood and other fuel contained in the pit, provided there is sufficient draught below the carcass to fan the fire.

Chemical disinfection

1 Three basic phenomena are of importance in disinfection by chemical means. First absorption of a chemical compound through the pathogen's cell wall, secondly its penetration into the cell cytoplasm and thirdly its reaction with one or more of the constituents of the cell.

2 There are numerous proprietary preparations and instructions for their use should be followed strictly.

3 Chemical agents do not function effectively in the presence of organic matter such as dried grass, manure, dust and other extraneous material found around buildings and yards. Proper cleaning is essential before applying a disinfectant and this action will destroy a major proportion of pathogenic organisms. Most disinfectants will not, however, kill spores.

4 Complete disinfection is not immediate; it takes place gradually, although it is most effective in the early stages of its application.

5 Many disinfectants have selective action; microorganisms respond favourably or adversely to changes in pH; most, but not all, have increased activity at high temperatures. Some chemicals are bactericidal, i.e. they actually kill the pathogen, whereas others are bacteriostatic, i.e. they merely prevent growth or proliferation of the organism.

Commonly used disinfectants

Hypochlorites Chlorine or hypochlorite is widely used because it is cheap, powerful and convenient to use and has a wide antibacterial spectrum, i.e. it destroys many different species of bacteria and other pathogens. It is however, corrosive and must therefore be used with care; it has a strong odour and is more easily neutralised by extraneous organic matter such as dirt and faeces.

Alkalis Hot caustic soda solutions at 1–3 per cent are most useful for destroying spores and worm eggs resistant to other chemicals. It is, however, corrosive and must be used with care. Its activity is markedly reduced by lowered pH of the environment.

Quaternary ammonium compounds These are still very popular since they are of very low toxicity to animals when compared to many other disinfectants and they are easy to use and without appreciable odour or taste. They are especially useful for disinfection of utensils at concentrations of 1:1 000 to 1:20 000 parts, depending on which compound is used.

Phenols These are derived from coal tar. A common commercial product is lysol, which is derived from the cresol fraction. They are irritant to live tissues and are now less used than other compounds because of this although the chlorinated phenol is less irritant and is widely used in proprietary preparations for disinfecting buildings, etc. at recommended strengths. Ordinary lysol, for example, used in a disinfectant foot bath outside a stock yard, is effective at a strength of 3 to 5 per cent.

Methanol (formaldehyde) Used in the form of formalin which is 40 per cent methanol. It has excellent penetrating power in the presence of organic matter, is most effective when used warm or hot at a 1–5 per cent solution and will destroy most viruses, fungi and bacteria including bacterial spores. It is widely used in a foot bath outside buildings and enclosures where there is an outbreak of foot-and-mouth disease; canvas sheets or sacking soaked in formalin are also put outside gates so that vehicle tyres are disinfected as they pass over them.

Sodium carbonate Another virus-destroying disinfectant used widely against food-and-mouth disease, for example, is sodium carbonate (washing soda) placed on wet sacks as above. It is much more lasting than methanol and is standard practice for foot-and-mouth disease in Europe.

Miscellaneous compounds Iodine, although a useful antiseptic, has disadvantages as a sterilant because of its strong odour and because it stains badly. It is most useful as a tincture (mixed with alcohol) but is expensive and can be irritating to the skin. Iodophores are becoming popular and have both detergent and sterilising properties. Ethyl alcohol in 70 per cent solution is an effective antiseptic and is used especially for cleaning skin before incising and for quick disinfection of syringe needles, scissors and other instruments.

Desirable features in disinfectants

These may be summarised as follows. They should:

1 be free from strong or objectionable odours;
2 not be corrosive or otherwise destructive;

3 not remain toxic for too long lest it be dangerous
to stock;
4 be effective at ordinary temperatures;
5 be effective with and mix easily with water; and
6 be of reasonable price.

Further reading

BVA (1976). *Handbook on animal diseases in the tropics.*
3rd edn. British Veterinary Association: London.

Hall, H. T. B. (1985). *Diseases and parasites of livestock
in the tropics.* 2nd edn. ITAS, Longman: London.

ILCA (1979). *Trypanotolerant livestock in West and
Central Africa.* Vol. 1: *General study.* Vol. 2: *Country
studies.* ILCA Monograph no. 2. International Livestock
Centre for Africa: Addis Ababa.

Keating, Molly I. (1983). *Tick control by chemical ixodi-
cides in Kenya: a review 1912–1981.* Trop. Anim. Hlth
Prod. 1983 Vol. 15 p 1–6.

Lindley, E. P. (1978). Maintenance of health (including
Parasitism, by R. P. Lee). In *An introduction to animal
husbandry in the tropics*, ed. G. Williamson and W. J. A.
Payne. 3rd edn. Longman: London. 29–61.

Mackenzie, P. Z. and Simpson, R. H. (1964). *The African
veterinary handbook.* Pitman: Nairobi.

9 Slaughter methods, meat hygiene and carcass quality

Meat inspection

In the English-speaking Commonwealth countries the laws governing meat inspection were based originally on two types of ordinance, namely:

1 diseases of animals – concerned with the control of stock movement, quarantine and impounding; and
2 public health – concerned with meat inspection, export handling and conveyance.

All aspects of animal disease control are the responsibility of national veterinary services; public health aspects are administered either by the national health services, or as a combined operation by both the medical and veterinary services. But whatever the organisation, the duties of a state-appointed meat inspector include:

1 the inspection of meat and decisions on what is and what is not, fit for human consumption;
2 the overseeing of preparation, storage and distribution of meat, including attention to buildings, utensils and vehicles; and
3 the enforcing of proper legal standards of food hygiene among those engaged in food preparation.

Conditions pertaining to meat export
There has been a strict embargo for many years, except in the case of internationally accepted live animal and meat exporting countries, on exports of chilled or frozen meat for fear of the world-wide spread of animal diseases. After the end of the Second World War, however, the acute shortage of meat in many countries necessitated some degree of relaxation of these embargos. There are, nonetheless, still many dangers accompanying the export of chilled and frozen meat, although this does not apply to canned meat. The European Economic Community (EEC) agreed in 1972 on the establishment of a Community Directive responsible for the sanitary requirements applied to the importation of live cattle, pigs and fresh meat from non-member to EEC member countries. This organisation provides a list of eligible exporting countries, states what part or parts of an animal may be imported and the specific sanitary requirements in respect of such imports. Approved world-wide standards for meat hygiene and slaughter house procedures are set out in the framework of the Joint FAO/WHO Food Standard Programme, supported by an established Codex Committee on Meat Hygiene. However, the recognition of what are termed 'disease-free zones' and the development of a meat export trade is determined, in the long run, between potential exporting and importing countries.

Movement of meat animals

It is the responsibility of the animal and/or health services in any country to observe the following requirements for livestock transport:

1 prevention of the spread of disease;
2 observance of the necessary standards of hygiene; and
3 avoidance of unnecessary suffering during transport.

Losses can occur during transport. There can be decreases in body weight, or losses due to injury, suffocation, or diseases contracted en route. The effectiveness of measures adopted to control such losses depends upon:

1 the efficiency of the services responsible e.g., economic considerations, number and effectiveness of personnel involved;
2 the type and condition of transport used;
3 distances to be covered;
4 the reactions of the animals during transport; and
5 environmental hazards.

Driving on the hoof (trekking or droving)
Cattle accustomed to extensive pastoralist conditions and continually on the move for food – often covering 5 to 10 ha per day – are not greatly inconvenienced by long treks on foot to markets since they can pick up enough feed from grazing and browse plants during the trek to provide some degree of maintenance, although there will inevitably be weight losses. In the dry season these are

estimated to be 15 to 20 per cent. In much of tropical Africa there is the additional hazard of the tsetse fly, cattle frequently having to trek through fly belts to reach their destination. Under such conditions, where infection from trypanosomiasis provides an additional burden, losses in liveweight are accentuated and can be as high as 30 to 40 per cent. In addition there are also losses from death when infections are severe. The use of trypanoprophylactic drugs at the beginning of the trek has been introduced in some areas but 'there are still problems regarding removal of the meat from the drug injection site and questions to be answered regarding possible residual effects of the drug used on meat destined for human consumption. This is not to say that the situation is static; work is continuous on this type of problem and improvements in the control of such problems as trypanosomiasis infection as a hazard to trade cattle movement are being tackled at both national and international levels.

Cattle trekking on the hoof to market sources follow recognised paths known in much of tropical Africa as trade cattle routes (fig. 9.1). These are well defined routes which are used regularly and may vary only with seasonal changes. Trekking herds may wander off them for peripheral grazing and browsing, but to maintain a constant movement of some 19 to 32 km a day (the total journey may be over 1 280 km) there is little time for feeding outside the route. Furthermore, there is opposition from local farmers to such a practice during the cropping season, although less so when trade cattle use the dry season stubble and thus provide some manure to the land.

Watering and inspection posts Trek cattle can manage adequately from water points situated some 19 to 24 km apart, but in many countries these may be considerably further spaced, involving maybe two day treks between watering. This matters less in the wet season when much of the water intake comes from grazing and browsing on trees and shrubs and indigenous grasses. It has been stated that if cattle are not to suffer serious liveweight shrinkage water should be available at no less than 8 km intervals and in addition to this there should be grazing facilities and some conserved forage en route. In the arid tropics such conditions are virtually unattainable and the often comparatively good condition of the stock on arrival at markets for slaughter serves as a reminder of the resistance and adaptability of most indigenous tropical breeds under the rigours of prevailing conditions.

Trade cattle control posts These operate in many countries in the tropics at both the state and para-statal levels. The system applies to cattle in transit by any of the land routes and involves the use of transit papers from the place of origin which are endorsed or renewed from station to station as the cattle progress to their destination. Sick or lame or otherwise incapacitated animals are pulled out at the relevant post and slaughtered and/or sold locally at villages or townships along the route. Where infectious enzootic conditions such as foot-and-mouth disease or contagious bovine pleuropneumonia are encountered, quarantine and other control measures are imposed on the affected group. Transport on the hoof thus entails loss from shrinkage, death or culling en route, as well as drovers' pay, taxes, tolls and inevitable extortions. Because of its comparative simplicity, however, and the availability of willing and highly capable drovers in pastoral cattle countries, this method is still widely used.

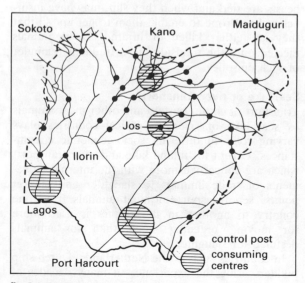

fig. 9.1 Cattle trade routes in Nigeria

Rail transport

Loading at the railhead Provision should be made as far as possible at the railhead for watering and feeding of the stock before loading. Feed may be provided from grazing in the vicinity of the loading area – a situation quite common to the more humid areas – or from forage cut locally and hand fed, say, a minimum quantity of 10 kg per day for an average 350 kg liveweight animal. Water should be provided in troughs, situated on firm and well drained ground in sufficient quantity to allow for an average of 23 litres per animal per day.

A reception yard off-loading and loading ramp should be provided according to the number of cattle normally handled daily, with sorting pens and chute for directing the correct number and size group into the rail truck. The yards may be built according to the specifications described for yards in Chapter 7. However, being in close proximity to a railhead means that old sleepers and discarded rails may be available and these make admirable yard structure material. If additional horizontal bars are added to the lower half of the standard cattle yard fence, the yard is also then suitable for sorting and loading of smaller stock, such as sheep and goats. Chain-link fencing may also be added for this purpose. Loading, as far as is possible, should not take place more than one hour before the rail journey commences.

Over long distances rail transport effects saving on maintenance and handling charges, toll, and other incidental expenses as well as greatly reducing losses from shrinkage and deaths. Shrinkage losses under severe hot and delayed conditions, especially in the absence of good watering facilities, may be up to 10 per cent or more, but should normally not be more than 3 to 5 per cent for two to three day journeys. Losses from bruising may still be considerable, although far less so than in road transport. Nonetheless reports of downgrading of some 7 to 8 per cent of carcasses of cattle transported by rail in Kenya have been reported.

The synchronisation of shipments by sex and horn character can not as yet be envisaged in much of the African continent, where, as in West Africa for example, the majority of trade cattle have medium to very large horns and there is a preponderance of males. Fortunately, the inherently docile nature of the African Zebu makes him a long-suffering and docile passenger, able to withstand the most rigorous hardships. As production systems tend more towards extensive ranch management, involving less personal day-to-day handling of stock from birth, or where the more fractious and agile semi-dwarf trypanotolerant breeds are marketed off range, both loading and transport facilities will need to be improved to guard against bruising and other damage en route.

Railway trucks which are to carry livestock should be roofed, provide for free passage of air and have battened or non-slip floors. On journeys lasting for more than three days the trucks should be off-loaded and the stock allowed yard feeding or local grazing before re-loading.

Road transport

Road transport is becoming increasingly used in those countries where major inland road networks are being developed. A major advantage is that animals can be loaded at the farm, holding yard, or ranch and delivered directly to the sales market, local village slaughter slab or abattoir. Losses from shrinkage are also greatly reduced. Ideally, trucks should be covered, have non-slip slatted floors and be suitably partitioned. All too often, however, beasts are tied and when they slip, may have insufficient head rope to enable them to get up, so that they are either killed or injured. Dead animals ejected onto the roadside are a frequent reminder of such episodes.

Sea, lake or river transport

Transport of cattle, buffalo and other meat animals by sea, lake or river in tropical countries plays varying roles in differing socio-economic circumstances. Except for inland lake and river transport, which are concerned more with the internal movements of trade animals to slaughter and market points, sea transport of meat animals from one country to another in the tropics is used more for moving breeding stock than for animals destined for slaughter.

In countries such as the Netherlands, Dutch ship builders using the experience of many decades of livestock transport by sea, have designed vessels and equipment with specially constructed gang-ways, loading crates and other facilities to suit many different loading and off-loading situations. This is not the case in the tropics, where merchant vessels loading palm oil, groundnuts and other agricultural commodities, may also take special consignments of breeding and foundation stock from one country to another. Under these circumstances any free deck space is provided with improvised corrals or pens, into which cattle are either jumped from the quayside, or lowered by crane or derricks in crates. It must be admitted that, under some tropical climate conditions, accommodation on deck is often more satisfactory than it is below deck, even in elaborately contrived stalls. Fig. 9.2 shows a group of some 70 N'dama foundation stock heifers and bulls being transferred on deck from a ranch in Congo (Brazzaville) via the port of Matade to the port of Lagos, Nigeria, for final transfer to a ranch in the derived guinea savanna zone. These cattle were at sea for three weeks in an environment of high temperatures and humidity.

Under such management conditions it is better to allow the stock free movement and not to tie cattle up by the head or horns. Experience shows that cattle will climb a gangway sloping up to a maximum of 45° without trouble. Getting cattle from the gangway onto the deck may be a problem; a good gangway leading onto the deck and wide enough to avoid obstacles is essential. Range cattle, however, may be less disturbed on reaching the ship's deck and may even jump heights of 1 to 1.3 m from the ramp onto the deck if there is something soft such as sacks of grass or grain for them to land on.

Air transport
The air transport of livestock is a very specialised business and it is normally only used for the transport of valuable breeding stock. In all forms of livestock transport, disinfection of equipment and vehicles after transporting the livestock and of holding yards, etc. is an essential component in good hygiene and management.

The effect of transport on meat quality
Before the introduction in more developed countries of road and rail transport of cattle destined for the market, the beasts were herded on foot, as is still the case in many parts of the tropical world. In fact, the mode of transport of cattle has in many ways dictated the sort of beast that was considered most suitable to cope with local market and transport conditions. In Great Britain, for example, where cattle two centuries ago might be trekked for hundreds of miles to market, the older, larger and fatter animal was considered most suitable. This was because during the long treks to market, cattle would need to depend upon their own bodily reserves of energy to enable them to survive the arduous journeys on the hoof. The ideal type of animal in Great Britain in those early days was a large framed, well muscled beast, with an adequate reserve of fat to provide the energy fuel for long treks to market towns and cities.

In a tropical environment these conditions still pertain. In Nigeria, for example, over 45 per cent of trade cattle still trek southwards on the hoof,

fig. 9.2 Transporting cattle by boat

while the remaining 55 per cent are carried by road and rail. In the wet season the well-fattened beast can reach the southern markets on the hoof in quite surprisingly good condition, despite trekking for several weeks for distances of over 1 000 km. But the less well-nourished animal in the dry season, where food on trek is scarce, may be very poor by comparison. Similar conditions of trade cattle management persist in parts of Northern Australia and South and Central America, where thousands of trade cattle off range, destined for stocker or finishing regimes, are still trekked on foot to the sales yards.

By contrast, beef cattle managed under semi-intensive or intensive conditions are not subject to the rigours of their range-reared mates. Local market and management facilities allow for a more compact and faster maturing animal that can provide meat of an adequate quality and quantity in the shortest possible time. Such market conditions, however, depend upon the demand of consumers with sufficient income.

The most important item governing meat quality is the amount of glycogen available in the muscles at the time of slaughter. After slaughter the available glycogen allows for the anaerobic formation of lactic acid-forming bacteria with consequent lowering of the pH and breakdown of connective tissue in the meat. Furthermore, when the meat is exposed to the air after butchering, lowered muscle glycogen interferes with the formation of oxy-haemoglobin, which gives the pleasing bright red colour to fresh meat. Lack of oxyhaemoglobin results instead in a dark purple-red colour, unattractive to more selective buyers.

Fortunately, cattle and buffalo can withstand considerable fatigue before these undesirable changes in the meat after slaughter take place. It is known, however, that excitement and fear, inducing muscle tension and even shivering, can cause reduced muscle glycogen reserves. Rough handling during loading or off-loading will also reduce meat quality by bruising and in those countries where electric goads are used to make cattle move through chutes or to raise collapsed beasts from the ground, this can also bring about 'dark-cutting' meat. Temperament is, of course important, for docile beasts, those handled by pastoralist herdsman, normally behave quietly and respond to command by word-of-mouth even up to the time of slaughter. The nervous beast, however, particularly those coming from managed ranges, may react strongly when moved from its accustomed habitat to the market. In such cases, an adequate rest of three to four days prior to slaughter is needed if muscle glycogen reserves are to build up again.

Pre-slaughter holding
It is not sufficient simply to get the animal from its source to the point of slaughter. In practically all trade cattle movement there is a waiting period of days before the animal is slaughtered. When trade cattle that have not passed through Veterinary Control Posts reach the holding yards, the following minimal requirements are necessary to avoid stress and possible spread of disease:

1 adequate space in holding pens to avoid overcrowding;
2 shade and water;
3 provision of forage (in some urban or suburban areas peripheral grazing may still be available); and
4 veterinary surveillance to detect possible disease carriers of, for example, contagious bovine pleuro-pneumonia, foot-and-mouth disease, tuberculosis, salmonellosis, etc.

Slaughter facilities

Ideally, slaughtering facilities should be adequate to ensure minimum risk of contamination of the meat by insects, parasites and micro-organisms from the surroundings and the subsequent growth of some of these contaminants within the carcass meat. In a tropical environment this is easier said than done, but whatever the circumstances, whether the animal be slaughtered for market on the open slaughter slab floor, or in fly-proofed modern abattoirs, examination of the meat during and after slaughter, as well as veterinary public health inspection of the live animal and, after slaughter, of the carcass, are essential. Unhealthy meat at slaughter can be condemned on the spot, but undetected contaminated meat during slaughter and in processing procedures may harbour micro-organisms that will later multiply. Such contamination not only reduces meat quality, but also constitutes a public health hazard.

There are many social and religious customs, food taboos and economic and climatic factors that mitigate for or against the improvement of slaughter facilities. The basic slaughter techniques and descriptions of facilities detailed in this chapter, may or may not be suitable in all cases and it is for the reader to decide their suitability. It should also be borne in mind that the attitude of most livestock traders, butchers and hide traders is so conservative that great care must be taken in recommending any new or apparently revolutionary procedures. This is understandable for new methods, however advantageous from the meat quality and public health standpoint, may involve changes that might not at first sight appear to help them. One cannot lose sight of the fact that in some countries, where slaughter facilities, though efficiently run, may still be classed as primitive, many people are involved; some may remove the offal, others the head and feet, and still others the tail and hide, as well as blood. One cannot disrupt such age-old practices as these without exercising due caution, and it would seem that the inevitable compromise must still lie between the old and the new methods of cattle movement, slaughter and subsequent processing.

Simple slaughter slabs and slaughter houses

The most basic facility is a slaughter slab, which consists simply of a hardened or concrete floor and rudimentary drainage. Such slaughter slabs are regularly found in remote or sparsely populated areas and sometimes in the larger towns (fig. 9.3). They may be erected by the butchers themselves, or by the local authorities. A slight improvement on the slab is the simple slaughter house, which may provide a few simple facilities for more humane slaughter and better hygiene and some sort of roofing or shelter (fig. 9.4).

The basic principle of hygiene in any method of slaughter of animals is to raise the carcass from the floor. This is often not done, however, and many butchers insist on continuing with the traditional methods of slaughtering on the floor, even when hoisting facilities are available.

fig. 9.3 Slaughter slab

fig. 9.4 Simple slaughter house

There are three methods of raising the carcass. These are:

1 Two sets of block-and-tackle (fig. 9.5a). As the carcass is raised, the legs are pulled apart to facilitate splitting.
2 Chain block-and-tackle and gambrel (fig. 9.5b). The gambrel or 'beef tree' parts the legs of the carcass to facilitate splitting. This can be made of wood, but steel is preferable.
3 Winch or wall hoist (fig. 9.5c) also using the gambrel. Hoists to support the carcass can be made from good strong timber or from tubular metal.

185

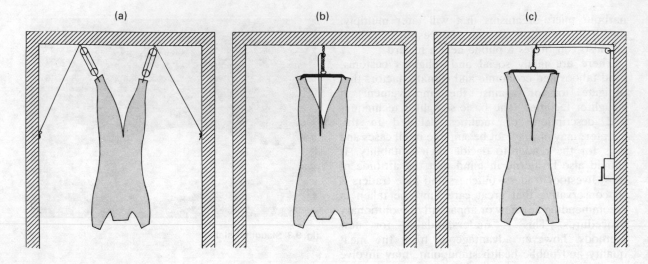

fig. 9.5 Different types of hoist

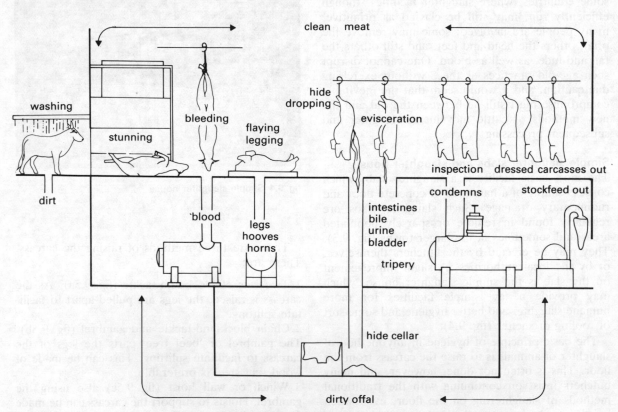

clean meat

washing

bleeding

stunning

flaying
legging

dirt

blood

legs
hooves
horns

hide
dropping

evisceration

inspection   dressed carcasses out

condemns

stockfeed out

intestines
bile
urine
bladder

tripery

hide cellar

dirty offal

fig. 9.6 Diagram showing division between clean and dirty operations in a double-storied slaughter house

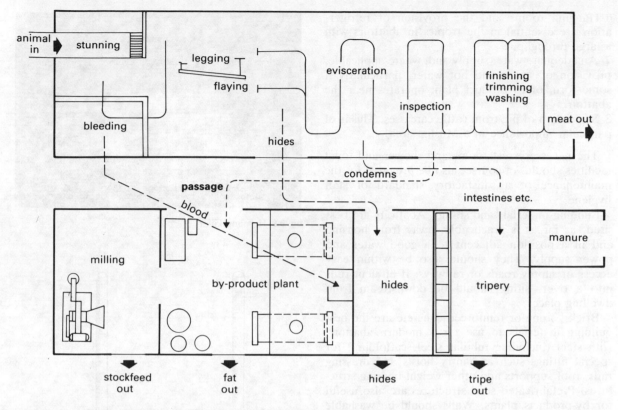

fig. 9.7 Division between clean and dirty operations in a single-storey slaughter house

Abattoir design

The slaughter facilities described above suffice in most cases to meet the requirements of rural areas, where few animals are slaughtered at any one time and where fresh meat is removed almost immediately. Overhead operating costs are very low. Larger slaughter houses (figs 9.6 and 9.7) or abattoirs are necessary to serve larger communities and handle large numbers of animals. They need to provide space for large amounts of offal and in more elaborate abattoirs, meat storage and processing facilities. The following common features apply to any abattoir layout, irrespective of its size or design:

1 Pre-slaughter facilities should include off-loading ramps and adequate resting space and room for veterinary inspection and isolation of sick animals.
2 Slaughtering procedures should be humane, so that animals may enter from the lairage to the stunning area without seeing blood, carcasses and offal of other animals.
3 There should be division between what are known as 'clean' and 'dirty' procedures to avoid contamination of the carcass (clean) by the offal (dirty). The latter include the hide, feet, tripe and guts.
4 The building should provide a meat inspector's office, including space for records, specimens and some laboratory equipment for preliminary diagnostic purposes. Carcasses hanging on rails, with the offal hanging opposite, provide the easiest access for the meat inspector. A separate rail should be provided for detained carcasses, or condemned carcasses not fit for human consumption.
5 Triperies, or the area used for the preparation of offal for human consumption, should be separate.

6 Hanging rooms and the provision of refrigeration are essential in the tropics in abattoirs with a large throughput.

7 An adequate water supply and, where applicable, provision of steam and hot water, particularly if some form of by-product plant operates near the abattoir.

8 Separation of pig from cattle carcasses. This is of particular importance in a Muslim area.

The necessary rest rooms and shower and toilet facilities should, of course, also be provided for the maintenance of a satisfactory standard of staff hygiene.

Building materials and siting Abattoirs are best sited, as far as is practicable, away from housing and in a position adjacent to a good water and power supply. They should also be within easy access of supply roads or railways. If effluent runs into a river, siting should be downstream from dwelling places.

Bricks, stone or reinforced concrete are the best building materials to use for a modern abattoir, with steel (including tubular steel scaffolding) for special fittings such as gantry hoists and dressing rails, roof supports and other weight-bearing structures. Prefabricated steel structures are also useful for by-products plants. Walls should be washable and the junction with the floor should be rounded so as to facilitate drainage. They should also be hard, impervious to things such as blood or excreta, easily cleaned, properly drained and quick drying.

Humane slaughtering

As already stated, animals awaiting slaughter should be kept apart, where possible, from animals being slaughtered and from carcasses or carcass by-products. The principle of slaughter with the least possible cruelty should be the aim. This can be achieved by the procedure known as stunning, that is, rendering the animal unconscious before it is subsequently killed and bled.

Stunning is usually carried out using the humane killer (fig. 9.8), the knocking hammer (fig. 9.9) or electricity, after which the unconscious animal is immediately hauled to the killing area where its throat is cut for bleeding. Thus the animal

fig. 9.8 Humane killer

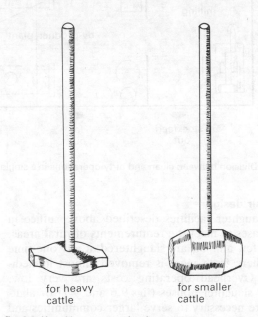

for heavy cattle   for smaller cattle

fig. 9.9 Knocking or stunning hammers

is not distressed or struggling at the time of killing and this allows for more complete bleeding. The old method of stunning by pole-axing is still used in some parts of the world and consists of striking the animal on the forehead with a type of axe, that renders it unconscious. The practice of pithing that consists of sticking a sharp knife into the space between the skull and the first bone of the neck, the atlanto-occipital space, is cruel and is to be condemned. Although it paralyses the motor nerves controlling muscle movement, it leaves the animal fully conscious and thus sensitive to fear and pain.

The entrance to the stunning and killing area from the holding pens should be narrow enough to prevent the animal from turning round. The width will therefore need to be suited to the type or breed being slaughtered. For example, the passageway for the small N'dama should be narrower than one for the Brahman or other large Zebus.

Stunning pens should be approximately 0.4 m × 0.9 m in area or smaller, according to the size of the animal to be stunned. The animal enters through a side door and stunning is performed. The animal is then ejected from the stunning pen onto the killing floor, the next one enters the pen and the process is repeated. Where the pen is not fitted for ejecting the animal it may be shackled for casting from under the gate, stunned, cast, and then pulled out. Types of stunning or knocking, and casting pens are shown in figs. 9.10, 9.11 and 9.12.

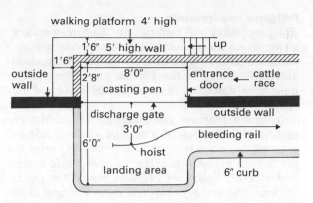

fig. 9.11 Plan of arrangements of a casting pen

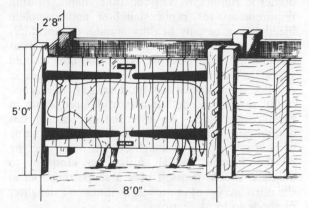

fig. 9.12 A casting box made of wood, not fitted for ejection, which is recommended for use in the smallest slaughter house and suitable also for Muslim slaughter

Bleeding should be conducted so that the animal is bled to the fullest extent and with the least possible contamination. Although many traditional butchers are loath to bleed except on the floor, the ideal way is to hoist the stunned animal quickly onto an overhead rail or gantry post. The hide on the dewlap area, just above the sternum at the front of the neck is cut and the knife directed toward the throat, thus severing the main blood vessels. Bleeding should be done as soon after stunning as possible because the heart rate and blood pressure are high only at this time and thus aid maximum and rapid bleeding. Bleeding is decreased the longer the delay after stunning.

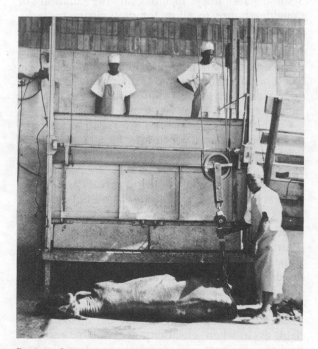

fig. 9.10 Stunning pen

189

Religious requirements

The procedures and facilities for slaughter outlined so far do not meet entirely with the specific requirements of certain religious communities. Methods of animal slaughter in the Islamic and Jewish faiths have been described in detail by the FAO and are summarised below.

In mixed religious communities, where Muslim and non-Muslim butchers may be working side by side, all processes relating to pig slaughter must be carried out in separate areas, using separate knives and utensils. Followers of Islam regard the pig as unclean and consequently all items relating to its slaughter, including lairage, transport and personnel involved must be separated from the slaughter of domestic ruminants. On the other hand, Muslim requirements for rapid slaughter and complete bleeding out of only healthy animals do not differ from the basic requirements of modern meat hygiene. Where possible, only Muslims should supervise such slaughter procedures, although in practice some sort of compromise may be reached in this respect among butchers of different faiths in rural communities. An essential element of this compromise is that all will have invoked the name of God at the time of slaughter. The basic teaching of the Prophet, which insists on kindness to animals, should in itself play a supporting role in the introduction of improved facilities and slaughter methods to local abattoirs.

Jewish slaughter procedures are not dissimilar to those of the Muslim system, in which the live animal is cast and the throat cut. The animal is cast onto its back by hobbles or side ropes and the throat cut with a very sharp knife by the *sochet*. To reduce panic in the animal as it is turned on its back head masks may be used in a modern abattoir. Special casting crates that rotate and tip the animal onto its back are also used.

Other creeds, for example certain Hindu sects, may accept humane *halal* slaughter methods, but the Sikhs and some other non-Muslim communities will not. In its place they adopt the Jhatka method in which the head is severed from the body with one single blow of a very sharp knife. This practice is confined to sheep and goats since cattle are not slaughtered. This method, if efficiently carried out, at least has the attribute of being swift in despatching the animal.

Whatever the slaughter methods used, several principles need to be observed that do not offend both local customs and religious beliefs. Local authorities should demand that knives and other instruments be sharp and handled only by experienced butchers. Where possible lairage and other facilities should be well constructed, well screened and the blood drained away in such a manner as to reduce as far as possible panic among animals awaiting slaughter.

Postmortem inspection procedures

As with antemortem inspection of animals, whether conducted at control posts or at the holding ground, adequate postmortem inspection is necessary in order to reduce public health risk from consuming what may be infected meat.

Adequate postmortem inspection depends upon:

1 properly trained personnel;
2 reasonable facilities for carrying out postmortem examination; and
3 some laboratory facilities at the abattoir or slaughter house to allow for preliminary bacteriological, parasitological or biochemical examination of suspect material.

Final confirmation of preliminary findings will in many instances necessitate further analysis in more adequately equipped and staffed diagnostic laboratories.

Certain guiding principles are required for postmortem procedures which may be adapted to suit local conditions. For the purposes of this brief discussion, these will relate only to postmortem examination procedures on the carcass and not to more sophisticated laboratory diagnostic work.

Type of premises and amount of light

There should be sufficient space for the inspector to examine both carcass and offal and good light is essential for these purposes. Imperfect bleeding, jaundiced or yellow meat and a possible greenish colouration of muscle or fat indicating bacterial or other changes, may be missed in bad light even when electricity is available, so that daylight is best. In tropical countries, where slaughter and preparation of the carcass and offal is usually complete by the time it is light, there are usually no problems in this respect.

Time of postmortem examination
This should be as soon after slaughter as is possible. In most cases, since inadequate storage and other facilities makes it essential to distribute the fresh meat for sale without undue delay, this usually presents no problem. Even where there are by-product processing or refrigerator facilities, post-mortems can best be carried out on the fresh carcass, soon after slaughter.

General examination of the carcass
This should be done in a methodical manner, what-ever the status of the slaughter house or abattoir facilities. The criteria laid down, for example in the UK, regarding methods and stipulations of meat inspection can also apply to meat inspection in a tropical environment. Every carcass should be examined for the following:

State of nutrition Physiological leanness resulting from lack of feed and water must be differentiated, as far as is practicable, from pathological leanness due to disease. In trade cattle in the tropics this may be difficult since, in many cases, cattle on long treks are not only deprived of food, but exposed to tick and tsetse-borne diseases. In a temperate climate the percentage of water within the meat of normal cattle is not above 76.5 per cent and the percentage of protein about 22 per cent or a ratio of less than 4:1. In extremely emaciated animals the ratio may be 80 per cent water and 19 per cent muscle, or greater than 4:1. Such criteria may be of little consequence for the local market, but where a quality product is sought after, especially for the export market, the emaciated carcass has no place, either as saleable fresh meat or for its storing qualities.

Bruising, haemorrhage and discoloration Where there has been excessive trauma, as may occur with severe trampling, beating or crushing during transit, this can be seen on the surface of the dressed carcass after removing the hide. The joints of meat below these bruised areas should be cut out and sold as soon as possible, otherwise serum from the bruised muscles may infiltrate down through the adjacent unbruised meat and reduce the market value of the carcass as well as its storage quality.

Local or general oedema This condition is undesirable in any carcass, whether it be due to some localised condition, or more generalised conditions, such as helminthiasis, trypanosomiasis and the tick-borne diseases. Oedema reduces carcass quality and saleability as well as storage quality of the meat.

Efficiency of bleeding This is pertinent to any community since it affects both keeping quality and flavour of the meat. Reference has already been made to meat that is dark because of its low glycogen content; the result of exhaustion before slaughter. This should not be confused with dark meat caused by poor bleeding-out methods. Most consumers in the tropics will not eat meat that is improperly bled and because of this local butchers are often highly suspicious of stunning and new slaughter methods. They insist on casting the beast and cutting the jugular vessels or cutting off the head, pithing, or some other slaughter method that ensures good bleeding-out. This is discussed more fully in the next section.

Swelling or deformities These receive much less attention under slaughter conditions in the rural tropics, where meat is more of a luxury and for special occasions, than in the larger abattoirs adjacent to urban communities.

Age and sex These items are also not considered in most tropical meat markets unless, of course, quality meat is required for elite households or special occasions.

Abnormal odours These do not arouse particular attention in the cattle and buffalo meat market unless, for example, there is some specific odour encountered, as in putrefying meat or in the sweet-smelling meat of rinderpest-infected animals.

Detailed inspection of the carcass
After a general examination the carcass is subjected to a more detailed examination. The following is a summary of procedures applicable in a tropical environment.

The head
1 The tongue should be loosened but not detached and the surface and substance (i.e. deep structures) inspected.
2 The gums and roof of the mouth should be inspected.
3 The lymph glands around the pharynx and large

salivary (parotid) gland behind the angle of the jaw are examined. Lymph glands act as filters of disease agents and if swollen, haemorrhagic or abscessed indicate disease in the tissues that they drain.

4 The cheek muscles should be examined by incisions parallel to the lower jaw.

5 The eyes should be examined.

NOTE: In young or 'bobby' calves, the above examination should be suitably modified, or ignored, where animals of this age are not considered fit for human consumption.

The abdominal cavity

1 Stomach, intestines, and spleen: the outer, and when necessary, the inner surfaces of the stomach and intestines, the surface and substance of the spleen, and the surfaces of the omentum or loose covering over the stomach, should be examined. The lymph glands related to these organs are also examined.

2 Liver: the surface and substance of the liver should be examined and the bile ducts incised to check for the presence of the liver fluke, *Fasciola gigantica*. The thick end of cattle livers should be incised, and examined in detail, also the hepatic lymph glands.

3 Kidneys: the renal lymph glands and the adrenal glands should be examined and, when necessary, the kidneys should be exposed and incised.

4 Uterus and ovaries: the substance of the uterus, its outer surface and, if necessary, its inner surface should be examined as should the substance of the ovaries.

The chest cavity
The 'pluck' (fig. 9.13) should be examined in the following manner before the organs are separated from each other.

1 Lungs: they should be examined by observation and by palpation and, unless obviously diseased, they should be incised at the base. The bronchial and mediastinal lymph glands, those lying between the lungs, should be examined in detail.

2 Heart: the heart covering should be opened and the heart examined and, if necessary, incised.

The udder
This should be incised and examined by observation and palpation and the associated supramammary lymph glands should be examined in detail.

The testicles and penis
The outer surface and substance of the testicles and penis should be exam-

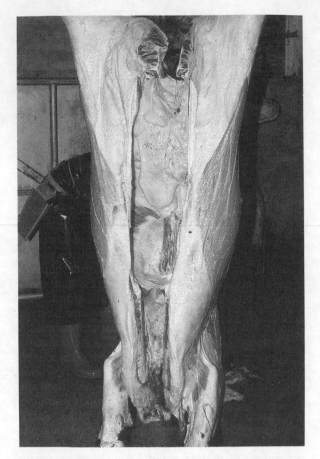

fig. 9.13 The 'pluck'

ined in detail. The superficial inguinal lymph glands or those situated under the skin in the groin area should be examined in detail.

The feet
The feet should be examined, especially for lesions suggesting foot-and-mouth disease.

The zoonoses

The zoonoses may be defined as those diseases of animals that are transmitted to man. This is a subject of considerable complexity and it can also, in the case of the anthropo-zoonoses, refer to diseases of man that are transmissible to his domestic livestock. The whole concept and basis of meat hygiene and inspection relates to the fundamental principle that the meat reaching the market is sufficiently well examined before and after slaughter, as well as during the process of cutting, despatching and retailing to ensure, as far as possible, freedom from diseases which can be transmitted to man.

In developed countries optimum precautions can be taken at all stages, both during ante- and post-mortem inspection and transport and processing stages of the carcass and by-products. In developing tropical countries the rigid criteria of inspection accepted in the developed world cannot be applied to local marketing, although much can be and is being done by local authorities to protect the consumer and abattoir workers from exposure to infection.

Of a somewhat formidable list of the zoonoses, five have been selected for brief discussion.

Anthrax

This is a highly infectious bacterial disease of animals, quite commonly encountered in tropical countries. Man can acquire the disease from infected carcasses or by-products by handling, inhaling contaminated air, or eating infected meat. Anthrax can often be detected by proper ante-mortem inspection, but the disease can be overlooked. Even an experienced inspector may have difficulty under certain conditions in differentiating anthrax from other septicaemic diseases. For these occasions minimal laboratory facilities for early on-the-spot provisional diagnosis are essential. Once an infected anthrax carcass has been removed unnoticed from the abattoir the disease can spread rapidly. The anthrax bacillus forms resistant bacterial spores which can remain viable in the soil and elsewhere for very long periods. Care should be taken to remove a suspected carcass from the abattoir floor. To avoid further contamination the premises should be disinfected with a 2 per cent caustic soda solution.

Carcasses infected with anthrax should be destroyed completely, if possible by burning. If buried, the pit should be sufficiently deep to prevent the carcass being dug up by dogs or other predators. Lime sprinkled on the carcass before burial also helps reduce the danger of the disease spreading.

Cysticercosis

This condition is prevalent in cattle in many tropical areas and is a particular health hazard to man because infected cattle and buffalo muscles contain the cysts, an intermediate or developmental stage of *Taenia saginata*, one of the large tapeworms of man. Cattle and buffalo grazing on pastures contaminated with human faeces containing these tapeworm eggs can become infected. The muscular tissue of the cattle and buffalo then become infected with the tapeworm cysts and if man eats improperly cooked beef he becomes infected and the cycle of development can re-occur.

Meat inspectors usually cut into the cheek muscles and heart muscle to check for the presence of cysts. In Zebu-type cattle the hump is also a further useful site for muscle incisions.

Hydatidosis

The importance of this disease lies in both its human health and economic aspects. The dog is the most important link in the biological cycle of this tapeworm and for this reason control should be directed at proper treatment of dogs with anthelmintics, keeping them out of slaughter premises, and the proper disposal of the viscera of all slaughter animals. The hydatid cysts are intermediate developmental stages of the dog tapeworm. These cysts can develop not only in large and small ruminants and swine, but also in man, where they may even locate themselves in the brain.

From the human infection standpoint, the hydatid cysts in the viscera of sheep and swine are the most dangerous as far as potential infection of scavenging dogs is concerned, because cysts in these animals are much more fertile than those found in cattle and buffalo.

Bovine tuberculosis

There is increasing evidence that this disease, which is also transmissible to man, is becoming more prevalent in the tropics. This may be due to an actual increase in the incidence of the disease, or an indication of improved detection. Since infection is by ingestion of infected meat or milk, adequate inspection of the carcass, with particular reference to the lymph glands, is essential.

Tuberculosis is a bacterial disease of both

animals and man and causes gastro-intestinal infections as well as lung infections. Meat-borne infections can occur from contamination of meat by tuberculosis-infected human carriers such as butchers and handlers and by contact with meat derived from infected animals during the abattoir routine. Careful antemortem and postmortem inspection combined with good slaughter hygiene are essential to reduce the danger of widespread contamination.

Salmonellosis
Salmonella bacteria affect a wide range of wild and domestic animals, as well as man. They cause mainly enteric infections and in the tropics human gastro-intestinal infections caused by salmonellae are common. Meat-borne infections can frequently occur, not only by contact with meat derived from infected animals, but also from meat which has been contaminated by human carriers of salmonellae during slaughter procedures. Contamination of meat from infected animals during slaughter is a considerable problem and careful ante- and post-mortem inspection combined with a satisfactory standard of slaughter hygiene are essential to reduce the danger of widespread contamination and subsequent dissemination of the bacteria.

Other diseases
The importance of adequate inspection for other diseases such as rinderpest, contagious bovine pleuro-pneumonia and foot-and-mouth disease, while they may not be a direct public health hazard, must still be emphasised. A careful watch for these diseases and their proper reporting to the authorities concerned can do much to improve the effectiveness of control procedures.

Trypanosomiasis, the tick-borne diseases and many other tropical diseases of bacterial or viral origin are often encountered at ante- or postmortem inspection. Many of these diseases are not directly dangerous to man, but they do pose problems of judgement for the meat inspector for he must decide on the fate of carcasses showing some considerable degree of emaciation, as well as minor lesions. Market demand and the quality of meat acceptable to a particular community will help decide the fate of such carcasses.

Preservation of meat
Although fresh meat has the highest nutritional value and is preferred by most consumers, it is frequently preserved and stored for future consumption. The four most widely used preservation methods are drying (including smoking), curing, canning and refrigeration. In many cases, combinations of these, for example, drying and salting, are used together in producing the desired result.

Drying
Air drying of meat dates back to the early history of mankind and although commercial techniques for the preparation of dehydrated (dried) meat are available, these are generally very costly to operate. Air drying, on the other hand, is a comparatively simple process, provided it is done in hot, dry weather. It has been shown, in East Africa, that physiological emaciation of cattle, commonly found in starved animals, does not interfere with the final dried product, although the yield from such carcasses may be low. One of the best known of dried meat products is biltong, used extensively in South Africa. Although simple and cheap to prepare, pre-slaughter care of animals is essential for the production of biltong that has good keeping qualities. Strict adherence to such procedures as proper bleeding and evisceration, as described earlier, are necessary. The procedures for biltong production are as follows:

1 The carcass meat is cut into long strips of equal thickness, cutting the fibres lengthwise. The best dried meat is obtained by physically tearing rather than cutting the muscles so that groups of fibres can be dried as a unit.
2 Strips of meat are then salted; either the salt is rubbed in by hand just before hanging or strips are left covered with salt overnight. Spices and peppers may be added, according to local taste, also salt-petre, which is a mild preservative and which also imparts a good red colour to the meat.
3 The strips of meat are then hung in the sun on galvanised wire or on separate S-shaped hooks some 7 cm in length. The strips should not touch one another, to allow free circulation of air.
4 After about 12 hours drying the strips should be

removed, straightened and turned round for the other side to be properly dried. The time taken for good drying will depend upon the weather.

5 Where dried meat is to be kept for periods longer than four to six weeks, it may be necessary to smoke it or to add surface insecticide in low concentrations, if this is allowed by local ordinances. Such dried meat is best stored in polythene bags.

The advantages of dried meat are due to its high content of protein, its good keeping qualities if protected from moisture and the attacks of insects such as beetles, and its retention of minerals and vitamins after processing. The disadvantages are that exposure to air and light can bring about rancidity of the fat. Exposure to moisture will also lead to decomposition and/or mouldiness. Naturally dried meat continues, however, to be one of the most popular meat products. It can be eaten dry, or raw, or it can be treated as fresh meat, after soaking in water.

Salting and drying

The salted meat known as *charqui* is first cured in salt and then dried, and differs from biltong in that it contains more moisture. When processed, it resembles dried salted fish in appearance. Pieces of fresh meat for initial curing should be 1.5 to 2.5 kg in weight and about 2.25 cm thick. These are first hung for a period of about one hour to cool, after which they are immersed in brine for a further hour. They are then allowed to drain off on slats. Final curing consists of placing the pieces of meat in a series of layers with about 2.25 cm salt between them, to make up a series of meat/salt layers some 1.25 m high. The pile of layers is then covered with planks and heavy stones to press the pile. The next day the layers in the pile are reversed in position, and this reversal of the position of the layers continues for five days, after which the meat is ready for drying. This is done by pressing the meat between planks, or by passing it through a sort of wooden mangle. In hot, dry climates, sun drying on bamboo slats or on chicken wire in the early morning and evening is sufficient. The meat should not be allowed to overheat, otherwise the fat is melted.

This type of dried, salted meat has good keeping qualities. Before eating it should be soaked in water, which is then poured away in order to get rid of excess salt.

Biltong has a higher protein content than charqui (68.8 and 46.2 per cent respectively) and more B group vitamins. Charqui on the other hand, contains more fat and is saltier. Generally speaking, people accustomed to dry salted fish prefer charqui to biltong, whereas biltong, after it has been soaked in water, resembles more closely fresh meat.

Dehydration

Dehydrated meat is prepared using special equipment to control temperature and humidity, as well as being carried out under a vacuum. The process is generally not suited to the developing stages of beef and buffalo meat industries. The chief advantages of dehydrated meat are its light weight, ease of storage and packing, and the reliability and excellence of the water-reconstituted product.

Two major processes of preparation are the vacuum contact plate process and the Platt or Zimmerman process. In the latter fresh meat is immersed in heated oil under vacuum, the oil acting as a medium for the transfer of heat to the meat. There are certain technical difficulties in removing all the oil from the meat by centrifugation, but this method is cheaper than the vacuum contact plate process.

Smoking

Smoking is one of the oldest methods of preserving meat, the simplest method being to hang slices above an open fire. Smoking imparts good keeping qualities and, provided the right woods are used, a pleasant flavour. Smoked meat does not easily go bad and it is also resistant to flies and beetles. Its longer keeping properties, nevertheless, can be improved by a combination of curing and smoking. Smoked meat is often prepared for export in developed countries. For these purposes the meat is hung on a rotating shaft and heat is applied by steam coils and burning sawdust. The latter is blended from selected hardwoods and fired by a gas burner. Suction fans are used to draw the smoke evenly over the hanging meat.

Simple smoke houses are in use in many tropical

countries. They can be made from local materials, using wattle and mud for the top and sides, and wooden lattice work to support the meat, which is covered by local woven matting to protect it from flies, vultures, etc. and to dampen down the smoke. An alternative method is to use a large oil or petrol drum, the bottom of which is removed and the top made into a lid. A fire pit is dug near the drum and the smoke from the pit is directed through a covered trench into the base of the drum, in which the meat is hung. The smoke escapes through the top, where the lid can be adjusted to control its rate of flow. Fig. 9.14 illustrates a simple design for a wattle and daub smoke house.

Meat for smoking must not come from fevered or emaciated animals. Such meat remains wet and flabby and does not smoke well. Meat may be smoked raw or after being cured or previously cooked. It should be cut along the muscle fibres into flat slices to allow good smoke penetration. Large pieces of meat need higher temperatures and a longer period of smoking. Where salt-cured meat is used for smoking the brine should be washed off the surface of the meat with clean water, otherwise

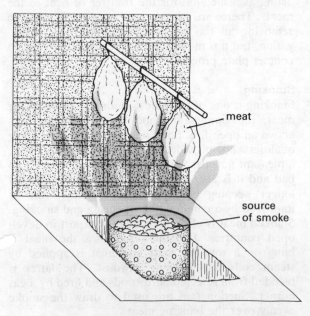

meat

source of smoke

fig. 9.14 Wattle and daub smoke house

the salt will form a crust on the surface of the meat during smoking.

Curing and pickling
There are several methods and substances used for preserving by curing. Some of these are used for curing pork and other meats, but only those relevant to beef and buffalo meat will be briefly mentioned here. Curing is not the same as preserving meat by the use of antiseptics. Curing agents such as salt, sugar or vinegar are harmless for the consumer, and while they do not kill micro-organisms they prevent their multiplication. At the same time, they may also impart special flavours or even improve the flavour of some products. Antiseptics and certain other chemical preservatives may kill micro-organisms, but if improperly used may be harmful to the consumer, so that there is strict legal control over their use.

The following ingredients are used for curing and preservation: salt; sugar, used in high concentration and also jointly with other curing ingredients; Bengal saltpetre or potassium nitrate; Chile saltpetre or sodium nitrate; vinegar, and various spices. Although spices are used mainly to impart flavour, they also have some inhibitory action in high concentrations on micro-organisms.

Cures may be either used dry, in which the dry ingredient is rubbed into the surface of the meat, or in solution as in pickling and brineing, or as a mixture.

Heat sterilisation (canning)
The principle of this process is that the produce is sealed in a container after applying heat to kill micro-organisms which may cause spoilage of the product. The process is not dissimilar to that of home bottling of fruit. The basic principles involve heating the food product sufficiently to kill the micro-organisms, followed by sealing in a vacuum. The length of time of heating will depend on several factors, including the type of micro-organisms to be destroyed, the moisture content and acidity of the product, the amount of protection offered by fats or oils and the quantity of other substances, such as salt, that may be present.

Meat for this process must be properly prepared before canning and, if necessary, precooked.

Oxygen and air are driven off to provide the vacuum, either by closing the can under vacuum, or by passing the can through an exhaust box, where the air and oxygen are driven off by heat and the can sealed before cooking.

Refrigeration

The preservation of meat and fish by refrigeration was first used on a commercial basis in northern Europe, using natural ice shipped from the Arctic. Mechanical refrigerators came into use during the latter part of the nineteenth century in order to ship meat from the Argentine, Australia and New Zealand to Europe. There are now rapid developments in refrigerator transport of meat carcasses from production areas to internal consumer markets and for export in some tropical countries.

There are three major temperature ranges at which meat is processed by cooling. These are: the initial cooling range (0 to −5 °C), the chilling range (−3–10 °C), the freezing range (−10 to −18 °C).

Initial cooling Since the temperature of freshly killed meat is generally about 40°C, quick cooling is desirable in order to prevent what is called 'bone taint' caused by anaerobic micro-organisms and spoilage on the surface of the meat during storage. A great deal of water can be lost from the superficial carcass tissues through rapid desiccation at atmospheric temperatures. Initial cooling reduces loss of water. In some cases, however, the carcass is put straight into the cold room without prior cooling.

Storage of meat in the chilled state This process can be used for meat storage for one or two weeks prior to marketing, or for overseas or overland transport. In those countries where meat can be marketed within a few days, chilling allows the meat to 'ripen', thus increasing tenderness. Meat can also be ripened at freezing temperatures, but this can cause 'drip' and consequent reduction of juiciness of the meat. For transport of chilled meat by road or rail wagon, trucks are fitted with bunkers containing blocks of ice. Special refrigerated trucks and wagons can be used for chilling warm carcasses direct from slaughter houses which have no chilling facilities – a situation frequently encountered in the tropics.

Freezing of meat Chilling of the carcass is carried out for three days, prior to storage at temperatures of −10 to 18 °C. However, freezing of the whole or half beef carcass may take four to six days and this may cause 'drip' in which a red viscous fluid drains out from the unfrozen meat. The system of quick-frozen meat cuts, as distinct from freezing the whole or half carcass, at −20 to −30 °C causes the bulk of water in the tissues to be frozen in 30–60 minutes. Meat frozen in this way is usually cut into slices some 3.5 to 5 cm thick.

Microbial inhibitors and radiation

Of the various gases or liquids tried for meat preservation, carbon dioxide gas, added at a concentration of 8 to 10 per cent of the storage atmosphere in the hold of ships, is now the most commonly used. Ultraviolet lamps are also used to control microbial spoilage. However, penetration of the meat by the ultraviolet light is only superficial. Such lamps are quite commonly used above meat display cold cabinets and counters in retail stores.

The carcass

There is some variation in the use of the words carcass and carcase. This has led to differences in reports on carcass yields due, especially, to different methods of dressing the carcass. It is therefore proposed to follow the definitions used by Ross Cockrill. The word 'carcase' is used for the whole dead animal while the word 'carcass' represents the dead animal after head, hoofs, hide, intestines, blood, genitalia, etc. have been removed. The 'carcass' as a percentage of the 'carcase' is known as the 'dressing percentage', 'dressing out percentage' or 'killing percentage'.

The dressing percentage can be criticised as an expression of meat yield since it is based on the liveweight of the animal before slaughter and thus includes the gut fill, which, in the ruminant animal, is considerable. A difference in dressing percentage of 11.6 per cent between empty and full animals was found in a group of 8 British beef steers. Differences ranging from 8.3 to 12.3 per cent between empty and full West African N'dama steers on mixed grass/legume pastures are shown in Table 9.1. The composition of the carcass fill and

Table 9.1 The relationship of 'fill' to body weight and dressing percentage

Treatment item	B	C	D	General mean
Full body weight (lb.)	704.3	724.5	652.3	693.7
Empty body weight (lb.)	573.2	604.5	563.2	580.3
Cold carcass weight (lb.)	375.9	391.5	343.1	370.2
'Fill'				
Amount (lb.)	136.1	122.5	99.1	119.2
Full body weight (%)	19.1	16.6	15.3	17.1
Empty body (%)	24.1	19.9	17.7	20.6
Final total weight gains of steers (lb.)	1376.0	1290.0	1350.00	1338.6
Final total weight gains corrected for 'fill'	1110.4	1075.5	1143.5	1109.8
Dressing (%)	53.3	54.0	52.6	53.3
Dressing percentage corrected for 'fill'	65.6	64.8	60.9	63.8

Table 9.2 Composition of carcass, edible offal and fill of 10 White Fulani and 10 Sokoto Gudali Zebu bulls

	Average weight (kg)	Percentage of carcass (%)
Left side	90.23	29.14[1]
Right side	94.98	30.42[1]
Head	16.20	5.17
Hide	30.30	9.68
Shanks	7.47	2.38
Tongue	2.17	0.69
Liver	5.04	1.60
Lungs	3.13	1.00
Heart	1.25	0.39
Rumen (empty)	10.22	3.26
Intestine (empty)	11.00	3.50
Fill	41.01	12.77
Dressing percentage	52.95%	

[1] As a percentage of the empty carcass.

offal of Nigerian Zebu cattle managed in a feedlot are provided in Table 9.2.

Carcass dressing

The best and most hygienic way to dress a carcass is with the carcass hanging from some kind of hoist. Whether or not the carcass is hung, the nature of the dressing technique and the way that the carcass is cut will depend upon local custom and, of course, upon variations in marketing techniques which may differ even within a community. In the latter case, one may find different categories of butchers, working with different facilities and often situated adjacent to each other, preparing different cuts of meat to suit a particular market.

In major meat producing countries the whole side of meat is dressed and cut, but in many tropical countries this is not practical. The hot carcass is cut into several recognisable pieces that facilitate transport which may be on a man's head, on a cart or even in the boot of a taxi. Whereas such methods expose the carcass cuts to contamination, they do at least ensure rapid distribution of the fresh meat. Most consumers in the tropics still demand fresh and not chilled or frozen meat.

Although practised mainly on sheep and goats there are some tropical countries where the tissues under the skin of the slaughtered beef animal are inflated by passing compressed air through a needle inserted through the skin. This facilitates removal of the hide. The gaseous pockets on the surface of the carcass are also reported to make the meat more attractive in appearance to local consumers. The danger of contaminated air penetrating the deeper parts of the carcass is considerable, however, and even more so when, instead of using a pump for inflation, air is forced through by the mouth of the butcher.

In any event, hides should be carefully removed, using the proper knives (fig. 9.15), to avoid damage to this valuable by-product. In many countries

fig. 9.15 Skinning knives

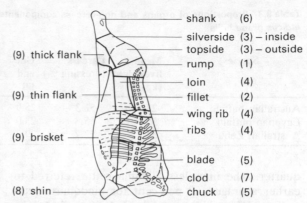

shank — (6)
silverside (3) – inside
topside (3) – outside
rump — (1)
loin — (4)
fillet — (2)
wing rib — (4)
ribs — (4)
blade — (5)
clod — (7)
chuck — (5)

(9) thick flank
(9) thin flank
(9) brisket
(8) shin

Figures in parentheses indicate relative commercial market values of various 'cuts', the highest being (1).

fig. 9.16 The carcass 'side': a method of cutting used in the UK

there are strict regulations governing removal of the hide and butchers may even be penalised by a fine for inflicting unnecessary damage. In some countries those parts of the hide that are not sold for curing and subsequent use in the leather industries are sold for eating, especially in communities where large quantities of starchy foods are eaten and where animal protein chewiness is a desired quality.

Where possible, carcasses should be washed after dressing. The various offals, such as stomachs and intestines, are cleaned out and washed, the contents and washings being disposed of separately as is the blood. Stomachs and gut casings may be processed in the tripery.

Carcass composition

There are several methods of assessing the composition of the carcass including the use of sample joints, testing the specific gravity of the meat and chemical analyses. All are somewhat slow and tedious. From the practical standpoint, methods are based upon the degree of finish or fatness of the carcass, the balance of side and the fleshing of the hindleg and forequarters. Colour, texture and odour are also taken into account. What might be called a semi-objective method, developed in New Zealand, combines measurement of carcass components and judgement of the carcass by eye. Measurements include that of the 'eye' muscle when the carcass is cut between the tenth and eleventh rib.

The retail butcher's chief concern is with the

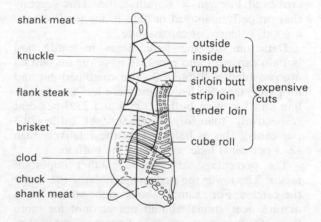

shank meat
knuckle
flank steak
brisket
clod
chuck
shank meat

outside
inside
rump butt
sirloin butt
strip loin
tender loin
cube roll

expensive cuts

fig. 9.17 The carcass 'side': a method of cutting for the USA market

amount of meat in the carcass and, for the more selective customer, the percentage of choice – hence more expensive cuts (figs. 9.16 and 9.17). Since these are contained in the hindquarter and back, a carcass with the hindquarter heavier than the forequarter is desirable. In the USA, where the quarters are severed between ribs 12 and 13, at least 48 per cent of the carcass weight is required in the hindquarter. In the British method of severing the quarters between ribs 10 and 11 about 54 per cent of the carcass weight is in the hind-

Table 9.3 Proportions of organs and non-carcass components to body weight in buffalo males compared with *Bos indicus* grade bulls

Species	Mean liveweight (kg)	Carcass (dressing %)	Gut and fill	Body components as percentage of liveweight					
				Hide	Head	Heart	Loin	Spleen	Shanks
Australian buffalo	282	52.3	25.9	10.7	5.9	0.6	1.6	0.2	2.8
Egyptian buffalo	359	55.8	23.0	10.8	5.6	0.4	1.4	0.3	2.7
Australian Zebu	343	52.7	29.3	8.7	4.9	0.5	1.2	0.3	2.4

quarter. The humpless N'dama cattle referred to earlier averaged 52 per cent for hindquarter carcass weight. Unimproved Zebus tend to be heavier in the forequarters, though this is not the case in beef-type Brahman and the improved Brazilian Zebu. Work in Egypt on the buffalo has indicated that there is a higher percentage of their meat plus bone in the more expensive cuts than in crossbred Friesian × Baradi cattle. This suggests that properly managed buffalo in the feedlot have a good 'balance' of carcass side.

Data on dressing percentages in cattle and buffalo carcasses and proportions of organs and fill are provided in Table 9.3. The combined gut and fill percentages of liveweight were less for Australian and Egyptian buffalo (25.9 and 23.0 per cent respectively) than for Australian Zebu cattle (29.3 per cent). This is balanced by the relatively high (2–3 per cent) hide weights of the buffalo.

The percentage of bone is another important factor. The lower the percentage of bone the better the carcass. For example, bone in the well selected mature beef animal should not account for more than 14 per cent of the carcass weight. The percentage bone will depend on the degree of finish of the carcass so that, the more fat, the less bone. However, the distribution of bone in any individual beef carcass is very unequal. This accounts for

Table 9.4 Ratio between meat, fat and bone in three-rib samples

	Cattle	Buffalo
Meat (%)	61.9 ± 5.35	52.9 ± 5.06
Fat (%)	17.2 ± 2.90	24.5 ± 4.10
Bone (%)	20.9 ± 5.10	22.6 ± 2.38

Table 9.5 Proportions of muscle weight in 'expensive' regions of the carcasses of buffalo males and *Bos indicus* grade bulls

	Proximal hind limb (%)	Around spinal column (%)	Proximal forelimb (%)	Total muscle in 'expensive'[1] groups (%)
Buffalo 1	34.1	10.5	13.4	58.0
Buffalo 2	33.4	10.2	12.7	56.3
Buffalo 3	32.6	10.4	11.9	54.8
Mean	33.3	10.4	12.7	56.4
Bos indicus 1	30.7	12.0	12.1	54.8
Bos indicus 2	32.4	12.4	12.8	57.6
Bos indicus 3	33.1	11.1	11.8	56.0
Mean	32.1	11.8	12.2	56.1

[1] Those muscles which fetch high prices in developed meat producing countries.

variations in monetary value of different carcass cuts and generally speaking the cuts with the least bone are the most valuable.

The percentages of meat, fat and bone and their ratios in cattle and buffalo sample cuts are given in Tables 9.4 and 9.5.

Fat distribution and quality

Fat deposition in relation to age, growth and nutrition in beef cattle and the buffalo were discussed in Chapter 6. The following concerns the role of fat in carcass quality.

It is not practicable to apply uniform standards of beef carcass quality to suit all customers; these will vary with tastes, local economies, social prejudices and the like. In traditional beef producing countries there is, however, general agreement where quality is of special importance on a number of factors which affect it. In wild animals fat is the chief source of reserve energy. In domestic animals fat also has far-reaching effects upon the nutritive value, quality and palatability of meat.

In addition to the amount of fat, its distribution is also important in carcase quality assessment. There is a definite order of growth in the deposition of body fat. In early growth fat is laid down in the mesentery and kidney fat. In small dairy cattle and other improved milking or primarily non-beef breeds fat deposits rarely pass beyond this stage. In beef animals the next area for fat deposit is directly under the skin. This gives the smooth, rounded, or well finished look to a steer. The dairy cow should never look this way since it means that the feed provided for milk production is being synthesised into body fat instead of milk. In the last stage the fat in improved beef breeds becomes deposited between the muscle fibres themselves (fig. 9.18). This is called 'marbling'. Tropical breeds do not generally exhibit this phenomenon, their meat fibres being closely adhering. This type of meat is often preferred to the more tender marbled meat, particularly in areas where much starchy and/or oil-cooked food is consumed.

Effects of age and fatigue In beef cattle age also has a secondary effect on fat deposition in various parts of the body. Younger animals have less fat in their fatty and muscular tissues than do

fig. 9.18 Marbling

older beef animals. There is also a breed effect. The early-maturing European beef breeds such as the Aberdeen Angus have more intramuscular fat than do slow-maturing breeds such as the Hereford. Improved dual purpose breeds also have more fat in the muscles than do the dairy breeds.

Fat plays a prominent role in terms of taste in the assessment of the palatability of various grades of beef carcasses. Marbling is said to increase meat tenderness by breaking up the lean fibres, improving flavour. Excess fat, however, in carcasses over about 58 per cent dressing weight is said to reduce palatability. Colour of beef fat is of little importance from the nutritional point of view, although it may affect the visual quality in that highly coloured yellow fat in the carcass and deepening yellowness of fat occurs with age. In certain Channel Islands dairy cattle breeds, such as the Jersey and Guernsey, however, the fat is always yellow.

Buffalo carcass fat In the Australian work described in Chapter 2, 65.5 per cent of the fat in the buffalo carcasses was found in the inter-muscular depots and 19.3 per cent was subcutaneous. The percentage of subcutaneous fat in beef cattle carcasses is markedly higher and since the present international trend is towards leaner meat the buffalo may yet assume a more important place on the international meat market. Buffalo fat is white and of good firm texture. Freshly cut muscles in young buffalo carcasses present a rich red colour, slightly darker than that of cattle and like Zebu and some other tropical cattle virtually devoid of intra-muscular fat. Palatability tests in Australia showed that the buffalo meat from the trial was very tender and palatable, but not juicy. Juiciness is character-istic of marbled beef but this particular quality is unlikely to be found in cattle reared on tropical ranges, although some degree of inter-muscular fat can most certainly be generated under inten-sive management conditions.

Lean meat

Lean meat, that is, muscle, is made up of minute fibres which can be seen under the microscope. These small fibres are grouped together by connec-tive tissue into bundles. In young animals the muscle fibres and bundles are small, improving tenderness. In old animals the meat becomes coarser and tougher.

Fatigue is especially important in the young animal since muscle fibres are more quickly fatigued than those in the older animal. The colour of the muscle deepens in the older animal due to an increase of the respiratory pigment haemoglobin or myoglobin in muscle, thus making it darker and more attractive and palatable. In the very young animal, such as the veal calf, the muscle is pale and has a less strong flavour. Public tastes vary considerably and consumers in many beef producing countries object to the deeper coloured meats because this may also depict age and thus poor meat quality, though in many parts of the tropics such considerations are of no consequence.

Buffalo meat is similar to cattle meat in many basic properties such as structure, chemical composition, nutritive value and palatability. Nevertheless, where cattle are the traditional beef producing animal, consumers will tend to give first choice to beef. The popularity of the buffalo as a meat animal depends upon acquainting consumers with its value as a source of animal protein. The whole carcass is little different in terms of overall conformation, muscle distribution and structure, tendons, bones, etc.; the major differences rest with fat and connective tissue distribution.

Effects of hormones on the carcass

In cattle, whether used orally or as implants under the skin, hormones cause an increase in growth rate with preferential formation of protein and bone at the expense of fat. The use of natural and synthetic hormones in fattening animals has caused great controversy, particularly in Europe and North America. It is claimed that the residues of these hormones may persist in the carcass or in milk, or in the soil contaminated with faeces from the hormone-treated animals. Workers handling hormone-treated feedstuffs may also absorb the hormone through the skin. The dispute is not settled and in some countries there is strict legislation regarding their use. Newer and safer synthetic products are constantly being tested, or are already in use.

There are three growth promoting compounds available in implant form in the USA, in addition to several compounds which can be given by mouth. These include such commercially produced compounds as DES (diethylstilboestrol) and MGA (melangostrol acetate), and compounds of progesterone and oestradiol benzoate for implanting into steers between 45 and 180 kg liveweight, and testosterone and oestradiol benzoate for heifers 180 to 360 kg liveweight. Other growth stimulants include substances such as zeranol, which is non-hormonal. Despite the controversy engendered these growth stimulants continue to be used in many countries and results indicate an increased average daily gain in liveweight, as well as improved feed efficiency following a period of 90 to 120 days of use. Table 9.6 shows the daily weight gain of buffalo in Brazil. A much shorter beneficial period of 56 to 63 days using zeranol implants in Zebu bulls from pastoralist herds finished on feedlot on a ranch in Nigeria has been observed in a 112 day feeding trial.

Choice of hormone and hormone combinations

The natural male sex hormone testosterone and the female sex hormones oestradiol and progesterone are too costly for commercial use. Synthetic substances are much cheaper and equally active. These include the synthetic oestrogens diethylstilboestrol, usually called stilboestrol, and hexoestrol.

The earliest one used in the USA – stilboestrol – is still one of the most widely used in that country both for implantation or orally. Another form of the same hormone, hexoestrol, is now the hormone of choice for animal use. It is less active for man when ingested orally as residues in treated meat and is therefore much less of a public health risk.

The dose rate for hexoestrol implants, given about 100 days before slaughter, is 60 mg or less for steers fattened intensively indoors and 30 to 45 mg for cattle on grass. The lower rate for cattle on grass is probably because cattle ingest some oestrogenic material from the pasture. The time of administering the hormone prior to slaughter can be worked out according to carcase finish requirements. If more finish is required, the hormone should be given early to obtain optimum body growth, followed by more fat deposit when the effect of the hormone treatment wanes.

Site and mode of implantation

The implantation site of choice is at an inedible part of the animal, for example at the base of the ear (fig. 9.19). Any pellet residues are thus located at this point and the ear removed at slaughter with the hide. When, as in Australia, ear cartilages are used for gelatine manufacture, very little residue of oestrogen is reported. The caudal fold or skin fold under the tail can also be used but is more liable to contamination from faecal matter at the time of implantation. Both the pellet and solid paste forms may be used for implants. The latter method is simple in that a single, total estimated dose can be injected under the skin by syringe. The paste is liable to be more quickly absorbed and so the effect wears off more rapidly. On this account many beef producers prefer to use the pellet implant.

The oral method avoids the need for handling of the animals; on the other hand up to 20 times higher doses are required for the desired effect. There is also the public health risk for staff handling the medicated feedstuff.

Hormone combinations

The male sex hormone testosterone also has growth promoting properties and has been used alone, or in combination with oestrogen. Tranquillising drugs such as promazine are also said to have growth promoting qualities and can be used either alone or in combination with the hormones.

Side effects

The most pronounced side effect in steers is that in which the testes may be twice the size of those of untreated animals. The udder may also enlarge. In cattle there is also a noticeable elevation of the tail head, a slackening of the pelvic ligaments and a depression of the loin. Such changes, however, are not seen in all animals, or they may appear for a time and then disappear. Changes in the loin and tail head are most noticeable in the carcass but are not usually detrimental to carcass value.

Growth effects and carcass value

Oestrogens produce true growth by improving the retention of nitrogen in the body which is used to lay down more body protein. There is also increased body retention of calcium and phosphorus which brings about more bone or skeletal growth. Animals treated with oestrogens also eat 5–10 per cent more food and use this food more efficiently than untreated animals. They also attain market weight earlier. The cost of the hormone implant or hormone-treated food is quite low so that there is some profit to be made from the quicker weight gain and earlier sale of the treated animal.

In the USA most grain-fattened cattle receive stilboestrol either as ear-implanted pellets or in the feed. Certain uses of stilboestrol are permitted by the Food and Drug Administration of that country. Stilboestrol used in the permitted manner leaves no detectable residue in the edible flesh. It is reported to increase daily gains in weight and efficiency of feed utilisation by about 10–15 per cent in most cases. Use of stilboestrol does not, on the other hand, shorten the period required to reach the desired degree of finish, although it does accelerate the rate of increase in lean meat.

Further reading

Berg, R. and Butterfield, R. M. (1976). *New concepts of cattle growth*. Univ. Press: Sydney, Aust.

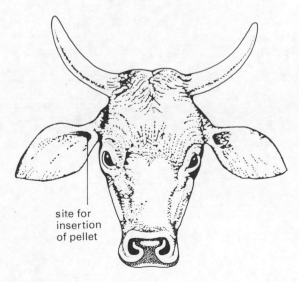

site for insertion of pellet

fig. 9.19 Site for implantation of hormone at the base of the ear

Charles, D. D. and Johnson, E. R. (1975). Liveweight gains and carcass composition of buffalo (*Bubalus bubalis*) steers on four feeding regimes. *Aust. J. Agric. Res.*, 26, 407–413.

Eriksen, P. J. (1978). *Slaughterhouses and slaughterhouse design and construction*. FAO Anim. Prod. and Health Paper no. 9. FAO: Rome.

Mann, I. (1960). *Meat handling in underdeveloped countries*. FAO Agric. Devel. Paper no. 70. FAO: Rome.

Obi, T. U., Daniyan, M. A. and Ngere, L. O. (1980). Response of Nigerian Zebu cattle to zeranol implants. *Trop. Admin. Health Prod.*, 12, 224–228.

Olayiwole, M. B., Buvanendran, I. J., Fulani, I. J. and Ikhatua, J. U. (1981). Intensive fattening of indigenous breeds of cattle in Nigeria. *Wld. Rev. Anim. Prod.*, 17, (2).

Olayiwole, M. B. and Fulani, I. J. (1978). *Economics of commercial beef production under the feedlot system of management*. Nat. Anim. Prod. Res. Inst., Ahmadu Bello Univ.: Zaria, Nigeria.

Preston, T. R. and Willis, M. B. (1982). *Intensive beef production*. 2nd edn. Pergamon Press: Oxford.

Roy, J. H. B. (1980). *The calf*. 4th edn. Butterworth: London.

Index